# SIDNEY HOOK

## on

## PRAGMATISM, DEMOCRACY, and FREEDOM

The
Essential
Essays

# SIDNEY HOOK
on
## PRAGMATISM, DEMOCRACY, and FREEDOM

edited by
### ROBERT B. TALISSE
### & ROBERT TEMPIO

foreword by
### ALAN RYAN

 **Prometheus Books**
59 John Glenn Drive
Amherst, New York 14228-2197

Published 2002 by Prometheus Books

Inquiries should be addressed to
Prometheus Books
59 John Glenn Drive
Amherst, New York 14228–2197
VOICE: 716–691–0133, ext. 207
FAX: 716–564–2711
WWW.PROMETHEUSBOOKS.COM

06  05  04  03  02      5  4  3  2  1

Library of Congress Cataloging-in-Publication Data

Hook, Sidney, 1902–
    Sidney Hook on pragmatism, democracy, and freedom : the essential
essays / edited by Robert B. Talisse and Robert Tempio ; foreword by Alan
Ryan.
        p.  cm.
    Includes bibliographical references.
    ISBN 1–59102–022–0 (alk. paper)
    1. Political science—Philosophy. 2. Pragmatism. 3. Naturalism.
4. Communism. 5. Democracy. 6. Liberty. I. Talisse, Robert B. II. Tempio,
Robert, 1975– III. Title.

JC251 .H66  2002
320'.01—dc21

                                                                                    2002031827

Printed in Canada on acid-free paper

To *Angelo Juffras* and *John Peterman*,
*for making us pragmatists.*

"More important than any belief a man holds is the way he holds it."
—Sidney Hook

# CONTENTS

## III.  DEMOCRATIC THEORY

## IV.  DEMOCRATIC PRACTICE

## V.  IN DEFENSE OF A FREE SOCIETY

# FOREWORD

## BY ALAN RYAN

Sidney Hook very much admired Bertrand Russell and John Dewey; he and they contributed essays to *The Meaning of Marx*, a work published in 1934, in which Russell, Morris Cohen, and Dewey wrote variously persuasive accounts of why they were not communists or Marxists, and Hook wrote unhappily of the extreme contrast between the authoritarian and intellectually liberticide regime instituted by Stalin and the intelligent social democracy envisaged by Marx. It was characteristic of Hook that he wrote in defense of Marx but against all the likely promoters of Marx's ideas, just as it was characteristic of Dewey and Russell that the latter sympathized with the anger of revolutionaries but not with their ideas, while Dewey just kept insisting that smashing things up was bad for the insurrectionists as well as for their prospects of bringing about reform.

As the essays reprinted here show, Hook spoke neither more nor less than the truth when he said in later life that he had never undergone a political change of mind, that he remained a social democrat, and that he was committed to economic as well as political democracy. Shortly before he died, he wrote me an engaging letter, saying how much he liked the book I had just written on the politics of Bertrand Russell, and how impossible it was that I should ever write the book I had in mind—on John Dewey. His reasoning was all his own. No Englishman could read

Dewey; whatever language it was that Dewey spoke, it was not English prose as the English knew it.

It was notable that Hook's complaints against Russell were against Russell's *style*; the aristocratic *hauteur* that Hook disliked meant that Russell was always prone to set himself up as a philosopher-king. It was not Russell's political *theory* that he disliked, but Russell's frailty of judgment and his readiness to accept undemocratic expedients. What Hook's critics saw as a move to the right, when he abandoned the Marxist groups with whom he had worked in the 1930s and argued for the banning of communists from teaching in schools and universities, was not a theoretical move. It was a political judgment. Hook thought that the enemies of freedom were duplicitous and well organized; to fight them with one hand tied behind one's back was silly. Their appeal to liberal values was either hypocritical—supposing that they understood the contempt for those values felt by their communist masters—or naive.

Hook's politics were, if one might risk a paradox, a street fighter's version of Dewey's pragmatism. (The paradox is, of course, that Dewey's pragmatism is so nearly pacifist that it is hard to think there can be a street fighter's version.) But Hook was quite right that Dewey's ideas about the logic of inquiry were what the young Marx might have thought out if he had not been so busy as a revolutionary; Dewey, of course, brushed aside the thought along with the implied compliment. And Hook saw, as almost nobody else did for another sixty years, that Dewey's emphasis on fulfilling work, and his emphasis on the idea of an individualism that could only be fulfilled in the appropriate sort of community, developed Marx's thought that social democracy was liberalism fulfilled.

The essays here, now that they can be read independently of the political conflicts that provoked them in the half-century between 1930 and 1985, reveal that the philosophical Hook was alive and well alongside the street-fighting Hook throughout those years. It is good to see him more clearly now that the dust has settled.

# EDITORS' INTRODUCTION
## THE LEGACY OF SIDNEY HOOK

Sidney Hook is arguably the most controversial figure in the tradition of American philosophy. After completing his degree under John Dewey at Columbia in 1927, Hook embarked upon a campaign of political and intellectual activism that placed him firmly among the fellow travelers of the Communist Party in America. By the early 1930s, Hook had established himself as the most important Marxist scholar in America and one of the leading philosophical voices of the Left.

Hook's sympathies with Communism began to languish, however, as news of the Moscow purge trials of 1936–37 reached the West.[1] Hook's experiences in defending Leon Trotsky's right to a fair and public trial served to confirm his suspicions that the American Communist Party was actually a conspiratorial organization under the direct control of Stalin that aimed to infiltrate and ultimately dismantle the political structure of the United States.[2] This realization led Hook to take what many consider a drastic shift to the political Right. Around 1938, Hook adopted the vehement anti-Communist and anti-Soviet stance that he sustained until his death in 1989.

Hook's anti-Communism drove him to defend positions unpopular with the Left on issues regarding academic freedom, the employment of Communist Party members in public educational institutions, and—during the Vietnam years—the methods and rights of student war protesters.[3] The coup de grâce of Hook's long career for those who would demonize him as the quintessential turncoat came in 1985 when he was awarded the Medal of Freedom by President Ronald Reagan.

Despite what seems to constitute incontrovertible evidence of a shift from radical Marxist to neoconservative cold warrior, Hook maintains in his autobiography that he is "not aware of having undergone any serious conversions from the days of [his] youth, or of having abandoned [his] basic ideals. . . ." (Hook 1987, 596).[4] This surprising claim so begs for philosophical elucidation—which Hook curiously does not proffer—that it is a wonder that no philosopher has undertaken an earnest study of Hook's political thought, in the decade since his death.[5] If the current scholarly literature is any indication, Hook has been completely forsaken by the philosophical community at large.[6] We hope that the current volume of Hook's essential political writings will help to reestablish Hook as an enduring source of vital insight into both the theory and the practice of the democratic way of life.

## HOOK'S CONCEPTION OF DEMOCRACY

Central to Hook's political philosophy is the radical conception of democracy that he inherited from John Dewey. It is with this conception that one must begin, and it is in the context of this conception that one must understand Hook's other political commitments.

The Deweyan slogan, "democracy is a way of life," is notoriously ambiguous.[7] What, *exactly*, does it mean to live democratically? The difficulty is compounded by critics who understand the proposition to be offering a novel *definition* of democracy. Actually, our discussion may begin with a strikingly ordinary formula: "a democratic society is one where the government rests upon the freely given consent of the governed" (277).[8] This minimal conception loses its air of triviality upon an analysis of the term "freely given consent."

A government rests upon the consent of the governed when (1) political mechanisms exist by which the governed may at regular intervals register their approval and disapproval of proposed government action and policy, and (2) the government acknowledges a prima facie duty to conduct itself according to the consent of the governed (277). That is, a basic condition for consent is *participation* on the part of the governed in the processes of government. This much is, again, commonplace. But what of the qualification that the consent of the governed must be "freely given"?

A convenient response is that consent is freely given only when it is "voluntary [and] not subject to coercion" (Hook 1959d, 54). Surely, this is a platitude, not an analysis. There are a variety of conditions to be met if consent is to be given freely. Beginning with the most obvious of these, Hook observes:

> An election held in the shadow of bayonets, or in which one can vote only "Yes," or in which no opposition candidates are permitted is obviously one which does not register freely given consent.[9] (Hook 1959d, 54)

Minimally, then, there must be no *procedural* obstructions to participation if consent is to be free.

There are, however, more subtle forms of interference. As "there are few things to which a starving man will not consent" (259), we also may speak of *economic* obstructions to free consent. For example:

> A threat to deprive the governed of their jobs or means of livelihood, by a group which has the power to do so, would undermine a democracy. (278)

This consideration may seem a variation on the foregoing examples of procedural obstacles; however, Hook goes beyond cases of blatant and direct economic manipulation. Hook notes that

> Differences in economic power make it possible for the more powerful economic group to exercise a much greater influence upon decisions that affect public welfare than their numbers or deserts warrant. (Hook 1959d, 54–55)

Hook fears that unchecked economic power will be employed to "render nugatory even legislative action" (Hook, 1959d, 55). Moreover, the economically powerful enjoy "greater advantages in mobilizing resources to influence public opinion and consent" (Hook 1959d, 55). Hook concludes:

> Where the political forms of democracy function within a society in which economic controls are not subject to political control, there is always a standing threat to democracy. (278)

That is, democracy requires not only protection of the general populace from the direct domination of the economically powerful, it requires that steps be taken to ensure that economic power is not employed to control or undermine democratic procedures.

Finally, we may speak of *epistemological* impediments to free consent. "Even in the absence of physical and economic coercion, consent is not free if it is bound or blinded by ignorance" (259). The operative epistemological principle is elementary: one's consent to a political proposal is free just in the degree to which one does not misunderstand the meaning and relevant implications of the proposal. Access to relevant sources of information is certainly not a sufficient condition for understanding a proposition, but whatever the sufficient conditions are, it is clear that understanding the meaning of a political proposal requires information. Thus democracy requires that the governed's access to information be unrestricted. Hook writes:

> The expression of consent by the majority is not free if it is deprived of access to sources of information, if it can read *only* the official interpretation, if it can hear *only* one voice in the classroom, pulpit, and radio. (278–79)

> If one is kept ignorant of alternatives, denied access to information, deprived of the opportunity to influence and be influenced by the opinions of others, consent is not free. (Hook 1959d, 54)

The commitment of a democratic society to freely given consent requires that there is no hindrance to access to relevant sources of information and to the agencies of critical discussion. Without such minimal provisions, consent is unfree since "the individual has no more freedom of action when his mind is deliberately tied by ignorance than when his hands are tied with rope" (279).

Our analysis has shown that the very concept of "freely given consent" demands that we broaden our conception of democracy beyond the minimal procedural level with which we began (Hook 1959b, 62; Hook 1944, 50). That is, we must acknowledge that the mere *existence* of democratic procedural devices such as open elections and periodic referenda are necessary, but not sufficient conditions for democracy. As we have seen, other conditions are necessary such as the absence of economic pressures and epistemological impediments to free consent. Democracy as a way of life begins to emerge once it is recognized that the requisite procedural mechanisms cannot be understood as free-standing institutions to be established and then left alone. Threats to democracy cannot be abolished once and for all; democracy must be *maintained*. Democratic procedures must be continually protected from any force—internal or external—that would frustrate their registering of the governed's free consent.

We have so far focused upon only the negative conditions for democracy, namely, the absence of obstructions to free consent. These conditions are in themselves insufficient. Even in the absence of impediments, democracy may not be realized. An election in which every negative condition has been satisfied may yet fail to register free consent if the governed are generally illiterate or incapable of open and critical discourse. Under conditions such as these, manipulation of public opinion and the production of artificial consent is easy; there is democracy in name only. Thus, we must also identify the positive conditions for democracy, the elements that must be in place if democracy is to prevail.

Just as there are economic and epistemological *obstructions* to democracy that must be guarded against, there are economic and epistemological *requirements* for democracy that must be provided for. It is through an examination of these positive requirements that the full meaning of democracy as a way of life surfaces. We cannot here examine Hook's proposals for "economic democracy";[10] we here focus upon the epistemological requirements for democracy that, according to Hook, are of primary importance.[11]

It has already been suggested that a positive condition for democracy is general literacy among the governed. A democratic society must therefore provide public education. But basic *literacy*, command of a language, is not enough (299). The principle that persons must discern the meaning and implications of a proposal before they can freely consent to it requires something beyond literacy. One's consent to proposal $x$ is free just in the degree to which one has examined $x$ in some critical way; that is, one needs to have considered implications of $x$, entertained objections, and evaluated alternative proposals. Examining a proposal critically requires free public discourse. It follows that a "democratic society cannot exist without free discussion" (289) since free discussion is a necessary condition for free consent.

However, "wherever discussion flourishes, controversy is sure to arise" (290). In the midst of controversy, free discussion can be as great a hindrance to free consent as any overt obstruction. Certain modes of discourse tend to silence debate, generate confusion, discredit dissenters rather than dissenting views, suppress relevant information, encourage dogmatism, and establish on the basis of an appeal to loyalty to tradition that which cannot be established by an appeal to evidence and analysis. That is, "Some kinds of discussion tend to undermine democratic society" (289). Democracy therefore requires that public discourse and deliberation be conducted according to a specific method by which conflicts may be judiciously resolved. Hook writes:

> What is required to live prosperously and peacefully together is not a fixed common doctrine or a fixed body of truths, but a common method or set of fixed rules under which we can live with our differences. (264)

What is this method? Following Dewey, Hook offers what he calls the "method of intelligence," or the "experimental method." What are the principles of this method? According to Hook, its principles are derived from the experimentalist epistemology embodied in the methods of science.[12] Most generally, the experimental method treats all proposals as hypotheses to be tested. It recognizes only experimental results as reasons in favor of or against a proposal. It acknowledges challenges, suggestions, and alternative proposals from every quarter of the community. It opposes dogmatism and authoritarianism in all its forms. It is progressive in that it never closes itself to further debate and experiment. It is self-corrective in that it is willing to revise or even abandon any principle or policy if experimental conditions so require.

Like any method, experimentalism embodies certain values that can be formulated as procedural rules. In an essay titled "The Ethics of Controversy," Hook outlines the "ground rules" for democratic discourse:

1. Nothing and no one is immune from criticism.
2. Everyone involved in a controversy has an intellectual responsibility to inform himself of the available facts.
3. Criticism should be directed first to policies, and against persons only when they are responsible for policies, and against their motives or purposes only when there is some independent evidence of their character.
4. Because certain words are legally permissible, they are not therefore morally permissible.
5. *Before* impugning an opponent's motives, even when they legitimately may be impugned, answer his arguments.

6. Do not treat an opponent of a policy as if he were therefore a personal enemy of the country or a concealed enemy of democracy.
7. Since a good cause may be defended by bad arguments, after answering the bad arguments for another's position, present positive evidence for your own.
8. Do not hesitate to admit lack of knowledge or to suspend judgment if evidence is not decisive either way.
9. Only in pure logic and mathematics, not in human affairs, can one demonstrate that something is strictly impossible. Because something is logically possible, it is not therefore probable. "It is not impossible" is a preface to an irrelevant statement about human affairs. The question is always one of the balance of probabilities. And the evidence for probabilities must include more than abstract possibilities.
10. The cardinal sin, when we are looking for truth of fact or wisdom of policy, is refusal to discuss, or action which blocks discussion. (294–95)

Hook admits that these principles may sound like truisms (294). However, what is often not apprehended is that experimentalism presupposes a *community* that is committed to the project of cooperatively inquiring into common problems to reach tentative but workable solutions. Understood in its communal aspect, experimentalism is

a perpetual invitation to sit down in the face of differences and reason together, to consider the evidence, explore alternative proposals, assess the consequences, and let the decision rest—when matters of human concern are at stake—with the consent of those affected by the proposals. (264)

When considered at the level of an entire community, the radical implications of experientalism are revealed. Hook observes:

how revolutionary the impact would be of giving the method of intelligence institutional force in education, economics, law, and politics. Policies would be treated as hypotheses, not as dogmas; customary practices as generalizations, not as God-given truths. A generation trained in schools where emphasis was placed upon method, method, and more method, could hardly be swayed by current high-pressured propaganda. (286)

Hook's conception of democracy now comes into full view. Our examination has shown that the slogan "democracy is a way of life" means that democracy—understood in a minimal procedural sense—implies a more extensive conception according to which democracy is primarily an epistemological proposal that requires a certain kind of community for its realization. A community is democratic in the degree to which its institutions and forms of public and personal association are arranged according to experimentalism and the principles and procedures it involves. A democratic community must identify as its essential and defining feature its commitment to the processes of experimentalism rather than its commitment to any particular results of those processes (Hook 1959d, 58).[13] That is, it must employ experimentalism as its primary method of deciding and revising its policies and of resolving its controversies. Most important, it must be always prepared to revise its most traditionally sanctioned principles in the light of new evidence. As such, it must be perpetually engaged in the project of reorganizing its institutions according to the most current results of experimental cooperative inquiry.

In light of these considerations, it follows that no existing community is perfectly democratic. The final step in our analysis is the realization that democracy as a way of life is an *ideal*. A community is democratic in the degree to which it strives toward the ideal of full experimental participation of every citizen in the processes of governing the social forces that affect his life.

Hook is no utopian. He recognizes that a democratic community is "sometimes foolish, sometimes callous and hostile to the underprivileged" (Hook 1962, 64). Democratic government is not necessarily good government; a democratic community will make mistakes. Yet this is hardly a defect of democracy; it is the standing condition of life.[14] However, as experimentalism is by its very nature self-corrective, democracy's commitment to experimentalism makes correction and progress possible. Hook writes, "the cure for the evils of democracy is better democracy" (283). "Better democracy" means more extensive application of the experimental method: more critical analysis and more public discourse with more participation from more sectors of the community. Insofar as it is committed to experimentalism, "democracy, with all its imperfections, possesses the instruments by which it can move toward the realization of the promise of equality and freedom" (Hook 1959d, 58). The instruments and processes of experimentalism are the essential agencies of the democratic way of life. They are therefore the features which must be most widely adopted and most vehemently protected, for they alone constitute the difference between an open, but imperfect society that is nevertheless able to progressively improve and tyranny (Hook 1962, 128).

## HOOK'S LATER POLITICAL COMMITMENTS

With these points about the nature of democracy established, we may now address Hook's political commitments. Though a full argument cannot be launched here, our suggestion will be that Hook was correct to deny that his thinking took a turn to the Right.

As was indicated above, Hook maintains that the essential feature of a democratic community is its commitment to the methods and processes of experimentalism rather than its commitment to any specific principles derived therefrom. For a democracy, the epistemological method of deciding policy and resolving conflict is supreme (Hook 1977, 236). This emphasis upon the processes and methods of democracy leads Hook to a further distinction between opposition that may be called *internal* to democracy and that which is *external* to democracy.

Opposition to a policy or action of a democratic community is internal if it complies with the "rules of the game" of democratic discourse (264). Most simply, opposition is internal to the democratic framework if it is expressed in a way which honors the ten principles of democratic controversy (16–17). Opposition is external to the democratic framework if it violates these principles. Hook writes:

> Opposition of the first kind, no matter how mistaken, must be tolerated, if for no other reason than that we cannot be sure that it is not we who are mistaken. Opposition of the second kind, no matter what protective coloration it wears . . . must be swiftly dealt with if democracy is to survive. (287)

Hook's distinction between internal and external opposition is essential to understanding his political commitments. As a careful survey of his work on the political controversies of his day will show, Hook's principal objective always is to preserve the *processes* of democracy. As such, he opposes any movement or faction that operates outside of those processes as well as any principle or policy that cannot be established by them.

Hook opposed the student antiwar movement *not* on the grounds that he thought American intervention in Vietnam was justified but rather because the students employed antidemocratic methods of expressing their objections.[15] Hook aptly characterized the student protests as an attack on the democratic process (Hook 1969, 112). Similarly, Hook's opposition to the employment of Communist Party members in public educational institutions is *not* grounded in his opposition to communist ideas. Rather, Hook's opposition stems from the authoritarian character of the Communist Party, especially its requirement that all members accept the official party line without question.[16] Hook thought Communist Party members unfit to teach in public schools *not* because they were communists but because they belonged to an organization that dictated beliefs to its members and tolerated no opposition. Finally, consider Hook's opposition to the Supreme Court decisions of the early 1960s banning voluntary prayer and Bible reading in public schools. Hook's opposition is not based in a belief that prayer is wholesome or necessary for the cultivation of virtue.[17] Instead, Hook objects to the process by which the secular position was secured. Hook writes:

> Since what one Court can do, another can undo, in the long run it seems to me that those who wish to keep religion out of the public life of a free society should look primarily to the educational processes of democracy itself rather than to the decrees of the Court to strengthen and extend the secular position. (Hook 1967, 63)

Additional texts can be cited that testify to Hook's overriding commitment to democratic processes and the way of life they require. This feature is constant throughout all of Hook's writings. Certainly, his dedication to democracy as process led him to some positions that today are associated with the Right. However, we have shown that Hook was motivated by a radical conception of democracy and a concern for its continued expansion rather than by the sentimental devotion to "tradition" that typically characterizes conservative thought.

## CONCLUDING REMARKS

Hook once said, "More important than any belief a man holds is the *way* he holds it."[18] There is a profound insight in this. Hook's political views are to be understood as the tentative products of the kind of inquiry that exemplifies the democratic way of life. Such a life is characterized by a willingness to follow an argument to wherever it leads, even if this requires that some most-cherished belief be revised or abandoned, or some revered allegiance be dissolved, or some unfashionable view be adopted. We live at a time in which political discussion is dominated by sloganizing sound bites; platforms and party lines have replaced critical discourse and acute analysis. Democratic participation has been reduced to responding to corporate-sponsored opinion polls and "sounding off" on afternoon talk shows. Academics and other intellectuals have run to the foothills of textual criticism and professional conferences, while a host of other diversions abound for the rest of society. Democracy dissipates. It is not *what* Hook believed but the *way* he believed, his constant engagement with political dialogue, that constitutes the radical element in his thought. Here lies the legacy of Sidney Hook and the perpetual challenge of the democratic way of life.

These remarks constitute only the preliminary steps toward a reevaluation of Sidney Hook's political thought. The materials collected in this volume put at the reader's disposal the fundamental tools with which to undertake a fuller study.

## NOTES

1. Hook writes, "The Moscow Trials were . . . a decisive turning point in my own intellectual and political development" (Hook 1987, 218).
2. Hook's ordeal with the Moscow Trials and the Commission of Inquiry is documented in Hook 1987, chap. 17. Hook 1937 is also instructive. See also Phelps, chap. 4. Hook's case for the conspiratorial nature of the Communist Party is most clearly articulated in Hook 1953. See also the essays in part II of the current volume.
3. See Hook 1974; Hook 1969; and chaps. 15 and 17 of the current volume.
4. Compare Hook 1985, 15.
5. The philosopher who comes closest to a serious study is Cornel West. The purpose of West's short discussion, it seems, is to demonstrate by means of Hook's "ideological trajectory" that by midcentury, pragmatism was in "deep crisis" (West, 124). The only other recent examination of Sidney Hook's political thought comes by way of an intellectual biography by historian Christopher Phelps. In *Young Sidney Hook*, Phelps attempts to locate Hook's turn within an essential tension between Hook's Marxism and his pragmatism (a conclusion which we believe cannot be sustained by a philosophical analysis of Marxism and pragmatism as Hook understood them). A distinctly philosophical reexamination of Hook's political philosophy remains to be undertaken.

6. The degree to which Hook is neglected is most clearly evidenced by the new books by Matthew Festenstein and Richard Rorty. Festenstein's book claims to survey pragmatist political theory *from Dewey to Rorty* but contains no discussion of Hook. Rorty's *Achieving Our Country* is subtitled *Leftist Thought in Twentieth-Century America* but mentions Hook only in passing. The phenomenon is typical. Neither H. O. Mounce, who claims to cover pragmatism *from Peirce to Rorty*, nor John Murphy, who discusses pragmatism from *Peirce to Davidson*, includes a substantial treatment of Hook. Hart and Anderson's recent collection of essays dealing with the future of the American philosophical tradition makes no acknowledgement of Hook. Brint and Weaver's collection of essays on pragmatist legal thought contains no examination of Hook's major contribution to legal philosophy, *The Paradoxes of Freedom* (1962). Similarly, James Campbell's study of *The Meaning of Pragmatist Social Thought* ignores Hook entirely. The sole exception we have been able to locate is John Stuhr, who favorably cites Hook in a footnote, claiming that it is "unfortunate that Hook's work now is generally neglected and not well-known" (Stuhr 1991, 56).

7. Compare some of Dewey's own expressions of the principle: Dewey 1939, 155; Dewey 1937, 182; Dewey 1935, 25; Dewey 1927, 325; Dewey 1916, 93.

8. Unless otherwise specified, page citations are keyed to the current volume. Compare Hook 1977, 235; Hook 1976, 98; Hook 1967, 51; Hook 1962, 64; Hook 1959b, 60; Hook 1959c, 43; Hook 1959d, 52; Hook 1944, 48.

9. Compare Hook 1938, 286.

10. Hook writes, "Genuine political democracy, therefore, entails the right of the governed, through their representatives, to control economic policy" (Hook 1938, 286). Those interested in "economic democracy" may consult Hook, 1985, 19–20; Hook 1978; Hook 1977, 240; Hook 1976; Hook, 1963; Hook 1959e; and Hook 1938, 290–91. As the dates of these selections suggest, despite his supposed turn to ultraconservatism, Hook remained a socialist throughout his life (compare Hook 1987, 600).

11. I am not here offering epistemological considerations as *justifications* for democracy. The question of democracy's justification has been foregone; I am here interested in the epistemological requirements of democracy. The project of justifying democracy by an appeal to epistemology has recently been undertaken by Habermas and Putnam. For Hook's view, see Hook 1959b.

12. Like Dewey, Hook often identifies experimentalism with scientific method (for example, Hook 1956; Hook 1954, 122; Hook 1940b, 7–8; Hook 1938, 295–96). This characterization leads to unfortunate misunderstandings, as in Rorty 1983 and Rorty 1991. In the interest of avoiding confusion, we here drop reference to scientific method.

13. Compare Hook 1977, 236; Hook 1959c, 49; Hook 1944, 50.

14. The record of history shows that humans are fallible. Note also that even Plato, hailed by some as the archenemy of democracy, recognizes this. In the *Republic,* the *kallipolis* dissolves because the Philosopher Kings err (546b).

15. According to Hook, the tactics of the student movement included the seizing and destruction of research materials and notes of allegedly pro-war professors, disruption of their lectures, demolition of university property, and threats of personal violence (Hook 1969, 77 ff.). See also Hook 1987, chap. 33; Hook 1974; Hook 1969, especially chap. 6 ("The War against the Democratic Process") and Appendix I ("Second Thoughts on Berkeley"); Hook 1967a; and Hook 1962, chap. 3. Note also that Hook himself opposed American intervention in the conflict, though he also opposed American withdrawal before the South's independence was recognized by the North (Hook 1987, 583).

16. It is often claimed that Hook's position violates the academic freedom of communists. Wilkerson provides the standard arguments of this sort. Hook's actual position is much more subtle than his communist critics acknowledge; see Hook 1953, chap. 1 ("Heresy and Conspiracy"). For Hook's evidence of the authoritarian nature of the Communist Party, see Hook 1987, chaps. 13 and 14; Hook 1955, 229–39; Hook 1953, 23.

17. Hook remained a secular humanist throughout his life.

18. Reported by Capaldi, p. 18.

# WORKS CITED

Brint, Michael, and William Weaver, eds. 1991. *Pragmatism in Law and Society.* Boulder: Westview Press.

Campbell, James. 1992. *The Community Reconstructs: The Meaning of Pragmatist Social Thought.* Champaign: University of Illinois Press.

Capaldi, Nicholas. 1983. Sidney Hook: A Personal Portrait. In *Sidney Hook: Philosopher of Democracy and Humanism.* Edited by Paul Kurtz. Amherst, N.Y.: Prometheus Books.

Commission of Inquiry. 1937a. *The Case of Leon Trotsky.* New York: Harper.

———. 1937b. *Not Guilty.* New York: Harper.

Festenstein, Matthew. 1997. *Pragmatism and Political Theory: From Dewey to Rorty.* Chicago: University of Chicago Press.

Dewey, John. 1939. *Freedom and Culture.* In *The Later Works of John Dewey.* Vol. 13. Edited by Jo Ann Boydston. Carbondale: Southern Illinois University Press, 1988.

———. 1938. Means and Ends. In *The Later Works of John Dewey.* Vol 13. Edited by Jo Ann Boydston. Carbondale: Southern Illinois University Press, 1988.

———. 1937. The Challenge of Democracy to Education. In *The Later Works of John Dewey.* Vol. 11. Edited by Jo Ann Boydston. Carbondale: Southern Illinois University Press, 1987.

———. 1935. *Liberalism and Social Action.* In *The Later Works of John Dewey.* Vol. 11. Edited by Jo Ann Boydston. Carbondale: Southern Illinois University Press, 1987.

————. 1927. *The Public and Its Problems*. In *The Later Works of John Dewey*. Vol. 2. Edited by Jo Ann Boydston. Carbondale: Southern Illinois University Press, 1984.

————. 1916. *Democracy and Education*. In *The Middle Works of John Dewey*. Vol. 9. Edited by Jo Ann Boydston. Carbondale: Southern Illinois University Press, 1980.

Habermas, Jurgen. 1996. *Between Facts and Norms*. Cambridge: MIT Press.

Hart, Richard, and Douglass Anderson, eds. 1997. *Philosophy in Experience: American Philosophy in Transition*. New York: Fordham University Press.

Hook, Sidney. 1990. *Convictions*. Amherst, N.Y.: Prometheus Books.

————. 1987. *Out of Step: An Unquiet Life in the Twentieth Century*. New York: Harper and Row.

————. 1985. Convictions. In *Convictions*. Amherst, N.Y.: Prometheus Books.

————. 1980. *Philosophy and Public Policy*. Carbondale: Southern Illinois University Press.

————. 1978. Capitalism, Socialism, and Freedom. In *Philosophy and Public Policy*. Carbondale: Southen Illinois University Press, 1980.

————. 1977. How Democratic Is America? A Response to Howard Zinn. In *Convictions*. Amherst, N.Y.: Prometheus Books, 1990.

————. 1976. The Social Democratic Prospect. In *Philosophy and Public Policy*. Carbondale: Southern Illinois University Press, 1980.

————. 1975. *Revolution, Reform, and Social Justice*. New York: New York University Press.

————. 1974. The Ideology of Violence. In *Revolution, Reform, and Social Justice*. New York: New York University Press, 1975.

————. 1969. *Academic Freedom and Academic Anarchy*. New York: Cowles.

————. 1967. *Religion in a Free Society*. Lincoln: University of Nebraska Press.

————. 1963. The Rationale of a Non-Partisan Welfare State. In *Convictions*. Amherst, N.Y.: Prometheus Books, 1990.

————. 1962. *The Paradoxes of Freedom*. Berkeley: University of California Press.

————. 1961. *The Quest for Being*. New York: St. Martin's Press.

————. 1959a. *Political Power and Personal Freedom*. New York: Collier Books.

————. 1959b. The Justification of Democracy. In *Political Power and Personal Freedom*. New York: Collier Books.

————. 1959c. Democracy or Republic? In *Political Power and Personal Freedom*. New York: Collier Books.

————. 1959d. Are There Two Kinds of Democracy? In *Political Power and Personal Freedom*. New York: Collier Books.

————. 1959e. Bread, Freedom, and Free Enterprise. In *Political Power and Personal Freedom*. New York: Collier Books.

————. 1955. *Marx and the Marxists: The Ambiguous Legacy*. Melbourne, Fla.: Krieger.

————. 1953. *Heresy, Yes—Conspiracy, No*. New York: John Day.

————. 1944. Naturalism and Democracy. In *Naturalism and the Human Spirit*. Edited by Y. H. Krikorian. New York: Columbia University Press, 1944.

————. 1940a. *Reason, Social Myths, and Democracy*. New York: John Day.

————. 1937. Liberalism and the Case of Leon Trotsky. *Southern Review* 3 (autumn): 267–82.

Mounce, H. O. 1997. *The Two Pragmatisms: From Peirce to Rorty*. London: Routledge.

Murphy, John. 1990. *Pragmatism: From Peirce to Davidson*. Boulder: Westview Press.

Phelps, Christopher. 1997. *Young Sidney Hook: Marxist and Pragmatist*. New York: Cornell University Press.

Plato. 1992. *Republic*. Translated by Grube and Reeve. Indianapolis: Hackett.

Putnam, Hilary. 1990. A Reconsideration of Deweyan Democracy. In *Pragmatism in Law and Society*. Edited by Michael Brint and William Weaver. Boulder: Westview Press, 1991.

Rorty, Richard. 1998. *Achieving Our Country: Leftist Thought in Twentieth-Century America*. Cambridge: Harvard University Press.

————. 1991. The Banality of Pragmatism and the Poverty of Justice. In *Pragmatism in Law and Society*. Edited by Michael Brint and William Weaver. Boulder: Westview Press, 1991.

————. 1983. Pragmatism Without Method. In, *Objectivism, Relativism, and Truth*. Cambridge: Cambridge University Press, 1991.

Stuhr, John. 1993. Democracy as a Way of Life. In *Philosophy and the Reconstruction of Culture: Pragmatic Essays after Dewey*. Buffalo: SUNY Press.

West, Cornel. 1989. *The American Evasion of Philosophy*. Madison: University of Wisconsin Press.

Wilkerson, Doxey A. 1953. Marxists and Academic Freedom. Reprinted in *The American Left: Radical Political Thought in the Twentieth Century*. Edited by Loren Baritz. New York: Basic Books, 1971.

# I

# PHILOSOPHICAL CONTEXTS

## PRAGMATISM AND NATURALISM

# 1

# EXPERIMENTAL NATURALISM

W ere the phrase not so encrusted with misleading associations, I should call my philosophy "dialectical materialism"; materialism, because its explanations make no appeal to entities or processes which are not empirically verifiable by scientific method or logically inferrible from experienced data; dialectical, because it holds (a) that there is an implied temporal reference in every description or generalization, (b) that the processes of discovery and interpretation—as distinct from the validity of their results—cannot be completely dissociated from the socio-historical culture of the age, and (c) that under certain conditions, human thinking, construed as meaningful selective behavior and not as a passive reflection or image of the external scene, plays a creative role in the world. The vested interests, however, of a political church, and factional sectarian controversy motivated by everything but a desire for the truth, have incurably ruined the phrase "dialectical materialism" as a clear-cut differentiating mark of one's philosophic allegiance. I prefer, therefore, for the sake of accuracy, to select a more neutral characterization.

Since I have elsewhere developed my philosophical position in more technical form, and encouraged by editorial prescriptions as well as by the presumable interests of a lay audience, I shall take the liberty of presenting my views in a kind of philosophical autobiography. In this way

From *American Philosophy Today and Tomorrow*, eds. Horace M. Kallen and Sidney Hook. Reprinted by permission of Ardent Media Inc., 522 E. 82nd St., Ste. 1 NY, NY 10028–7118.

not only will the formal concatenations of my beliefs be made clear but
their history, cultural context, and probable development.


# I


My earliest interest in philosophy arose in the course of my reading when
still a boy, and was strengthened soon thereafter by active participation
in the socialist movement and the study of its literature.

I can still recall the day when a few snatches of amateur epistemological discussion in *Martin Eden*—used by Jack London to flavor a
scene in an artist's crowded kitchen—fired my imagination and I set out
to fathom the mysterious terminology which, I felt, must have, despite
its tantalizing obscurity, worlds of meaning. When I finally learned to my
astonishment that the existence of the external world was a problem, I
resolved to save the foundations of the universe, and for a long time wor-
ried over the question of how to answer Berkeley. Unable to refute
Berkeley I resolved that none of my friends should enjoy the luxury of
unapprehensive dogmatism, and set about infecting them with the virus
of doubt. I found that it was just as difficult to convert people to subjective idealism—even after their first contemptuous shrugs or flashes of
indignation—as it was to unconvert them if, for any reason at all, they
fled to this formally impregnable position. The sides taken did not seem
to depend upon the strength of the arguments used to support them.

This was my first philosophical seizure but my last one with epistemology. Although I was always a realist, and with a great deal of moral
fervor, it was not until I read Dewey and Woodbridge that I realized why
the problem—how is knowledge of the external world possible—was
insoluble in its own terms. Like every other process, once the process of
knowing was dissociated from its specific beginnings and endings, from
its relation to other activities and modes of experience, especially the
need for acquiring reliable information and principles to settle concrete
problems and fix belief, it was possible for a philosopher to raise more
questions about it than a host of wisemen could answer. Once the initial
and final phases of any temporal process are split into isolated and independent states, how can they ever be coherently related, especially by a
logical analysis which treats all terms as if they had no temporal character? The futility of this approach seems to me to be evident not only
in epistemology but more particularly today in sociology where the social

whole is first broken down into sharply separated factors and then "understood" in terms of a mechanical cause and effect relation between the parts. In the social realm such a technique is both muddled and dangerous, for it leads not only to sweeping dogmatisms when explanations are offered but to fanatical practice when social control is attempted by those who accept the explanations.

My social interest, although motivated by entirely different considerations, fed into my technical philosophical interest. Always a voracious reader, I devoured the literature of the socialist movement at an age when righteous passion at the indignities of the existence which surrounded me in the proletarian slums where my family lived, helped me to understand and to fix firmly in my mind the fundamental truths of the class-struggle. But there was more in the literature of the movement than a concern with economics and politics. Engels' *Anti-Dühring* and *Feuerbach*, the fragmentary discussions of philosophy scattered through the writings of Marx, the discussions of Labriola, Dietzgen, and other critics and commentators, raised questions which seemed to be interesting on their own account and at first blush to have precious little to do with the theory and practice of social revolution. And as subsequent reflection convinced me, many of them actually did not. I could not see, for example, what social consequences one way or the other flowed from the hotly disputed question, "whether oats grow according to the Hegelian dialectic or not"; or what political effects were bound up with Engels' acceptance of the mistaken theory of infinitesimals as a foundation of the differential calculus. But although I was later to discover that considerable portions of the so-called socialist philosophy were cultural survivals of the cosmic evolutionary optimism of the nineteenth century and at best superfluous baggage for a movement which aimed at revolutionary transformation of the social order, at the very outset I recognized its fundamental premises as closer to the position of naturalism—or scientific materialism—than any other regnant doctrine. About its naturalism I was extremely keen. An early revolt against supernaturalism and all organized religion, induced by a reading of Lecky, Lea, and Draper, and fortified by my own boyhood experience of religious discrimination and persecution, led me to appreciate the tremendous secular and humanizing impact of a thoroughgoing naturalism upon all phases of culture. That is one of the reasons, besides its demonstrable falsity, why I could never share the position of those who called themselves *orthodox* Marxists—people who having given up the traditional religions still believed in a church, the Party, and who, when challenged, fell back upon a new religion based on the inevitability of socialism.

However, I could never see that the specifically philosophical problems which faced the naturalistic outlook—the nature of time, causality, and logical implication—had any relevance to concrete problems of political theory and practice. Yet it was their pursuit which fascinated me most. And so, although I found political activity with its jealous absorption of all one's time and energy to be bad for one's philosophy, and any attempt at philosophical clarification of fundamental ideas to be anathema in politics, I could give up neither, which probably accounts— kind friends have suggested—for certain difficulties in both.

I came to adolescence during the War and the post-War period when the educational system of the country was in the throes of a collective obsession. My high school teachers, in those days a miscellaneous lot of men who had failed to get into other professions, ranted against everything German. Without ever having read a line of Kant, Hegel, or Nietzsche, they bandied their names about as being indirectly responsible for the War. (I couldn't say that I had read them either, but the *Nation* and G. H. Lewis' *Biographical History of Philosophy* supplied me with my ammunition for classroom war.) Every critical attitude in the social sciences was suspect as Bolshevism. Mathematics classes were occasions for fervent pleas to plant potatoes and to save peach pits, and in all other subjects every opportunity was seized to turn the recitation into a kind of psychic war-dance. Inside the schools, students were terrorized by teachers and student-patriots for discussing the merits of a capital tax over Liberty Bonds as a method of financing the War, for quoting the Declaration of Independence to speakers sent by the National Security League and the Daughters of the American Revolution, for pointing out that the canards about the leaders of the Russian Revolution, Lenin and Trotsky, solemnly taught as part of modern European history, were so contradictory that they could not all be true—in short, for trying to carry on the educational process which their teachers had funked. Things were not much better in the colleges. I still recall that during my first college year—a year after peace had been declared—I was stopped by a professor in the midst of a report in which I had claimed that Calhoun's logic was superior to Webster's, with the words: "When you are not preaching sedition, you are preaching secession." Outside of school, any peaceful meeting called to discuss or debate the issues of war and reconstruction was enough to bring down the Gegans and Scullys and Browns of Palmer-

Lusk fame, whose unwelcome acquaintance on several occasions I was compelled to make. Perhaps I was young and foolishly impetuous, but I believe it would have been difficult for any inquiring student, on the basis of my experience during those years, to avoid the conclusion that most of his teachers were fools and the rest cowards.

It was during this period that I picked up a copy of Bertrand Russell's *Justice In War-Time*, and learning more about the fortitude with which he had sustained unpopularity and imprisonment, continued to read his more popular works. There was nothing he wrote on social subjects which I did not already believe; but what fascinated me beyond all else was the method by which he got at his conclusions and the simple shining clarity of the arguments with which he would eliminate opposing views. Fortunately for me, I soon afterward began the study of philosophy with Professor Morris R. Cohen, himself a great admirer of Bertrand Russell but convinced, however, that Russell's philosophical power had declined in direct proportion to the growth of his civic zeal and social interest. My sense for method and evidence was strengthened by Professor Cohen's teaching and my enthusiasms, although disciplined, were not dampened. His was the first critical mind I had encountered in the educational wilderness and I revised my hasty judgments about the function of schools and teachers in society. From an educational point of view, his only philosophic infirmity was a tendency, bordering on genius, to distort the positions of eminent contemporary philosophers with whom he disagreed.

Logic for some years thereafter became my driving philosophic interest. Like all initiates into its easy mysteries, I made a perfect nuisance of myself by the indefatigable spirit with which I pointed out, classified, and held up to public light the fallacies in the perfectly comprehensible speech of my friends. To their protests that I knew what they meant, I responded that I wasn't interested in what they meant but in what they said. But behind all this was the feeling that logic, and particularly the logic of scientific method, was the only method by which the raging fevers of stupid and cruel intolerance could be diminished. All the fanatics I knew, whether they were professional patriots or heresy-hunting Communists, were either completely impervious to logic or conspicuously lame in following an argument. When they talked themselves into glaring contradiction either they did not know it, or were completely unabashed, acting as if their inconsistency reflected a higher law of nature. The notion that fanatics are too logical and suffer from too great a desire for consistency rather than too little is a sheer superstition. Most

of them are not even aware of the plainest implications of their statements. In the joy of my first discovery, I leaned over backward and tried
to assimilate scientific method to formal logic rather than vice versa. In
the murky atmosphere of a world in which there were so many different
variables influencing each other, so much uncertainty and confusion, I
had a hunger for something one could be sure about. One could be sure
about logic even at the price of not saying much. And in those days, with
the memory of the intellectual nightmare of the war and the post-war
period still fresh in my mind, I was not as interested in saying things as
in exposing the vicious nonsense which was being said. I knew that logic
was no substitute for insight and vision, but I knew then, and still
believe, that nothing significant could be accomplished in the world—
even in the social world—by an open defiance of the implications of what
we believe or do. Men may be controlled by blind passion but not the
material things and situations upon which they ultimately depend.

As a Marxist, I knew that history is not to be understood in terms of
the thoughts and passions which move men but in terms of the conflicting
group pressures and interests which express themselves through them
now in one way, now in another. But there is nothing incompatible with
Marxism in realizing and emphasizing that *how* these interests express
themselves makes a genuine difference. Whether the presumed interest is
the same as the real interest, and whether the real interest can be furthered by one mode of activity rather than another, are questions which
can be truly settled only when interests, so to speak, become self-conscious, when they are logically formulated, appraised, and tested in action.

Whatever may be the relevance of logical thinking as an historical and
social influence, there can be no question of the importance of its presence or absence in individual life, unless one is prepared to assert that a
man's ideas are self-contained entities separated by non-osmotic tissues
from the world in which he lives, enjoys, and suffers. But if we take
thoughts to be the motor cues of planned, executed, or suppressed
actions, then ideas are not feeble rays thrown off by a kind of phosphorus
substance in the brain, but ways of living and acting. What is called character in a man's life—and no character is fixed—can either be read
directly from the pattern of his activities, or since the pattern by itself
tells us little about the future, from the integrating ideals which he professes, under suspicious scrutiny, to be carrying out. Without some integration of the conflicting desires which solicit him, no man can achieve
the honesty of purpose that represents the whole of morality's demand.

Without some ability to do logical sums and exercises, to weigh alternatives and see implications, the self-consciousness necessary to integration in a world suggesting many possible paths of development for a sensitive and complex organism to follow is impossible. Indeed, it is no paradox but a reliable generalization that the man incapable of thinking, of knowing what he wants and what he means, cannot be honest either to himself or others. No matter what its role in social life, in individual life a modicum of logic is necessary for integrity of intellect and character. Is it not true that by a man's logic we judge him? But, of course, not only by his logic.

Further interest in, and reflection upon, logic led me to metaphysics. And like most young students of philosophy who have read the early Russell and savored the flavor of logical propositions whose validity is independent of experience and true for all possible worlds, I became, for a while, a staunch Platonic realist. This is an interesting phase in the development of students of philosophy today and I have watched many of my own go through it. Platonic realism seems to be a necessary transitional stage in the attempt to achieve philosophical clarity. Whoever remains stuck in it, I have noticed, seems to be rendered intellectually sterile. It makes, however, a many-sided appeal. Not only does it deal with eternal certainties so dear to men in a social crisis, not only has it the prestige of the exact disciplines of mathematics and logic which philosophers neglected in the nineteenth century, but it gratifies the insistent demand of youth—and its greatest weakness—the demand for intellectual simplicity. According to Platonic realism, what is intelligible can be grasped by an immediate intellectual intuition, and is capable of being broken down upon analysis into ultimate logical truths. Existence is essentially unintelligible. Nothing can be said not to have Being which can be the subject of a sentence. If the being it has is not existent, it is subsistent. A particular wheel exists, but "roundness" subsists; so does "a wheel whose like has never been seen before." Round-squares, golden mountains, the integer between 2 and 3, subsist too. The existential context of meaning, communication, intent, and history are dismissed as so much irrelevant psychological data and no problems are left to be solved—except all the important ones.

Another characteristic feature of Platonic realism—and this, I think, is a significant clue to its acceptance—is the generous contempt in which it holds most other philosophies. This comes about as follows. The problems which Platonic realism ignores (not to speak of those which its easy dualism creates) are the knottiest and most difficult problems of philosophy since they concern the relationship between form, content, process, and time. So complicated are these problems that it is often difficult to tell whether those whose philosophy is based upon the assertion of their metaphysical union and primacy are really talking sense or not. It is not Bergson, it is not James, it is not Bradley, it is not Dewey who repel the logical realists—when they actually get to reading them—but the hosts of their hangers-on, who enunciate in the name of their alleged masters and with an air of making new discoveries, propositions which were already commonplace truths or falsehoods in antiquity. Who does not know the flock of dabblers in philosophy whose stock in trade consists of statements like: "Everything moves," "Truth is what any culture says it is," "The law of identity is false," "Reality is spirit, mind, this, that, or something else"? I know that it was a great relief to have at hand the sharp instruments of logical realism with which to scalp all the nonprofessional prophets of the philosophy of gush and go. Logical realism will always make a call upon tough-minded students of philosophy until they learn that one can avoid uttering nonsense without thereby acquiring any great wisdom.

It was as a rather militant logical realist that I left college for graduate work at Columbia where for one year I constituted myself the official opposition to what I called "the psychology which was being passed off as philosophy." But a sad fate was in store for me. One day I sat down to write a definitive refutation of Professor Dewey's pragmatism. Of pragmatism I was a sworn enemy, having heard it refuted time out of hand by former teachers but never expounded. Nor did the reading of James or Schiller make me relent. James seemed to me to skirt all the difficulties, particularly those pressed against him by the philosophical formalists as well as those created by himself when any one of his books was compared with any other. Schiller's offer of pragmatism to the theologians as the best device for saving their religion scandalized me as such a piece of philosophical prostitution that I was blinded to the worth of his writings on the nature of hypotheses. Peirce, although brilliantly suggestive, never seemed to me a consistent thinker. Dewey, whom I could not answer, nonetheless could not convince me.

All of Dewey's contentions about the processes of thinking I was willing to grant, but I could not see how the formal characters of logic and the criteria of logical validity could be derived from empirical considerations. John Stuart Mill, I thought, was an illustration of the blind alley into which all empirical approaches to logic and mathematics led. Starting then from the fact that there were certain formally valid propositions, I raised the question as to the source and test of their validity.

The question, however, of the validity of any set of formal, presumably non-existential, propositions turned into a question of their consistency. The only proof of the consistency of propositions with which I was acquainted introduced empirical considerations. How, then, establish their validity? The only recourse was to fall back upon inspection and immediate intuition. But immediate intuition smacked dangerously of the psychology I was trying to avoid. I was compelled to ask myself what a valid intuition was and how I recognized it as such. With this the question of "meaning" became focal and it began to grow upon me that without some ultimate denotative reference to events or processes, one could never tell whether propositional functions were nonsense syllables or not. The non-existential logicians had gone from the unquestionably true statement that their meanings were independent of *any* particular exemplification to the highly dubious statement that they were independent of *all* possibility of exemplification. And with this, the game of Platonic realism was up and I found myself in the camp of my enemies. For if the meaning of a proposition necessarily involved the possibility of performing some operation to reveal its denotative range, the truth or falsity of a proposition could only be defined in terms of the predictive functions of meaningful statements, and determined by examining the consequences of the actions they pointed to.

It was not easy to surrender the paradise of subsistence and the comforts of truths necessary and universal in all possible worlds. I contested every inch of the way, but all my reading, arguing, and consultation with my logical realist friends proved to be fruitless. I was converted to pragmatism in a very unpragmatic way. Dewey's writings took on a new significance as treatises on the theory of meaning, and the last vestiges of supernaturalism—for that is what Platonic realism is—disappeared from my thought.

The weakness of Platonic realism becomes most apparent when the questions of meaning, consistency, and applicability are raised. For once challenge the assumption that terms can have meaning independently of the possibility of exemplification in some event, process, or operation, then the inevitable retort that these are "mere" matters of psychology and history can be met by showing that the Platonic realists have a definite psychology based upon the dogma of immediate knowledge and a definite theory of time according to which only the present exists.

The naturalistic approach to logic regards logical principles either as the formal expressions of the structure *of* some subject matter in space and time and, therefore, in some sense historical, or as the leading prin-

ciples of the methods and techniques of inquiry which have enabled men
to solve specific problems or difficulties. This approach has its difficuties
—difficulties, of course, which are not solved by pointing to the weaknesses of Platonic realism. For there seems to be a great many mathematical and logical principles which have no reference to existential subject matter even at many removes and do not function as principles of
inquiry in solving specific problems. But the very claim to be dealing
with a subject matter at no point infected with "the evil" of existence is
at the source of many of the difficulties and paradoxes of contemporary
foundational logic and mathematics. It is in this field that the experimental or operational theory of meaning permits not only a defense of
the naturalist approach but, as the work of Dewey, Bridgman, Nagel, and
the logical positivists shows, makes possible a beginning in clearing up
some of the mysteries clustering around the concepts of infinity, zero,
irrationals, and classes which contain themselves as members.

The question may be asked, why such concern with saving naturalism against all varieties of *a priorism* whether it be Platonic realism,
Hegelian idealism, conventionalism, or mechanistic materialism?
Although it was the intrinsic inadequacy of these positions—and this was
the only relevant philosophical ground—which led me to reject them, I
must confess that here, too, there were at least two other nonphilosoph-
ical motives which sharpened my critical zest. *A priorism* always seemed
to me to be associated with theology and social conservatism. The sharp
separation between existence and validity, and the problem to which this
gave rise, of accounting for the ontological status and truth of universal
and necessary propositions, made it particularly easy to postulate a
cosmic consciousness—in short, the mind of God—as their locus and
guarantee of validity. Descartes' dualism led him to base the necessity of
the truths of arithmetic upon God's mind and God's goodness. That
absolute idealism was an implicit theology did not have to be argued in
view of the admissions of Schelling, Hegel, and their followers. Nor can
any view which holds that every segment of the world, past, present, and
future, is part of one great machine of interlocking mechanisms escape
the plausible, even if logically unjustified, analogy to the existence of a
supreme machine-maker. By different routes, then, all *a prioristic*
philosophies seem to converge on God.

The social uses of *a priorism* have been clear, I think, from the days
of antiquity when Plato deduced the aristocratic rule of philosophers
from the idea of true knowledge, and Aristotle provided eternal justifica-

tion for slavery on the basis of disparity in human talents. My Marxism had taught me to be suspicious of absolutisms of every kind, and although I could not find any Marxist who could give even a remotely plausible historical interpretation of the specific varieties of *a priorism*, their general function as rationalizations for entrenched conservatism was clear. Indeed, one did not have to be a Marxist to see this. There is a passage in John Stuart Mill's *Autobiography* which has always seemed to me not only to explain a great deal about Mill's philosophy but to state effectively the point I am making:

"The notion that truths external to the mind may be known by intuition or consciousness, independently of observation or experience, is, I am persuaded, in these times, the great intellectual support of false doctrines and bad institutions. By the aid of this theory, every inveterate belief and every intense feeling, of which the origin is not remembered, is enabled to dispense with the obligation of justifying itself by reason, and is erected into its own all sufficient voucher and justification. There never was such an instrument devised for consecrating all deep-seated prejudices. And the chief strength of this false philosophy in morals, politics and religion, lies in the appeal which it is accustomed to make to the evidence of mathematics and of the cognate branches of physical science."

## II

I had now to come to grips with the different varieties of naturalism, to set them in their historical context, to work out their fundamental motivation and relate them to the conflicting group values, which struggled for domination in the social scene. Under Professor Woodbridge I got still further away from the baubles of essence doctrine. His method of analysis always took as its point of departure some concrete situation and his insistence upon control by subject matter was the best antidote to that lingering fever of philosophical adolescence which might very well be called "dialectic flutter." Universals and essences were naturalized as the structural principles of the concrete. Logical order could be discovered in nature; there was no need to look for it elsewhere. This emphasis upon structure was in line with the rationalistic naturalism of Professor Cohen, for whom logical principles represented the most general metaphysical invariants of all being, out of time because they held for time, and necessarily true because they could not be confronted with a significant alternative.

Again it was the influence of Professor Dewey which led me away from the modified Aristotelianism of Woodbridge and the ambiguous rationalism of Cohen to a further development of my naturalism. The analysis of the concepts of invariance—in use in any fruitful inquiry—convinced me that it was unnecessary to attribute an absolutely fixed ontological status to them. In nature there was warrant only for relative invariants. To isolate them from their knowledge-getting context and set them up as a kind of grammar of eternity seemed to me to be playing God to creation. *Relative* invariants, I could see as the indisputable necessary condition for prediction and control in all fields of nature and society. Emphasis upon them was justified in view of the uncritical tendencies toward a free and easy temporalism which exalted novelty, discontinuity, and chance to a point where the recurrent connections, patterns, and organization of events—upon which all intelligible explanation depends—disappeared. And for purposes of calculation, invariants could be abstracted from the existential complex in which they were found and considered by themselves. But when it was forgotten that these abstractions were the working rules of various formal and material branches of knowledge, and converted into imperatives of all thought and practice in all fields for all time, it prepared the way for that metaphysical isolation and hypostasis of the criteria of logical validity, upon which traditional dualisms have fed. It was this hypostasis which seemed to me to be behind the periodic resurgence of scholasticism, the easy flights to eternity on the borrowed wings of Spinozism, and the revival of neo-Platonic mysticism even among mathematical physicists—in short, the most important currents of what goes by the name of the classic tradition in philosophy.

What can an "invariant" be from the point of view of the experimental theory of meaning? It is either a resolution to handle particular situations in a certain determinate way or it is some structural or functional fact discovered whenever certain relevant operations are performed. The most general invariants—logical invariants—are those that always turn up whatever the technique of inquiry might be. Experimentally, the concept "always" has meaning only because of its reference to a temporal process or operation, necessarily incomplete. Let us not mistake this experimentalism for arbitrary relativism. Against all species of conventionalism and "pure" dialectical method, which deny all objectivity to truth, accept all starting points as equally valid because they are all undebatable axioms, and which are therefore, prepared to sell any picture of the world modeled to any heart's desire, the experimental philosophy in its sober materialism contends that resolutions to treat things in a certain way can only succeed when they yield to the structural features of the subject matter treated. But the materialism of experimentalism is historical and evolutionary. For the structural features of any subject matter in this world is of a subject matter which is itself a segment of space-time, considered not as substance but as process. Consequently, unless it is proved that the temporal nonformal aspects of subject matter can never affect the formal, logical aspects, allegedly eternal, no absolute invariants can be established.

Until I could emancipate myself from the fear of verbalisms which gave the appearance of self-contradiction, I could not assert this position. Translated into the language of orthodox nontemporalism, I knew it did not make sense. For, after all, how could one speak about an invariant changing, or a law having a history, except in terms of a more inclusive invariant or law? And how could logical principles have temporal coefficients when no significant alternatives to them could be formulated? But this was letting language impose upon me and forgetting that the appearance of verbal contradiction only reflected the attempt to catch up, so to speak, with the character of time. To put descriptions into fixed symbols and then, not merely to disregard their temporal contexts but to deny their existence, was equivalent to treating time as if it had no temporal qualities at all, as if it were something which was all run out, a series of befores, heres, and afters with no pasts, presents, and futures. Of course, the opposite of a logical proposition cannot in the nature of the case make sense. For that would demand finding a case to which it did not apply and it has been so formulated as to assume that all the cases are in. But the nonsense which now results from negativing a logical proposition is no guarantee that the original proposition will "always" make sense, i.e., operationally speaking, that it will always enable us to organize our experiences. However, there is a shorter way out of the difficulty. No claim should be made to the title of absolute invariants for the widest structural relations of experience. Our task is to analyze and organize them into a hierarchy of levels of generality. Each level would be relatively invariant to the one above it.

The fundamental issues between rationalistic and experimental naturalism, I now believe, can be traced to differences in emphasis which are motivated more by cultural and personal considerations than by strictly logical ones. Both admit that there is a legitimate distinction between the unique, specific, irreducible, on the one hand, and the repetitive, general, typical on the other; between propositions whose opposite is unintelligible and those whose opposite is meaningful. Both accept the dialectic polarity (in the sense of Hegel's doctrine of Essence) of the fundamental metaphysical categories: term-relation, continuity-discontinuity, particular-universal, concrete-abstract, so that any discussion of one involves necessary reference to the other. But in the face of concrete problems it is not enough to recognize that polar categories are necessarily involved in order to solve them. The necessities of action compel the acceptance of one series of categories rather than another; and contemplation, the favorite activity of philosophers, since it has definite consequences, is one form of action. Depending upon the *purposes* of action, so manifestly conditioned by the culture, country, and class in which we live and by the personalities we are, one set of decisions rather than another will result. Reflection upon decisions already taken and to be taken, determines the selection of, or rather the emphasis upon, one cluster of categories instead of the other. It is this accenting of the categories of movement over those of stability, of the freshly occurrent over the old recurrent, or vice versa, which is the foundation stone of a man's metaphysics. And although the difference in emphasis may in the beginning be slight, when the structure of thought is completed that difference makes all the difference in the world to the kind of life and the kind of society we know.

What kind of philosophers—really what kind of men—lay their foundation stones one way rather than another? No very accurate generalizations can be made. But substantially, there is a rough correlation between social attitudes and metaphysical bias. Those philosophers, who in any definite age are prepared to support the status quo on the ground that the imperfections of today, because they are known, are more tolerable than the dangers of tomorrow, are likely to stress the categories of invariance. Those who are more sensitive to the remediable evils of today and are optimistic about the possibilities of human intelligence contriving techniques with which to grapple with the problems of tomorrow are apt to be experimental in their metaphysical outlook. Where conflict arises between these groups for social support, the philosophers of invariance are more likely to receive the official blessings and sugar plums than the others. Governments are always on the side of eternity. Today, however, it is not social and political allegiances which can be significantly correlated with different philosophical views. And for a simple reason. Practically all schools of philosophy in America have the same middle-class outlook upon social affairs. The significant connection must be sought elsewhere. I believe that the connection between temperament and philosophy is more fundamental and more readily ascertainable than that between class allegiance and philosophical belief. The temperament which loves peace above all other values and sees in the ordered routines of professional, social, and personal life the best methods of achieving it, is likely to embrace in thought the calm options of eternity and invariance, if not the consolations of outright theology. The temperament which enjoys battle, for which variety is a genuine good, which values the perplexities that attend the pursuit of incompatible goods as the opportunities for creative action, is likely to follow the vital option of experimentalism. Of course no philosopher is either purely one thing or another in all his interests. The boldest experimentalist, Santayana somewhere suggests, had better draw the line rather narrowly in his cooking. And absolutists have been known to experiment with new arguments for self-defense. The dominant patterns, however, as James so wisely saw, will assert themselves, even if the types be different from those he classified. Since most philosophers by training, selection, and the mechanisms of academic preferment have been timid, peace-above-all loving creatures, the history of philosophy, in the main, has been a history of dogmatic rationalism, mysticism, and religious apologetic. The most beaten paths have been made by unidirectional tracks toward the One.

The metaphysical program of experimental naturalism recognizes, as its fundamental task, the exhaustive analysis of all the primary categories with especial reference to temporal context and experience. Here not more than a beginning has been made.

# III

During the course of these years my strong social interests kept on interweaving with my technical ones. When Marx's early philosophical manuscripts were published, I took the occasion to make a systematic restudy of all his works. I was impressed by the presence in his thought of points of view—undeveloped to be sure—completely incompatible with the orthodox exegsis. After further research which took me into Germany and Russia, into the history of Marx's times, his intellectual development and the doctrines of his opponents, I became convinced that his dialectic method by which he strove to combine realism and activism, to do justice to the facts of objectivity and relativity, and to explore the logic of the process, involved a nascent experimental naturalism. This was essentially the same position which John Dewey had independently arrived at in a different idiom and developed so impressively in psychology, logic, science, and esthetics.

Since many critics have insinuated that I have read Dewey into Marx, I wish to point out that nowhere and at no time have I claimed that Dewey was a Marxist or Marx the John the Baptist of pragmatism. Their social and political philosophies are quite different in spirit and emphasis. All I have asserted is that their fundamental metaphysical and logical positions are the same but developed as differently as we would expect a great social revolutionist and a great professional philosopher to develop them. From a naturalistic point of view agreement upon fundamental metaphysical doctrines does not univocally determine any *one* social doctrine, and certainly not a specific class allegiance. And as for the fundamental agreement between Marx and Dewey, I need only point here to their common left-Hegelian derivation and naturalization of the Hegelian dialectic, common criticism of atomism, sensationalism, Platonism and formalism, and a common wholehearted acceptance of the philosophical implications of Darwinism. Any philosopher who takes these three positions seriously is an experimental naturalist whether he knows it or not.

Since I have described my social philosophy elsewhere,[1] I shall not dwell upon it here except to say that I regard the social problem as the most important, and at the same time philosophically the least interesting, of all problems. It should be solved in order that mankind may devote itself to art, science, and pure philosophy which can never be really autonomous disciplines in a class society. When one reflects upon the extent to which philosophy has been an apologia for some vested social right, when one recalls the undistinguished role philosophers played during the World War, it will be admitted that no more than any other branch of culture can it pursue its professional task independently of the economic and political miasmas bred by capitalist society.

As to what the task of philosophy is, philosophers themselves seem to be in quite a quandary. Judging by the amount of time consumed in apologizing for the way in which they earn their living and in the variety of the extra-philosophical justifications offered in defense of their activity, one would suspect that philosophers themselves are doubtful as to whether they have a specific subject matter. It seems to me that philosophy at its best is not a hand-maiden to politics or theology, nor an instrument of moral edification, but a *critical activity* which aims to clarify to ourselves what we know, what we live for and die for, what we do, and what we say. It is critically relevant to the whole of life's activities and its exercise creates a value and adds a dimension to experience obtainable in no other way. This is the professional task of philosophy even though philosophers need not be professionals. It is through philosophical activity that mankind becomes conscious of itself—of its possibilities and its limitations.

[1935]

## NOTE

1. Compare the symposium volume, *The Meaning of Marx* (New York: Farrar and Rinehart, 1934).

# 2

# NATURALISM AND FIRST PRINCIPLES

I n this chapter I shall discuss what seems to me to be one of the most fundamental problems in the intellectual enterprise which goes by the name of philosophy, viz., what it means for human behavior to be reasonable or rational. It is a question which arises even when we have no doubt that a person is logical in the sense that he draws conclusions which are implied or entailed by certain premises. A paranoiac is nothing if not logical when he spins the strands of unrelated events into a web of conspiracy of which he is the presumed victim. Some philosophers have raised the question in connection with a discussion of the nature of intelligibility when the meaning of the thought or conduct of others is puzzling or in doubt. I have been led to it because of some recent criticisms of naturalism which charge that it arbitrarily imposes its own canons of rationality or intelligibility on human behavior and therefore denies certain important truths about the world and human experience on *a priori* grounds.

A similar question has also been raised by some fashionable sociological views of knowledge according to which there are irreducibly different modes of knowing illustrated in different cultures and which suggest, and sometimes explicitly affirm, that there is no such thing as a universally objective, valid method of determining rational or intelligible conduct, independent of time or society or class, or even of party. On this latter view, it is sometimes argued that moral, social, and political conflicts are the results of conflicting logics of inquiry. Sometimes the converse is argued, i.e., irreducible social conflicts give rise to irreducibly different criteria of truth. In either case no one method can claim universal and exclusive validity. Indeed, to claim that any one method of establishing truths is better than another is to be guilty of philosophical imperialism almost in the same way that the claim of superiority for the institutions of modern Western, democratic society evinces cultural imperialism.

My argument will make the following points: (1) despite all the basic conflicts over first principles of thinking or evidence, there are working truths on the level of practical living which are everywhere recognized and which everywhere determine the pattern of reasonable conduct in secular affairs, viz., the effective use of means to achieve ends. Rationality on this level is not merely as Charles Peirce suggests "being governed by final causes" but so using the means and materials of the situation in which final causes are pursued as to achieve a maximum of functional adaptation between means and ends. (2) Second, this conception of rationality is not limited to our culture and to our time but is supported by the available anthropological evidence. The mind of primitive man, medieval man, communist man, for all the claims that have been made about their differences, is no different from our own. This is not incompatible with believing that in respect to discovering new truth one or another group of men, in virtue of *historical*, perhaps genetic reasons, at a given time may be in possession of superior powers. (3) Third, scientific method is the refinement of the canons of rationality and intelligibility exhibited by the techniques of behavior and habits of inference involved in the arts and crafts of men; its pattern is everywhere discernible even when overlaid with myth and ritual. (4) Fourth, the systematization of what is involved in the scientific method of inquiry is what we mean by naturalism, and the characteristic doctrines of naturalism like the denial of disembodied spirits generalize the cumulative evidence won by the use of this method. (5) Fifth, that the criticisms of naturalism from which the paper takes its point of departure can be met by showing that, although the assumptions of naturalism are not necessarily true, they are more reasonable than their alternatives.

If it is true, as Peirce says, that "Every reasoning itself holds out some expectation," the validity of rules of reasoning is not a matter of fiat but depends upon the fruits of inquiry. Ultimately the rules of logic are instruments of discourse which enable us to avoid the shocks and surprises, the disasters and disappointments in attempting to understand the nature of the world and our own intentions and purposes. One method of reasoning is more valid than another because its use enables us to make the knowledge we have today more coherent, and especially because it more easily facilitates adding *new* knowledge to it.

# I

That first principles must be justified before we can achieve assured knowledge is a view seemingly held by some philosophers but rarely by anyone else. Scientists, for example, have satisfactorily solved problem after problem without feeling called upon to solve the problem of justifying their first principles. Not only scientists but people of ordinary affairs generally know when something is truer than something else without knowing, or even claiming to know, what is *absolutely* true. To say that we do not have to know what is ultimately or absolutely true or good in order to know what is truer or better, sounds dialectically impossible. But I submit that this is actually the way common sense and science operate. Even the most rationalist of philosophers in their nonprofessional capacity make effective use of everyday knowledge long before they reach their uncertain conclusions about the validity of first principles. It isn't necessary to assert that we know what is absolutely true about the cause of tuberculosis to know that a certain germ has more to do with it than climate. Similarly, few people know what their "ultimate" values are, and yet almost everyone will claim to know that it is better for human beings to do productive labor for a living than to be recipients of charity. Deny propositions of this sort and insist that declarations of the truer or better must wait upon knowledge of *the* true or *the* good, and the whole of human inquiry anywhere would come to a halt.

This is not to assert that there is no problem concerning the justification of first principles or of those rules of procedure which we follow when we reach the knowledge about which there is a maximum of agreement among human beings. What I am asserting is that the justification of rules of procedure in inquiry is not of a different logical order, possessing so to speak another or higher type of necessity than the actions of which they are the rule. More specifically what I am asserting is that there is no such thing as strictly logical justification of first principles in science or common sense since proof by definition involves the reduction of all statements to indefinable terms and undemonstrable propositions or to propositions themselves so reducible. And secondly, what I am further asserting is that in the sense in which justification of first principles is an intelligible question—as when someone asks me why I regard naturalism as a truer or more adequate doctrine than its rivals—the answer will take the same *general* form of the answers given by those who do the world's work—the cobblers, the carpenters, and gardeners—when they are asked to justify one set of procedures rather than alternative ones.

In other words I am saying somewhat differently what William James observed in *The Problems of Philosophy* although it is alleged he sometimes sinned against the meaning of his own words. "Philosophy," he there says, "taken as something distinct from science or human affairs, follows no method peculiar to itself. All our thinking today has evolved gradually out of primitive human thought, and the only really important changes that have come over its manner (as distinguished from the matters in which it believes) are a *greater* hesitancy in asserting its convictions, and the *habit* of seeking verification for them when it can." [my italics]

Such an approach, as I understand it, is the only one that can consistently be advanced by naturalists in justifying their first principles. This has provoked the retort that it is essentially question-begging, that since the methods and categories of common day activity and science—upon which naturalism relies—are designed to take note only of the existence of certain things, the existence of other things like immaterial entities, cosmic purposes, Gods, and disembodied souls are ruled out *a priori*. The assertion of their existence on the naturalist's view must therefore be assumed to be not merely false but meaningless or contradictory. Since we are concerned here with questions of existential fact, the naturalist who naïvely believes himself to be imbued with a spirit of natural piety for a world he has not created, is taxed with the ironic charge of legislating for all existence.

Before evaluating the charge of circularity it is important to realize that if valid, it holds for *every* philosophical position. We cannot break out of this circularity by invoking only the law of contradiction, unless we are prepared to hold that all knowledge is analytic and that the differences between nature and history, with all their contingency, and mathematics and logic disappear. Certainly, whatever falls outside the scope of the basic explanatory categories of any philosophical position cannot be recognized. This is a tautology. That these categories are restrictive follows from their claim to be meaningful since a necessary condition of a meaningful statement is that it should be incompatible with its opposite. The only legitimate question here is whether they are narrowly restrictive, whether there are matters of knowledge in common experience which they exclude or whose existence they make unintelligible.

Since every philosophic position must start somewhere and make some preliminary or initial assumptions that can be challenged at least verbally by other philosophers, it is always possible to level the charge of circularity. But what shall we therefore conclude? That these assumptions are mere stipulations or arbitrary postulations which express nothing but the *resolutions* of philosophers? This would be voluntarism gone mad. Philosophers might just as well close up shop insofar as they claim for their position some objective validity in reporting or interpreting the facts of experience. For even voluntarism could not sustain itself against the charge of circularity.

The naturalist does not despair because he cannot demonstrate what is by definition indemonstrable. Nor can he rely upon intuitions or revealed dogmas because of their irreducible plurality. He believes he can show that although not demonstrable, his assumptions can be made reasonable to "reasonable" men. And the mark of a "reasonable" man is his willingness to take responsibility for his actions, to explain why he proceeds to do one thing rather than another, and to recognize that it is his conduct, insofar as it is voluntary, which commits him to a principle or belief rather than any form of words where the two seem at odds with each other. The naturalist does not speak, as one of its critics does, in large terms of "justifying philosophical categories as rationally and comprehensively as possible," and then fail to tell us in what specific ways philosophical rationality and comprehensiveness differ from scientific rationality and comprehensiveness. Are the laws of logic and the canons of evidence and relevance any different in philosophy from what they are in science and common sense?

To every critic of naturalism who has charged it with circularity I propose the following. Consider someone who comes to you and proclaims on the basis of some special personal experience that an all-pervasive R substance exists. It is neither physical nor psychical nor social, neither natural nor divine, nor can it be identified by, defined in, or reduced, in any sense of reduction, to any physical, psychical, or social terms. It is subject, so you are told, to no material conditions of determination whatsoever. The very request that these conditions be indicated is brushed aside as revealing a constitutional incapacity or blindness to grasp this unique entity to which all sorts of edifying qualities are attributed in an analogical sense, including a triune gender. It is granted by the believer in R that its existence cannot be logically inferred from whatever *else* is experienced, but he is quick to add that its existence cannot be logically *disproved* without assuming a questionbegging philosophical position which rules out the possibility of this unique cosmic process. The next day he reports personal contact with another presence which he calls the analogical father, and the day after, the analogical grandfather, and so on, until even the most fervent supernaturalist finds himself confronted with an embarrassment of supernatural riches.

Embroider the fancy as you will. It is obvious that he can repeat almost word for word the points in the indictment of those who charge naturalists with circular reasoning.

Even if all philosophical positions are *au fond* question-begging, there would still remain the task, pursued by all philosophers of determining which of all question-begging positions is more adequate to the facts of experience. Every philosopher who seriously attempts an answer does assume *in fact* that there is some common method of determining when a position is adequate to the facts of experience and when not. The contention of the naturalist is that this common method is in principle continuous with the method which we ordinarily use to hold individuals to responsible utterance about the existence of things in the world—a method which is preeminently illustrated in the ways in which men everywhere solve the problem of adaptation of material means to ends.

## II

The procedures which are the matrix of reasonable conduct everywhere seem to me to be clearly involved in what broadly speaking we may call the technological aspect of human culture. It is not necessary to maintain that tool using is the only characteristic which differentiates human society from animal societies to recognize that whereas only some non-human animals occasionally use natural objects as tools, all human animals, wherever they are found, *make* their own tools. What distinguishes modern society from primitive society is not the presence of inventions but the organization of inventiveness.

Anthropological evidence leaves no doubt that primitive man wherever found solved tremendous problems of adjustment and survival. With a little imagination we can appreciate that starting from scratch such things as the invention of fire and the wheel, the cultivation of plants, domestication of cattle, and the smelting of metal represent inventive feats of a high order. There is an obvious continuity between our own technology and that of our primitive ancestors. "The sapling," says A. A. Goldenweiser, "bent out of its natural position to provide the dynamic factor in a primitive trap, is the remote forerunner of a spring which runs untold millions of watches and performs numerous other tasks in modern technology. The achievement of Alexander the Great in cutting the Gordian knot, though dramatic, did not equal that other achievement—the tying of the first knot. And this knot, in the midst of an ever-growing family of knots, is still with us."[1]

One can multiply illustrations indefinitely of the ingenious ways in which primitive man everywhere chooses between alternate means to achieve the particular end, improves upon these means and tests them by their relative efficacy in achieving determinate results. What stands out in my mind particularly is the impressive functional economy of the Eskimo's composite harpoon, that marvelous contrivance by which he spears seal, walrus, and whale, and especially the way in which the precious point is recovered. Hundreds of decisions must have been made and tested by their consequences before the instrument finally took shape.

The pattern of rationality does not extend of course to all aspects of primitive life any more than it does to our own life, but it points to a universal pattern of intelligibility understood by everyone who grasps the problem which the tool or technical process is destined to solve. Where religion or myth does not influence technology, the indefinite perfectability, so to speak, of the particular instrument is recognized or another one is substituted which gives more reliable results. Thus, for example, the Eskimo will abandon his ingenious harpoon for a gun when he can procure one.

The contention of Levy-Bruhl that primitive man thinks prelogically, that he denies the law of contradiction, that he is unable to isolate and distinguish logically unrelated things or ideas, that he understands by a kind of "participation" is not borne out by a study of primitive technology. Levy-Bruhl's observations are valid enough for the religious beliefs and social customs of the primitives, for their "collective representations" but not for the individual behavior of the primitive in war or hunt or in the field. One might add that Levy-Bruhl's observations can be extended to much of the religious beliefs and social customs of modern society, too. Even if all of Levy-Bruhl's claims are granted they do not invalidate Franz Boas' plausibly argued conclusion that the mental processes of primitive man in respect to inhibition of impulses, power of attention, logical thinking, and inventiveness seem essentially like our own.[2]

Despite their differences on other questions there is fundamental agreement among Levy-Bruhl, Boas, Goldenweiser, and Mahinowski concerning the universality of the experimental, commonsensical, practical approach to the environmental challenge. Malinowski points out that the realms of the profane or secular, and the realms of the religious or supernatural are not confused even when their respective activities are conjoined. The native plants his sweet potato with the most exacting care for the conditions of soil, moisture, and other elements which affect its growth: but in addition, he goes through some religious ritual, supported by a myth, before he believes he has a right to expect a successful crop.

> "Can we regard primitive knowledge," asks Malinowski, "which, as we found is both empirical and rational, as a rudimentary stage of science, or is it not at all related to it? If by science be understood a body of rules and conceptions, based on experience and derived from it by logical inference, embodied in material achievements and in a fixed form of tradition and carried on by some sort of social organization—then there is no doubt that even the lowest savage communities have the beginnings of science, however rudimentary."[3]

Similarly, Goldenweiser:

> "Technique on the one hand, and religion and magic, on the other, present from one angle the opposite poles of the primitive attitude. Industry stands for common sense, knowledge, skill, objective matter of fact achievement. Religion stands for mysticism, a subjective translation of experience, a substitution of mental states for external realities and a reification of such states into presumed existences in a realm which in part is 'another' world but in part also belongs to 'this' world insofar as the two worlds interpenetrate."[4]

What all modern anthropologists seem to agree on, as I interpret them, is that the religious or mystical elements in primitive experience, with their myths and religious rites, arise not in competition with the secular knowledge of technology or as a substitute for such knowledge but as a "complement" in situations in which all the available technical means and know-how are not adequate to a desired end, or where events do not clearly or always prosper when the proper instrumentalities are employed. In a world full of dangers and surprises, in a world of time, pain, and contingencies, it is not hard to understand the psychological place of religion. It is a safe generalization to say that the depth of the religious sense is inversely proportionate to the degree of reliable control man exercises over his environment and culture. In this sense religion is a form of faith, emotion, not knowledge: when it is something more than this and competes with science or technology it becomes superstition.

We may restate this a little differently. Science or technology and religion represent two different attitudes toward the mysterious: one tries to solve mysteries, the other worships them. The first believes that mysteries may be made less mysterious even when they are not cleared up, and admits that there will always be mysteries. The second believes that some specific mysteries are final.

This relation between technology and religion is not restricted to primitive societies. Somewhere in the Talmud it is written that if a man's son is ill, the correct thing for him to do is not merely to call a doctor or merely to pray to God but to call a doctor *and* pray to God. And in our own culture this seems to be the function of nonsuperstitious religion. The theology comes as an afterthought. Even those who do not believe in God often look around for Him to thank or to blame somewhat like the atheist in the well-known story who when asked why he nailed a horseshoe over his door replied, "I really don't believe in it but I've heard it brings luck even if you don't."

In modern societies our attitudes are more complex. There is religion and religion. If you pray to God expecting rain or a baby boy, that is one thing. It is bad science, although if Rhine establishes the existence of psychokinesis (the PK effect), a power which some subjects allegedly have to influence the way dice will fall by wishing or willing, this kind of praying may not be bad science. If you pray in order to relieve your mind that is another thing. It is good psychology although there may be better psychology. If you pray without any purpose at all but out of a sense of relief, gratitude, awe, or fear—that is not science at all but pure religion or art. "If scientific statements are to be called truths, religious statements should be called something else—comforts, perhaps."[5]

## III

I turn now to a brief consideration of the nature of technology and technological behavior. All technological behavior is purposive behavior; the purpose provides a test of relevance, and the achievement of purpose, a test of the adequacy of alternative means suggested. Its every feature takes note of the compulsions of the environment as well as the much more limited powers of man over the environment. Its knowledge is a form of *ack*nowledgment—an acknowledgment of the nature of materials, the effect of motor action on the redistribution of materials, the importance of sequential order and spatial configuration. It is obviously reconstructive in intent, and makes of a natural order one that is also reasonable. It discounts the immediate qualities of use and enjoyment for the sake of anticipated consequences. Wherever we have a tool or technique, it refers not to a unique situation but a class of situations so that it has a kind of implicit universal import not separable from ultimate individual applications. The better instrument recommends itself to us to the extent that it enables us to make a more reliable prediction of *observable* effects that bear on the the purpose in hand—the resolution of the problem. Learning from these simple inductions of experience is usually the first manifestation of intelligence. The violation, or rather the attempted violation of established inductions, like walking off a roof or out of a window, is sometimes the first evidence of insanity.

Technological behavior may be overlaid with all sorts of propitiatory rites but it is usually possible to distinguish between the functional and ritualistic aspects of the use of instruments. In its purely functional aspect every feature of the technique can be justified by its normal fruits or consequences. In time the process of adaptation tends to give us structures that are as simple and beautiful in their economy as the axhandle and oar, turbine and jet plane.

An analysis of the implicit logic of technology and the commonsense operations it involves, reveals that no hard and fast line of separation can be drawn between the general pattern of scientific method and reasonable procedures in the primary knowledge-getting activities of men struggling to control their environment. With the development of new instruments of discovery and measurement, and the use of mathematical notation, science becomes more abstract, more systematic, more precise, more complex. But wherever a man has had an idea sufficiently clear to enable him to draw a valid inference from it, the truth of which he sought to test by some controlled observation or experiment, he was proceeding—no matter how primitively—in a scientific way. The continuity between reasonable procedures in reaching conclusions about matters of fact of everyday concern and the procedures by which we make the most esoteric discoveries in the advanced sciences cannot be breached without making the whole enterprise of science a mystery, for every science starts from, and returns to, some of these reasonable procedures. If the commonsense world is radically unreliable or illusory, every theoretical construction which is based upon it or which it tests, is no more credible.

What we might call the first order facts of science are drawn directly from the world of commonsense experience—e.g., that a sponge holds more water than a cloth, that a polished surface is a better reflector than an opaque one, that white clothing is cooler than black—all of which were once discoveries. In the development of science no matter what the succession of theories, these first order facts are the last to be challenged. Whether the wave theory or corpuscular theory or any other theory of light is defended, the law which states the inequality of the angles of incidence and refraction when a ray of light passes from one medium to another is not questioned. For the class of phenomena it characterizes must be accounted for irrespective of what other predictions are made. From this point of view the laws of nature may be plausibly interpreted as instrumental devices to bring within the largest explanatory scheme our empirical knowledge of first order facts and successfully to predict future experiences which then become first order facts for all other theories.

Science differs from technology in two important respects. First in generality, and second in purpose. Technology is restricted in its practical reference to useful results; whereas the practical purpose of science, if we choose to use this language, is "the advancement of knowing apart from concern with other practical affairs," i.e., the building up of a systematic body of knowledge.[6]

# IV

If there is no break in the continuity between life sustaining technological and vocational activities anywhere, and developed scientific activities, there is still less to be said for the view that science is so intimately tied up with culture that we must in Spenglerian fashion speak of Apollonian science, Magian science, and Faustian science with irreducibly different criteria of scientific validity. This is carried to extreme lengths by the current dialectical materialistic interpretation of science which denies its classless, international character and asserts that all sciences, social as well as physical, are class sciences and party sciences. More is meant here than the obvious view that social and political circumstances, interests, and ideas have influenced the kind of scientific problems considered, and the direction of their application. The actual content of science is allegedly dependent upon a class or party approach, and the philosophy of dialectical materialism is recommended because by following its lead, problems within science can be presumably solved which defy solution on the basis of other philosophies. It would follow from this, to paraphrase Mannheim, that different classes think differently about everything, or at least everything important, which is manifestly false. There are no "national truths" in science, and Pierre Duhem is obviously right in his claim that it is only by its deficiencies that a science can become the science of one nation rather than another. The belief that there are "class truths" or "party truths" in science rests upon the elementary confusion between the objective evidence for a theory, which if warranted, is universally valid, with the uses, good, bad, or indifferent that are made of it.

Much more worthy of notice is the claim made that what constitutes "objective evidence for a theory" is an historical conception. The history of science reveals that the conditions which a scientific theory must fulfill to be accepted have been more rigorous at some times than at others. It becomes pointless to speak, then, of scientific method *überhaupt*; there are only scientific methods.

This is a very difficult and interesting question which I can treat only briefly and with the appearance of a dogmatism I do not feel. As a possible solution of this problem I venture the following: At any given time scientists accept as working truths hypotheses of varying degrees of generality and strength. They are more firmly convinced of the genetic theory of heredity than of the theory of organic evolution. They would be less surprised if the general theory of relativity were abandoned than the special theory. The degree of confirmation which a theory must pass muster at any time seems to be a function of the fruitfulness of previous theories in the field with similar degrees of confirmatory strength in extending our knowledge of the unknown. In addition the strength of an hypothesis is a function of the number of alternative hypotheses that are available as explanations. As a rule the more numerous the confirming instances the stronger the hypothesis. But if there are no alternative hypotheses present, we may be satisfied with far fewer confirming instances than where alternative hypotheses are present.[7] Further, the bearing of an hypothesis upon the direction of inquiry, the leads it opens up to new ways of experiment, must be taken into account.

To use a distinction of Peirce, in science a *valid* reason for believing a theory may not be a conclusive reason or even a strong reason. My contention is that what makes any reason in science a *valid* reason for believing an hypothesis is not historical, but invariant for all historical periods in the growth of science. But whether a reason is a strong reason for believing an hypothesis varies with the presence or absence of other leads and the evidence for them. This is an historical matter since no one can predict how many creative, competing insights will be current when an hypothesis presents its credentials for confirmation. I therefore do not believe that the variations in the degree of confirmatory completeness which scientific hypotheses have had to meet at different times relativizes in any way the logic of scientific method.

In passing it should be noticed that even in the history of mathematics standards of rigor seem to have varied, and for centuries mathematicians believed propositions which were only conclusively proved in the nineteenth and twentieth centuries. No one would infer from this that the notion of mathematical validity is historically conditioned, for despite the variations in rigor they progressively illustrate one underlying logical pattern of proof to which no alternative has ever been formulated.

If the foregoing is sound then I think it constitutes some reason for believing that there is only one reliable method of reaching the truth about the nature of things anywhere and at any time, that this reliable method comes to full fruition in the methods of science, and that a man's normal behavior in adapting means to ends belies his words whenever he denies it. Naturalism as a philosophy not only accepts this method but also the broad generalizations which are established by the use of it; viz, that the occurrence of all qualities or events depends upon the organization of a material system in space-time, and that their emergence, development, and disappearance are determined by changes in such organization.

Common sense takes the word "material" as loosely equivalent to the *materials* with which men deal as they go from problem to problem; naturalism as a philosophy takes it to refer to the subject matter of the physical sciences. Neither the one nor the other asserts that only what can be observed exists, for many things may be legitimately inferred to exist (electrons, the expanding universe, the past, the other side of the moon) from what is observed; but both hold that there is no evidence for the assertion of the existence of anything which does not rest upon some observed effects.

The objections that have recently been urged against naturalism sometimes proceed from the notion that a philosophical position must justify its general assumption in some absolutely unique way. This is, as we have seen, a blind alley. Naturalism makes no assumptions over and above those that have been made every time the borders of our knowledge have been pushed back. It therefore has the cumulative weight of the historic achievements of common sense and science behind it. *If* we want to acquire new knowledge, the naturalist asserts, we should follow the basic pattern of inquiry—recognize the problem, state the hypotheses, draw the inferences, perform the experiment, and make the observation. There is no logical necessity or guarantee that we will achieve new knowledge this way but it is reasonable to act on the assumption. If one chooses to call this faith, it is certainly of a different order from the faith that new knowledge will suddenly be won in some other way—as different as the faith that "if I sow, reap, mill, and bake the wheat, I shall get bread" is from the faith that "manna will fall from heaven." This difference would remain even if men decided not to reach for new knowledge, and depressed by Hiroshima, were to cry "Sufficient unto the day is the knowledge thereof." The connection between the method that one could follow and the conclusions that depend upon its being followed, remains unaffected by what one wants or does not want.

It is all the more surprising therefore to hear from one critic that "the most fundamental objection to the naturalist's procedure is that in Peirce's words it 'blocks the path of inquiry' in that it seeks to settle by stipulation the very issue that we need to be reasonable about if we can." Why? Because, he answers, "having committed themselves in advance to a position which identifies reasonable procedure with that which does not differ 'sharply' from that of the more developed sciences, they (the naturalists) will limit the scope of reasonable inquiry to what can be settled by the methods these sciences employ."[8]

This charge rests upon a double confusion—one of interpretation and one of observation. It is not reasonable procedure—what Dewey calls the basic pattern of inquiry—of which the naturalist says that it does not differ sharply from the more developed sciences. It is the techniques and body of knowledge which enable us to control everyday affairs of which he says that they do not differ sharply from the techniques and body of knowledge that the sciences have developed. For some of the techniques and parts of the body of knowledge of the former are always incorporated in the latter. The reasonable procedure—which according to naturalists is emphatically *not* a special technique of any special science—is *identical* in every formal aspect in every field in which we can lay claim to tested and universally agreed on knowledge about the world. How, then, can it serve as an obstacle to further inquiry, unless it is held that some disciplines have a basic pattern of inquiry quite different from that employed by critical common sense and science. What are these disciplines? What is this pattern? And what tested and universally agreed upon knowledge about this world or any other has been won by it? We are not told.

The error of observation derives from the failure to note that the driving motivation of modern naturalism has been not to block but to open up the paths of inquiry into whole fields which until now have not been investigated scientifically—especially the social disciplines. If this criticism of the danger threatened by naturalism were just, we should expect to find naturalists opposing attempts to employ scientific method in anthropology, history, and economics on the ground that the methods and techniques of mathematical physics—"the more fully developed sciences"—were not applicable to them. But it is precisely the naturalists who by distinguishing between the basic pattern of inquiry and the special techniques applicable to different subject matters have been trying to banish methodological purism.

It is true that there have been occasions in the past when those concerned with the logic of scientific method have seemed to show excessive caution in evaluating the first efforts of scientific theories struggling to be born. Before the theory of evolution was buttressed by the findings of experimental genetics some biologists regarded its claims as too speculative. Today many scientific psychologists are very dubious about the validity of psychoanalytic theories which are somewhat in the same state as theories of magnetism at the time of Oersted and Oken. But all of these doubts, including those that follow from a too rigorously formulated canon of verifiability, far from obstructing inquiry are a challenge to it, and melt away as fruitful results are achieved and systematized. Such hypercritical doubts about evidence usually lead to suspension of *judgment* not of inquiry; they do not establish or enforce non-trespass signs. The dogmatism of a Comte who ruled out the possibility of our ever learning anything about the internal constitution of the stars, derided the undulatory theory of light, and professed skepticism about the results of microscopic investigation is as rare as it is inconsistent, and was repudiated by his scientific colleagues as soon as his views were made known.

If we take a long view of the history of scientific inquiry, the evidence is overwhelming that it has not been the naturalists who have obstructed investigation into new fields by insisting that the methods of the more advanced sciences be taken as paradigmatic for all inquiry, so much as those who have contested the validity of the naturalist position, particularly in the study of the human body and mind. The deliverances a few years ago by high church dignitaries against psychoanalysis follow a precedent established by a long line of more distinguished predecessors. An interesting chapter remains to be written on the distortion produced in other fields of science by those who took mathematics as the *model* of all knowledge. But the mathematical ideal for all human knowledge was held by comparatively few naturalists. Those thinkers who took it seriously tended to regard scientific knowledge as mere opinion lost in the welter of appearances and unable to grasp reality.

The most powerful opposition to naturalism comes not from those who feel that it obstructs the path of inquiry and closes the gates to new knowledge but from those who fear that it arbitrarily excludes from the realm of existence and knowledge something which we actually have good reason to believe in, viz., God and man's immortal soul. Naturalism *arbitrarily* excludes the existence of God and man's immortal soul, it is alleged, because its first principles and categories of explanation are such as to make the very assertion of their existence meaningless. If true, this charge would be serious indeed, for the naturalist professes to be open-minded about the possibilities of existence in a world in which his greatest efforts seem so modest in the cosmic scale.

There are many conceptions of God and the soul which are unintelligible because they involve the attribution of contradictory qualities to Him; and there are other conceptions which are so vague and indeterminate in meaning that nothing significant can be affirmed or denied of them. But it is not difficult to find conceptions that are sufficiently meaningful to make the contention of the *impossibility* of their existence arrant dogmatism. Are naturalists guilty of this kind of dogmatism?

I do not believe this to be the case. For one thing this would remove the sting from naturalism. Its criticisms of the belief in Deity have not been based on semantic considerations but on what it presumed to be the weight of scientific discovery. Some theologians and even some Catholic scientists like Duhem have sought to bolster the beliefs in God precisely on the ground that in relation to the categories of naturalistic science, the affirmation as well as the denial of God's existence would be meaningless. Such a view of naturalism is more devastating to atheism than to theism because the atheist does not profess to have any other categories at the disposal of his understanding while the theist emphatically does.

Secondly, wherever declared naturalists assert that the existence of God is impossible, it will usually be found they are using the term impossible not in the logical or mathematical sense but in the physical or medical sense in which we say that it is impossible for anything to burn or for a man to breathe without oxygen. Neither Professor Ducasse in his recent discussions of immortality nor Professor Ewing in his discussions of the body and its mental attributes have established anything more than what a sophisticated naturalist is prepared to grant them *to begin* with, viz., that God's existence and personal survival are synthetic propositions and that therefore their denial cannot be contradictory or a matter for logic alone to settle. G. E. Moore once observed that the fact that one needs one's eyes for seeing is an empirical discovery, and this is obviously true for more recondite matters like the role of the brain in thinking and of the nerves in feeling. To see without eyes is physiologically impossible but every believer in immortality known to me is convinced that in his disembodied state he will see at least as well as he sees now. The two assertions are not *logically* incompatible for obviously the believer in immortality expects the laws of physiology to be suspended in the hereafter. This is not logically impossible but the absence of a logical impossibility does not constitute a scintilla of evidence against the usual validity of physiological law as we know it. Every reasonable person in his behavior denies the assumption "that we have no right to disbelieve in anything which cannot be logically disproved."[9]

The history of naturalism, it seems to me, has been marked by two main tendencies. The first has interpreted God in the same way as the great historical religions; viz., as an omnipotent personal power who guides the destinies of the world He has created—and concluded that the evidence does not warrant belief in the existence of anything corresponding to this conception. The second has reinterpreted the conception of God and used the term "God" to signify a principle of order in the universe, the totality of all things, the possibility of good in the world, or the object of human allegiance. Karl Marx once observed that even the profession of belief in deism on the part of scientists was motivated by a desire to win freedom to continue scientific inquiry and to escape molestation from those whom we would today call religious fundamentalists. But in most cases the attribution of such motives seems to be entirely gratuitous even though a greater freedom from interference by revealed religion may have been among the effects of the profession of deism.

Whatever the historical facts, the charge of dogmatism against naturalism on the ground that it rules out by definition the possible existence of God and the soul has often been made. Recently it has been renewed and fortified by quoting from an essay by Professor W. Dennes some ambiguous passages which are interpreted to mean that all things in the world *must* ultimately be described and explained in terms of the categories of quality, relation, and event. One critic then asks, "How do we know that the world consists of events, qualities, and relations, and nothing more? We know that we must so describe it if we are committed to basic categories of a naturalistic philosophy. . . . But would the nature of a spiritual substance be so determinable?"[10] Another critic referring to the same point writes, "If everything has to be an event, the idea of a timeless God is excluded from the outset and without argument. The writer asserts that his list of categories makes no demand upon the metaphysical commitment of the reader, as though giving up one's belief in God were nothing."[11]

These questions seem to me to misconceive both the meaning of the text criticized as well as the position of naturalism. I shall, however, discuss only the latter.

(1) Naturalism is not committed to any theory concerning which categorial *terms* are irreducible or basic in explanation. Naturalists differ among themselves about this in the same way that scientists may differ among themselves as to what terms in the language of science should be taken as primary. What all naturalists agree on is "the irreducibility" of a certain method by which new knowledge is achieved and tested. The analysis of this method may be made in terms of categories like thing, structure, function, power, act, cause, relation, quantity, and event. The choice of which categories to take as basic in describing a method depends upon the degree to which they render coherent and fruitful what we learn by the use of the method. Historically, and up to very recently, the most widely used category among naturalistic philosophers has been matter or substance. It is a complete non sequitur to assume that because one asserts that the fundamental categories of description are X and Y and Z, and that they hold universally, he is therefore asserting that the world cannot be significantly described *except* in terms of X, Y, and Z, or as so many critics assume, that the world consists of "nothing but" X and Y and Z. One may use categorial terms A and B and C that are not fundamental and maintain either—what most naturalists do *not*—that they are logically definable in terms of X, Y, and Z or—what most naturalists do—that the conditions under which any existing thing is signifi-

cantly describable in terms of A, B, and C are such that they are always describable in terms of X, Y, and Z.

This gives us two possibilities in respect to a term like substance. It might be defined as a constellation of events instead of a substratum in which predicates inhere, and all statements about substances translated without loss of meaning into statements about organized sets of events or processes. Or second, an attempt might be made to show that whatever else a substance is, its manifestations or appearances can always be described in terms of activities or operating powers, themselves definable as events or powers. This does not require that substances whether material or spiritual have to be directly observed, but it does require that their presumed manifestations or effects must be observable in our experience, else we can populate the world at will with the creatures of our fancy.

Whether the existence of the identifiable "effects" of an allegedly spiritual substance justifies our belief in the existence of a separable and immortal soul rather than our belief that they are "effects" of a highly organized body in a given culture is something which the naturalist proposes to solve, either (i) by proceeding in the same way and with the same logic that he makes inferences from the presence of certain observable occurrences to the presence of other unobserved occurrences, or (ii) by examining the experimental evidence for the survival of the soul or personality after the death of the body, which brings us into the field of parapsychology and psychical research.

That the choice of which categorial terms to use in description is a problem independent of determining what actually exists in heaven or earth may be clear if we bear in mind that even if we were to conclude that man has an immortal soul, that would not by itself answer the question whether it was to be described as a spiritual substance or an organized set of spiritual functions. Conversely, Whitehead denies the explanatory primacy of the category of substance, and using the categories of event, quality, and relation reaches altogether different conclusions from naturalism.

(2) Nor does naturalism exclude the very idea of a "timeless" God at the outset and without argument, as Professor Raphael Demos alleges. Otherwise, as I have already indicated, it could not deny his existence or be denounced for its atheism. Naturalists use the term "timeless" to designate traits and qualities in existence which either do not change or to which the predication of temporal quality is irrelevant. Circular things exist in time but their circularity is timeless. Before we can assert that

there are timeless "entities" in existence which do not change, we should need some experience of them in time in order to distinguish them from what lacks changeless character. The point is not whether timeless nonexistential entities can be conceived without contradiction. Assume that they can. But Mr. Demos is talking not of a purely conceptual or logical construction from whose meaning we can deduce existence. He is talking about a timeless entity whose existence must be inferred, as in orthodox theology (e.g., the Aquinate proofs of the existence of God) from a series of temporal and contingent events. And he must meet the naturalist contention that there is neither empirical nor logical warrant for the leap from what we can observe in our experience in time to a creature outside of time. That there must be some disclosure in time of what is presumed to be outside of time is a starting point of the argument, Mr. Demos must admit, else the whole concept of God is useless for the purposes for which Mr. Demos and orthodox theology invoke him.

(3) If God and man's immortal soul are so conceived that they have no empirical effects, then there is nothing to prevent anyone from imputing any set of logically consistent attributes to them. They would then take their place with other imaginary creatures in the realm of mythology. I can very well understand the refusal of historical religions to take such conceptions of God and the soul seriously, since it makes them completely otiose in understanding the world, superfluous entities that can be shaved away with a flick of Occam's razor.

It is of course true that in modern philosophy the term "God" has stood for many different ideas—natural structure, the order of cause and consequence, the principle of concretion or logical limitation, the experience of value and righteousness. Avowed atheists, like Morris R. Cohen, have described their dedication to truth, and not only out of piety to the memory of Spinoza, as "the intellectual love of God." Naturalists are under no more compulsion to observe terminological taboos than other philosophers although one would expect them to be more careful of the context of familiar terms used to convey new meanings. If anyone gets particular satisfaction out of the use of the term God, then fortunately or unfortunately, he can find it in the writings of most naturalist philosophers. Naturalism, as a philosophy, however, has nothing to do with such linguistic matters important as they may be in other respects. Naturalism as a philosophy is concerned only with those assertions about existence from which something empirically observable in the world follows that would not be the case if existence were denied. And it proposes to treat assertions about God's existence in the same generic way that it treats assertions about the existence of invisible stars or hidden motives or afterimages or extrasensory perception. Critics of naturalism who regard this as dogmatic might put their charge to the test by furnishing the reasons or evidence which *they* hold warrant belief in the existence of God or gods, cosmic purpose, or personal survival after death.

Some beliefs are reasonable even if we cannot finally confirm or disconfirm them. But if we take technological and practical behavior as the matrix of the reasonable, then beliefs in the existence of supernatural entities are not reasonable. They are not warranted even if they turn out to be true, just as a guess is not warranted knowledge even when it turns out to be true. Santayana somewhere suggests that the reason most people believe in immortality is that they cannot imagine themselves dead. This raises an interesting methodological point since only if we are immortal can we prove it, while the naturalists who deny the immortality of the soul will never have the satisfaction of saying, "We were right." "Wouldn't naturalists be surprised," a critic of the position once observed, "if after they died they woke up in the presence of God." They certainly would be surprised. The degree of their surprise would be the measure of the unreasonableness of the belief. Unreasonable behavior or conduct may sometimes turn out right—e.g., if I gave six to one odds on the toss of a well-made coin—but it is no less unreasonable for all that. And what is true for conduct is true for belief. Consequently, in respect to the available evidence in our possession, the naturalist is reasonable in his belief even if it turns out he is wrong about God and survival, while the supernaturalist in respect to the same data is unreasonable even if it turns out he is right. "Faith in the supernatural," says Santayana, "is a desperate wager made by man at the lowest ebb of his fortune." The scientist who predicts that life will disappear because of the second law of thermodynamics will never be around when the last flicker of life dims. The logic of the argument is no different in the case of immortality.

In conclusion, the naturalist believes that his assumptions are reasonable because they express, in a more general way, no more than what is expressed by any nonphilosopher as well as by all philosophers, whatever their school, in their successful working practice in solving problems concerning the nature of things. And by successful is meant here something independent of the categorial terms of naturalism or any other philosophy, something as simple, naïve, and indefeasible as discovering a substance that subjected to friction will burst into flame, building a house that will withstand an earthquake, producing a seed that will yield a better harvest. Naturalism, as a philosophy, is a systematic reflection upon, and elaboration of, the procedures man employs in the successful resolution of the problems and difficulties of human experience. To use a phrase of Peirce, without giving it necessarily his special interpretation, it is "critical commonsensism." But it is more than this. It is a proposal. It is a proposal to continue to follow this general pattern of procedure in all fields of inquiry where it has enabled us to build up a body of knowledge, and to extend it to fields where we have not satisfactorily settled questions *of fact* of any kind. As a proposal it seems hardly less reasonable to the naturalist to follow than, when thirsty, under normal circumstances, to look for some liquid to quench one's thirst. Could any other procedure be more reasonable or as reasonable? Or must we solve *the* problem of induction first? But to raise the problem of induction no less than to solve it assumes that we are already in possession of undisputed although not undisputable knowledge. And to facilitate the transition from the problematic to the undisputed in human affairs has been one of the underlying purposes of all historical forms of naturalism.

[1956]

# NOTES

1. Alexander A. Goldenweiser, *Anthropology* (New York: Crofts & Co., 1937), 134.
2. Franz Boas, *Mind of Primitive Man,* 2d ed. (New York: Macmillan), 131.
3. Bronislaw Malinowski, *Science, Religion, and Reality* (New York: Macmillan,1929), 35.
4. Goldenweiser, *Anthropology,* 420–21.
5. W. Cranshaw-Willams, "True Truth: or the Higher the Deeper," *Rationalist Annual* (London), 1948, 28.
6. John Dewey, in *Journal of Philosophy* 42 (1945): 206.
7. Charles Peirce, *Collected Works,* vol. 2, pt. 2 (Cambridge: Harvard University Press,), 780.
8. Arthur Murphy, in *Journal of Philosophy* 42 (1945): 413.
9. Cranshaw-Williams, "True Truth: or the Higher the Deeper."
10. Arthur Murphy, in *Journal of Philosophy* 42 (1945): 411–12.
11. Raphael Demos, in *Philosophy and Phenomenological Research* 7 (1946–47): 271.

# 3

# PRAGMATISM AND THE
# TRAGIC SENSE OF LIFE

I n the realm of thought and culture America has largely been a colonial dependency of Europe. Its own authentic history—the conquest of a virgin continent, the bloodiest of all civil wars, the technological revolution, the extension of social democracy—has not been reflected in a characteristic philosophy of life. As the pioneer settlements struggled across river and mountain, New England divines were still wrestling with age-old problems of freedom and predestination. When the nation was locked in arms over the issue of slavery, its leading teachers were still justifying the ways of God to man while the more daring were beginning to unwind the cobwebby speculations of German idealistic philosophy. Only toward the end of the nineteenth century did a distinctively American philosophy emerge. The names associated with it were Charles Peirce, William James, and John Dewey. This philosophy was labeled pragmatism or instrumentalism or experimentalism.

Pragmatism was regarded as a distinctively American philosophy, despite its European congeners, because it stressed three things: the universe was open—therefore possibilities were real; the future depended in part upon what human beings did or left undone—therefore man was not a slave of scientific or theological necessity; ideas were potentially plans of action—therefore thinking could and did make a difference to human affairs. This emphasis on action became central in the interpretation of

Reprinted from *Commentary*, August 1960, by permission; all rights reserved.

pragmatism and before long action was identified with practice and—fateful step!—practice with usefulness. Since Americans were considered a practical people with a highly developed sense of the concrete and useful, pragmatism was played up abroad as the American philosophy par excellence. Its claim that all thinking which aimed to win new knowledge involved some practice or experiment was transformed into the belief that all thinking was for the sake of practice. And since the chief practice of Americans seemed to be, in the eyes of their poorer neighbors, the making of money, pragmatism was cried down as the typical philosophy of a parvenu people, insensitive to tradition and culture, and devoted only to the invention of machines to make more machines by human beings who acted as if they were themselves only complicated machines.

This European conception of pragmatism reached American shores and infected some of the more tender-minded intellectuals who attributed their ineffectuality not to their own failings but to the addiction of the American people to the philosophy of pragmatism. It is now an almost unchallenged commonplace that pragmatism is a superficial philosophy of optimism, of uncritical adjustment and conformity, of worship of the goddess success. Such an interpretation of pragmatism not only runs counter to what we know of the personalities of Peirce, James, and Dewey, but is based upon a tendentious reading of their work.

What was overlooked in this caricatured account is that the very nature of philosophy, as the pragmatic philosophers conceive it, makes it a method of clarifying ideas and therefore preeminently a method of *criticism*. It is death on bunkum and pretentious abstractions especially when they are capitalized as Success or Historical Destiny or Reality. It clarifies the meaning of ideas by uncovering their consequences in use—not merely consequences in linguistic use but in the behavior of things and people in the concrete situations in which language functions. Long before Wittgenstein, pragmatists believed that language was a form of life. They sought to reduce differences concerning supposed first principles and ultimate necessities to their varied fruits and consequences in experience.

Pragmatism was not only a method of clarifying ideas by exploring their consequences in behavioral use. It was also a temper of mind toward the vital options which men confront when they become aware of what alternative proposals commit them to. It stressed the efficacy of human ideals and actions and at the same time their inescapable limitations. It forswore the promise of total solutions and wholesale salvation for piecemeal gains. Yet far from embracing easy formulae of the ultimate reconciliation of conflicting interests and values, it acknowledged the reality of piecemeal losses even when we risk our lives to achieve the gains. No matter how intelligent and humane our choices, there are, William James insists, "real losses and real losers." We live in a dangerous and adventurous and serious world and "the very 'seriousness,'" James goes on to say, "we attribute to life means that ineluctable noes and losses form part of it, that there are genuine sacrifices, and that something permanently drastic and bitter always remains at the bottom of the cup."

This aspect of the philosophy of pragmatism has been almost completely ignored by its critics. It seems to me, however, to be central in pragmatism, and to provide an illuminating perspective from which to survey the problems and predicaments of men. It is grounded in a recognition of the tragic sense of life.

Despite its criticism of the detailed claims of traditional philosophy, pragmatism has a certain kinship with some classical conceptions of the role of philosophy, but not with their methods and manners of thought. Although it recognizes the importance of precision in the analysis of problems, it is not a "minute" philosophy charting the refinements of linguistic usage while other disciplines stride forward. And although vitally concerned with normative problems of individual and social ethics, it does not seek necessarily to reform or revolutionize the world. It tries to undercut the rather tedious disputes about what philosophy is or should be by calling attention to its plural historic roles. "Logic is the essence of philosophy," some philosophers of our time have declared. Yet Plato is surely more notable for his vision and as a dramatist of the life of reason than for his logical analyses. "The function of philosophy is not to understand the world but to change it," say some other philosophers. But neither Aristotle nor Hume was a reformer or revolutionist. Yet each enriched the stores of human wisdom even if we believe that we have gone beyond them.

Pragmatism is a philosophy which does not rule out the right of other philosophies to be legitimately regarded as philosophies on the basis of some "proper" definition of philosophy which cannot be defended without circularity. It does not take as its own norm the positivistic criterion of whether philosophy is a science or a body of knowledge of comparable objectivity. It asks only whether what passes for "philosophy" in any historical period is worth doing, whether there is sufficient illumination in pursuing certain themes, ignored by other thinkers, to justify continuing concern with them, especially in the light of their bearing on basic issues in other disciplines, and on the conduct of social and personal life. Sufficient for its importance is that it makes a difference, good or bad. After all, no one really believes that only science is a self-justifying enterprise.

In this sense pragmatism is as catholic in its conception of philosophy as the great classical views of philosophy, although it regards the a priori and deductive methods employed by most philosophies of the past as inadequate, their conclusions false or misleading, obstacles rather than aids to the extension of knowledge and the further enrichment of experience. Because of current misconceptions of the nature of pragmatism, it may be helpful to call attention to some of its neglected aspects.

For many years I have concerned myself with problems of social and political and legal philosophy, with "problems of men" as authentic as any of those recognized by thinkers who would reform modern philosophy. But I find myself increasingly out of sympathy with those who have impugned the whole philosophical enterprise because of its failure to serve as a beacon to mankind in distress. When I ask myself why I feel uncomfortable and at odds with those who attack philosophers because they have nothing of immediate, practical moment to say, I find that my conception of philosophy, although stated sometimes in words similar to theirs, differs in important ways. Put most succinctly, although I believe that philsophy is a *quest* for wisdom, many of those who cite this phrase, too, speak and act as if they already had it. The difference may be only of nuance and emphasis, but it has a profound bearing on one's conception of the appropriate role of the philosopher in the culture of his time. It is the difference between being a moralist and being a moralizer. The moralizer may be called "the shouting moralist," of whom Santayana somewhere says that he "no doubt has his place but not in philosophy." It is a difference, on the one hand, between *analyzing* specific and basic social problems and conflicts, and *clarifying* the issues in dispute with all the tools at one's command—and, on the other, *proclaiming* solutions and programs on the basis of antecedent commitments which one shares with some faction of his fellow men. It is the difference between approaching problems of human experience in terms of one's vocation as a philosopher, which is to do intellectual justice to the varied and conflicting interests present or discovered, and one's vocation as a citizen limited by specific duties he must fulfill. It is the difference between intellectual concern which may or may not lead to programs of action, and commitment to programs of action which by their very nature estops self-critical thought.

In the course of its history philosophy has been many things. But its distinctive concern at all times *has* been the quest for wisdom. Otherwise there would be no point in including thinkers like Descartes or Leibnitz in the history of philosophy in addition to the history of science or mathematics. What distinguishes the philosopher as a moralist from the philosopher as a mathematician, logician, or natural scientist, and from the ordinary man as a philosopher, is his sustained reflective pursuit of wisdom. This means two things. The systematic study of the knowledge which is relevant to wisdom; and the analysis of the commitments we assume and rule out when knowledge is related to policy. All of us know that wisdom and knowledge are not the same thing, but we sometimes mistakenly speak as if they are opposed. A man may have knowledge of many things and not be wise, but a wise man cannot be ignorant of the things he is wise about. He must have knowledge of the nature and career of values in human experience; knowledge of the nature and history of the situations in which they develop and conflict; knowledge of the minds and emotions of the carriers of value; knowledge of the consequences of actions taken or proposed. The wise man is not one who merely recites moral principles and applies a ready-made schedule of moral obligations to the problems and perplexities of value conflict. He is one who on the basis of what he already knows, or believes he knows, makes fresh inquiry into the situations which define alternatives and exact their costs. "Only the conventional and the fanatical," observes Dewey, "are always immediately sure of right and wrong in conduct." This means that a philosopher must earn his title to be wise not by right of philosophical tradition or philology but by the hard work of acquiring relevant knowledge and by hard thinking about it.

Here lie important tasks for the philosopher. To be wise he must immerse himself in the actual subject matters (not necessarily experiences) out of which life's problems arise. To be wise about economic affairs he must study economics, to be wise about problems of law he must study law, to be wise about politics he must study history, sociology, and other disciplines. To be wise about war and peace he must study military technology and the theory of and practice of communism, including its strategic exploitation of peace movements to disarm the free world. Indeed, these subjects are so interrelated that to be wise about any one of them he must study them all. And I might add, in view of some current writing, to be wise about education it is not enough merely to rebaptize the ends of the good life as ends of a good education, too, as if without operational application to concrete historical situations they had any but a peripheral bearing on the great, current problems of education. One must study social history, the psychology of learning, the methods and techniques of pedagogy to achieve educational wisdom. To enumerate the ends of the good life is not enough. Nor is a primer on logical analysis which can serve as an introduction to the study of *any* subject sufficient for a study of the distinctive issues in the philosophy of education.

All of these problems are of tremendous complexity because of the number of independent variables they contain, because they rarely permit of controlled experiment, and because the community must sometimes act upon them in desperate urgency before the analysis is complete. This should make for humility among philosophers even as they bring to the study of these problems the methodological sophistication, the arts and skills of analysis which are the hallmarks of their profession. This is what *I* mean by "the problems of men." It is philosophy not as a quest for salvation but as a pursuit of understanding of great cultural issues and their possible upshot. It does not start from a complete stock of philosophical wisdom which it dispenses to others with hortatory fervor but with an initial sense of concern to meet the challenge of the great unresolved problems of our time, offering analysis of these problems which will win the respect of the specialist and yet command the attention of everyman, e.g., how to preserve peace *and* freedom, achieve adequate production and meaningful vocations for all, design patterns of creative leisure, effect desegregation if possible without coercion, establish a welfare state and a spirit of enterprise, preserve national security and the right to dissent. It is philosophy as *normative* social inquiry. And it is *not* social reform. How could philosophy be identified with social reform in view of the existence of many esteemed philosophers from Aristotle to Santayana whose judgments of wisdom were conservative, hostile to social reform? Such identification would be comparable to defining a physicist as one who was committed to a specific hypothesis in physics.

At this point my inner ear senses unspoken murmurs of surprise. "Surely," some of you must be saying, "this constitutes a repudiation of John Dewey's conception of philosophy, for, after all, does not Dewey call upon philosophers as philosophers to do precisely what is being urged they should not do? Does not Dewey call upon philosophers to play the role of social reformers?" My answer is: "Not as I understand him and not as he is to be understood in the light of all he has written."

Here is not the place to provide the documentation. I content myself merely with saying that Dewey has a very *complex* conception of philosophy. Philosophy is indeed concerned primarily with what I call normative problems of social inquiry. But its function is also to provide leading, speculative ideas in science—natural and social. And a third function is to weave together certain families of ideas into a philosophical synthesis. "There is a kind of music of ideas," he says, "which appeals, apart from any question of verification, to the mind of thinkers!" Nor is this all. The philosopher must bring some perspective or vision to bear upon the world which is related to issues of value and hence makes the analysis of normative problems of social inquiry more sensitive. "Philosophies," declares Dewey, "are different ways of construing life."

There is more, then, than problems of normative social inquiry which falls within the province of the philosopher's concern. There is the illuminating perspective in which they are seen which is metaphysics. "If philosophy be criticism," Dewey asks in *Experience and Nature*, "what is to be said of the relation of philosophy to metaphysics?" His answer briefly is that metaphysics is a description of those gross features of the world which constitute the backdrop of the theater of human activity against which men play out their lives. The conduct of life and the analysis of its problems, however indirectly, will reflect what we believe to be the generic features of human experience in the world. In this sense, as ultimately related to the human scene and the adventure of human life, but not to ontology, metaphysics is "a ground map of the province of criticism establishing base lines to be employed in more intricate triangulations."

This brings me finally to my theme of the tragic sense of life as a feature of human experience which provides an illuminating perspective upon the analysis of man's problems. The juxtaposition of the expressions "pragmatism" and "the tragic sense of life" may appear bewildering to those who understand "pragmatism" as a narrow theory of meaning and "the tragic sense of life" as the hysterical lament that man is not immortal—the theme song of Unamuno's book of that title. To speak of pragmatism and the tragic sense of life is somewhat like speaking of "The Buddhism of John Dewey" or "The Dewey Nobody Knows."

I am not aware that Dewey ever used the phrase "the tragic sense of life," but I know that growing up in the shadow of the Civil War he felt what I shall describe by it and that it is implied in his account of moral experience. At any rate, nothing of moment depends upon whether the view is actually Dewey's or Hegel's or William James's or Nicolai Hartmann's, in all of whom it can be found. I take the responsibility of the interpretation and its application. It is a perspective which seems to me to illumine the pragmatic view that problems of normative social inquiry—morals in the broad sense—are the primary—not exclusive—subject matter of philosophy, and that reason or scientific intelligence can and should be used to resolve them.

By the tragic sense of life I do not understand merely sensitivity to the presence of evil or suffering in the world, although all tragic situations to some degree involve one or the other. And since I have mentioned Buddha I should like to say that the presence of the evils in the world which led Buddha to surrender his Kingdom in order to seek salvation for himself and mankind are not to me the realities fundamental to the tragic sense of life. There were three things in Buddha's experience, reflection upon which led him to a renunciation of his princely lot and a quest for liberation from desire and incarnate existence—sickness, old age, and death. One can very well understand why, in the world in which he lived and for many centuries thereafter until our own, these phenomena loomed so large in the overpopulated and poverty-stricken areas of Asia. Nonetheless if we are to distinguish between the sense of the *pitiful* and the sense of the *tragic*—sickness, old age, and even many forms of death, despite their numbing effect upon human sensibility, are not necessarily to be classified as tragic.

First, given the rapidly expanding horizons of knowledge in our age, there is nothing in the nature of things which requires that the sick, any more than the poor, must always be with us. If scientific medicine develops at the same pace in the next few hundred years as it has in the last century, it is not shallow optimism to anticipate that the most serious forms of sickness will disappear and not be replaced by others. Even where sickness is present it may be the occasion of tragedy, but by itself is not an illustration of it. In relation to the forces of nature man's lot may appear pitiful. The tragic is a moral phenomenon.

What is true of sickness is true of old age. The aged arouse our compassion because of their feebleness and fragility—and the mulitplicity of their aches and pains. When these are absent—and this, too, is a concern of scientific medicine—there is a chance for serenity, wisdom, and beauty of spirit to manifest themselves. There is sometimes a grandeur and stateliness about an old tree which aged persons do not possess because the processes of physical degeneration, and the consequent weakening of the vital powers, make man pitiful. There is no tragedy in growing old biologically, but only sorrow; the element of the tragic enters in the defeat of plans or hopes, in the realization that in much grief there is not much wisdom, and that we cannot count merely upon the passage of time alone to diminish our stupidities and cruelties.

But what of death—Buddha's third appalling discovery—preoccupation with which has become so fashionable today among some European existentialist philosophers that their philosophy seems to be more a meditation upon death than upon life? Is not death the ultimate source of whatever is tragic in life? I cannot bring myself to think so. Nor can I convince myself that its nature and significance in life waited to be discovered by Kierkegaard and Heidegger and their modern disciples.

It is the reflective attitude toward death, not the popular attitude or the one displayed by those in its last agonies, which throws light on its nature and place in life. The attitude exhibited by Socrates in facing it seems wiser than that expressed by the contemnors of the rational life who, not content with talking about what they find when they look into themselves, inflate it into a universal trait of the human psyche. So Tolstoy, who is quoted by existentialist writers, writes: "If a man has learned to think, no matter what he may think about, he is always thinking of his own death. All philosophers are like that. And what truth can there be, if there is death?" Logically, of course, this makes no more sense than the even more extreme statement of Sartre that "if we must die then our life has no meaning," which to those who solve some problems in life and therefore find some meaning, might be taken as a premise in a new short proof of human immortality. All this, it seems to me, expresses little more than a fear of death and a craving for immortality. It is a commonplace observation, however, that most human beings who desire immortality desire not unending life but unending youth or other desirable qualities which life makes possible. The fable of Juno and her lover in which Juno petitions the Gods to take back the gift of eternal life they had conferred upon a mortal indicates that the Greeks knew that a life without end could be a dubious blessing. In this respect the Hellenes were wiser than the Hebrews, whose God drives Adam from Paradise after he had eaten of the fruit of the tree of knowledge to prevent him from eating of the fruit of the tree of eternal life. Agony over death strikes me as one of the unloveliest features of the intellectual life of our philosophic times—and certainly unworthy of any philosophy which conceives itself as a quest for wisdom. It has never been clear to me why those who are nauseated by life, not by this or that kind of life but any kind of life, should be so fearful of death.

Wisdom is knowledge of the uses of life and death. The uses of life are to be found in the consummatory experiences of vision and delight, of love, understanding, art, friendship, and creative activity. That is why in a contingent world of finite men, vulnerable to powers they cannot control which sometimes rob them of the possibility of any justifying consummations, death has its uses, too. For it gives us some assurance that no evil or suffering lasts forever. To anyone aware of the multitude of infamies and injustices which men have endured, of the broken bodies and tortured minds of the victims of these cruelties, of the multiple dimensions of pain in which millions live on mattress graves or with minds shrouded in darkness, death must sometimes appear as a beneficent release not an inconsolable affliction. It washes the earth clean of what cannot be cleansed in any other way. Not all the bright promises of a future free of these stains of horror can redeem by one iota the lot of those who will not live to see the dawn of the new day.

It is nobler to exist and struggle in a world in which there is always a vital option to live or die. The fear of death, the desire to survive at any cost or price in human degradation, has been the greatest ally of tyranny, past and present. "There are times," says Woodbridge, "when a man ought to be more afraid of living than dying." And we may add, there are situations in which, because of the conditions of survival, the worst thing we can know of anyone is that he has survived. We have known such times and situations. They may come again.

Even in a world in which all injustices, cruelties, and physical anguish have disappeared, the possibility of withdrawing from it makes the world in so far forth a better and a freer world. So long as we retain possession of our faculties, our decision to remain in the world indicates a participating responsibility on our part for those events within it which our continuance affects. If human beings were unable to die, they would to that extent be unfree. Man shares a *conatus sui esse perseverare* with everything else in the world, or at least with all other sentient beings. But just because he can on rational grounds give up his being, choose not to be, he differentiates himself most strikingly from his fellow creatures in nature. I conclude, therefore, that death as such is not a tragic phenomenon and that its presence does not make the world and our experience within it tragic. It would be truer to call tragic a world in which men wanted to die but couldn't.

What, then, do I mean by the tragic sense of life and what is its relevance to pragmatism? I mean by the tragic sense a very simple thing which is rooted in the very nature of the moral experience and the phenomenon of moral choice. Every genuine experience of moral doubt and perplexity in which we ask "What should I do?" takes place in a situation where good conflicts with good. If we already know what is evil, the moral inquiry is over, or it never really begins. "The worse or evil," says Dewey, "is the rejected good," but until we reject it, the situation is one in which apparent good opposes apparent good. "All the serious perplexities of life come back to the genuine difficulty of forming a judgment as to the values of a situation: they come back to a conflict of goods." No matter how we resolve the opposition, some good will be sacrificed, some interest, whose immediate craving for satisfaction may be every whit as intense and authentic as its fellows, will be modified, frustrated, or even suppressed. Where the goods involved are of a relatively low order, like decisions about what to eat, where to live, where to go, the choice is unimportant except to the mind of a child. There are small tragedies as there are small deaths. At any level the conflict of values must become momentous to oneself or others to convey adequately the tragic quality. Where the choice is between goods that are complex in structure and consequential for the future, the tragic quality of the moral dilemma emerges more clearly. And when it involves basic choices of love, friendship, vocations, the quality becomes poignant. The very nature of the self as expressed in habits, dispositions, and character is to some extent altered by these decisions. If, as Hobbes observes, "Hell is truth seen too late," all of us must live in it. No matter how justified in smug retrospect our moral decisions seem to have been, only the unimaginative will fail to see the possible selves we have sacrificed to become what we are. Grant that all regrets are vain, that any other choice would have been equally or more regretted, the selves we might have been are eloquent witnesses of values we failed to enjoy. If we have played it safe and made our existence apparently secure, the fascinating experience of a life of adventure and experience can never be ours, and every thought of a good fight missed will be accompanied by a pang. It is a poor spirit, William James reminds us, who does not sense the chagrin of the tardy Crillon, who, arriving when the battle is over, is greeted by Henry IV with the words: "Hang yourself, brave Crillon! We fought at Arques, and you were not there!" On the other hand, if we have scorned to put down our roots, hugged our liberty tightly to ourselves by refusing to give hostages to fortune, become crusaders or martyrs for lost causes, we have thrust from ourselves the warmth of sustained affection and the comforting regularities which can best heal the bruised spirit.

There is a conflict not only between the good and the good but between the good and the right, where the good is a generic term for all the values in a situation and the right for all the obligations. The *concepts* of good and right are irreducible to each other in ordinary use. We are often convinced we must fulfil a certain duty even when we are far from convinced to the same degree that the action or the rule it exemplifies will achieve the greatest good. The "good" is related to the reflective satisfaction of an interest; "the right" to the fulfilment of a binding demand or rule of the community. There is no moral problem when in doing the right thing we can see that it *also* leads to the greatest good or when striving for the greatest good conforms to our sense of what is right. But the acute ethical problems arise when in the pursuit of the good we do things which appear not to be right, as, e.g., when in order to avoid the dangers of war a nation repudiates its treaty obligations or when in order to win a war noncombatants are punished who are in no way responsible for the actions of others. They also arise when in doing what is right our actions result in evil consequences, as, e.g., when a dangerous criminal, set free on a legal technicality, kills again or when the refusal to surrender to the unjust claims of an aggressor results in wholesale slaughter. Many have been the attempts made to escape the antinomies between the right and the good by defining the good as the object of right or the right merely as the means to the good. All have failed. To act upon the right no matter what its consequences for human weal or woe seems inhuman, at times insane. The thirst for righteousness has too often been an angry thirst satisfied if at all by long draughts of blood. On the other hand, the attempt to do good by *any* means, no matter how unjust, is subhuman and usually irrational.

As compared to traditional ethical doctrines, ideal utilitarianism reaches farthest in our quest for an adequate ethics, but in the end it, too, must be rejected. And it was the pragmatist and pluralist, William James, long before Pritchard and Ross, who indicated why in the famous question he asked: "If the hypothesis were offered us of a world in which Messrs. Fourier's and Ballamy's and Morris' Utopia should all be outdone, and millions be kept permanently happy on the one simple condition that a cer-

tain lost soul on the far off edge of things should lead a life of lonely torture, what except a specifical and independent sort of emotion can it be
which would make us immediately feel . . . how hideous a thing would be
its enjoyment when deliberately accepted as the fruit of such a bargain?"
The situation is unaltered if we recognize that there are other goods
besides happiness and that justice is itself a good, because in that case the
conflict breaks out again between good and good. In this connection I
would venture the statement that it is the failure to see the radical pluralism in the nature of the goods which are reckoned in the consequences
of an action that accounts both for Moore's view that it is self-evident that
it can *never* be right knowingly to approve an action that would make the
world as a whole worse than some alternative action and for Kant's view
that there are some duties that it would *always* be right to perform, even
if the consequences of the action resulted in a worse world or in no world
at all. No specific rule can be laid down as absolutely binding in advance
either way. Nothing can take the place of intelligence; the better or the
lesser evil in each situation can be best defined as the object of reflective
choice. Even the decision in the stock illustration of the textbooks
whether to execute an innocent man or turn him over to be tortured in
order to save the community from destruction, would depend upon a
complex of circumstances. It is perfectly conceivable that an unjust act
will sometimes produce the greater good or the lesser evil. It is sometimes
necessary to burn down a house to save a village. Although when applied
to human beings the logic seems damnable, few are prepared to take the
position of Kant in those agonizing moral predicaments that are not
uncommon in history, especially the history of oppressed minority peoples, in which the survival of the group can be purchased only at the price
of the pain, degradation, and death of the innocent. No matter how we
choose, we must either betray the ideal of the greater good or the ideal of
right or justice. In this lies the agony of the choice.

Many have been the attempts to escape the guilt of that choice. I cite
one from the past. During the Middle Ages, Maimonides writing on the
Laws of the Torah to guide his people discusses what a community is to
do when it is beset by enemies who demand the life of one man with the
threat to kill all if he not be turned over to them. Maimonides teaches
that they are to refuse to turn over any man even if all must die in consequence, except if their enemies call out the name of a specific person.
I had heard this teaching defended on the ground that if the community
itself had to make the decision who was to die, it would be taking the

guilt of an innocent man's death upon itself, which is impermissible. But if the enemy names the man, then he can be turned over because the guilt and sin fall now on *their* heads. By this miserable evasion it was thought that the tragic choice could be avoided. But it turns out that Maimonides has been misread. What Maimonides really taught is that only if the name of the person who has been called out is of one already under the death sentence for his crimes should he be surrendered. But never an innocent man. "Never," however, is a long time. It is problematic whether the Jews would have survived if they had always abided by Maimonides' injunction.

If anything, human beings are more readily inclined to sacrifice the right to the good than the good to the right especially in revolutionary situations which have developed because of grievances too long unmet. It can easily be shown that it was Lenin's conception of communist ethics which implicitly defined the right action as consisting in doing *anything*—literally anything that would bring victory in the class struggle— which explains the transformation of a whole generation of idealists into hangmen. In fact, the health of the revolution, whether in the times of Robespierre or Castro, never really requires the holocaust of victims offered up to it. But no revolution including our own has ever been achieved without injustice to someone. However the conflict between the principles of right and the values of good be theoretically resolved, in every concrete situation it leads to some abridgment of principle or some diminution of value.

The most dramatic of all moral conflicts is not between good and good, or between good and right, but between right and right. This in its starkest form is the theme of Sophoclean tragedy, but the primary locus of the tragic situation is not in a play but in life, in law, and in history. Innocence in personal matters consists in overlooking the conflict of moral duties and obligations. Innocence in political matters, the characteristic of ritualistic liberalism, consists in failing to see the conflicts of rights in our Bill of Rights and the necessity of their intelligent adjustment. In our own country we have witnessed again and again the antinomy of rights revealed in divided loyalties, in the conflict between allegiance to the laws of the state and allegiance to what is called divine law or natural law or the dictates of conscience. On the international scene it is expressed in the conflict of incompatible national claims, each with *some* measure of justification, as in the Israeli-Arab impasse.

One of the noteworthy features of moral intuitionism as illustrated in the doctrines of Ross is this recognition that prima facie duties conflict and that every important moral act exhibits at the same time character-istics which tend to make it both prima facie right and prima facie wrong, so that although we may claim certainty about these prima facie duties, any particular moral judgment or action is at best only probable or con-tingent. As Ross says, "There is therefore much truth in the description of the right act as a fortunate act." From this the conclusion to be drawn, it seems to me, is that the most important prima facie duty of all in a sit-uation requiring moral decision is that of *conscientiousness*, or reflec-tive assessment of all the relevant factors involved, and the searching exploration of our own hearts to determine what we sincerely want, whether we really wish to do what is right in a situation or to get our own scheming way come what may. As much if not more evil results from confusion of our purposes and ignorance of our motives than from ruth-less and clear-eyed resolve to ignore everyone's interests but one's own. This emphasis on the importance of reflective inquiry into the features of the situation which bear on the rightness of an action seems to me to be more important than Ross's conception or interpretation of the intu-itive apprehension of our prima facie duties. It is easier to doubt that we have this faculty of infallible intuition than that our intelligence has the power to discover our conflicts and mediate between them.

Irony is compounded with tragedy in the fact that many of the rights we presently enjoy we owe to our ancestors, who in the process of win-ning them for us deprived others of their rights. In some regions of the world the very ground on which people stand was expropriated by force and fraud from others by their ancestors. Yet as a rule it would be a new injustice to seek to redress the original injustice by depriving those of their possessions who hold present title to them. Every just demand for reparations against an aggressor country is an unjust demand on the descendants of its citizens, who as infants were not responsible for the deeds of aggression. That is why history is the arena of the profoundest moral conflicts in which some legitimate right has always been sacri-ficed, sometimes on the altars of the God of War.

The Christian and especially the Buddhist ethics of purity, which seek to transcend this conflict and avoid guilt by refusal to violate anyone's right in such situations, can only do so by withdrawing from the plane of the ethical altogether. This may succeed in God's eyes, but not in man's. The Buddhist saint or any other who out of respect for the right to life of man or beast refuses ever to use force, or to kill, even when this is the only method, as it sometimes is, that will save multitudes from suffering and death, makes himself responsible for the greater evil, all the more so because he claims to be acting out of compassion. He cannot avoid guilt, whether we regard him as more than man or less than man. No more than we does he escape the tragic decision.

There are three generic approaches to the tragic conflicts of life. The first approach is that of history. The second is that of love. The third is that of creative intelligence in quest for ways of mediation which I call here the pragmatic.

The approach of history is best typified by Hegel precisely because he tries to put a gloss of reason over the terrible events which constitute so much of the historical process. Its upshot is woefully inept to its intent. It suggests not only that whatever cause wins and *however* it wins is more just than the cause which is defeated, but that the loser is the more wicked and not merely the weaker. Further, it calls into question the very fact of tragic conflict from which it so perceptively starts. No one has seen more profoundly into the nature of the tragic situation and its stark clash of equally legitimate rights than Hegel. But his solution, expressed in Schiller's dictum *Die Weltgeschichte ist das Weltgericht*, as Hegel develops it, makes the philosophy of history a theodicy. It thereby vulgarizes tragedy. For it attempts to console man with a dialectical proof that his agony and defeat are not really evils but necessary elements in the goodness of the whole. The position is essentially religious. No monotheistic religion which conceives of God as both omnipotent and benevolent, no metaphysics which asserts that the world is rational, necessary, and good has any room for genuine, inescapable tragedy.

The approach of love is incomplete and ambiguous. It is incomplete because if love is more than a feeling of diffused sympathy but is expressed in action no *man* can love everyone or identify himself with every interest. Empirically, love has produced as much disunity as unity in the world—not only in Troy but in Jerusalem. Injustice is often born of love, not only of self-love but of love of some rather than others. Love is not only incomplete but ambiguous. There are various kinds of love and the actions to which they lead may be incompatible. An order of distinction is required. A man's love for his family must be discriminatory; his love of mankind not. He cannot love both in the same way without denying one or the other. The quality of love is altered with the range of its generalization. In one sense love always shows a bias which reinforces some conflicting interest; in another it gives all conflicting values its blessing without indicating any specific mode of action by which conflict can be mediated. Love may enable a person to live with the burden of guilt which he assumes when he sacrifices one right to another. But it is no guide to social conflict as the last two thousand years have shown. Because the Lord loves man equally nothing follows logically about the equality of man before the Law. "The *Agape* quality of love," says Tillich, "sees man as God sees him." But what *man* can tell us how *God* sees man? "Agape," continues Tillich, "loves in everybody and through everybody love itself." Karl Barth speaks more simply and intelligibly, and with a basic brutality which is the clue to his crude neutralism, when he claims that such has no bearing whatever for the organization of any human society. For Barth, God loves Stalin no less than Stalin's victims.

Finally there is the method of creative intelligence. It, too, tries to make it possible for men to live with the tragic conflict of goods and rights and duties, to mediate not by arbitrary fiat but through informed and responsible decision. Whoever uses this method must find his way among all the conflicting claims. He must therefore give each one of them and the interests it represents tongue or voice. Every claimant therefore has a right to be heard. The hope is that as much as possible of each claim may be incorporated in some inclusive or shared interest which is accepted because the alternatives are less satisfactory. To this end we investigate every relevant feature about it, the conditions under which it emerged, its proximate causes and consequences, the costs of gratifying it, the available alternatives and *their* costs. Every mediation entails some sacrifice. The quest for the unique good of the situation, for what is to be done here and now, may point to what is better than anything else available, but what it points to is also a lesser evil. It is a lesser evil whether found in a compromise or in moderating the demand of a just claim or in learning to live peacefully with one's differences on the same general principle which tells us that a divorce is better for all parties concerned than a murder. In every case the rules, the wisdom, the lessons of the past are to be applied, but they have presumptive, not final, validity because they may be challenged by new presumptions. "The pragmatic import of the logic of individualized situations," says Dewey, "is to transfer the attention of theory from preoccupation with general conceptions to the problem of developing effective methods of inquiry," and applying them. It is a logic which does not preach solutions but explores the suggestions that emerge from the analyses of problems. Its categorical imperative is to inquire, to reason together, to seek in every crisis the creative devices and inventions that will not only make life fuller and richer but tragedy bearable. William James makes essentially the same point as Dewey in the language of ideals. Since in the struggles between ideals "victory and defeat there must be, the victory to be philosophically prayed for is that of the more inclusive side—of the side which even in the hour of triumph will to some degree do justice to the ideals in which the vanquished interests lay. . . ." But prayer is not enough. He goes on: "*Invent some manner* of realizing your own ideals which will also satisfy the alien demands—that and that only is the path of peace." To which we must add, provided there is a reciprocal will to peace in the matter, and even then, your own or the alien demands or both must be curtailed.

As one may have gathered by this time, I have been concerned to show that this pragmatic approach to the moral problem can be squared not only with the recognition of tragic conflicts, of troubles, minor and grave, which dog the life of man in a precarious world, but that it gets its chief justification from this recognition. Intelligence may be optimistic when it deals with the control of things but the moral life by its very nature forbids the levity and superficiality which has often been attributed to the pragmatic approach by its unimaginative critics.

Indeed, I make bold to claim that the pragmatic approach to tragedy is more serious, even more heroic, than any other approach because it doesn't resign itself to the bare fact of tragedy or take easy ways out at the price of truth. Where death does not result from the tragic situation, there are always consequences for continued living which it takes responsibly without yielding to despair. It does not conceive of tragedy as a preordained doom, but as one in which the plot to some extent depends upon us, so that we become the creators of our own tragic history. We cannot then palm off altogether the tragic outcome upon the universe in the same way as we can with a natural disaster.

Contrast this attitude toward tragedy with the Hegelian fetishism of history, which in the end is but the rationalization of cruelty. Contrast it with the Judaic-Christian conception which offers, at the price of truth, the hope that the felicities of salvation will both explain and recompense human suffering. Contrast it with the attitude of Unamuno, whose hunger for immortality is so intense that he sees in intelligence or reason the chief enemy of life, both in time and eternity. For him the joy and delight of life is the conflict of value and value no matter what the cost. "The very essence if tragedy," he tells us, "is the combat of life with reason." And since the Inquisitor is concerned with the eternal life of his victim's soul, the potential victim must defend the Inquisitor's place in society and regard him as far superior to the merchant who merely ministers to his needs. "There is much more humanity in the Inquisitor," he says. Crazed by this thirst for the infinite, Unamuno glorifies war as the best means of spreading love and knowledge. He illustrates the dialectic of total absurdity and caprice in thought which often prepares the way for atrocity in life. Here is no quest for the better, for the extension of reasonable controls in life and society, for peace in action.

To be sure, Unamuno is so horrified by the flux of things in which all things are ultimately liquefied that he expresses pity for the very "star-strewn heavens" whose light will some day be quenched. But this cosmic sentimentality is disdainful of the vexatious, unheroic daily tasks of mediating differences, even of mitigating the consequences of irreconcilable conflicts, of devising ways to limit human suffering whose ubiquitous presence is the alleged cause of spiritual agony.

No two thinkers seem so far removed from each other as Miguel de Unamuno and Bertrand Russell—and as philosophers they are indeed related as a foothill to a Himalayan peak. But this makes all the more significant the similarity of their attitude toward the arts of social control which require the extension of man's power over nature. For Russell, any philosophy, and particularly one like Dewey's, which interprets ideas as implicit guides to activity and behavior, and knowledge as dependent upon experimental reconstructive activity in the situation that provokes it, exhibits "the danger of what may be called cosmic impiety." It is an arrogant power-philosophy whose insolence toward the universe is hardly less objectionable when it stresses social power than individual power.

It is fortunate that Russell's attitude—in which he is not always consistent—toward scientific power and control of our natural environment has not prevailed, otherwise the whole of modern civilization including modern medicine would never have developed. The charge of megalomania against any view of knowledge just because it is not a pure spectator view is absurd. For the pragmatic view accepts the Spinozistic dictum that nature can be changed only by nature's means. The problem is to discover or devise these means. This cannot be intelligently done without experimental activity. According to Russell's own position, power itself is neither good nor bad but only the uses and ends of power. But since he also tells us that there is no such thing as a rational or irrational end, that intelligence or reason is helpless in determining what we should do with our power, one can argue with much better warrant that it is *his* view, *if acted upon*, that increases "the danger of vast social disaster" rather than the pragmatic view, which believes that by changing nature and society men can to some extent change themselves in the light of rationally determined ends. No humane person can read history without being moved more by man's failures to use the knowledge he has had to remove the evils and sufferings which were remediable than by his attempt to achieve too great a control or power over nature. It was not science that was responsible for the use of the atomic bomb. It was politics—a failure of politics to understand the true situation. The pitiful disparity at any particular time between what we know and what we don't know is sufficient to inspire a sense of humility in the most intellectually ambitious. But it is only in the most vulgarized sense of the term "pragmatism," a sense which Russell helped to popularize by flagrant misunderstandings, that the adequacy of a theory of knowledge, which regards activity or experiment as integral to the achievement of knowledge of fact, can be judged by its alleged social consequences.

I am more interested here in stating a position than establishing it. As I understand the pragmatic perspective on life, it is an attempt to make it possible for men to live in a world of inescapable tragedy—a tragedy that flows from the conflict of moral ideals,—without lamentation, defiance, or make-believe. According to this perspective, even in the best of human worlds there will be tragedy—tragedy perhaps without bloodshed, but certainly not without tears. It focuses its analysis on problems of normative social inquiry in order to reduce the costs of tragedy. Its view of man is therefore melioristic, not optimistic. Some philosophers belittle man by asking him to look at the immensities without; others belittle him by asking him to look at the perversities and selfishness within. Pragmatism denies nothing about the world or men which one truly finds in them, but it sees in men something which is at once, to use the Sophoclean phrase, more wonderful and more terrible than anything else in the universe, viz., the power to make themselves and the world around them better or worse. In this way pragmatic meliorism avoids the romantic pessimism of Russell's free man, shaking his fist in defiance of a malignant universe, and the grandiose optimism of Niebuhr's redeemed man, with his delusions of a cosmic purpose which he knows is there but knows in a way in which neither he nor anyone else can possibly understand.

To the meliorist the recognition of the gamut of tragic possibilities is what feeds his desire to find some method of negotiating conflicts of value by intelligence rather than by war or brute force. But this is not as simple as it sounds. There is no substitute for intelligence. But intelligence may not be enough. It may not be enough because of limitations of our knowledge, because of the limited reach of our powers of control. It may not be enough because of the recalcitrance of will—not merely the recalcitrance of will to act upon goods already known and not in dispute, but because of unwillingness to find out what the maximizing good in the situation is. And although we are seeking to settle conflicts of value by the use of intelligence rather than by force, is it not true that sometimes intelligence requires the use of force?

Let us take this last question first. Faced by a momentous conflict of values in which some value must give way if the situation is to be resolved, the rational approach is to find some encompassing value on the basis of some shared interest. This, as we have seen, involves willingness to negotiate—to negotiate honestly. The grim fact, however, is that there is sometimes no desire to reason, no wish to negotiate except as a holding action to accumulate strategic power, nothing but the reliance of one party or the other upon brute force even when other alternatives may exist. In such cases the moral onus rests clearly upon those who invoke force. Their victory no more establishes their claim to be right than a vandal's destruction of a scientist's instruments of inquiry has any bearing on the validity of his assertions, evidence for or against which could have been gathered by the instrument destroyed. The intelligent use of force to *prevent* or crush the use of force, where a healthy democratic process, equitable laws, and traditions and customs of freedom make it possible to vent differences in a rational and orderly way, is therefore justifiable even if on prudential grounds one may forgo such action. This means that tolerance always has limits—it cannot tolerate what is itself actively intolerant.

There is a tendency in modern philosophical thought which, in rejecting too sweeping claims for the role of intelligence in human affairs, settles for too little even when it does not embrace a wholesale skepticism. Of course, a man may know what is right and not do it just as he may know what is true and not publicly assert it. In neither case is this a ground for maintaining that we cannot know what action is more justified than another or what assertion is more warranted than another. The *refusal* to follow a rational method, to give good reasons, is one thing; the claim that there are different rational methods, different *kinds* of good reasons each with its own built-in modes of validity, is something else again—and to me unintelligible. To be sure, the acceptance of rational method is not enough. Men must have some nonrational element in common. Hume is on unquestionably solid ground in asserting that reason must always *serve* a human need, interest, or passion. But his mistake outweighed his insight when he contended that rational method could only be a servant or slave of what it served and that needs, interests, and passions could not be changed or transformed by the use of intelligence. In our flights into space if we encounter other sentient creatures capable of communicating with us, it is more likely that their logical and mathematical judgment will be the same as ours than their ethical judgments, because we can more readily conceive creatures of different needs than of different minds.

At any rate the world we live in is one in which men do not share all their needs and interests and yet it is one in which they have sufficient needs and interests in common to make possible their further extension, and to give intelligence a purchase, so to speak, in its inquiry.

The most difficult of all situations is one in which even the common use of methods of inquiry seems to lead to conclusions that are incompatible with each other although each is objectively justified. There is always an open possibility of ultimate disagreement no matter how far and long we pursue rational inquiry. We can conceive it happening. In such situations we must resign ourselves to living with our differences. Otherwise we must fight or surrender. But it is simply a non sequitur to maintain that because no guarantee can be given that there will not be ultimate disagreement, penultimate agreements cannot be validly reached and justified.

In any case we cannot in advance determine the limit of reason or intelligence in *human* affairs. So long as we don't know where it lies, it is sensible to press on, at the same time devising the means to curb the effects of the refusal to reason when it manifests itself. Above all, we must avoid oversimplifying the choice of evils and encouraging the hope that to be unreasonable will pay dividends.

We are moving into another period of history in which freedom once more is being readied for sacrifice on the altars of survival. The Munichmen of the spirit are at work again. The stakes are now for the entire world. Our task as philosophers is not to heed partisan and excited calls for action, but rather to think through the problems of freedom and survival afresh. In a famous pronouncement some years ago Bertrand Russell declared that if the Kremlin refused to accept reasonable proposals of disarmament, the West should disarm unilaterally "even if it means the horrors of communist domination." Although he no longer believes this, there are many others who do. I know that common sense is at a discount in philosophy, but in ethics it should not be lightly disregarded. A position like this obviously can have only one effect, viz., to encourage the intransigence of those who wish to destroy the free world without which there cannot be a free philosophy. You cannot negotiate successfully by proclaiming in advance that you will capitulate if the other side persists in being unreasonable. Our alternatives are not limited to surrender and extinction of freedom on the one hand and war and the danger of human extermination on the other. There are other alternatives to be explored—all tragic in their costs but not equally extreme. The very willingness, if necessary, to go down fighting in defense of freedom may be the greatest force for peace when facing an opponent who makes a fetish of historical survival. On pragmatic grounds, the willingness to act on a position like Kant's *fiat justitia, pereat mundus* may sometimes—I repeat, sometimes—be the best way of preserving a just and free world—just as the best way of saving one's life is sometimes to be prepared to lose it. The uneasy peace we currently enjoy as a result of "the balance of terror" is tragic. But it may turn out that it is less so than any feasible alternative today. If it endures long enough and it becomes clear to the enemies of freedom that they cannot themselves survive war, they may accept the moral equivalents of war in the making. The pragmatic program is always to find moral equivalents for the expression of natural impulses which threaten the structure of our values.

I have perhaps overstressed the sense of the tragic in human life in an effort to compensate for the distortions to which pragmatism has been subject. There is more in life than the sense of the tragic. There is laughter and joy and the sustaining discipline of work. There are other dimensions of experience besides the moral. There is art and science and religion. There are other uses for intelligence besides the resolution of human difficulties. There is intellectual play and adventure. But until men become gods—which will never be—they will live with the sense of the tragic in their hearts as they go in quest for wisdom. Pragmatism, as I interpret it, is the theory and practice of enlarging human freedom in a precarious and tragic world by the arts of intelligent social control. It may be a lost cause. I do not know of a better one. And it may not be lost if we can summon the courage and intelligence to support our faith in freedom—and enjoy the blessings of a little luck.

[1960]

# 4

## THE PLACE OF REASON IN AN AGE OF CONFLICT

Traditionally, man has been defined as a rational animal. Spectators of the human scene, however, have in irony or jest observed that for a rational being, man's behavior is strange, indeed. In matters of comparative unimportance he acts reasonably enough; and in some fields, as the history of technology shows, with admirable ingenuity. But on all the great issues of life and death, whether they call for social or personal decision, he often seems to be a creature of impulse or mechanical habit, of instinct or fanatical allegiance to the traditions in which he was cradled. Not infrequently men meet crises by not doing anything about them, hoping they will go away, forgetting that a refusal to act has consequences, too. In the end decisions of moment often seem to be the result of chance or caprice. How many individuals looking back on the course of their lives can say that they planned it "this" way, that the choices which proved crucial in retrospect were made on reasonable grounds?

There is a striking paradox about the use of reason or intelligence in human life. On the one hand, we are enjoined almost from infancy to think before we act, to reflect carefully on our ends and goals before undertaking important affairs. All education at some point stresses the necessity of developing powers of thought. Think or be damned! is the dernier cri in some current campaigns of educational salvation. And indeed it hardly makes sense to urge anybody to act thoughtlessly. It requires considerable philosophical sophistication to offer such advice. What it amounts to when it has the semblance of sense is the realization that there are occasions which are more appropriate for action than for continued talk or thought.

On the other hand, the more we learn about human beings, the more it seems that man's reason is not an independent power but an instrument of what is not and cannot be reasonable. Because he is an animal and not an angel, man is a creature of biological impulse and need, of self-centered desires, emotions, and interests. His impulses and needs largely determine the direction his intelligence takes; his emotions and desires, not all of which he is aware, determine the goal of his actions; his interests, derived from his cultural tradition, economic class, and social status, determine a bias that is always peeping out from behind the grandiose rhetoric in which he expresses his demand for justice and fair play. Man's reason, some scientists tell us, does not officiate like an umpire over conflicting passions but is the executor of the stronger passion or group of passions; they deny what some moralists assert, viz. that man can sometimes act in favor of the weaker passion.

Even theologians and philosophers have joined the chorus to deny that reason is sovereign in human affairs. Martin Luther once referred to reason as "the Devil's Whore" in the cause of human desire. David Hume proclaimed that "reason is and ought only to be the slave of the passions." This view in our own time is urged not only by all existentialists but by Bertrand Russell, a philosophical descendant of Hume, who assures us at the very time he is vehemently condemning the ends of others as foolish that "reason has nothing to do with the choice of ends." This carries even further the half-serious dictum of another philosopher, of whom Russell is an arch-opponent—F. H. Bradley who said: "Metaphysics is the finding of bad reasons for what we believe on instinct," which is hardly tempered by his qualification that the seeking of reasons is itself an instinct.

Sociologists recognize many things in addition to instinct as causes of our beliefs about the ends of life. Social conditioning, for example, is even more powerful than biological predispositions. But most of them are one with the dominant schools in holding that the ends of life are beyond the reach of reason or intelligence. And to show that this apparent denigration of the function of reason is not restricted to theoretical studies, we may cite from the discipline of law which is so intimately concerned with regulating human conflicts. Justice O. W. Holmes, the grand old man of American jurisprudence, described the law as a calling for thinkers. But he advised judges that in hard cases decisions guided by their feelings about justice were more likely to be sound than the legal reasons offered for them.

There is no doubt that reasons are often masks hiding the face of passion and privilege, and we need no Solomon or Freud come to tell us this. We are all expert about other people's rationalizations. And it is not for nothing that the word "ratio" is the root of the term "rationalization," meaning a process of thinking by which we half-consciously deceive ourselves and others.

But is the function of reason always and only to be the servant of desire? Is it unable to reconstruct our desires, distinguish between what is desired and desirable, hold some desires in check and reinforce others, recognize the varied springs of human action and still judge between reasonable and unreasonable ends?

If the answers to these questions are affirmative, then the prospects of human life in this world are dark indeed. All moral decisions become mere thrusts for power among superior beasts of prey; all social alternatives like democracy and communism are on the same plane; "saint" and "sinner" are only emotive terms of praise and abuse; the murderer and his innocent victim have the same moral posture.

Because the consequences of a proposition are disagreeable in the extreme, does not mean it is therefore false. The truth sometimes hurts. But is it true? Or does it leave out something as true and as important, if not more so, as what it states?

Let us begin by examining a series of simple situations in which reason appears to play a role in the decisions made by ordinary people, and observe its use and limitations. These situations will not prove anything but they will illustrate certain principles, reflection on which will enable us to assess varying conceptions of the place of reason in the life of man.

A is a schoolteacher earning a modest salary who has to skimp to make ends meet. She is offered a position selling books, which pays much more money than she can ever make as a teacher. What should she do? How can reason help her to decide? Note the obvious thing that she will not toss a coin to decide. She assumes naturally, as we all do, that one decision will be wiser than another. Nor will she automatically accept the offer merely because it pays more money. For if she were interested only or mainly in money, it is hardly likely in the first place that she would have selected the vocation of teaching. She will begin by asking whether she enjoys selling as much as teaching; whether she can acquire a job security comparable to her academic tenure; whether the benefits of travel, which she loves, in conjunction with business are the same, fewer, more or less intense than the benefits of the long school vacation travel on a restricted budget. She will make inquiries and seek advice. She will try to discover what the requisites of becoming a good salesman are, whether she possesses them and what the consequences of preparing oneself for becoming one will be on her other interests. She will observe what the prospects are of the improvement in the status of teachers in the community. She will recognize her obligations to her charges not to desert the classroom until a substitute is available. Can she leave without violating her contract and without leaving bad will behind her?

Answers to these questions can be found which are more reliable than guesses. Even when she has them, however, she will not know how to decide. She must also ask some searching questions of herself. How important is marriage to her? Granted that she will meet more men selling books than in teaching, are they likely to be more congenial? It may be her social life is so rich as to make these considerations irrelevant. But there remains the question: in which pursuit can she more easily combine marriage and a vocation?

No matter what decision she makes, it will be a more reasonable one in virtue of this process of inquiry than if she had acted on the spur of the moment, or consulted a horoscope, or decided blindly on someone's say-so. Nor would it have been reasonable to ask in this case: what would happen if all teachers were offered more money and deserted the classroom? For there is no danger of that happening. And if it did, the consequences might not be calamitous. Further, if our teacher decided to accept the offer, it would be more reasonable on her part to take a leave of absence for a year from teaching than irrevocably to cut her ties. She would be leaving a door open for return in the event that she found she had erred about what gave her the profoundest satisfaction or about the rewards of business life. Her decisions, whether to go or remain, would be reasonable even if an accident subsequently befell her as a result of making it. For there was no evidence that one profession was more hazardous than another.

Before going on to our next illustration, three general observations are in order. First, the situation described is typical of many that confront all of us in the course of our lives. Everyone can think up his own examples. But in relation to any particular life, no matter how humble, the choice can be just as *momentous* in its promise or menace as any faced by the exalted captains of the world. In their case the scope and consequence of the decisions are far more vast. This is not the important difference but rather that their decision involves many others. The question is: can reason, which obviously should, and sometimes does, help us make decisions in relation to *our* personal interests, also possess the authority and power to exercise the same function when the interests of *others* are involved?

The second observation is suggested by the reader's probable reaction to the case of A. He will say that he can easily imagine a change in the condition of the illustration which would require a different decision from the one made, whatever it was. This does not refute the main point but confirms it. For the point is that changed conditions, whether in the self or environment, provided they are among those established as relevant, will very probably make a difference. That is why a reasonable decision for one person in situations of this sort will not necessarily be a reasonable decision for someone else. That is why each situation, with its complex of relevant changes, requires thought; why no recipe, formula, or copybook maxim can be used as a substitute for fresh thinking. In this sense every decision is *relative*, meaning that it is warranted in relation to the particular state of affairs which has provoked our inquiry. But because the decision is warranted, it is *objective*. A judgment therefore may be both relative and objective and the easy view which identifies the relative with the subjective and implies that any man's judgment in any case is as valid as any other's is shown to be false. Those who claim that reason plays no role are not being empirical. They are committed to a theory which must explain certain easily confirmable phenomena.

The third observation is equally important. A did not know what her ends really were before she began thinking. She found out something about herself in the course of thinking matters through. It is easy to settle questions when our ends are predetermined, but the poignancy of moral choice arises from the fact that we are not sure of our ends, not sure that they can be reconciled as they stand. Notice, too, that A's decision, whatever it is, has consequences for the kind of person she is going to be ten or twenty years hence—depending upon her choice. Her interests, friends, ideas, values, commitments—even her vocabulary—are likely to be significantly different in view of the new behavioral patterns required for her to make good. What she will consider of most worth in the future is largely implicit in what she considers of most worth now. In this way she recreates to some extent her own personality. She must accept some responsibility for what happens to her.

B is a young man very much in love with a young woman who cannot leave her aged parents. He is offered a unique opportunity to fulfill his deep professional ambition by going abroad. It is obvious that she will not wait the many years required for him to complete his service abroad. The nub of this situation is that his desire to fulfill his life-long ambition and to marry this girl are incompatible. If he marries, he will have to take a job he doesn't like, live with his wife's family, and probably brood about what he might have been. If he goes abroad, he will be heartsick for the girl he loves. There is no happy solution here in the way some movies and novels contrive. Nor can he make a tentative choice, leaving a door open. Here, too, he is not sure what he really wants except that he can't have both. The chances of a mistake are greater than in the case of A. He will suffer in any event. The reasonable decision will be the one for which he will suffer least. This will be determined by whether it is easier to resign himself to the loss of a great opportunity or a great love. At the very least he must reconstruct his interest in one or the other. His parents will usually advise him one way, his friends another. It is safe to say that if the agony of doubt is prolonged, this in itself is weighty but not conclusive evidence that it would be more reasonable for him to go than to stay. The younger he is, the more likely it is that he will recover from love's arrows than from a frustrated life's ambition. There are hard decisions in most people's lives and quiet deaths of the spirit from which reason cannot spare us even when it points out the road of the lesser evil. "Why isn't a decision to blow his brains out just as reasonable?" sneers an existentialist philosopher. "Because he loses both options and much more beside" is a sufficient answer.

C is a married woman, the proud and not unpretty mother of two small children, whose husband has been unfaithful. The affair was not casual; neither was it enduring. What is the reasonable thing for her to do? She may be too hurt to use her reason. Her own feelings to her husband have become ambiguous, and he is apparently indifferent and unrepentant. As usual, some kind friend advises her that the only dignified thing is to get a divorce and a good settlement. There is a certain dignity in such a procedure. Were she without children, younger and prettier, this might also be the reasonable thing to do, especially if there is reason to believe that such lapses were chronic. But the presence of children who are fond of their father makes a great difference. It is so great as to be the overriding consideration in the decision to make every effort to keep the family together—short of the humiliations that a faithless husband may impose on a wife which poisons the relationship between parents and children. In that case it is more reasonable to dissolve a marriage. There are some fathers children are better off *not* growing up with. In general, however, women are more forgiving of men's infidelities than vice versa; sometimes the situation gives them a certain strength of outraged virtue which they exploit with dexterity to reestablish the family until the children are grown. By that time most couples have achieved an understanding that brings them together again. The point here is that every choice is one of misery but not all choices are equally reasonable.

D is a member of a school board whose vote will determine whether to permit an agitator for some minority cause to speak before a club in a local high school. Such issues should be left to teachers and students' groups to settle. But often pressure groups or newspapers succeed in putting the problem into the laps of the school board, the P.T.A., and kindred organizations. What would a reasonable decision be for a member of such a group and how would it be reached?

What about our Bill of Rights? Doesn't that altogether settle the question? Not completely. Because a man has a right to speak on a street corner denouncing Jews or Catholics or Negroes, and can claim legal protection in the exercise of that right, does not of itself give him a right to the use of public facilities to reach students even if they are not a captive audience. The problem is primarily an educational one. Since we are committed to developing the intellectual independence of our students, if the theme of the speaker has a bearing, even a peripheral one, upon the intellectual concerns of the students, there is a strong presumption that he should be heard. After all, what can they hear in an hour's talk, followed by questions and critical discussion and an occasion to continue the discussion with their teachers in subsequent class periods, which will lead them to abandon the good sense or the values and ideals they have until now acquired? When they are older, won't they hear peddled outside the school buildings pretty much the same messages of demagogy and salvation to which irate parents and citizens now object to students listening? How will they best be able to meet it—by critical exposure to it or intellectual isolation from it? What have the consequences been of permitting these occasional talks in other schools? Of denying them? What do the teachers themselves say? Can they make the entire question, subject, speaker and all, a peg on which to build a stimulating educational experience?

Nonetheless, this does not mean that any speaker on any subject should automatically be extended the same privilege as the unpopular heretic. If the talk is likely to precipitate violence in consequence of the speaker's incitement, he should be barred. The line may be hard to draw but it is the precise task of intelligence to draw it. Principles are a necessary but not a sufficient guide, for the simple reason that more than one principle is involved. Depending upon the occasion, the emphasis goes to one or another. In time of war we may decide a case differently from the way we would in time of peace. It is one thing for a speaker to present a position; it is another if he tries to recruit for a subversive group. Intelligence involves not only insight into the changed conditions but the courage to make the new decision, even if it means breaking a rule. *Sometimes* it is necessary to pass a red light to avoid a disastrous accident, and to fight fire with fire.

E is a well-known safecracker—the most intelligent rogue in town. The case of the intelligent rogue is always cited in discussion of the place of reason in human affairs as the clinching evidence that intelligence is the mere tool of desire. We can only give it a few words.

What is E really intelligent about? Cracking safes. But is he intelligent about human relations or about himself or even about how to make money? He is always on the run; always under suspicion when a crooked job is done; a source of acute embarrassment to his family and children. He has friends only when he has money. And how much money has he? It has been computed by someone that most intelligent rogues of this type earn far less in the course of a lifetime by their depradations than they could earn by using their indisputable skills and still enjoy their freedom. Most crooks are intelligent about things and money but not about human beings, and about themselves least of all.

We now take a giant stride from these situations of ordinary life to world problems. Can reason help to make decisions here? What, for example, can it do with the enormously complicated question of disarmament. We can take for granted that we require reliable knowledge of political, social, and scientific realities just as scientific decision about the choice of vocation, marriage, and divorce requires reliable knowledge about job, personalities, one's temperament, and the prospects of change in the behavior of others.

It always comes with an impact of surprise to discover that a person who is highly knowledgeable and eminently reasonable in one domain may be an extraordinary fool in other domains. The very virtues of a scientist in a laboratory, his openness and trust in the reports of his colleagues, may be drawbacks at a conference table with Communist or Fascist diplomats. Nor does a wise and exemplary life as head of a family or business fit a man for the complexities of foreign policy. Oddly enough, complicated problems like those of foreign policy are questions which almost all literate persons feel called upon to judge without specially qualifying themselves by long and patient study. "We tend to be most dogmatic about what we know least about." Then again, the very complexity of world political affairs, the great number of variables interacting with each other, make it difficult to tell whether a person is speaking out of expertness or ignorance. The fact is that experts are sometimes wrong. This does not prove that amateurs are as good or better than experts but only that experts are not infallible and therefore, where our own welfare is at stake, we must do our own thinking. Fortunately, one does not have to be an expert to judge experts. We can tell who the expert cooks are by tasting what they concoct, not by cooking better.

A reasonable decision about disarmament must be based upon knowledge of the cost and deadliness of modern war. This knowledge is widely known although there is some dispute about the details. But disarmament is not merely a technical scientific matter. It is a political, historical, and psychological matter. We must also have knowledge of the thought ways of the Communist world; its ethics and history, and especially its record of promise-keeping. For there is much truth in the Chinese proverb: "No man can have more peace than his neighbors will allow him."

On the one hand, there is the obvious risk that increasing armaments may lead to war and bankruptcy. This is not inevitable; else the world would always be at war or always bankrupt.

On the other hand, genuine disarmament depends upon a mutually agreed upon system of control. The catch is that the other side may refuse to accept any effective system of inspection without which disarmament is a farce. How can any nation, or group of leaders, sincerely desire peace and refuse the necessary means to it? Here the refusal to accept the necessary means may lead to doubts about whether peace is the genuine goal, but it is more likely to indicate that peace, as desirable as it is, is of subordinate importance to other values.

Very well, some have urged, if the United States truly desires peace, why does it not disarm unilaterally and give the world a convincing spectacle of our courage and devotion to peace? If the only mighty powers in the world with which the United States had to contend were like England, this would be a reasonable proposal, and probably effective, too. The history of England in the thirties, both with respect to nonintervention in Spain and rearmament in the face of Hitler's growing power, and earlier of China with respect to Japan, point up the risks of such a strategy. It is also noteworthy that some of our Indian friends who have urged this course upon us did not themselves advocate or follow it themselves in relation to Pakistan. Far more reasonable is to pursue the path of mutual or mulilateral disarmament, taking small risks for limited periods in the absence of adequate safeguards of inspection and closely monitoring developments. Agreements can then be extended or cancelled when the negotiated time period has lapsed.

This brings us to the most difficult problems of all. They are typified in extreme situations in which even men who regard themselves as reasonable sometimes declare that reason must abdicate. How can reason help decide when the choice is between life and death?

The first pertinent observation is to deny that such situations constitute the paradigm of moral choice. Most moral problems do not confront us with such grim alternatives. Even if it were true that all extreme situations are beyond the jurisdiction of reason, which I shall challenge, most of us live most of our lives without having to make such heroic or desperate decisions. Suppose it were true that in extreme situations reason is helpless to guide us. All that would mean is that the sovereignty of reason is not absolute. But what has absolute sovereignty? Reason would still be necessary in enabling us to distinguish between what is and what is not an extreme situation, whether our alternatives are truly exclusive and exhaustive. To escape the flames it is not always wise to jump off the roofs of buildings.

Nonetheless, the nature of our life today is such that anyone may be confronted with a choice between life and death. In situations of this kind what can reason tell us? In general, it tells us to choose life rather than death if life holds out any joy or hope. That is why it is foolish to lose one's life in order to save one's private purse or watch or any other material possession, especially if one's life is important to the welfare and happiness of others. Does this mean that one must always submit to the demands of a man with a gun, that one must choose survival in all circumstances and conditions regardless of any consequences? Obviously not. What shall we say of those who have died for their faith or in the cause of human freedom or to save the lives of others? "The more fools they," replies the cynic, the egoist, and the man whose discretion is a mask for his cowardice. The wisdom of the race as reflected in the traditions of all literate communities recognizes that it is a poor sort of creature for whom there is nothing more in life than bare life itself. With rare exceptions, human beings are not so simply organized that they can live at peace with themselves if, for the sake of survival, they betray friends, family, country, and the very ideals and values that are integral to their personalities. Death is not beyond human judgment when it is a consequence of human action. The fact that we can say that a man died foolishly or unnecessarily in a barroom brawl he could easily have avoided, or that Ferdinand Lasalle was unwise to imperil the German working-class movement he so brilliantly led by risking his life in a duel, shows that we do not consider such deaths as independent of the lives of which they are a part and of the lives of others they affect. From one point of view every death voluntarily chosen, even under a forced option, is an act of suicide. Suicides may be noble or ignoble, good or bad, foolish or wise.[1]

Many individuals are willing to risk their lives for what they believe or love because it is a *risk* of death they face, and not its certainty. If so, then the calculation of the risk can be intelligent or foolish. But can one intelligently choose the certainty of death? If we grant that one can choose it foolishly, why not? A variety of causes is behind the decision of individuals of the past who chose death rather than renunciation of their ideals or betrayal of comrades. But to the extent that their decision was freely made, reasonable grounds of two kinds entered. One was the general effect of their action upon the cause for which they were fighting. The second, if they were ever tempted to yield, was the realization that they could not live with themselves and bear the cross of their betrayal to the grave even if they escaped public obloquy. Men and women have chosen to die in the face of far less radical threats to or violations of their integrity.

This is not to say that reason alone determines the course of action in extreme situations. Character, habit, locale, audience, "the eye of history," all play a role. But reason is still operative, still relevant even if the individual is overwhelmed by emotions of fear or religious ecstasy to a point where he cannot grasp its relevance. Nor does reason always counsel death. One may confess to no more than what the enemy knows already in order to escape it. We must make a further distinction between the decision of a man under torture or, what is worse, confronted by the torture of his wife and children, and the decision when these are absent. We may praise or even revere the person who has the fortitude to withstand these agonies, but we have no moral right to condemn the actions of those who are broken by it—and not merely because we cannot be sure how we would behave in similar circumstances.

Karl Jaspers somewhere claims that no sensible person would sacrifice his life rather than renounce some truth that everyone knows. If a tyrant demanded of one that he deny the truths of mathematics or science or else face a firing squad, compliance would be more reasonable than defiance. These truths remain true regardless of what anyone says about them. On the other hand, were one asked, under threat of execution, to renounce certain beliefs one holds on faith, beliefs about persons, friends or family, or ideals, justice or love, about which one can never have the same degree of objective evidence as for scientific statements, we could recognize the reasonableness of the refusal. Why? Presumably because the second involves the integrity of one's personality in a way that the first does not. This would make Giordano Bruno's fateful decision foolish and Galileo's wise.

This distinction seems questionable. One's personal integrity may be bound up in the discovery of a mathematical or objective truth, and the future of its development may depend upon its publication. The number of relevant factors that may enter into a decision are so many, regardless of whether the issue is political, personal, or scientific, that one cannot formulate a rule prescribing reasonable behavior in all conceivable circumstances. What seems warranted is the assertion that given the concrete circumstances of any decision, investigation will show that all possible decisions are not equally justifiable, that some are better than others in the same sense, if not the same degree, as in problems arising in situations that are not "extreme." The only exceptions are those in which a blind guess is the only guess that can be made. And, as we have already seen, the determination that the guess can be only a blind guess and not an informed one presupposes some rational exploration of the situation. That our previous experience, memories, and guiding maxims should have absolutely no bearing on our new experience is extremely unlikely although not impossible. Were the world to dissolve in chaos, intelligence would avail us nothing. But it is only ex post facto, after we have found that our intelligence has been systematically frustrated, that we can discover the absence of any order or, alternatively, an order of such great complexity that it is unpredictable.

Sometimes the difficulty in recognizing the jurisdiction of reason or intelligence consists in a failure to distinguish between the legitimacy or justification of resort to the processes of reasoning and the validity of the specific reasons given. This difficulty is compounded by uncertainty about what constitutes a reason and the failure to recognize that the criteria of acceptability depends upon the class of phenomena we are inquiring into. To the question "Why do you eat avocados?" the answer, "Because I like or enjoy them," is a good and sufficient reason to anyone who does not know they are edible or who has a distaste for them. It would not be a reason in answer to the question "Why do you believe avocados are nourishing?" or to any other question about causes or consequences. *De gustibus non disputandum est* is true enough when we are discussing tastes in food or drink but not any question in the moral economy. Whenever an issue of good taste arises, something more is involved than the occurrence of taste itself. How much more so is this the case when we must choose between life and death. Such choices, when they must be made, are more fateful than others but not more ultimate. They can be social or personal. When personal, no one can make them for us. It would be wrong to call them arbitrary or absurd. But they can be mistaken. A wise man knows when to die and how to die—and this means that he also knows when not to die, when he must yield in order to win the space and time to fight more effectively for a freer and better life, when he must compromise in order to save the things that may not be compromised.

In these grave and far-reaching decisions as well as in the ordinary circumscribed decisions of daily life, reason never operates alone but always in relation to our fears and hopes, desires and passions. But it is not their slave because, as we have seen, its insight and foresight give us some power to reconstruct them and to modify the attitudes we bring to the assessment of fact. There is a continuum of ends and means in our attempt to think our way out of our predicaments. The means we select to realize our ends redetermine the ends which in turn lead us to modify the means.

There is a simple argument against the view that reason can enable us to make decisions when values are at stake. It asserts that since we can make decisions only in the light of the consequences of alternative modes of conduct, we must know in advance which consequences are good. Doubt about the validity of these consequences can be allayed only in terms of other consequences; and so on until we reach a point where some consequences are considered absolutely valid. Beyond them we cannot go, and about them we cannot be mistaken. Otherwise, we are embarked upon a vicious infinite regress. If the method of reason or intelligence is here equated broadly with the method of science, then as an editorial in *Science* once put it: "Science in pursuit of values is much like a donkey in pursuit of a bunch of carrots that has been suspended in front of its nose from a twig fastened to its harness." The conclusion is:

either we never reach a firmly grounded value by reason or, if we do, its validity does not depend upon reason.

This argument is mistaken on many grounds. It overlooks the fact that our value-problems are specific and that if we take them one at a time, we do not have to settle questions about so-called ultimate values or goals. Our problem is always what to do in this particular case; if I discover that this action rather than another will win friendship (or health or knowledge or money), I do not have to inquire what these are good for or whether they are worth having. Of course these *may* become problematic but not necessarily. We can agree with each other that some steady employment is desirable without agreeing, if someone asks us why, on the reasons therefore. We do not have to go all the way to the end of the road in order to travel together a part of the way. Perhaps there is no end of the road. Just as I do not have to have an ultimate destination in order to take a worthwhile trip, so I do not have to be in possession of an ultimate or absolute value in order to choose what is desirable among possible alternatives. We can put this in another way. We have *many* "ultimate" values: love, work, knowledge, family, friendship, art, country. Our problems result because they conflict with each other. How do we choose intelligently among them except by reference to the way they affect other values?

When our values are at variance with the values of others, as so often happens in human affairs, can the use of reason help us avoid overt conflict? Here, too, we must not claim too much; but neither should we settle for too little. That there will always be differences among human beings—differences in tastes and preferences, feelings and claims—is as certain as anything can be. Since there is joy in variety, we should not try to banish or even reduce them. But a distinction must be made between difference and conflict. Some differences are complementary to each other; some are compatible with each other; some are incompatible. Some incompatible differences may be resolved by compromise, separation, or by the creative intelligence which devises "soundproofing" and the other amenities that extend the area of privacy in a crowded world. There are differences, however, which may not be resolvable by reason and which can be settled, if at all, only by conflict. Sometimes the only reasonable course is to fight—particularly if one is confronted with a persistent refusal to use reason. Reasonableness is not synonymous with sweet compliance nor does it exclude the judicious use of force. What it requires only is the offer, continued and renewed until the last

possible moment, to negotiate conflict in the hope of reaching an acceptable, even if not ideal, solution.

Something must be said about the pathology of reason. One can often
reason at will. But there are times when reason does not respond when
summoned; yet at other times, one reasons when there is not further
need of it. There are few human beings who will not be roused occasionally to unreasonable fury when some vital interest of their life is threatened. It would be too much to expect it to be otherwise. The only question is whether their fury can be kept within reasonable bounds, i.e.,
whether it can be checked before it proves counterproductive or even
suicidal. There are some human beings chronically unable to reason
about themselves or about the consequences of their furious reactions.
They don't want to find out about themselves out of fear or shame at
what they will find. There is no remedy here except possibly some form
of psychotherapy or religious conversion or the simple courage to accept
oneself as a basis for desirable change.

There are individuals whose ailment is different, in whom reason, so
to speak, has no terminal facilities. They keep on reasoning long after
they have reached a reasonable decision. This is usually attributable to a
desire to avoid action, especially a bold stroke which will irrevocably
transform the securities, such as they are, of the status quo. But the life
of reason is not the same as a reasoning life any more than the joy of life
is a life of joy (which is notoriously joyless) or good talk is compulsive
talking. Reason is the judge of its own legitimate use and limitation.

Reason is not so much *reasoning* as it is good sense, and like a sense
of tact or humor it has as deep a root in our genetic structure as in our
learned behavior. This should not be a cause of despair except where an
individual is born devoid of a capacity to think. Whatever our capacities
to think, and they are at least as widely distributed as our other natural
capacities, they can always be improved. Irrationalists and mystics to the
contrary notwithstanding, we suffer from too little thinking rather than
from too much. Until we find ways of directly influencing the genes of
intelligence, our only hope for improvement of the powers of human
understanding lies through the processes of critical education.

But is not the entire position here viciously circular? When we
choose to rely on reason rather than on intuition, revelation, authority,
tradition, or whatnot, are we not guilty of the most obvious question-begging? If we ask, "Why reason?" how can we invoke reason to answer the
question? Is not a simple voluntarism, an exercise of arbitrary will,

inescapable? It would be scoring an easy dialectical victory to point out, as Russell once did to Bergson, that it is incoherent to reject the use of reason on reasonable grounds. It is no less dialectical to indicate that anyone who asks, "Why should I be reasonable?" and expects an answer is not really asking a genuine question, since any intelligible answer one way or another would be put forward as presumptively reasonable. However, the question would be a straightforward one if the term "reasonable" here meant not a ground or justification but "conciliatory" or "considerate" or "prepared to negotiate or compromise."

Nonetheless, I do not believe that the proposal to use reason when we are concerned to find reliable methods of reaching the truth—regardless of how we define the truth—is viciously circular. For what we are doing is extending the pattern of reasonable decision that not only the skeptic but any normal person follows in ordinary life experiences. The condition of survival in a hostile world is the use of reason in at least some situations. If there are certain methods which men use to cure stomachaches, find their way out of jungles, grow food, win battles, catch fish that are obviously better than other methods, then once the pattern by which the superiority of these methods is established and generalized, is it not natural to extend this knowledge to the consideration of other problems? Granted there is no guarantee that the extension will be successful. Is it not reasonable to extrapolate?

Those who speak of the limits of reason must stake out and justify those limits. Usually what is meant by the phrase calls attention to the fact that different subject-matters require different techniques and determine different orders of exactitude in the conclusions drawn. But the limits of particular methods or techniques are not the limits of reason. Granted that reason always takes something else for granted. But the nonrational is not the irrational. Granted that there is always something more in life than reason, that most human beings are loath to reason most of the time. If this is what is meant by the limits of reason, then we may just as well speak of the "presuppositions" or "conditions" of reason as well as its "limits."

In reflecting upon the illustrations above a certain number of principles emerge which can be used as guidelines in the use of intelligence in human affairs, in the wise choice *both* of ends and means.

(1) Moral or ethical problems are those in which we find ourselves committed to plural ends, not all of which can be realized. The meaning of these ends is brought home to us when we discover the means neces-

sary to achieve them. Means are not merely means but integral parts of the end. The way one gets his happiness determines the quality of it, as so many have discovered who have built their happiness on the ruin of others' lives. Not only are ends which are impossible to realize irrational (except when taken as ideals to guide the direction of activity) but also those ends the means to which cost too much, hurt too much, bore us too much. No one can state precisely the exact weight we give the competing ends or means in a particular situation or work out in detail the calculus of our deliberation. But a reasonable choice can always support itself by offering good grounds for itself. If the good grounds are really sound, we need not worry whether they are the actual or real causes of the decision. A man may act out of fear, but if it is wise to act in a certain way in the face of a challenge or a danger, the wisdom of the action should determine whether he inhibits it or gives it full rein.

(2) Reasonable choice, like all choice, is between alternatives. But there is always a danger that we conceive alternatives too narrowly and overlook the multiplicity of alternatives in many situations where we imagine ourselves confronted by a stark either/or. The happiest discovery—alas! too rare—is that ends in apparent conflict do not really exclude each other, as when marriage and a career can be combined. But when ends do exclude each other they do not necessarily exhaust all the alternatives. We cannot go to two different places at once, but we may go to a third place or nowhere at all. The broader the vision of alternatives, the more reasonable the decision. This applies to the consideration of means as well.

(3) The reasonable man has impulses but is not impulsive, has emotions but is not emotional, and understands what William James meant about the importance of moral holidays. The one thing he cannot be is a fanatic, either about virtue or reason. Santayana defines a fanatic as one who having forgotten his goal redoubles his efforts. This really characterizes some efficiency experts. Santayana to the contrary, a fanatic knows what his goal or end is: what makes him a fanatic is his willingness to sacrifice everything else to it, to repudiate all the other ends of life for the sake of one overriding concern or supreme end. No matter how exalted that supreme end may be—whether knowledge or art, love or friendship, pleasure or purity, justice or glory—whoever is prepared to sacrifice all other ends to it is a moral monster. He will make of his life a shambles, and when he has the power, of the world as well. Any one human value pursued with an exclusive intensity beyond a certain point turns sour and infects the others.

(4) There is no assurance that a decision, reasonable at the time we make it, will always turn out to have been for the best. In a contingent world reason is only an insurance policy, not a ticket to felicity. Everyone will admit that it is reasonable to take shelter when bombs begin to fall. Yet some people have been killed in bomb shelters who would have remained alive had they been less cautious. This is a poor argument against bomb shelters.

More important, the self grows and develops with its choices. There is a limit to our power and wisdom in foreseeing at twenty what we will be like and need at forty or sixty. It would be foolish to forget that we live in the overlapping present and that although we must take thought *of* the future we cannot live *for* the future. Those who live for the future never live at all. Almost as bad is the dreamlike experience of living in the past. Those who escape from the challenges and problems of the present to the memories which rehearse past triumphs and satisfactions are destroying all possibilities of further growth.

The greatest provocation to escape into the past is through our regrets. Almost every major decision in personal life at some fleeting moment is sure to be regretted when contrasted with the rose-colored reconstruction of what might have been. But we can wager on it that if we really had made the alternative decision, we would have regretted even more bitterly not making the choice we actually did. Regrets are vain except as resolutions to avoid what is undesirable in the future.

(5) Finally, a reasonable decision in human affairs is not the less reasonable because it cannot be proved in strict logic, because it rests only on an estimate of probabilities.

Reason is not everything, but on every serious occasion it always has something to say. Catastrophes, natural or social, may be unavoidable even after reason has done its best. But we have a far way to go before we can claim that we have even begun to make habits of reason prevail in our schools, our homes, and our lives.

[1975]

## NOTE

1. See my article "The Ethics of Suicide," *International Journal of Ethics* 37 (January 1927): 173–88.

# II

## STUDIES IN
## MARX AND MARXISM

# 5

# COMMUNISM
# WITHOUT DOGMAS

## I

To begin with I wish to make it perfectly clear that if by communism one means an acceptance of the present principles and tactics of the Third International, or any of its affiliated organizations, I am not a communist. But to define communism in terms of membership in a specific organization is as inadequate as to define Christianity in terms of membership in any particular church. I believe that communist principles are more important than communist organizations, for they enable us to judge the theory and practice of existing communist organizations in their light. It is these principles I wish to make the basis of discussion—principles to be found in the writings of Marx and Engels, and in the economic and political works of Lenin and Trotsky. Here, again, some further distinctions are necessary. If by communism one means a form of social organization in which the associated producers democratically control the production and distribution of goods, then it is possible to be a communist without being a Marxist, although every Marxist must be a communist. Marxism, then, can only be significantly defined as *the theory and practice of achieving communism or a classless society.* When I speak of *Marxian* communism, again I do not mean the communism preached and practiced today by "official" and "orthodox" commu-

Originally published in *Modern Monthly*, April 1934.

nist parties in Europe and America. In fact, it seems to me that just as Marx and Engels in 1848 called themselves communists to set themselves off from bourgeois socialists who had debased the term socialism, so it may soon become necessary to find another name for communism to differentiate it from the Communist Party which has succeeded in corrupting the meaning of the term by its mistaken theories and tragically sectarian tactics.

I shall indicate the grounds upon which I accept Marxian communism and shall try to show that any other type of communism is doomed to remain an unrealizable dream. In the sense in which I have defined these terms Bertrand Russell, John Dewey, and Morris R. Cohen may, on the basis of their social writings, be regarded as communists of a sort, since they all subscribe to the ideal of a classless society. But they are clearly not Marxists.

It is a commonplace, however, of Marxist methodology—and indeed of experimental logic—that it is impossible to make a sharp division between means and ends; that the real meaning of any goal can be understood only in relation to the means necessary to attain it; and that intelligent choice of ends can be made only when the consequences of the use of our means have been taken into calculation. What we really want is not merely what we say we want but what the doing, which is always bound up with sincere saying, commits us to. From this point of view, when two parties say they want the same thing but disagree concerning the methods by which it may be attained, analysis will show that they do not really want the same thing. It is important to stress this because verbally all social classes and political parties profess to subscribe to the same ideals—security, order, happiness, peace, or whatnot. Thirty years ago it was possible for a leading statesman to say: "We are all socialists now." Tomorrow another one of his kind will say: "We are all collectivists now." Both "socialism" and "collectivism," in the abstract, function like the formulae proposed by the League of Nations and accepted by nations with conflicting interests. They conceal differences instead of expressing them. That is why it is possible for ministers to sign peace pacts with one hand and war budgets with another, and why statesmen who are self-declared socialists imprison those who are trying to bring socialism about. Unless in every definite socio-historical situation the ideal formulae are given specific content in terms of a program of *action*, it is impossible to take them seriously except as disguises of another kind of allegiance—one of which the proponents of the ideal formulae may be truly unconscious but which is unmistakably revealed in what they actively support or passively tolerate in practice. In a deeper sense, then, instead of Marxian communism being one species of communism sharing a great deal in common with other species but differing in a few important details, it may turn out that its differences from other types of communism are far more important than its agreements. This I believe to be the case.

I shall now proceed to state the general arguments for communism in such a way that the organic connection between communism as a philosophy of social organization and Marxism as the theory and practice of social revolution may be more apparent than appears in customary exposition. I shall attempt to meet the major arguments of Bertrand Russell, John Dewey, and Morris R. Cohen against communism, at the same time pointing out what in the principles and practice of orthodox Communist Parties today give the criticisms of these eminent men such force and apparent plausibility.

## 1. The Argument from Efficiency

The strongest justification ever offered for capitalism was its success in unlocking the great sources of energy which slumbered in nature and society. The classic tribute which Marx paid in the *Communist Manifesto* to the great historic function of capitalism in developing the forces of production and creating the conditions of modern civilized life is all the more significant because it came from one who was passionately aware of the human costs of the accumulation of capital, of the industrial and bourgeois revolutions. To all arguments against capitalism on humanitarian grounds the unfailing response came: "It works." Today no honest man in his senses can make a similar reply. Capitalism cannot even attempt to operate its production plants at full capacity without coming to a standstill almost overnight. Its further functioning is possible only by the retrenchment and destruction of already existing facilities. The signs of this appear on all sides—in fact, it has been elevated to a deliberate policy under the euphemism of "social planning." During the nineteenth century, economic waste might have been regarded as a by-product of necessary economic advance; today, it would hardly be an exaggeration to say that industry and agriculture can continue to function only as by-products of necessary economic waste. From the point of view of its productive efficiency not even the most brazen apologists of capitalists can say a word for it.

It is not only from the standpoint of the industrial engineer that capitalism appears to be wasteful and destructive; its waste of human
resources—which is a necessary consequence of its economic policies—
is just as irresponsible and even more criminal. Hand in hand with its
tendency toward industrial consolidation and capital concentration, it
slowly but surely destroys the lives of the great producing masses. And
this even without recourse to the "extraordinary" processes of war. Progressive unemployment on the one side and progressive speed-up for the
employed on the other, together with the demoralizing effect of insecurity on the mind, character, and life of almost the entire nation, produce
a mass of misery not less terrible for being long drawn out or expressed
in the monotonous rhythms of stupefaction, anxiety, and despair.

So much all socialists and communists must—and do—grant. Why,
then, labor the point, especially since the other contributors to the symposium admit it and have written with great eloquence about the manifold evils of capitalism? Because in evaluating the communist position, it
is precisely these factors which they have omitted from consideration.
The risks of revolutionary action are regarded without weighing the price
of the alternative paths of action, whether these be the passive
endurance of existing evils or the methods of evolutionary or parliamentary socialism. *It is the absence of a realistic alternative program and
path of action which makes the criticism of the communist position—*
justified as it may appear to be from an abstract ideal position—*irrelevant to the pressing tasks of combating capitalism, fascism, and war.*

## 2. The Argument from Democracy

Whatever may be the claims of capitalism to democratic forms of political
representation, there can be no denying the fact that the existence of economic class divisions in society makes genuine democracy impossible.
The power which the control of the means of production gives the ruling
class aver those who must live by their use extends to every phase of
social and personal life. Communism, despite the false emphasis of some
of its adherents, is not the negation of democracy but its fulfillment. The
right to determine our own social destiny—to go to heaven or to hell in
our own way—is an intrinsic good. It may be that in industrial society
most administrative tasks demand specialized knowledge and selection
on the basis of merit rather than election by popular favor. But in any
society there can be, from the communist point of view, no specialist in

social policy. Those who wear the shoe know best where it pinches. Unless provision is made at some point for the democratic control and check of social policy, mankind may be well-fed, it cannot be free.

The way to get genuine democracy—social democracy—is to take power and overthrow the economic system which makes the ruling class within it, together with its representatives, dictators of the national economy. When communists speak of taking power, they do not mean that a minority of the population is to seize control and hold it against the desire of the majority of the population. The theory of dictatorship of the proletariat, in its classic not degenerate form, presupposes that a majority of the population supports the working class and its political allies. The opposite of the dictatorship of the proletariat is not democracy but the dictatorship of the bourgeoisie. A good English synonym for the dictatorship of the proletariat is a workers' democracy.

The real question is, then, how a workers' democracy is to be achieved. All of the three distinguished contributors to this symposium believe that the policy of class collaboration will enable the masses to acquire social security, democracy, and peace. But this flies in the face of the actual historic experience of the last fifty years. It presupposes that under the existing economic setup it is possible both to increase the standard of living of the masses and to sustain the rate of profit and interest. It overlooks the thousandfold objective antagonisms which exist between the capitalists of the entire world and the international working class. It shuts its eyes to the fact that every concession which has been won from those in power has been forced by mass struggles and the threat of further struggles. It refuses to reflect upon the history, activity, and fate of the Social-Democratic Party in Germany and the Labor Party in England—parties which became the instrumentalities by which the dictatorship of finance capital lowered the standards of living, strengthened the national defense, continued the old shell game of diplomacy in foreign affairs and restricted, in the interests of national unity, militant working-class agitation.

To profess a love for democracy in the abstract and not to be willing to fight to give it concrete content, to take the rules of political democracy in a profit society—rules which are so flexible that they enable a Mussolini and a Hitler to come to power—as the *fixed* limits within which to struggle for a truly human society, is to give a lease in perpetuity to the capitalist dictatorship upon the lives of the people. According to the communist theory, political democratic forms are to be used for agitational purposes to the uttermost. But when the time comes when the capitalist dictatorship has plunged the country into chaos, when production has been disorganized, when hunger and despair eat out men's bodies and souls, when the great masses of people led by those who have social vision are already in action to protect themselves and to secure the future of their descendants, it is nothing short of calamitous to make a fetish of legality. The rising bourgeoisie never hesitated to set up its own revolutionary legality against the legal anathemas of an earlier dying social order. How much more justification has the working class, together with its allies—the farmers, the technicians, the professional groups—to do so. For it does not take power to visit vengeance upon anyone or to exploit another class but to abolish all economic classes. It cannot be too strongly emphasized that communists do not believe in a minority revolution. Nor do they believe in a revolution at any time or under any circumstances. Nor would they dream of urging the masses to make an open bid for power unless the general discontent with capitalist rule had penetrated every important group in the country including the armed forces which now stand ready to be hurled against them whenever their agitation threatens to be effective. *It is the consequences of the existing capitalist dictatorship which makes people revolutionary: the task of the communists is to educate them to proper class consciousness and to lead them.*

I stress these things because the other contributors to this discussion have misinterpreted the communist theory. They do not distinguish between a *putsch* or *coup d'état* and a social revolution. They attribute to communists the absurd belief that the working class by its own unaided power can achieve victory. They impute to communists the fantastic notion that every measure of social amelioration from the abolition of child labor to an unemployment insurance bill must be won by social revolution. Whatever occasion members of the official communist party may have given them to believe this, there is nothing in the theory of communism to justify it. When communists ask: "When has any ruling class voluntarily surrendered its power?" Professor Cohen offers to tell them. But his illustrations show that he is unaware that the question refers to periods in which the important issue concerned the overt change in property relationships and not measures of reform. The bourgeois revolution took place in England in the Cromwellian wars and not in the period from 1832 to 1884. The bourgeois revolution took place in France in 1789–1793 and not with the fall of the Third Empire. Even the

English reform bills were yielded by the Tories only because of their fear of a revolution induced by the semi-insurrectionary demonstrations of the English working class. The strength of the revolutionary movement was indicated not only by the flaming portents of burning hayricks, clashes with the constabulary, and seditious slogans but by the frightened alacrity with which the English middle classes deserted their working-class allies. The liberation of the serfs by Alexander II was a move to consolidate his own rule which had been undermined by the reverses in the Crimean War and subsequent revolutionary ferment. The terms of the liberation were such that the power of the Russian landlords was not diminished nor the lot of the serf improved; only the development of capitalism was made easier. The real bourgeois revolution in Russia took place in February 1917. It would be no exaggeration to say that most of the significant reforms granted by ruling classes in history have either been measures taken to strengthen themselves against eventual attack or have been forced from them by the fear of having to surrender more to revolutionary forces.

Those who have power are not afraid of the liberals but of the actual or potential revolutionary forces behind them. Liberalism becomes a political power only when it can point to the danger of something "still worse" in the offing.

Let us admit, however, for the sake of the argument, that some ruling classes in the past have peacefully abdicated their power. And certainly both Marx (in 1872) and Engels (in 1886) believed that a peaceful revolution was possible in England and America. Does that mean that the working class must cultivate the faith that when a revolutionary situation arises the state will act any differently than it now does in strikes, evictions, and mass protests? Consider what is at stake. Socialization of the means of production does not mean the substitution of one class for another in the ownership of private property; it means the abolition of all private property of a social nature. In past revolutions it was possible for members of one class to save their property by shifting their class allegiance. And by the time the bourgeois revolution broke out the interests of the entrepreneurs, the landlords, and the monarchy interlocked at many points. Yet how bitterly the feudal classes fought against the rising bourgeoisie who were often more than ready to compromise. Is it romanticism or merely sober wisdom to expect that the ruling classes today will fight even more fiercely against any proposal which makes forever impossible the arbitrary exercise of power over human beings through the possession of private property? Is it far-fetched to imagine that once a workers' democracy were set up, even peacefully and legally, that almost overnight a counterrevolutionary Defense Guard would spring into existence to defend "home, country, and honor"? The Finnish Socialists who had a majority in the parliament of 1918 were swept out of power by a bloody counterrevolution. Communists demand—I had almost written common sense demands—that the working class be ready to defend itself when a revolutionary situation arises. And an effective defense cannot be conducted—as the Austrian Social-Democracy learned—by waiting until the enemy has made its position impregnable by disarming and surrounding the workers. At certain times successful defense is only possible by strategic offense. Communists do not create civil war: they merely fight to a finish the civil war which in one form of the class struggle or another is always going on.

The argument may be summarized as follows: Objections against the use of force as always intrinsically wrong cannot be consistently made except by those who make a fetish or religion of nonresistance. But whoever supports any state and pays the taxes which subsidize the military and police arm of the state, is barred from using the plea of nonresistance. If the use of force is justified only when it has the sanction of legality—which seems to be the position which the other contributors take—then it can be pointed out that those who have the legal power can always change the forms and meaning of "legality." The consequence would be a necessary acceptance of any régime so long as it abided by its own shifting forms of legality. When it is realized that the social revolution is not a minority revolution, the use of force does not constitute a special moral problem but a problem in effective and intelligent application. Renan was undoubtedly justified in saying: *"Happy are those who inherit a revolution: woe to those who make it."* A Marxist might reply that a social revolution is one way of repaying the debt we owe for reaping the advantages of past revolutions. But his real answer would be to show (see point 5 below) that under capitalism it is even truer to say: *And greater woe to those who do not make it.*

## 3. *The Argument from Morality*

It is commonly assumed by a great many exponents as well as critics of Marxism that there is no place in Marx's critique of bourgeois civilization for a moral evaluation of the social order. This is an error. Marx denied the relevance of any abstract morality which merely juggles with formal concepts, to the conflict of class interests at the basis of social life. But each class interest generates its own morality. To deny this is to deny that history is made by men. In almost every one of his works Marx scathingly criticizes the dominant morality of society and indicates the general character of the morality which should replace it. In the *Communist Manifesto* he points out how almost every value of life—love, marriage, art, science, and vocational activity—has been clouded over and degraded by the "morality of cash-payment." Against the ideals of a social order in which the possession of property gives power over others and hampers their free development, he counterposes the ideal of a society "in which the free development of each individual is the condition for the free development of all."

Marx was impatient with the easy equalitarianism which sought to minimize individual differences and reduce personalities to a symmetric democracy of ciphers. Certain human differences in capacity, vision, and creation may be irresolvable: but Marx held that these differences cannot be exploited, by those upon whom nature has lavished them, to the cost of the rest of the community, which supplies the opportunity for their expression. Human talents which draw their nutriment from social life must be put to the service of the whole. But the only social condition under which this is possible, under which the possessive and exclusive tendencies of men can be channeled into creative and shared activities, is a classless society. Do we hold "intelligence and free experimental inquiry" in all fields to be genuine goods? Then the existing social order which makes it impossible to apply intelligence to human problems, which calls for a moratorium on technical ingenuity, which employs myth, magic, chicanery, and force to mediate human conflicts, must first be fundamentally transformed. Substitute for "intelligence" any other value in the previous question and it will be seen that its concrete realization presupposes an anterior change in the material institutions of social life.

Professor Cohen declares the communist criticism of liberalism to be altogether baseless and worthless. But he defines the essence of liberalism to be freedom of thought and inquiry, freedom of discussion and criticism. Now communism, as I understand it, would not dream of denying the value of liberalism in this sense. It points out, however, that in a profit society inequality of economic status makes it impossible for all classes to enjoy this freedom, that just as soon as the freedom of discussion and criticism begins to bear fruit disapproved by those who have a monopoly of political power, it is abridged and finally revoked. Genuine liberalism in the sense in which Professor Cohen defines it, is possible in *all fields* only when vested interests have been abolished. Some restraints may always be necessary but they should flow not from extrinsic considerations, such as those derived from economics and politics, but from the necessities of fair and free discussion itself. As a matter of fact, however, by "liberalism" communism understands something quite different from what Professor Cohen intends. Liberalism is the social philosophy of *laissez-faire*. The only connection between liberalism, as the theory and practice of bourgeois society, and liberalism, as free inquiry, is that the first, in the interests of the needs of its own expanding economy, made possible the wider extension of free inquiry than any previous social system. But as fascism shows, in the period of the decline of capitalism when the falling profit rate and interest rate compel rationalization and coordination not only in industry but in politics as well, free inquiry is scrapped together with all other obsolescent economic and governmental machinery. It is legitimate, however, to challenge Professor Cohen's right to define liberalism in the way he has. It is just as if someone, after having described Professor Cohen's opposition to radicalism, were to go on to define radicalism as "an attitude which went to the root of problems." Communism is no more opposed to liberalism in Professor Cohen's sense than he is opposed to radicalism in this last sense.

But how reconcile this belief with the well-known position of the communists that a transitional period must intervene between the capitalist dictatorship and the classless society in which illiberal methods must be used against those who obstruct the processes of building the conditions under which liberalism (in Professor Cohen's sense) is possible, in which force must be used against those who will not keep the peace? Is there not a contradiction here? Not if we first ask ourselves how else peace and the widest degree of free inquiry can be achieved. The notion that all matters can be settled by free discussion today presupposes that it is possible for both sides to engage in it, that they are willing to do so, that they are pledged to abide by the consequences of the discussion, and that the fundamental class conflicts over the distribution of the social product and social power can be affected by such discussion. The lessons of Italy and Germany must still be learned by the spokesmen of liberalism. During the transitional period the denial of liberties is directed, in theory at any rate, only against those whose activities are such as would restore the old order and therewith destroy the new freedom and liberties which the social revolution has won. The restrictions last so long as the class enemy exists, and only against the enemy on relevant political matters. But, objects Professor Cohen, this is just what the militarists say; for them, too, the suppression of civil liberties is temporary. Certainly they say it. But the real question is whether the militaristic wars aim to remove the sources and causes of future wars and, therefore, the evils which flow from war including the denial of civil liberty. If they did, I, for one, would not be opposed to them. But no militarist or imperialist war can do this or even aim to do this. That is why we do not put any stock in what the militarists of the world *say*. However, that there are greater difficulties and dangers involved in the conception of a transitional period than most communists realize, I shall point out below in my discussion of the "dogmas" of orthodox communism (Section II, Part 3).

In this connection it cannot be too strongly emphasized that communism does not believe that the end justifies the use of *any* means. If some communists talk that way, they are simply mad and belong in the fascist camp. For it is precisely in their refusal to employ *any* means to win a victory that the political strategy of communism distinguishes itself, among other things, from the tactics of fascism. Communists would not martyrize an entire people as the fascists have done, they would not countenance wholesale massacres of innocent victims, they would not pound and torture women and children in order to achieve power. The use of means to attain an end, which have as their consequences the violation of still more important ends, is forbidden not only by elementary decency but by considerations of expediency. To win the confidence of the working class and its potential allies, communists must be the living exemplifications in both person and practice of the highest ideals—the most important of which are courage, intelligence, and honesty. The fact that the official communist parties in the Western world despite their desperate heroism have fallen far short of the ideals of communist behavior is only a measure of the extent to which they have abandoned the true communist position in this as in other matters of principle. It is not an argument against communism. I admit with shame that I have no answer to Professor Dewey's charges against the official communist party practice of deceit, misrepresentation, disruptive hooliganism, character assassination, and downright lying about those who have honest differences with them. This is especially true of their attitudes to those other communist groups which do not believe that a political party is a church and that its leadership is infallible. I know from personal experience the infinite capacity of the official communist press to invent, distort, and slander—in short, to drag the name of communism down to the level of the bourgeois gutter press. But this is no part of the philosophy of communism, no communist party ever came to power by such practices, and the emergence of a mass revolutionary movement will sweep into the discard all who engage in such practices.

## 4. *The Argument from Art*

No matter how bad a social system is, it can never completely choke the creative impulses of man. But by providing a hostile or indifferent milieu, or by establishing social mechanisms which select both the artists and the type of art to be encouraged, a social system exercises enormous influence upon the character of existing art, the extent to which, and the classes among which it flourishes, and the functional role it plays in the processes of daily life. Under capitalism the professional artist without means can survive only by producing for a market or by receiving a subsidy from a patron. Where he produces for a market, his work is likely to reflect the cheap commercial values of a profit economy. When he produces for the select market of museums and private collectors, the shrinkage in the returns on capital investment, the vicissitudes of the business cycle, and the radical retrenchment on "cultural luxuries" which marks the decline of capitalism, progressively narrows his opportunities to dispose of his products. At the present time, except for a very few, most of them dead, this market has dried up. Dependence upon the capricious generosity of patrons, who in the best of times are hard to find, strikes at the very heart of a free creative art, and, what is more important, at the self-respect of the artist as a human being.

In a communist society, social control of the processes of production will enable us to break down the false separation between aesthetic significance and utility, between artificial museum art and the natural life of the people. When production is planned for beauty as well as for use, artists can be drawn into the productive processes in a way which is impossible in a profit society. This does not mean that all art will necessarily have a utilitarian or functional aspect any more than all science will. But in art as in other fields, communism will provide greater opportunities for all those who are especially endowed with creative talent than any other social system of the past. That there will be abuses, goes without saying. It is not undue optimism, however, once the social instrumentalities for planned production and democratic mass education are at hand, to expect that the aesthetic blasphemies and the waste of human talent, as we know them today, will be eliminated.

## 5. *The Argument from Necessity*

At no time in recent history has there been such alarming unanimity that the world is drifting toward war and fascism. And fascism, it must be remembered, is not a new social system but capitalism, *gleichgeschaltet* and armed to the teeth, compelled by the logic of a super-rationalized profit system and a frenzied religion of nationalism, to prepare for bigger and better wars. Russell, Dewey, and Cohen admit this as well as the fact that social revolution is a possible alternative. They deny, however, that social revolution is a desirable alternative and that fascism and communism exhaust all of the possible alternatives. *They do not indicate, however, what the third alternative can be;* nor can I infer from their words what differentiating social character they conceive this alternative to have, nor, further, what the methods of achieving it will be. I wish to argue, however, that no matter what alternative is imagined, the existing situation in the world today, which must always be the point of departure for realistic analysis, narrows "the vital option" mankind can exercise, to a choice between war and social revolution.

Before this can be done it is necessary to meet an important objection which Professor Dewey has raised. As a sincere opponent of fascism, he holds that he must oppose any revolutionary radical movement because the growth of such a movement will almost certainly unleash the forces of fascist reaction and counterrevolution. There is a semblance of plausibility about this argument, for it cannot be denied that the growth of revolutionary sentiment will accelerate the rate with which forces will be rallied to the defense of the existing order. Offhand one might respond that this danger makes it imperative to prepare even more widely and intensively. Certainly I know that this would be Professor Dewey's answer if one were to tell him that agitation against lynching was adding fuel to the fire of southern Negro prejudice. But there is a more fundamental assumption behind Professor Dewey's question which must be challenged, viz., that fascism is a superficial political form imposed upon the social processes of existing production and not a natural outgrowth of the latent tendencies of imperialist, finance capital. Psychologically, fascism is a reaction against the consequences of capitalist production; objectively and practically, it consolidates capitalist rule and dictatorship. Where there are strong labor organizations fascism must of course destroy them. But the social necessity of fascism is not explained merely by the *existence* of labor organizations but by the needs of capitalist economy which calls for the transformation of the "rationalized" state into a direct arm of the "rationalized" national plant. Even if all the opponents of fascism were to become followers of Gandhi overnight and forswear all active resistance, this would not check the fascization of the capitalist state, the germs of which are already in the NRA. I do not mean to imply, as some official communists do, that the existing state under Roosevelt is in essentials fascist, a view which follows *a fortiori* from the still wilder notion that, in the words of Stalin, "social-democracy and Hitler are twins"(!). What I am asserting is that fascism will have to be fought or have to be accepted. And if it is to be fought, what other way is more effective than the development of a mass revolutionary movement under intelligent and militant leadership? Would Professor Dewey suggest the way of German Social-Democracy which went down without even a struggle, or the way of Austrian Social-Democracy which waited until it was too late, and whose leaders argued from the same premises which he accepts? If so, historical events have spoken and the premises should be judged by their consequences.

In the modern world the ideals of national economic self-sufficiency or autarchy are unworkable. Few nations possess all the raw materials necessary for developed culture, and even if they did the fact that the gap between mass production and mass consumption cannot be dosed in a profit system compels them to seek foreign outlets, spheres of influence, and methods of breaking down their neighbors' economic isolation. Under these circumstances war is the only "economic" way out for the ruling classes since it destroys surplus stocks of goods and men and carries with it the promise of the reestablishment of the domestic and foreign market. Despite the pious sentiments of peace professed on all sides, the world today, both physically and psychically, has a higher potential capacity for war than at any other time in history. *When war comes—!* Everyone knows the answer. There is no longer any difference between the front and the rear, between combatants and noncombatants. I could quote eloquent passages from the writings of Russell and Dewey to prove that the next world war spells the end of civilization. The real question is what is to be done to prevent it, and how is it to be stopped once it begins. Whatever the costs of a social revolution may be, they will be far less than the costs of the major war into which the world is drifting. And whatever the chances of its success, it at least holds forth the promise of a new order in which war and the other barbarities of capitalism will be unthinkable.

With all respect to the arguments of Messrs. Russell,[1] Dewey, and Cohen, it seems to me that they have not established a case against the communist philosophy but against the official Communist Party. But even here the only valid criticism of the Communist Party is that it is not communist enough, so that the moral would be that the time has come to build a new organization which will represent in philosophy and action the genuine ideals of communism.[2]

# II

In this section I wish to address myself to those who either accept or are sympathetic to the ideals of communism and to raise certain fundamental questions concerning what passes for communism in many quarters. To such people, the contributions of Russell, Dewey, and Cohen constitute a unique challenge for several reasons. First, not only are these men among the leading intellectual figures of their time—so that on purely theoretical grounds they would have to be answered—but they are in the front ranks of that movement of social liberalism which affirms its agreement with the ultimate ideals of a communist society and from which recruits to the cause of communism may be drawn. Second, they represent the attitude of thousands of intellectuals and professionals—no matter what their social origins—who not so eloquently and not so cogently, but just as insistently have been saying the things which these men have expressed in such precise form.[3] And it goes without saying how valuable the accession of this group would be to the communist cause. Third, the force of the argument is sufficiently impressive to justify asking, what elements in the position of official representatives of communism lay their doctrines open to these attacks, whether the doctrines attacked are really valid and can be successfully defended, and finally, if these doctrines are false, whether they are essential components of the social and political philosophy of communism or foreign ideological excrescences engrafted upon it.

My own position is briefly that the fundamental doctrine of communism is sound but it has been so wrapped up in certain dogmas that its logic and force has been obscured. What I desire to do is to enumerate some of the more important dogmas of official communism, show that they are false, trace their baleful influence upon the existing theory and practice of communists, and point to the necessity of reformulating the communist position in such a way that, without surrendering in the slightest its revolutionary character, its appeal can be made both more widespread and efective than it has yet been in America.

1. The first dogma I wish to discuss is the view that communism is inevitable. Although in some of the practical analyses which communists make of daily affairs, the plain implication of their statements is that communism is not inevitable, yet the canonic doctrine of official communism, as well as of old line orthodox socialism, leaves little doubt that this view is not merely an expression of an emotional faith or a devout hope, but a fixed article of belief.[4] It requires very little analysis to show that no proof can be offered of the inevitability of the victory of a proletarian revolution; and indeed all that Marx established was that the functioning of an economic order which fulfilled certain ideal conditions would in the course of time (1) lead to a progressive inability to dispose of commodities produced, to provide employment, and to make a profitable return upon invested capital, and (2) result, in virtue of the processes of concentration and centralization, in the generation of the objective conditions for a new social order. Where he speaks of the expropriation of the expropriators in the "future present" tense, it is either dramatic, revolutionary prophecy or a prediction on the basis of certain psychological assumptions whose truth and invariance are by no means self-evident. The spatial metaphor of the collapse and breakdown of capitalism has been taken too literally. Capitalism may break down in the sense that the mechanisms of production, circulation, and credit no longer function in a way to keep the majority of the population adequately fed or housed. But the social order which is ultimately based on human activities never breaks down. Human beings never cease their functioning; they go on from one act to another—either to a defense of what has broken down, in the sense considered before, or to attack.

To deny that communism is inevitable is not to deny the existence of social determinism any more than the scientist's denial of inevitability in nature implies the denial of causality. No. What is denied is that the conjunction of all the different factors (objective and subjective) which are necessary for social revolution can be deduced from an analysis of any unique set of economic data. Stated concretely, a Marxist examining the structure of the NRA can predict that in all likelihood the NRA will fail to accomplish its purposes. He cannot say on the basis of the economic analysis alone whether this failure of the NRA will produce a psychological reaction toward fascism or communism. *That, in part, depends upon his own activities.* Nor can he say whether, if the class-conscious masses do rise up to seize power, they will win the victory. *That, in part, depends upon the intelligence and courage of those who lead them.* All the factors are determined, but there is no one independent variable of which all the others are necessary functions. And one of the factors which determines or fails to determine the conjunction of all the necessary conditions into one complex sufficient condition is the activity which we undertake *now* after reflection.

The theoretical and practical consequences of this false theory of inevitability are more momentous than the question of its intrinsic validity. The first of them is that it makes unintelligible any activity in behalf of communism. I am not saying that belief in inevitability paralyzes activity in behalf of communism. On the contrary. It has often been pointed out that men are more ready to fight, and will fight more vigorously, in a battle in which they are sure they will win. What I am saying is that the belief in inevitability makes that activity unintelligible and unintelligent. In assuming that the consequences of one action or another are the same so far as the coming of communism is concerned, it denies that there are *genuine* alternatives of action—something which its propaganda assumes. It denies that moral judgments and evaluations of social activity are meaningful—something without which its agitation could not be successful. It denies that thinking makes any difference to the ultimate outcome, yet it propagates a theory according to which theory and practice go hand in hand. It denies that mistakes are possible, or if possible that they are important, or if important that they could have been avoided. If the Panglosses believe (after Bradley) that "the world is the best of all possible worlds and everything in it is a necessary evil"; orthodox communists believe that communism is the only form of society possible after capitalism, and every mistake they make is a necessary means of achieving it.

The second consequence of the dogma of inevitability is that it strengthens the belief in the doctrine of "spontaneity," which teaches that the daily experiences of the working class spontaneously generates political class consciousness. If the economic consequences of capitalism

lead inevitably to communism, then, since it is admitted that the revolution—like all history—is made by men, it must be held that the economic consequences of capitalism inevitably give rise to revolutionary
class consciousness. In fact, this is the belief both of orthodox social-
democracy and present-day official communism, Lenin's *What's to Be
Done?* to the contrary notwithstanding. When it is believed that revolutionary consciousness develops spontaneously in the masses, there takes
place a systematic and wholesale overestimation of the readiness for revolutionary activity upon the part of trade unions, unemployed organizations, cooperatives, etc., a mistaking of restiveness for radicalism, a tendency to read into the masses the perfervid psychological intensity of an
isolated, political group which thinks that because it *calls* itself a vanguard it has thereby created a mass army behind it. Worst of all the doctrine of spontaneity is used as a justification for the policy of split and
schismatic fission. What difference does it make that the ranks are
thinned or if doctrinal content is watered down, when there is an unlimited reservoir of revolutionary energy which is sure to boil over as the
heat of the class struggle increases? The doctrine of spontaneity makes
it easy to mistake the wish for the deed, to rely upon the magic incanta-
tion of slogan and resolutions, and to take comfort in the "voice," the
"logic," the "dictates" of historic destiny or whatever other pious formula
may be found. These tend to become substitutes for the patient accumulation of organizational power, and for the development of realistic techniques of actually reaching the working masses, winning those who are
reached and holding those who are won.

A further consequence of the dogma of inevitability is that it makes
for an uncritical acceptance and imitation of the strategy and tactics
employed by the first working-class group which comes to power. If communism is inevitable, then everything leading up to it is regarded as
inevitable. Precedents of tactics which originally flowed from a special
historical situation are converted into precedents of principle. The Rus-
sification of the strategy, tactics, and very terminology of communist
parties of the world is a case in point. A theory which is avowedly scientific must approach the problem of the conquest of power with the same
care and regard for the national economic, cultural, and psychological
terrain as an army campaigning against another must consider the physical terrain. To be sure, if principles are lost, everything is lost,—but if
principles constitute our only knowledge in hand, nothing can be gained.
One could cite chapter and verse to show that these methodological

commonplaces are recognized on *paper* by orthodox spokesmen of communism. But what I am trying to call attention to is the fact that the theory remains a pious resolution—mocked at in practice—and to indicate one of the *contributory* causes therefor. The basic reasons for the spread of these dogmas in communist ranks are political. But this is another story.

The most fateful and pressing of all the immediate consequences of the dogma of inevitability is that there is observable on the part of communists throughout the world a tendency sometimes to speak, and more often to act (Germany, 1931–1933) as if fascism were inevitable, and to regard fascism as one more step, this time the last, toward communism, presumably because fascism succeeds in doing what the communists failed to do, viz., to wipe out social-democracy. The wildest confusion prevails in communist quarters on this subject, with unanimity on only two points: that the coming of fascism represents the realization of "one of the basic preconditions of the revolutionary crisis" (!); and that "the struggle against fascism is in the first place the struggle to defeat the social democracy," for which purpose a "united front" against fascism is offered to the social-democracy—with what sincerity can be imagined. But what the policy of the Third International is on the whole matter is clearly indicated by Mr. Walter Duranty, about whose reliability as a reporter on most matters official communists themselves harbor no doubts. In his dispatch on the last congress of the Russian Communist Party, Mr. Duranty wrote:

> It is noteworthy also that M. Molotoff spoke of the increasing strength of the Russian Bolshevist party as the "vanguard of the Communist International" and declared that the working masses and oppressed colonial peoples throughout the world were concerned in and encouraged by Soviet progress.
>
> This sounds strange in a period when fascism rather than communism appears to be the world answer to social crises, but it is explained by the fact that the Bolsheviki have succeeded in persuading themselves that fascism is not an obstacle but an inevitable step on the road to world revolution. Right or wrong, it is a comforting thought for the Bolsheviki at the present juncture and, anyway, it enables their congress to enjoy the full flavor of the undoubted successes in the building of socialism in the Soviet Union.[5]

Mr. Duranty, whom no one will accuse of being a "counterrevolutionary Trotskyite," has here put his finger on the chief political factor which accounts for the intensity with which these and other dogmas are held. If all energies are to be devoted to "building socialism in one country" and the function of other Communist Parties is primarily to serve as "frontier guards" of the USSR, so that Russia's successes may inspire other countries to believe in communism and follow its example (an amazing idealistic view of social causation)—what other dogmas can be so effective in enabling official communists, in Mr. Duranty's words, "to enjoy the full flavor" of the Russian successes and to dismiss as mere incidents the calamities in Germany, Italy, and Austria, and the diminishing influence of Communist Parties—and therefore even their effectiveness as "frontier guards"—throughout the world? And as if to elucidate the point, Mr. Duranty adds in a subsequent dispatch on Russia's surprise and confusion over the Austrian events:

> The only Communist party congress held in three and a half years has devoted itself to two questions which in a sense are one—the second Five-Year Plan and the organization of the party and governmental system to handle the same most efficiently. Foreign problems have been considered primarily in the light of the plan—that is, their possible effect upon it. It is true that the speakers, from M. Stalin down, have talked of world revolution and have even given the Communist International an occasional pat on the head. But that has been only a side issue.
>
> It was clear throughout to any impartial observer that 70 percent of Soviet interest was concentrated on the Five-Year Plan and its organization, 29 percent on foreign affairs in so far as they might hinder or help the plan, and maybe[!] 1 percent on foreign affairs in regard to world revolution.[6]

Mr. Duranty's "maybe" suggests that he does not know how to handle fractions. However, these important political problems cannot be further discussed here.

2. The second dogma which I wish to question is the view that all communists *must be* dialectical materialists and that all dialectical materialists *must be* communists. It is this proposition which is the source of that peculiar hodgepodge of politics, antiquated science, proletarian culture, idealistic philosophy, and mystical nonsense which goes by the name of the present-day party-attitude-in-philosophy. That it is not Marxian does not have to be argued, except against those who assume that Marx developed a philosophical attitude in violation of common sense, the laws of logic, elementary notions of scientific method, and the proposition that twice two is four. I believe it is possible to present

dialectical materialism as a plausible scientific philosophy which might be described in the technical idiom of contemporary Anglo-American philosophy as experimental, evolutionary naturalism; but here I merely wish to discuss that species of dialectical materialism which is regarded as the official communist brand today. The most authoritative spokesman for this species of dialectical materialism is L. Rudas of the Marx-Engels-Lenin Institute, Moscow. I quote some sentences from an exposition written especially for English readers:[7]

1. Dialectical materialism is cast from one mold, it is a strictly monistic theory.

2. Without dialectics there can be no scientific picture of the world, without dialectics the separate sciences are condemned to groping in the dark, without dialectics there is no correct method for investigation—of an individual or single region. Still less is it possible for the revolutionary struggle of the proletariat to exist without materialist dialectics.

3. *Without a recognition of the dialectical synthesis of the formation of new and higher unities in nature and society not a single step can be taken in science.*

4. And how could a non-Communist be a dialectical materialist. For dialectical materialism means recognition of the social revolution, of the dictatorship of the proletariat, as the concrete solution of the social contradictions.

5. In our epoch what Marx predicted by the aid of the dialectical method has been verified almost word for word; . . . the Communist Party is the only party which can truly forecast the course of events in capitalist society and which predicts and also realizes the inevitable social revolution.

6. It may be objected here that, granted that the recognition of the dialectics of society is inseparable from Communism, yet dialectical materialism is more than this, it is a philosophy which one can reject or partially accept without ceasing to be a Communist. It is easy to see that this objection does not hold water. The dialectics of society is only a special case of the *general dialectics* of the world, since society, in the last resort, is also part of nature, and has developed from nature. Whoever does not recognize the dialectics of nature, cannot recognize, without illogicality, the dialectics of society either.

7. The prerequisite for understanding dialectical materialism is a decisive break with the traditional mode of thought, *the revolutionizing of thinking*, and also sooner or later enrollment in the ranks of the revolutionary party.
8. Plekhanov and even Bukharin were not in a position to give an unexceptionable exposition of dialectical materialism, in the last resort also because they did not have an unexceptional line in politics.
9. Dialectics not only points out to the proletariat its historical task, but it gives the proletariat the certainty of victory, it is to a certain extent the *guarantee of this victory*.

It is hard to believe that Mr. Rudas and other orthodox dialectical materialists really subscribe to this philosophy, for some of the plain implications of the above statements are so astonishing that they may be said to constitute a *reductio ad absurdum* of the position. Look at statements 2, 3, 4, and 7. They furnish the major and minor premises of a neat little syllogism:

> None but those who have an adequate grasp of dialectics and dialectical materialism can have a correct understanding of the methods, the truths and achievements of science in nature or society;
>
> None but those who are sooner or later enrolled in the ranks of the Communist Party can have an adequate grasp of dialectics and dialectical materialism;
>
> Ergo, none but members of the Communist Party can have a correct understanding of natural or social science.

This surpasses anything that the Catholic Church at the heyday of its temporal power ever proclaimed. To hold seriously that a correct understanding of nature and society is possible only to members of the Communist Party is to say that only members of the Communist Party *can know the truth about anything*—whether it concern problems of mathematics, physics, psychology, art, or politics. To say this is to furnish the emotional premise for a ruthless policy of suppression and censorship in every domain of knowledge, since if we are convinced that we have the truth while others who are not members of the Communist Party *must* be in error, we are justified in protecting society by liquidating the sources of illusion, error, and deceit. And this is offered in the name of a "scientific" philosophy, a "critical" party which strives to preserve the best in human culture, and—of Marxism!

Now look at statement 8! The insane logic goes even further and revenges itself upon those who are victimized by it. It is not enough to be a member of the Communist Party—this is only a necessary condition— one must have an "unexceptionable line in politics" correctly to understand dialectical materialism. What does it mean not to have an "unexceptionable line in politics"? It means to be in disagreement with the views of the leader or leading group of the party. If one agrees with Bukharin about the rate of agrarian collectivization and not with Stalin, or with Trotsky's theory of permanent revolution and not with Stalin's theory of socialism in one country, one is not in a position to expound or understand properly dialectical materialism. True insight into *anything* is determined by a correct political line and a correct political line is determined by the enlightened leadership. There is only one step from this theory of the divine illumination of the bureaucracy to the theory of the divine right of bureaucracy. And I submit that this is more than a figure of speech, for as I shall show below, "nature" in the orthodox philosophy of dialectical materialism plays the same role as "God."[8]

That these implications will be denied by some members of the Communist Party does not alter the fact that they flow from their premises. On any monistic theory which holds that the universe is organically determined through and through—whether it be the absolute idealism of Hegel or orthodox dialectical materialism—it follows that we cannot know the truth about anything unless we know the truth about everything, that if we are wrong about anything we *must* be wrong about everything, that if any single event had turned out differently, every other event in the history of nature and man would have been different, that genuine possibility and novelty become mysteries whose existence can be admitted only at the cost of glaring contradiction. Fortunately, even those who refuse to learn from experience cannot believe such a philosophy to be true, for its very logic is self-defeating. Since at no time can anyone in his senses maintain that he knows the truth about everything, he must admit in accordance with the premises that the philosophy of organic determinism cannot be true nor, if true, can it be known to be true.

This is not the place to present a proof of the inadequacy of the fundamental propositions of the orthodox variety of dialectical materialism. Suffice it to say that it confuses the most elementary distinctions recognized in logic and scientific method and conceals this from itself by mistaking downright logical contradiction for an illustration of the higher dialectic. I need only point to the view (statement 6) that the dialectics of society is a *special* case of the dialectics of the world of nature on the ground that "in the last resort society is also part of nature." This is not merely completely un-Marxian, it is utterly unintelligible. The categories of history and society are not special cases of the categories of physical and natural science. In science the idea of a "special case" presupposes an identical categorial domain whose general laws, expressed in variables, receive specific application by the substitution of constant values, as when we say that Galileo's laws for falling bodies is a special case of Newton's laws of motion. But the class struggle is not a special case of "the struggle for existence" nor is either one of these, in turn, a special case of the fundamental "laws of motion." Engels may have defined dialectics as the science of the universal laws of motion and evolution in nature, human society, and thought, but he would have ridiculed out of court the notion that the laws of thought or human society are *special cases* of the laws of nature: If that were true we should be able to explain significant aspects of *human* history in terms of the most general field-equations of physics and approach the problems of *conscious* life and *meaningful* expression with the biological categories of stimulus and response. Even Mr. Rudas is compelled to criticize mechanism and behaviorism (with bad arguments, to be sure), but he does so in happy innocence of the fact that his premises logically do not permit him to do so. To speak of the laws of motion of consciousness is like speaking of the virtue of triangles. The shift in meaning from "nature," as that which is distinct from man and history, to "nature" as the inclusive totality of all existence including man and social life confounds the confusion. Characteristic shifts in meaning can be observed in practically all fundamental terms in the vocabulary of dialectical materialists with the result that most of their analyses end in muddles instead of clarification.

The practical consequence of the view that dialectical materialists must be communists, and vice versa, is that it tends to spread the superstition that there is such a thing as a class view or party line in all branches of science and art, and presumably even in logic. Thousands of intelligent people working in these fields who have broken with capitalist ideology are asked to subscribe to the alleged class or party view of their special subject as part of their acceptance of the social ideals of communism. Otherwise they are reproached for being still infected with "rotten liberalism," guilty of right backsildings or left deviations. And so this dogma is used as a club to drive away from the communist position all those who have refused to gouge their eyes and brains out of their heads.

What is the genuine Marxian view of the relation between communism and other fields and branches of science and philosophy? Surely there are some views which are necessarily implied, and others which are denied, by the communist position. What is the method by which this is determined? I wish to sketch briefly what I believe to be the true answer to these questions.

To begin with, we must ask what is the fundamental view which distinguishes Marxism from all species of liberalism and socialism. It is clear that the key proposition of Marxism, insofar as it is a touchstone of differentiation from other social philosophies, is the theory of the state. For from the proposition that the state is the coercive instrument of the ruling class there follow all the other essential propositions which deal with the manner in which it must be overthrown, what must take its place, etc.

But now the Marxian theory of the state presupposes other views. It is not presented as something self-evidently true but as a consequence of the application of the theory of historical materialism to social life. A Marxist, then, must be an historical materialist and cannot consistently adhere to any contrary or contradictory philosophy of history. But historical materialism is the belief that "the mode of production in material life conditions the general character of the social, political, and spiritual processes of life" (Marx). Now the extent to which this conditioning goes on is an empirical matter; different historical materialists have different theories which stress the influence of the mode of economic production in varying ways. Some admit an element of invariance in form in different material cultures; some deny it. Some exempt certain periods of music and fine arts from the scope of explanation; others include them. Some underscore reciprocal influences between different factors; others do not. *But it is interesting to observe that all species of historical materialism, whether it be that of Bukharin or Trotsky, Bogdanov or Gorter, Lukas or Korsch, are compatible with the view that the state is the coercive arm of the ruling class.* Consequently the acceptance of this last proposition does not necessarily imply *any particular one* of the different theories of historical materialism. I am not saying that all of these different theories of historical materialism are true. Only one can be true. But which one is true can be determined only by further historical research and analysis and not by a logical deduction from the Marxian theory of the state.

But now every historical materialist, no matter what his differences

with others of his school, is committed to the propositions which are presupposed by the theory of historical materialism. For example, he must
subscribe to a realistic theory of knowledge, for he holds that the social
relations into which men enter are indispensable to their existence and
independent of their individual wills and consciousness. All subjectivist
epistemologies are therefore ruled out. But there are at least twenty-
seven different realistic epistemologies which acknowledge the objective
existence of the external world and recognize the dependence of consciousness upon the structure of the nervous system. *All of them are
compatible with the theory of historical materialism.* Not all of these
realistic epistemologies can be true. Some realists believe that ideas are
reflex images of things, others that they are signs, still others that they
are outgrowths of things. Only one of these theories can be true. But
which one is true can be determined only by further philosophical and
psychological analysis and not by a logical deduction from the theory of
historical materialism.

A realistic theory of epistemology in the light of the development of
the nervous system presupposes an evolutionary biology. But whether
this evolutionary biology must be of a Lamarckian or Darwinian type it
leaves undetermined, *for both are compatible with it even though only
one can be true.* And the best proof of this that any Marxist can desire is
the fact that Marx sketched his realistic activistic theory of perception
and his theory of historical materialism fully fourteen years before
Darwin published his *Origin of Species.* How then can one claim that all
of these theories logically involve each other? An acceptance of a realistic evolutionary biology in turn presupposes a belief in the existence of
a physical world with a definite structure. But whether the structure of
the world be Newtonian or Einsteinian is irrelevant to biology, for both
are compatible with its findings even if only one can be true. None of
Marx's historical, economic, and political doctrines had anything to do
with the physics of his times.

It should be carefully noted that the combined implications of an
evolutionary biology and psychology with their naturalistic, functional
interpretation of purpose, are incompatible with any religious belief or
any doctrine of cosmic design. A Marxist, then, cannot consistently subscribe to any religion, and the essence of any religion, as creed if not
ritual, is belief in supernatural or cosmic purpose.

In addition to the argument above there is one simple fact which is
fatal to the conception that dialectical materialism is a monistic theory

which synthesizes all available knowledge from physics to the dictatorship of the proletariat into one organic whole. Marx's theories of historical materialism, surplus-value, class struggle, state, and proletarian dictatorship were developed at a time when the physics, chemistry, biology, geology, and anthropology of his day, and in which he naturally believed, had reached a certain stage. How can we hold that the first set of theories are still true today while the second set of beliefs (physics, etc.) are quite definitely false unless we admit that there is no *logical* connection between them? And if we admit this, why cannot a man be a communist who accepts all the distinctive propositions of Marx and yet disregards the pronouncements of the pundits of dialectical materialism on such questions as to whether light travels in waves, particles, or wavicules, or whether the geometry of space is describable in Euclidean, Lobochevskian, or Reimannian terms, or whether electrons take time in jumping from one orbit to another—questions which orthodox dialectical materialists have sought to answer with great courage but little knowledge?

To conclude this phase of the argument, then, a communist *must* be a dialectical materialist only in the sense that he is committed to all the necessary conditions which the affirmation of the communist position implies; but there is no intelligible sense, except by arbitrary definition, in which a dialectical materialist must be a communist.

The full significance of the dogma that dialectical materialism and the social philosophy of communism mutually imply each other can be grasped only when it is taken together with the previous dogma, already discussed, that communism is inevitable. For it now follows that dialectical materialism, as a synthesis of the material and methods of the sciences, necessarily implies the victory of the communist revolution. It not only gathers the relevant material on the basis of which valid social ideals may be formulated; it teaches that in the nature of things these social ideals *must* arise and *must* triumph. "Dialectics," says Rudas (statement 9), "not only points out to the proletariat its historical task, but it gives the proletariat the certainty of victory, it is to a certain extent the *guarantee of this victory.*" Whoever understands the universe properly then, i.e., from the standpoint of dialectical materialism, will see (1) that the world of nature and society could not have been different from what it is and the victory of communism still be possible, and (2) that the structure of the universe is such that that victory is logically already involved in the relationships discovered by dialectics. This is the promise of entire creation. The stars in their courses proclaim it; the ocean floor supports it; and man in his brief career realizes it. Even if life on this planet were destroyed, this philosophy offers the assurance that it would arise somewhere else and begin its pilgrimage to that one far-off event—or succession of events—toward which the cosmos is striving. Communism, it is admitted, will disappear but the same natural processes which insure its disappearance *necessitate* its coming—the Lord be praised!

> *But what passes away at one point of the universe, develops anew at another.* One solar system passes away, new ones develop. Life passes away from the earth, it arises elsewhere anew. *In this sense,* dialectical materialism asserts an eternal development; what exists evolves. It evolves because the dialectical self-movement of every thing which exists is a driving force towards development. *Decay holds in general for special cases, the endlessness of development holds only for the infinite universe sub specie aeternitatis.*[9]

This not only suggests the familiar consolations of religion; it is an outright expression of the theology of absolute idealism with all its attendant logical difficulties. What an ironic illustration of the alleged dialectic law of the transformation of a thesis into its opposite! Marxism, which is militant atheism, presented as sentimental theology! The indignant repudiation of this charge by Rudas and other orthodox dialectical materialists is only a measure of their inconsistency and of their failure to grasp the essence of the religious attitude. Because they eschew the use of the word *God* or *Absolute Spirit* and insist that there is no external source of movement but that every movement is *self-movement*, they feel that they have escaped religion when all they have done is to replace a transcendent theology with an immanent theology. For what is essential to religion is not the use of the term God but the belief that the universe is somehow friendly to man and human purpose, that natural processes are such that they must realize the highest human ideals (e.g., communism, if one believes in it), that these processes cannot be adequately understood without such reference, and that despite momentary defeats and setbacks the victory of the highest human ideals (i.e., the proletarian revolution) is guaranteed by the mechanisms of nature and society. To inspire this belief in the minds and hearts of its adherents is the precise function of the theology of orthodox dialectical materialism. It is as far removed from the philosophy of Marx as the philosophy of Marx is removed from the absolute idealism of Hegel which Marx criticized for its supernaturalism, mysticism, and logical inconsistency. This must be stressed not only against orthodox dialectical materialists but also against critics of Marx, like Max Eastman, who attribute to Marx the silly views of the present-day orthodox brood whom he would have been the first to disown.

3. The third dogma I wish to consider flows out of the confusion among official party communists on the nature of dictatorship and democracy. I have already argued that truly understood communism does not involve the negation of democracy but its fulfillment, and that one of the criteria by which a communist evaluates the culture of a civilization is by the character of its democratic processes and the possibility of their expansion. Such a statement, however, in its abstract form can be easily misunderstood. To noncommunists it will appear as a deliberate evasion of the true communist position; to communists as an inadmissible concession to bourgeois democracy. Lack of space prevents a proper concrete and historical analysis, for the question of what is a democracy cannot be settled by definitions. But I wish to point out that no matter how formal democracy be defined, the material conditions of social inequality make it impossible for political democratic forms to serve as the instrumentalities of a common welfare. Modern political democracy was the historical resultant of many interacting forces of which indisputably the strongest were the changes in the mode of production and the needs which they set up. The polarizing consequence of the further development and expansion of the underlying economy has been to widen the gap between the pretensions of formal democracy to serve all classes in the community and the actual operation of existing democratic forms. The mechanisms of inducing and registering "the consent of the governed" are derived from, and are continuously influenced by, the needs of the class which holds economic power and not vice versa. And when, as in capitalist countries throughout the world, the traditional democratic political forms turn out to be an inadequate brake upon the accumulation of social discontent and a needless expense and time-consuming luxury for the administralion of the economic plant, they are rapidly transformed or discarded. Corresponding to the acuteness of the economic contradictions—and in the absence of an *aktionsfähig* revolutionary movement, we get at one end the "gentle social planning" of MacDonald and Roosevelt and at the other, the fascism of Mussolini and Hitler.

According to communist theory, with the shift in economic power from the bourgeoisie to the proletariat, effected by the revolution, democracy is not destroyed but merely the old democratic forms, which at best served to conceal the brute facts of social inequality and which more often than not were flouted in a thousand different ways by those who gave them lip-allegiance. The new state bases itself upon the productive unit of socialized society and is administered by representatives of the producers organized into workers' councils. All those who are not producers (able but unwilling) are automatically excluded from the automatic processes; where they engage in any overt activity to overthrow the social conditions of the new democracy, they are naturally suppressed. The new state is not a complete democracy because not all elements of the population can be converted overnight into reliable producers. As distinct from all other states it does not conceal its class basis. But the workers' state claims to be more democratic than any other state which has hitherto existed (1) for since the overwhelming mass of the population is made up of producers, they have an opportunity to influence and check the social processes which affect them, and (2) because the workers' state aims at the progressive expansion of its democratic processes by drawing as soon as possible the whole of the population into the ranks of producers. What Engels describes as the "withering away of the state," i.e., the elimination of the suppressive functions of the state (army, prisons, etc.), is only the correlative aspect of the extension of the producers' circle to a point where it includes the entire able-bodied population.

Now the dogma I wish to challenge is that the state will necessarily wither away and that any automatic guarantees can be provided against the abuse of power by those who constitute the leadership of the Communist Party during this transitional period. I am particularly anxious to do this because there are some official communists who think that "the dictatorship of the proletariat" justifies the denial of democratic rights to dissenting proletarian groups which, although they accept the class basis of the state, may differ with certain policies of the Communist Party. Some go even further and justify the ruthless suppression of dissenting factions in the Communist Party and the abrogation of all party democracy except for those who agree with the leadership. In this way the political processes of the workers' state are corrupted and become the means by which a bureaucracy keeps itself in power. The only possible instrumentality by which the "withering away of the state" can be assured is discarded. The result is a degenerate workers' state in which the most important decisions are made by an uncontrollable bureaucracy. In such a state, the workers may be kept well-fed and housed because the social nature of production makes it impossible for the bureaucrats to accumulate capital although they can squander social wealth and human energy by costly mistakes. In such a state, however, the workers can never be free to criticize and control the bureaucracy nor individually free from the bureaucratic terror which can imprison or exile them at will. Let us remember that it was the materialist, Marx, who said that "the proletariat regards its courage, self-confidence, independence, and sense of personal dignity as more necessary than its daily bread."

According to communist theory, the Communist Party is the vanguard of the proletariat not only in the struggle to overthrow capitalism but in the transitional period as well. This means that the function of the Communist Party is not to exercise a dictatorship over the proletariat but to educate the proletariat to a consciousness of its class interest and to lead in the execution of the class will. In the transition period the necessity of preserving the workers' state against counter-revolution is so great that under certain historical circumstances the Communist Party may contest with some justification the right of other working-class parties to exist as political parties. *All the more imperative does it therefore become to permit the workers' councils or soviets, the trade unions, and other working-class associations the fullest freedom of discussion and criticism* so that the policies of the Communist Party may be checked by the experience of the class whose vanguard it proclaims itself to be. The Communist Party itself must be subject to some system of democratic controls, otherwise with what authority, aside from force, can it promulgate its own laws as the laws of the workers' state? Where the vital life of the workers' councils is throttled by the imposition of controls from the Communist Party, where the accounting for responsibilities in social production is made to the party and not to the executive organs of the councils themselves, where foreign politics are determined by the party—in short, *where the councils reign but the party rules*—there we may have a workers' state but not a workers' democracy.

Where the Communist Party preempts all the functions of the government, the social problems which arise receive articulate discussion not in the workers' councils but in the party circles. The same logic, however, which removes the power to make the important decisions from the hands of the representatives of the workers' councils, which reveals its distrust of the considered opinions and desires of the rank and file producers, leads to the abrogation of party democracy. Control is from "the leader" down who in the intervals between party congresses can always

insure, by virtue of the bureaucratic administration of the party apparatus and press, a chorus of *Vivas!* sufficient to drown out whatever mut-
tered opposition there is.

From whence, then, the certainty that the state and, therefore, the
political party will "wither away" unless the democratic institutions of the
workers' state are permitted to function and expand? The existence of a
bureaucracy means the existence, to be sure, not of an independent class
but of a social group capable of abusing power. That the possibilities of the
abuse of power in *economic* matters will be limited by the progressive
development of productive forces, which in time will provide material
necessities for all, is beside the point. There are abuses of power other than
economic—abuses to which the increasing complexity of personality in a
socialized society may make men peculiarly sensitive. Theoretically it is
not inconceivable that a bureaucracy may begin to restrict privileges of
higher education to its partisans, to develop a mythology which tends to
perpetuate its own rule, and to attempt to initiate government by experts.
There are no guaranteed safeguards against this eventuality except
untiring activity to make the proletarian dictatorship, not only in its *property form* but in its *political functioning*, a proletarian democracy.

It is for this reason that it seems to me desirable to counterpose "a
workers' democracy" to "bourgeois dictatorship." At certain times even
lexicography has political implications—and at no time more than today.
The slogan "a workers' democracy," on the one hand, marks off the true
communist from the official communist who uses the phrase "dictatorship of the proletariat" as a euphemism for the dictatorship of the Communist Party bureaucracy over its own members and over the working
class; and, on the other hand, the slogan "a workers' democracy" prevents the too-easy identification on the part of the unpolitical worker of
the proletarian dictatorship with the fascist dictatorships. The dictatorship of the Fascist Party is an essential part of the political system of fascism and is the only way by which capitalism can preserve itself against
disintegration; the dictatorship of the Communist Party bureaucracy is a
foreign excrescence upon the structure of the workers' state, as well as
upon the true communist party.

4. The fourth dogma I wish to discuss represents not so much a part
of the creed of orthodox communism but a tendency observable in its
cultural philosophy and practice. This is the dogma of "the collective
man." The Communist Party claims to have no official line for creative
artists to follow but the fact that, by its own theories, art is an expression

of social conditions, and therefore of politics, and the further fact that its politics leaves no room for any critical dissent, give a characteristic stamp to the literature, art, and very patterns of life which the official press approves.

From the premise that history can be most adequately understood, and made, by the guiding principles of the class struggle, some communists have inferred that the only valid ideals for life and letters are those that celebrate the achievements of the mass and the class. The "collectivity" as the hero of the novel, the objective political needs of the moment as the theme of poetry, the selected historical event as the subject matter of the play—all this of course is nothing new. It may be found in some of the great artistic treasures of earlier times. Nor is this emphasis peculiarly characteristic of what has been called "proletarian culture." The fascization of culture in Italy and Germany similarly attacks (from different ideological premises) individualistic and personal artistic forms as decadent, liberal, and smacking of petty-bourgeois anarchy. It, too, seeks to convert the politically exigent into the aesthetically relevant. In fact, it carries matters to absurdity by making political implications the sole consideration. But for historical reasons the cultural ideals of communism—even in "the transitional period"—have been interpreted as involving the glorification of the mass and the disparagement of the individual. Hostile critics who desire to lump fascism and communism together have not hesitated to say that the only difference between the cultural philosophy of fascism and communism is that where the latter says "proletariat," the former says "the state," and that what they both mean is "the political party."

It cannot be too much stressed, therefore, that communism is hostile to individualism, as a social theory, and not to individuality, as a social value. It seeks to provide the material guarantee of security without which the free development of individuality or personality is an empty or impossible ideal. But the *free development of personality remains its ideal*; difference, uniqueness, independence, and creative originality are intrinsic values to be fostered and strengthened; and indeed one of the strongest arguments against capitalism is that it prevents these values from flourishing for all but a few. Communists recognize, however, that the social content of these values, the forms and conditions of their expression, are historical variables. They therefore repudiate the notion that because the social content and patterns of personality in a communist culture will be different from those of the eighteenth-century country squire, the nineteenth-century industrial freebooter or the twentieth-century captain of industry—they are any less genuine and valuable. Communists grant—as every honest person must—that in any society where mechanical impositions of external constraints upon cultural activity or thought exist, where material deprivation and psychic lynching are the automatic consequences of cultural criticism, a premium is placed upon social conformity and upon that type of virtue which is made up of two parts inconspicuity, one part silence and one part diplomatic assent. That is why it is the duty of every principal communist to be sharply critical of the cultural excesses committed by the heresy-hunting orthodox Russian communists, especially in the fields of literature and technical philosophy.

Where the free development of personality remains the ideal, there can be no abridgement—even in the transitional period, only *one* of whose limits, let it be remembered, is determined—of the right to believe and actively hold independent or unpopular views in all cultural and scientific fields. That this right may sometimes lead to an expression of views which border on the *politically dangerous* is no more a justification for censoring critical and independent cultural thought than the fact that sometimes anecdotes circulate which undermine the prestige of the political leader constitutes a reason for declaring a political taboo against humor. One of the reasons why official communists do not see this can be traced to their uncritical assumption that the whole of culture is involved in, and relevant to, a criticism of any part of it. Consequently, to challenge the ruling dogma in philosophy or art is also to strike a blow at the foundations of the workers' state. This belief in a cultural monism will no more stand analysis than the belief in a metaphysical monism. It can flourish only when the fear of having to answer critical questions about the validity of the political line of the party is so great that all forms of criticism are discouraged, lest the habit of criticism spread. But where there is no criticism, intellectual life perishes.

One more word in conclusion. No matter what the cultural and moral philosophy of communists be, I do not think it is an exaggeration to say that communism, as a social system, will be an immense improvement over capitalism so far as the distribution of material goods and comforts is concerned. But the extent to which communism as a social system makes possible the development of a free culture for free and creative personalities—that does not depend upon the system of economic production but primarily upon the living communist men and women themselves, upon the type of leadership which arises and the type of membership which permits that leadership to develop. It seems to me that only communism can save the world from its social evils; it seems to me to be just as evident that the official Communist Party or any of its subsidiary organizations cannot be regarded as a Marxist, critical, or revolutionary party today. The conclusion is, therefore, clear: *the time has now come to build a new revolutionary party in America and a new revolutionary international.*

[1934]

## NOTES

1. I have not considered the arguments of Bertrand Russell against the Marxian economic analysis because their brevity has prevented me from understanding them. They seem to imply, however, that Marx held to the "subsistence theory" of wages which Marx specifically repudiated. At certain times the redistribution of surplus value depends *in part* upon the workers' own efforts in organizing themselves and fighting for higher wages and shorter hours. One of the uses of political mass agitation is to compel the bourgeoisie to return part of the surplus value in the form of social services. This does not imply, however, the possibility of the permanent improvement of the working class under capitalism.

2. An important step in this direction, I believe, has been taken by the organization of the *American Workers' Party*.

3. It is interesting to point out to those who confuse the social junction of an idea and its socio-biographical origin that Russell's origins are aristocratic, Dewey's lower middle class, and Cohen's proletarian.

4. *Communist* (March 1933): 300.

5. *New York Times*, January 28, 1934.

6. February 18, 1934.

7. All citations are from the article "Dialectical Materialism and Communism," *Labour Monthly*, September and October 1933. All italics in the original.

8. One of the minor dogmas which I have no space to treat and which strengthens the belief in the infallibility of leadership, derives from an abuse of the Marxian distinction between subjective intention and objective consequence. Official communists are quick to accuse other communists, who disagree with them and criticize the official line, as "counter-revolutionists" because their criticisms are sometimes seized upon by noncommunists. The ground offered for the use of such harsh terms is the principle: "Subjective intentions are irrelevant in judging an action; only the objective consequences must be considered." If this principle is assumed as a postulate then it requires only one plausible material premise to get both a startling and an amusing conclusion. The argument runs:

(1) Subjective intentions are irrelevant in evaluating an action; only objective consequences must be considered.

(2) A political mistake, by definition, has counterrevolutionary objective consequences.

(3) If *S.*, our leader, makes a political mistake, he is a counter-revolutionist.

(4) But *S.*, our leader, cannot be a counter-revolutionist.

(5) Therefore *S.*, our leader, is in political matters infallible.

The conclusion in a weakened form permits *S.* to make only little mistakes, i.e., those that have no serious consequences.

I submit that if postulate (1) and material premise (4) be granted, then the conclusion cannot be avoided. Official communists *insist* upon postulate (1); and the material premise (4) is assumed on psychologically necessary grounds by all who join a revolutionary party.

9. Rudas, *Labour Monthly*, September 1933 [italics in the original].

# 6

# WHAT IS LIVING AND DEAD IN MARXISM

O f Marxism as of Christianity it is easy to say that it has never been tried. There is some justification in speaking of Christianity in this fashion because, literally interpreted, it can never be applied. But by its own proud profession, Marxism is not merely a set of ideas but the theoretical expression and guide of an historical movement. Its validity can be tested only in historical practice. If events pass it by, that is to say, neither confirm nor invalidate it, one may still appeal to the pristine integrity of doctrines which, because they have never been understood, have never been acted upon. Such an appeal, however, is tantamount to a confession that these doctrines are historically irrelevant. And it is a good Marxian dictum that what is irrelevant for purposes of historical understanding and action is historically meaningless. For Marxism as the theory and practice of achieving socialism is not chiefly a method of reading history but of making it.

## 1. THE CRISIS OF MARXISM

The debacle of Marxist movements throughout the world may be only temporary. But at present their eclipse is almost complete. The "bank-ruptcy," "collapse," "degeneration" of Marxism is the theme of innumer-

Originally published in *The Southern Review*. Reprinted by permission of the Estate of Sidney Hook.

able articles and books. Even its "autopsy" has already been written, albeit prematurely. By itself the vogue of this critical literature testifies little concerning the actual state of affairs. From one point of view it indicates that Marxist theory, like every doctrine so often declared dead but which must be buried again and again, has considerable vitality.

More impressive evidence of the debacle of Marxism is to be derived from a direct examination of the dwindling influence of Marxist movements on contemporary social and political affairs. Such a survey will show that more than material power and strategic position have been lost. Confidence in the ideals of socialism has been undermined in quarters which had taken their validity for granted. For the first time in a century the Marxist movement in every country of the world seems to have lost that sense of direction and assurance which had sustained it in previous crises. Articles of faith and doctrine have been abandoned in a precipitate scramble for slogans and formulae that will work for a day, a week, or a month.

History itself has turned out to be the most deadly revisionist of Marxist theory and practice. Illusions which were already hoary in the time of Marx have been refurbished and set up as guides to political practice. The Stalinists, who have long since betrayed the ideals of socialism, still call themselves Marxists, just as in the past many groups that surrendered their Christianity still insisted that they were Catholics. Others, proud of their orthodoxy, are compelled to say as they run from the brutal blows of reaction, that it is all happening according to the principles of Marxism. Win or lose, their doctrines are right. Every defeat is an additional confirmation. "Events did not catch us unawares," writes Trotsky, "it is necessary only to interpret them properly."

The current moods of wholesale denial and skepticism are no more illuminating than uncritical reaffirmations. Those who in blind fury destroy the altars of the gods who have forsaken them are just as religious as the devotees who still remain rapt in their worshipful ignorance. They will find other idols and other Churches. They will not assay for themselves what is valid and invalid in the doctrines of Marxism for fear of discovering that what they have treasured is fool's gold.

In this chapter I wish to inquire into those doctrinal aspects of contemporary Marxist movements which seem definitely invalidated, and those aspects of the Marxist tradition, broadly conceived, which may still be integrated into a sound synthesis. Whether such a synthesis is *called* Marxist or not, is immaterial, as is the question whether it is "what Marx really meant."

## 2. SCIENCE, IDEALS, AND SCIENTIFIC METHOD

Everyone is acquainted with the proud boast of Marxism that it alone is "scientific socialism." Whatever the limitations of its conception of science, there is no questioning the *desire* of Marxists to be scientific, i.e., to base their judgment and action on verifiable evidence about the nature of man and the world. Scientific knowledge and valid knowledge were synonymous in Marxist literature. No popular movement ever surpassed Marxism in the intensity of its verbal appreciation of science both as a cultural force and as a basis upon which to project a philosophy of life.

The limitations of the orthodox Marxist conception of science were threefold—historical, analytic, and functional. What it meant for anything to be a science was determined by the nineteenth-century formulations of Engels which were already antiquated at the time he penned them. It was a deistic view of the world without Deity in which terms like infinity, necessity, universality were used in emotionally free but intellectually unprecise ways. The conclusions of science were celebrated but its methods hardly studied. And sometimes even these conclusions, as in anthropology and biology, became intellectual fixtures of the Marxist mind despite their untenability in the light of new scientific advances.

Analytically, the limitations of the orthodox Marxist view of science flowed from its lack of methodological clarity. It would assert: "Marxism is not a dogma" but it never made clear what the difference was between a dogma and an hypothesis. It looked to experience, but only to confirm Marxist pronouncements, not to test them. We search in vain in the canonic writings of the pre-war or post-war periods for any indication as to what empirical evidence Marxists were prepared to accept as constituting even a possible refutation of their doctrines. Yet without a clear conception of what would constitute a possible refutation of any particular view, we are without a clear conception of what would possibly constitute a confirmation. No adequate distinctions were drawn between what might be, what would be, what must be, even what we would like to be. "Cause," "condition," "occasion" were used interchangeably. *The* economic factor, usually undefined, was declared "fundamental," in an uninterpreted sense, in a "last analysis" or "long run" which remained unanalyzed.

The functional drawback of the Marxist conception of science was the most fateful of all its limitations, for it prevented Marxists from making clear to themselves the relation between their goals, the whole cluster of socialist ideals, and the means by which these goals were to be furthered. It is untrue to say that Marxists were not conscious of their socialist ideals or that they explicitly identified them with whatever the historical process brought forth. Before the first World War, the propaganda of the Marxist movement was infused with moral passion and idealism. It is true to say that with the coming of the Bolsheviks these ideals were taken for granted and policies were checked, when they were checked at all, by their bearing only on the conquest of power, and not in the light of the socialist ideals by which power was to be justified. For Lenin the proletarian power was its own justification. Whether the state power *in fact* was proletarian, needed no further proof in his eyes other than his own consciousness that he and his party "expressed" the "real" needs of the proletariat. If he had any doubts he settled them with the same decrees with which he silenced opposition parties.

Thinking back more than twenty years to American pre-war days, I recall the distinction which even youngsters in the socialist movement made (so invariably as to seem almost a stock response), between government ownership and socialism. The novice who defined socialism as *government ownership* of all means of production, distribution, and exchange would be carefully corrected. The post office and water works were government owned; even if the whole economy were organized and owned by the government, it would be a far cry from socialism. Socialism, we used to say, was collective ownership and *democratic control* of the basic means of production. Perhaps the influence of the I.W.W. with its exaggerated distrust of the state was reflected in this attitude; but whatever the causes of our belief, the ideals of personal and cultural freedom, of social and educational democracy, were considered as integral to socialism.

The ideals, then, were there; but not the habit of taking bearings by them or the courage to revise them in the light of what Marxists found themselves actually doing. Despite their vaunted scientific philosophy, Marxists never scrutinized their professed goals in terms of the programs and methods which they claimed the situation exacted from them, never criticized their ends-in-view by the consequences of their means in action. No matter what they did, no matter what the consequences of their doing, socialism was a valid ideal which would be somehow and sometime realized. The ideal of socialism, therefore, functioned as an absolute, as something that could always be saved despite the appearances. At most, Marxists were scientific about means toward limited objectives, never about ultimate ends, and yet their own *theory* stressed the interrelatedness of ends and means.

This fear of revising their ideals—a revision which is a natural phase of the process of understanding and criticizing them by consequences in action—led, on the one hand, to a terminological fetishism, and, on the other, to a vicious, because unacknowledged, revision of socialist ideals in practice. Socialism could not be touched, harmed, or discredited no matter what Marxists did or how historical events turned out. It fulfilled all the qualities of a dream.

Human beings will always dream. Dreams have their consolations, and sometimes, like religions, they may express edifying fairy tales. But to mistake a dream for a sober hypothesis about existence and history is madness. What is still living in Marxism, or more accurately, what can be brought to life in the thinking of Marxists, is the tradition of scientific criticism of all social dreams, so that the wishes behind them can be adjudged reasonable or unreasonable in the light of their contexts, and the possibilities and costs of achieving them. It is only then that dreams become ideals.

How much of traditional Marxism will remain after it is scientifically purged, cannot be foretold in advance. Even if everything cannot be saved, it is unlikely that nothing can be used. For psychological and historical reasons it may be necessary to discard the word "Marxism" as an identifying term.

## 3. CRITIQUE OF CAPITALISM

The perennial source of strength of all socialist movements is the inequities and inequalities of capitalist economy. By themselves, poverty, insecurity, unemployment, war, and their cultural effects do not constitute an argument *for* socialism, for there is always the abstract possibility that as bad as capitalism is, socialism may be even worse. But they are a compelling argument to look for something better, and insofar as Marxists can demonstrate that no fundamental improvement in these respects is possible under capitalism, they constitute the most powerful of all arguments *against* capitalism.

Stripped of the metaphysics of its value theory, the Marxian critique of capitalist economy still retains its validity. It is economically impossible for capitalist production under existing social and technological conditions to guarantee profits, employment, and an adequate standard of living for the working population, where "adequate" is not taken absolutely but relatively to the potential resources of wealth that are either not utilized or destroyed.

All proposals to effect recovery under capitalism turn out to be variations of three main lines of action—all of them sooner or later bound to fail, according to Marxist theory, because they cannot insure a profitable return on capital investment which is the only inducement to new investment.

*a.* Increases in prices relative to wages. This may reestablish profits in certain industries for a limited period. But before long a decline in the purchasing power of the consumers results in overproduction and depression. A decrease in wages relative to prices has the same effect.

*b.* Increase in wages relative to prices. This cuts the rate of profit to a point where there is no inducement to continued production. It also intensifies the quest for labor-saving devices in order to reduce costs, resulting in a higher incidence of technological unemployment. An increase of prices relative to wages likewise increases costs and reduces profits. An increase or decrease of both wages and profits cancel each other out.

*c.* Government spending on a large scale with no extensive regulation of prices or wages. This leads either to inflation or to increase in taxation which cuts profit and discourages new investment.

From this it by no means follows that capitalism is doomed to an automatic economic collapse. It can stagger along from crisis to crisis, "solving" its difficulties by destruction of materials, restriction of production, armament economics, and as a last resort, by war. The whole concept of "breakdown" is a mechanical and inept analogy. The transition from capitalism to another form of society, if it is made, is a *political* act, although not only a political act. This is recognized *on paper* by almost all Marxists. Were it taken seriously, it would follow that political prognosis could not be conceived as a corollary or addendum to an economic analysis. In actuality, however, instead of honestly facing the difficulties of political prognosis, and scientifically mastering as many of the relevant elements which time and the exigencies of intelligent action permit, stubborn intellectual habits persist. The future is read off on the basis of a simplistic economic monism. No matter how stormy the political weather, we are comforted with the assurance that some day all will be peace, plenty, and freedom.

## 4. THEORY OF THE STATE

Despite elements of exaggeration, and Utopian belief in its eventual disappearance, the Marxian theory of the state is fundamentally empirical. Many followers of Marx have attempted "to prove" that the state is an instrument of the ruling class by *definition*; but in the writings of Marx, this proposition appears as a generalization of analyses made of the specific activities of legislative bodies, courts, and the executive arm. Where there are conflicting interests, and where the regulation and the adjudication of these disputes are obviously the concern of the state power, it is legitimate to inquire in whose interests the state acts. And in principle, a determinate answer to such an inquiry can always be given.

Unfortunately, empirical analyses of state activity have rarely been undertaken. At best they can only yield answers of *degree* for various historical periods. Conclusions to the effect that the state "for the most part" or "in the main" serves as an instrument of the dominant class have little propaganda value. More important, they are formally irrelevant to the question of whether the state *here* and *now* and in respect to *this* proposal will act to further or frustrate the interests of a particular class.

Where Marxists have made a beginning at empirical analyses, their work has usually suffered from a threefold defect. They have often assumed, even when they have disclaimed doing so, that it is *only* economic interests which determine state activity; they consequently either discounted the influence of religious, racial, and sectional interests, or interpreted the latter as *mere* disguises of economic interests. Their conception of what constitutes a class has been so vague that no matter what the evidence, it could be claimed as a vindication of their thesis. Thus, if the farmers by high-pressuring the legislators, gained their point at the expense of the city consumer, or if one group of industrialists lost their advantage to another group by repeal of some discriminatory legislation, or if a government service or tax policy adversely affected a private monopoly, or if a Labor Relations act, helpful to workers, was adopted in the teeth of organized opposition by employers—all this would be taken as confirmation of the view that the state was an instrument of *the* dominant class. In these cases, it is explained, the "ruling class" yielded to pressure in order to escape more drastic demands being made upon it. But the fact that the "ruling class" could be made to yield is just as significant in understanding the nature of the state as its reasons for yielding. The third and crassest error was to assume that in a collectivized economy, differences in economic interests would disappear and therewith the necessity for any state power. This was more than a monstrous piece of question-begging. It estopped thought precisely at the point where it was most urgent, i.e., in relation to the question of how liberties and rights, which historically had developed with an unplanned capitalism, were to be preserved and extended in a planned collective economy.

Underlying all these errors was a momentous confusion between what may be called the *substantial* conception of the state and the *functional*. According to the latter, the state is what it does, and in any definite period, what it usually does gives it its class character. According to the former conception the state consists of a set of institutions whose *essential* nature is class-determined even when it expresses this nature in the most varied ways. The legislature, the courts, the army, police, and militia *cannot* change their nature by functioning differently or for different purposes. Now, historically, Marx may have been justified in asserting that in a given situation in a given country the state institutions, in virtue of their traditions and personnel, could not function to achieve socialist purposes, and that the workers and their allies, therefore, could not rest with capturing the state machinery but had to destroy it. But Lenin converted the conclusion of a specific analysis into a dogma and asserted that by its very nature, the existing state could never under any circumstances change its nature by new uses and new functions. He *defined* the state in such a way as to preclude this possibility. The result was that the road to power everywhere and everytime, in advance of specific historical situations and empirical analyses, was declared to be the road of dual power. This was a command concealed as a description or prediction. The slogan *Soviets partout!* became universal, and the enormous advantage in democratic countries of winning and using Parliaments in order to transform them into the instruments of socialist ideals and purposes was not even considered. Instead Parliaments were regarded as mere sounding boards from which to proclaim to the community their complete futility—a sentiment enthusiastically acclaimed also by Nazis and Fascists.

The confusion on this point was obscured by the completely independent question of whether the transition to socialism could be achieved peacefully. From Marx's point of view, it might be achieved peacefully; but peacefully or not, always democratically. According to Lenin's revision of Marx, the transition to socialism *cannot* be achieved either democratically or peacefully.

## 5. THE PARTY AS INSTRUMENT

Socialism is not inevitable. It is something to be accomplished when objective conditions are ripe. But how? By men and not by economic forces. Men may accomplish this spontaneously and with only a dim consciousness of what they are doing, or deliberately and through organization. The only form of organized political action we know is the action of a political party, a fact which is not altered by speaking of political "groups" or "associations." The character and functions of a political party are such that, if there are genuine alternatives of action, and there usually are, ideals may be perverted and instruments may corrupt ends. Nonetheless, to rely upon the spontaneous action of the masses, as a substitute procedure, in the hope of achieving the desirable features of political action without the risks of political bureaucracy, is unintelligent. Belief in the spontaneous and sustained wisdom of the masses is the sheerest mysticism. History is not like a gigantic roulette wheel which can be put into motion again and again until the favored number is drawn. Nor is it, as most believers in spontaneity hold, the unfolding of a benevolent cosmic dialectic.

For good or for evil, then, to the extent that social revolutions are political revolutions, they are organized by political parties. It speaks well for the scientific *intent* of Marxism that concern with the nature of the instrument—the political party—by which the socialist movement is to be led, has always been in the forefront of theoretical discussion. I say scientific *intent* because, here as elsewhere, the scientific analysis was cut short whenever conclusions emerged whose implications seemed to threaten the ends in behalf of which the party as a political instrument was to be used. Differences concerning the conception of the socialist party, its relation to the class, and its vocation of leadership proved to be the most *fateful* of all the causes of the Russian Thermidor. The party was conceived only as an instrument by which political power could be won, not as an instrument by which socialism could be achieved.

Despite its concern with organizational questions, the Marxist movement, particularly its most militant wing, showed itself singularly unaware of the far-reaching dangers to a democratically functioning socialism in the conception of a party of professional revolutionists. Its eye was fixed on the problem of how power could as soon as possible be wrested from those who had it, and not on the consequences to socialism of a view according to which a minority political party constitutes, by its own edicts, the vanguard of a class which in turn "expresses" the interests of humanity. The warnings of the syndicalists and the anarchists, the profound arguments of Mosca, Pareto, and Michels before the Russian Revolution, the criticisms of Martov, Rosa Luxemburg, and others after—were all disregarded. There is no more eloquent testimony of the practical ruthlessness and theoretical naïveté of Lenin than his reply to those dissident communists who warned against the cult of political leadership which was involved in the Bolshevik substitution of the dictatorship of the party for working-class democracy. "The mere presentation of the question," he says, "[of] 'dictatorship of the Party *or* the dictatorship of the class' is . . . childishness . . . evidence of the most incredible and hopeless confusion of mind." To contrast the dictatorship of leaders and the dictatorship of the masses, he adds, "is ridiculously absurd and stupid." It is worse. It is "repudiation of the Party principle and Party discipline . . . *for the benefit of the bourgeoisie*. It is to carry out the work of the agent-provocateur."[1] His discussion never even reached the level of an argument.

Lenin's naïveté was the reflection of his inability to imagine that *his* conception of the best interests of the workers could ever in fact be different from what their best interests actually were. His indignation was a reaction to a criticism which in virtue of his naïve Messianic faith, he could not interpret otherwise than as an attack upon *his* personal integrity. Stalin was the price that Lenin paid for this naïveté. And if we recall one of Lenin's own favorite maxims: "A political leader is not only responsible for the way he leads but also for what is done by those he leads," Lenin's responsibility for Stalin is absolute. Given this naïveté, it was perfectly natural for Lenin to charge that the Workers' Opposition which fought for more democracy *within* the Soviets was trying to overthrow the Soviet Power. It was perfectly natural for Lenin to hold that anyone who deviated from the consistent communist line (as *he* interpreted it), must end up as a Kronstadt mutineer, and that every Kronstadt mutineer, a "hero of the Revolution," when he aided the Bolsheviks, was now *malgré lui* a White Guardist.[2]

A final illustration of this simple-minded infamy will show the lengths to which Lenin was prepared to go. After the New Economic Policy had been introduced into Russia, Otto Bauer, one of the leading theoreticians of Western Social-Democracy, and a stanch opponent of any intervention into Russian affairs, wrote, "They are now retreating to capitalism; we have always said that the revolution is a bourgeois revolution." At which Lenin indignantly exclaims: "And the Mensheviks and Social-Revolutionaries, all of whom preach this sort of thing, are astonished when we say that *we will shoot those who say such things*."[3] One does not know whether to be more repelled by the actual murder of his working-class opponents because of their opinions than by the self-righteousness with which Lenin carried it out.

The alternative to the Leninist conception of the political party is not the traditional Social-Democratic conception. The latter assumed that a party dedicated to the heroic task of transforming existing society could succeed with the same organizational forms, the same leisure-time holiday effort, the same evaluation of electoral gains, which characterized capitalist parties for whom politics was, by and large, a business. The genuine alternative to the Leninist conception of the political party is a party not less disciplined but more flexibly disciplined in virtue of a better grasp of both scientific method and the democratic process. Its task will be to guide, and not to dictate, the organized struggle for socialism in such a way that "the conquest of power" becomes a phase in the unfolding of democratic institutions and tendencies already present in the community. It recognizes and respects the relative autonomy of the arts and sciences from politics, and thus avoids both the horror and foolishness of a "party line" in anything but politics. It is built around principles and not a cult of leadership. Its perspective is neither one of blood and thunder nor of milk and water. It must yield to none in realism which means nothing more than applied intelligence. It therefore will have no doctrinal dogmas, acceptance of which is a prerequisite of membership. Its confidence will extend to a point where it is prepared to take account of the dangers and obstacles which its own organized activities may create, even with the best of intentions, to the successful consummation of socialism.

## 6. THE ANATOMY OF REVOLUTION

Such a conception of the political party must face at least two severe criticisms. One is drawn from the alleged laws of social revolution according to which revolutions cannot be won except by a monolithic party which strives for a monopoly of political power. The other is drawn from another set of alleged laws, psychological and historical, according to which socialists (democrats) can be victorious, but socialism (democracy) never. We shall consider the first objection in this section, and the second in the subsequent one.

The difficulty of contending that there are "laws of social revolution" lies in the ambiguity of the key terms and, once they are univocally defined, in the indecisive character of the evidence that they actually obtain. To begin with, the denial that we possess verifiable laws of social revolution must not be taken to assert that social revolutions are uncaused. There may be a multiplicity of causes of such complexity that we cannot reduce them to general statements about invariable relationships between events. Moreover, what do we really understand by a "social revolution"? In the strict Marxist sense, a social revolution is a change in property relationships in the mode of economic production. Most discussions of social revolution, however, include political revolutions which do not involve changes in property relations. Even Marxists refer to the Paris Commune as an attempted social revolution although it made no effort to introduce socialism.

Professor Brinton in his *Anatomy of Revolution* tries to cut the Gordian knot of definition by saying that "since the movements with which we are concerned are commonly called revolutions, they may be so called once more." The only, but fatal, difficulty in this approach is that our choice of specimens is so wide that we can easily make a selection which would reveal quite a different set of simple uniformities from those Professor Brinton derives. If we take a functional approach to the question of property, i.e., in terms of actual control rather than paper decree, then the Fascist and Nazi revolutions must also be regarded as social revolutions. The German and Italian (and Russian) bureaucracies own the instruments of production in a more absolute fashion than the bourgeoisie in any capitalist democracy. These two revolutions fall outside the purview of Professor Brinton's survey and are rarely considered by Marxists as a test of their laws of social revolution. It is questionable whether any "law" according to which revolutions can be won only by a monolithic political party striving for a monopoly of political power, can be established except for illustrations already selected to conform to this "law."

Interestingly enough the Marxist conception of "historical laws" makes generalizations of this sort extremely risky. Marx does not deny that there are laws of production which hold for all epochs and without which production in any epoch is impossible. But he insists that "the conditions which generally govern production must be differentiated in order that the essential points of difference be not lost sight of in view of the general uniformity which is due to the fact that the subject, mankind, and the object, nature, remain the same."[4] These general laws of production do not tell us what the economic laws of slavery, or of feudalism, or of capitalism are. Similarly, even if there were laws of social revolution, it would not necessarily follow that the laws of capitalist revolution and the laws of socialist revolution would be the same. Nor, if there were laws of socialist revolution, need they necessarily take the same form in countries as different as France, Russia, China, and the United States.

All this was ignored or overlooked by the Leninists. It can be easily demonstrated that they based their conception of how political power was to be won on their study of the French revolutions of 1789, 1848, and 1871 (the Commune), and the attempted bourgeois-democratic Russian Revolution of 1905. Professor Brinton errs grievously when he asserts that "the Bolsheviks do not seem to have guided their actions by the 'scientific' study of revolutions to an appreciably greater degree than the Independents (Cromwellians) or the Jacobins. They simply adapted an old technique to the days of the telegraph and the railroad train." As a matter of fact, all the leading ideas of the Bolsheviks were drawn from their fancied "scientific" study of previous *bourgeois* revolutions. To be sure, there was the element of improvisation, including the public denial of their principles, and other Machiavellianisms. But this, too, was provided for by their organizational theory. After they won, their theory became canonic doctrine for *all* parties of the Communist International. They were shrewd enough to say on paper that since the conditions of the Russian Revolution could not be repeated elsewhere, there would be corresponding differences in strategy and tactics in other countries. But in fact the same tactical line, down to the very details of slogans and phrasing, was always imposed at the same time in all countries.

The success of the Bolsheviks by no means proved that their theory was scientific. For they won power, not socialism. Even if they had achieved socialism—an extremely unlikely event in view of their methods—this would not have proved that their methods could succeed elsewhere.

One further consideration, of no little importance, is overlooked by Leninists when they speak of the laws of revolution. It is an oversight also committed by Professor Brinton in his *Anatomy of Revolution*, a witty and readable book which shows genuine insight into all questions concerning social revolutions except the important ones. This is the influence of *knowledge* of the theories guiding those who lead social revolutions upon the methods by which such revolutions are combated. In no country of the world where the Bolshevik theory of the conquest of power is known by their opponents are the Bolsheviks likely to win again if they act on their theory. Present-day Stalinists, of course, who are merely the border guards of the Soviet Union, have no interest in winning power, except if and when it becomes necessary to safeguard the Russian bureaucracy. But other species of Leninists are doomed to failure precisely because of their unscientific disregard of the specific factors in each historical situation and of their underestimation of the historical effects of knowledge and ignorance.

## 7. THE FETISHISM OF POWER

The most powerful arguments against the possibility of democratic socialism have been advanced in the writings of Mosca, Pareto, Michels, and Nomad.[5] These arguments are all the more impressive if we recall that they were formulated long before the rise of totalitarianisms, and in a period when social optimism was as general as pessimism is today. They carry, therefore, the additional weight of predictions that appear to have been at least partially confirmed. In the light of recent events, the position taken by these thinkers has been revived in many quarters. If it is sound, then the social philosophy of Marxism is a pernicious illusion, a variant of a Utopian dream which must cost mankind dearly wherever an attempt is made to realize it.

Mosca's thesis is a simple one and recommends itself with a high initial plausibility to anyone who has had some political experience. It asserts that political power in actuality never rests upon the consent of the majority, that irrespective of ideologies or leading personalities, all political rule is a process, now peaceful, now coercive, by which a minority gratifies its own interests in a situation where not all interests can receive equal consideration. As Mosca puts it: "Political power always has been, and always will be, exercised by organized minorities, which have had, and will have, the means, varying as the times vary, to impose their supremacy upon the multitudes." In peaceful times, the means are public myths and legal frauds; in a crisis—force. Whichever side wins, the masses who have fought, bled, and starved, lose. Their "saviors" become their rulers under the prestige of new myths. The forms of mythology change but the essential content of minority control and exploitation remains. This is put forth by Mosca as a "law" of all social life which can be demonstrated to the satisfaction of everyone except the dull, the pious, and candidates for political leadership. It is a "law" accepted by every political partisan as obviously true for other organizations but as a slander when applied to his own.

Mosca's "law" appears in Pareto under the principle of "the circulation of the elite." Belief in the homogeneity of society is a fable for simpletons. According to Pareto, differences between groups, and conflicts between their interests, are always more pervasive than the harmonies which idealistic philosophers discover, more often than not, by definition. Every society divides roughly into two classes—an elite which includes all who enjoy the fruits of recognized excellence in virtue of their strength, cunning, valor, wealth, social origin—the lions and the foxes—and a non-elite which comprises the rest of the population—the sheep. The elite in turn subdivide into a governing elite and a non-governing elite which mutually support each other. A governing elite, like the poor, we always have with us. Whenever its members lack qualities of vigor, will, discipline, and *readiness to use force in an emergency*, new members are recruited from the non-elite, those who prove that they are not sheep after all. When this does not happen, the reins of power are torn from the hands of the ruling class by a revolution headed by a counter-elite. "History is the graveyard of aristocracies." But aristocracies there will always be. Power may be taken in the name of humanity, democracy, and freedom. It can only be wielded by a few.

Michels reaches the same conclusion through considerations that are more empirical. Political power in behalf of any ideal, no matter how exalted, can be won only by organization. All organization, no matter how democratically conceived, inevitably involves the emergence of a leadership which in the last analysis controls the organization. If it is defeated it is replaced, not by a functioning democracy, but by a new leadership. All democratic movements, therefore, are self-defeating. They are doomed by "the iron law of oligarchy." According to this law "the majority of human beings, in a condition of eternal tutelage, are predestined by tragic necessity to submit to the domination of a small minority, and must be content to constitute the pedestal of an oligarchy."

In the interests of clear analysis we must distinguish between the descriptive generalizations of Mosca, Pareto, and Michels concerning the actual uses and abuses of political power in the past and present, and the theoretical explanations they offer of them. As descriptive generalizations, their conclusions, after differences in the forms of political rule have been properly noted, are largely valid. It is true that every political organization is in effect run by a minority. It is true that vital lies, chicanery, and naked force have been almost always the three props of all political rule. It is true that all successful mass movements—even with democratic ideologies—have compromised some of their basic principles, sometimes all of them. The history of Christianity, German Social-Democracy, and Russian Communism indicate in a dramatic and focal way all this and more. But in explaining these phenomena and in predicting that the future *must* be always like the past, Mosca falls back upon a psychological theory of human nature as something given and fixed independently of its social context. Almost every one of his major explanations and predictions involves an appeal to an original nature, conceived as essentially unalterable despite its varying expressions. Mosca's antiquated terminology, has, and can be, brought up to date by translation into the language of dynamic psychology and psychoanalysis. But the controlling assumptions are the same. The laws of political power are frankly characterized as psychological. They flow from unchangeable elements in the nature of man. Mosca had no hesitation in sometimes referring to them as "wicked instincts." It is from this conception of original sin that his direst prophecies flow.

The same is true for Pareto, and in a lesser degree for Michels. The whole significance of Pareto's doctrine of the constancy of residues is summed up in the sentence: "The centuries roll by and human nature remains the same." Michels weakens the force of his arguments, which are drawn from the technical indispensability of all leadership in all political organization, by deducing therefrom the conclusion that "the majority is permanently incapable of (democratic) self-government." Even Crane Brinton, who is reluctant to state propositions in outmoded psychological terms, concludes his study of revolutions with the remark that "in some very important ways the behavior of men changes with a slowness almost comparable to the kind of change the geologist studies." Instead of saying "human nature never changes," Brinton is saying "almost never"! As far as historical understanding is concerned, the qualification is not very significant.

The fact that the argument from human nature must be invoked to support the sociological law that democratic socialism is impossible is *prima facie* evidence that the entire position is *unhistorical*. If it is true that history without sociology is blind, it is just as true that sociology without history is empty.

For the sake of the argument, everything Mosca and Pareto claim may be granted except when they speak in the future tense. The genuine problems of power are always *specific*, are always rooted in the *concrete needs of a particular* people at a *determinate* time. Any conclusion based on their finding (Michels is in a different category) about the futility of social struggle and revolution is a *non sequitur*. It betrays political animus, for to cultivate abstract suspicion of the excesses of all political power is often to encourage acceptance of the customary abuses of existing power. Insofar as the conclusion concerning the futility of revolution is grounded, it must be derived from other empirical, nonpsychological, considerations. Michels provides some of these considerations but it is noteworthy that he does not base any counsel of inactivity or despair upon them.

The belief that there is an invariant core of properties which constitute the "essential" character of human nature, rests on gross data drawn from history and a faulty technique of definition. Habits, historical traditions, and social institutions play a much more important role in political behavior, and are more reliable in predicting the future than any set of native impulses, residues, instincts, or urges. By isolating the latter from their objective cultural setting, selecting from among them an alleged impulse to dominate, to be selfish, to fight, love, or flee, the pattern of human nature can be cut to suit any political myth. The whole conception has received its definitive refutation in John Dewey's *Human Nature and Conduct*.

## 8. THE USES AND ABUSES OF POWER

Despite the fact that "the laws" of Mosca, Pareto, and Michels, when presented in psychological dress, have no empirical warrant, they can be reformulated *with supporting historical evidence*. Stated in such a way, they bear relevantly on particular situations in which intelligent choice is possible between accepting a given form of political rule, with its known evils, and struggling for a new form of political rule, with its menace of new evils. In such situations, these "laws" function as guides or cautions to possible dangers that attend the transference of power from one group to another. The task then becomes one of devising safeguards—an occasion for experiment, not for lamentation. And most safeguards do not make accidents impossible, they make them less frequent or less fatal.

Sometimes the prospect of social gain by change in political power may be so small that in face of our knowledge of the dangers of social revolution, we can easily reconcile ourselves to our existing condition no matter how deplorable. For example, if all that can be said of the gains of the French and Russian Revolutions is, to cite Brinton's wry speculation, "that it took the French Revolution to produce the metric system and to destroy *lods et ventes* and similar feudal inconveniences, or the Russian Revolution to bring Russia to use the modern calendar and to eliminate a few useless letters in the Russian alphabet," then to undertake revolutions would be criminally stupid. But the gains of the revolutions, as Mr. Brinton well knows, were much more extensive. Whether they were worth the price is another question. Whether the price was necessary is still another. Whether we must *continue* paying the price, or even a higher one, is a third question.

These questions must always be posed in a specific context. The present context is one in which we must consider the price that *may* have to be paid by an attempt to achieve democratic socialism. To the Marxist, indeed, to any intelligent person, that question presupposes another: What is the price of the *status quo*? If that price is war, it is hard, but not impossible, to conceive of any loss of life, freedom, and happiness attendant upon the abuse of power under socialism which will be worse than the losses suffered in a large-scale war. Further, we are now in a position to anticipate more adequately the probable sources of corruption and oppression under socialism, and to construct theoretical and institutional safeguards against them.

Without the consciousness of the dangers of a collectivized economy and the recognition of the necessity of establishing safeguards for freedom, criticism, personal independence, and all the other basic practices we associate with a functioning democracy, the case for socialism, it seems to me, is lost. For it would lead to another variant of Stalinism which costs too much no matter what its dubious gains. Russia under Stalin has lost many more dead than she lost in the World War under the Czar. No mass misery in her entire history, including the famines, begins to equal the distress and absolute political despotism which the Russian masses have endured in the last generation. As André Gide said, writing in the years before the great purges began, "In no country of the world . . . is thought less free, more bowed down, more fearful (terrorized), more vassalized."

We turn now to a brief survey of the dangers against which socialists must safeguard themselves. The first sphere of conflict and possible oppression in a socialist society—any socialist society—is the sphere of economic life. This may shock those uncritical socialists who believe that economic injustice is possible only under a system of private ownership of means of production. It is apparent, however, that under no system operated by finite creatures in a finite world can all men be equally served in everything. What is just as important, they cannot be equally served at once. Consequently there will be some differences in standards of living, no matter what level the productive forces of society will reach. To deny this is the veriest Utopianism. If Marx's dictum for a classless society be taken literally "From each according to his capacities, to each according to his needs," instead of as a guiding principle to reduce differences in living conditions (*while increasing their absolute minimum level*), it is a will o' the wisp. Differences there will always be; and because there are differences, conflicts. The kind of conflicts, their extent and intensity will depend largely upon the presence of specific mechanisms which will both reflect and negotiate the conflicting interests of different groups of producers and consumers. Among these mechanisms are working-class and professional organizations, trade-unions and guilds, *that are genuinely and permanently independent of the government.*

The second sphere of possible abuse of authority in a socialist society is administrative. Every administrator entrusted with responsibility for making decisions that may affect the jobs, pleasures, and life careers of other human beings, may function as a tyrant. The greater the area of administration, the greater the danger. Especially, when efficiency is a desideratum, is it easy to palm off injustice as a necessary evil. Here, too, the situation is one that must be met, for better or for worse, by contriving checks and controls. A vested interest on the part of the qualified worker in a job must be publicly recognized. Where administrative action affects civil or industrial rights they must be subject to review by democratically elected commissions, *independent of party affiliation.*

Finally, there is the multiplicity of individual psychological factors which make for oppression. It is extremely questionable whether there is any such thing as the love of power in the abstract. There is a love for a variety of things which, to be achieved or retained, require power in varying degrees. For some, the exercise of power is a compensation for frustration; for others, it is a way of acquiring prestige, glory, a sense of vitality or importance; for almost everybody, a temptation to favor those we like and overlook those we despise. Everyone has his own list of people whose absence he believes would be a boon to the world. But what follows from all this? Nothing that need dismay anyone who is not a saint or a fool. Here, as everywhere else, once we surrender the dogmas of an unalterable human nature or inevitable laws of organizational progress or corruption, we can do something to mitigate, counteract, and establish moral equivalents.

Whether we are talking of pain or injustice or power, there is no such thing as *the* problem of evil except to a supernaturalist. There are only evils. The more we know about the pathological lust for power, the conditions under which it thrives, the instruments it uses, the myths behind which it hides—*and the more public we make that knowledge*—the better can we cope with the problem of taming it. Skepticism is always in order; but no more than in science need it lead to paralysis of activity. More knowledge is required but we know enough to make at least a beginning.

Most of that knowledge is a knowledge of what to avoid, derived, in the main, from a close examination of Germany and Russia. It is clear that no monopoly of the instruments of education, including the press and radio, can be tolerated. More positively, the primary emphasis of all educational activity must revolve around the logic and ethics of scientific method. The meaning of democracy itself must be so conceived as to show that the methods of intellectual analysis to resolve conflicts of policy between minorities and majorities are an integral part of it. Freedom and authority can live together happily only in a society where scientific method is applied not merely to problems of physical control but to questions of human value.[6]

## 9.  HISTORICAL MATERIALISM

Despite theoretical recognition of the plurality of factors in history, Marxism as a political movement has tended to assign to the mode of economic production an overwhelming determining influence upon politics and culture not borne out by a scientific study of the facts. It has failed to realize that the economic organization of a society is often compatible with different alternatives of political rule and cultural behavior. This failure entailed an insensitiveness to the operation of other factors, including, as we have already pointed out, the historical effects of knowledge and ignorance, upon future events. Tested, therefore, by its ability to predict political and cultural changes, traditional Marxism has not been very successful. That other social theories have not been more successful is hardly an extenuation because Marxism has claimed to be the *only* scientific theory of social change.

Two conspicuous illustrations of the disproportionate influence assigned to the mode of economic production may be cited. Until recently most Marxists deduced the nature of the cultural superstructure of socialism—politics, law, and the family, religion, art, and philosophy—as a simple corollary from the character of socialist production. To say that they "deduced" anything is, in a sense, an exaggeration. It is more accurate to say that they took these matters for granted. The change in productive relations of itself guaranteed that social life, and even the soul of man, would be harmonious, just, and free. Concern with the constitution of the socialist commonwealth, with the problems of cultural and educational direction, with the possibilities of collectivist tyranny, was dismissed as, at best, a time-wasting absorption in empty possibilities. Often, reflections of this kind were considered as hampering the struggle for political power, instead of being evaluated for their bearing upon the way the struggle must be conducted in order to achieve the ideals of democratic socialism.

Even a more glaring example of the overemphasis of economic factors is the political position of Leon Trotsky, the most "orthodox" of contemporary Marxist-Leninists. Because he assumes that the Russian *economy* is socialist, he is prepared to defend the invasion of any democratic country by Stalin's armies, and the imposition of Stalin's absolute and bloody totalitarianism upon their citizens, including the proletariat. Trotsky does this not because he approves of Stalin's bureaucratic regime, fortified, as it is, by frame-up, purge, and cultural terror. Nor because he approves of the wisdom of such invasions. But solely because he expects the productive relations to be socialized. Even if the cultural and economic lot of the workers is worsened by this change, Trotsky is certain that the dialectical necessity of socialized economy will inevitably result in secondary political revolutions which will sweep Stalinism away. This mystic faith has nothing in common with a scientific analysis of politics but it is consistent with that view of historical materialism which is common to all schools of Marxist-Leninism.

If the truth be told, the very statement of the theory of historical materialism in the writings of canonic expositors suffers from several types of ambiguity which make it difficult to know how to go about testing its validity. Among them may be mentioned the equation between productive relations and productive forces, the shift from necessary to sufficient conditions, the meanings of the term "basic" and the phrase "in the last instance" in such statements as "the mode of production basically determines a culture in the last instance," etc. Here an important work of clarification must be done. The greatest obstacle to the task of clarification is the persistent contention among orthodox Marxists that they command a dialectic method which permits them to entertain without embarrassment doctrines that appear to others as downright inconsistencies.

## 10.  THE CRITICAL HISTORICISM OF MARX

The social philosophy of Marxism has been repeatedly declared to be historical. Historical in a twofold sense. First, in the obvious sense, that it arose in a definite historical period to articulate the interests and direct the struggles of the international working class. Second, in that it stresses what was once *not* a commonplace, viz., that all cultural activity, all norms and standards of social theory and practice are bound to a time and place.

If we take the term "historical" in the first sense, then to say that Marxism is historical is to state a fact. But what follows from it is by no means clear. Does Marxian socialism express the interests of the working class only or of the community as a whole? If of the community as a whole, why does it claim to be a class doctrine and why is the class struggle the central feature of that doctrine? If in liberating itself from the bonds of capitalism, the working class liberates the rest of humanity—as Marx himself asserted—then it would be just as true to say that in liberating itself from the bonds of capitalism, the rest of humanity liberates the working class.

Sometimes Marx speaks as if the rest of humanity, or that portion of it which finds its apparent present interests in irreconcilable opposition to those of the working class, does not truly appreciate what its "real" interests are. These are alleged to be harmonious with the "real" interests of the working class. Here Marx follows Hegel who follows Rousseau in the distinction between the general and individual will. The chief trouble, leaving the metaphysics aside, with this distinction between the apparent and real interests of the community, is that the same grounds which lead Marxists to make it, justify them in introducing a similar distinction between the real and apparent interests of the working class, i.e., between what the workers think they want and what Marxists *know* they really want. This distinction introduces the thin edge of totalitarianism into Marxism which Lenin drove home to a disastrous conclusion. It is diametrically opposed to Marx's oft-expressed view that the working class is the architect of its own political fate and that its victory must be democratically achieved with the uncoerced support of the majority of the population.

The only intelligible inference that can be drawn from Marx's writings on this point is that only the working class is in a position to lead successfully the struggle for socialism. The reasons adduced by Marx are many. Primary among them are that its most pressing difficulties—unemployment, insecurity, relatively low standard of living—cannot be met short of socialism, whereas this is not so true or as obvious, for other groups; and second, its strategic position in industry gives labor, once organized, a tremendous striking force both of defense and offense. Marx did not assert that the working class *alone* can achieve socialism but that it must constitute the chief base of a movement, uniting different groups of the population, to bring it about.

Let us grant for a moment Marx's claim that the working class is, and has been, in a position to lead a successful socialist movement. Unfortunately, being in a position and being able to move from that position are two different things. The test of events has shown that the working class has been petrified in its position of potential movement. Grant that if the working class does not lead the socialist movement, democratic socialism will not be achieved. True as that may be, it is no assurance that it will ever actually take the lead. The causes of the failure of socialist labor to win allies from middle class and professional groups, or even, in many countries, to align most of the workers under its banner, may be in dispute, but the facts themselves are incontrovertible.[7] The liquidation of peasants and intellectuals during the counterfeit socialist Russian revolution enhances, of course, the difficulties of united action between the working class and other sections of the population. No one really knows today how such fruitful united action is to be achieved. The time for it is very short, indeed. New political genius is necessary to develop the techniques of cooperation and persuasion.

The second sense in which Marxism is historical does not justify a belief in the relativity of truth as that phrase is customarily interpreted in popular literature. If we examine Marx's procedure, we will observe that his historical approach is not a substitute for scientific method but a concrete application of that method to the question of "universal" social laws and "abstract" ethical ideals.

As we saw in a previous section, Marx does not deny that certain uniformities of social behavior may be observable in all societies. What he insists upon is that for purposes of understanding and action in any historical period, an investigation must be undertaken of the historically differentiating factors in that period which may bear upon the extent and validity of the supposed uniformities. When we are dealing with the subject matter of history, we discover that there are many more variable factors that are relevant for our purposes than is the case in the materials of the natural sciences. The basic pattern of inquiry is the same in both fields. Whatever differences appear are differences not in general method but in the specific natures of what is being investigated. At any definite time, the conclusions reached by Marx are either true or false, once meaning can be assigned to them. To call them "historical" truths or errors does not add or take anything away.

Insofar as abstract ethical ideals are concerned, Marx follows the basic outline of Hegel's critique of Kant, substituting naturalistic theories of mind and human interest for Hegel's spiritualistic ones. The good and the right, or the better and the more just, are not expressions of arbitrary fiat drawn from intuition, revelation, or authority. Nor are they empty tautologies deduced from purely formal rules. They are evaluations and commitments based upon *knowledge* of (i) all the relevant interests involved in a particular situation, (ii) how they are related to the state of productive forces and relations, (iii) the alternatives of action open to men, and (iv) the consequences of the respective actions. The historical approach to ethical ideals is nothing more than intelligent criticism of ideals. And all ideals are subject to criticism. The process of criticizing ideals may include *more* than what Marx believed necessary. But it must include at least that. Only those are in fundamental opposition to Marx's critical, historical approach, who believe that some ideals or standards are above or beyond criticism at any time or place.

It should be noted that what is living and sound in Marx's critical historicism, as well as in his "rationalism" and "humanism" (discussed in the subsequent sections) are to be found not so much in contemporary Marxists or Marxist movements as in the thought of individuals who, identifying Marxism with Marx, naturally regard themselves as utterly opposed to him. The most outstanding figure in the world today in whom the best elements of Marx's thought are present is John Dewey. They were independently developed by him, and systematically elaborated beyond anything found in Marx. If ever a democratic socialist movement succeeds in striking roots in American soil, it will have to derive one of its chief sources of nourishment from the philosophy of John Dewey.

## 11. THE RATIONALISM OF MARX

Few of Marx's leading principles have been so severely criticized as his alleged rationalism. Not many have taken the trouble to specify what they meant by it. Marx is not a rationalist, if that means the belief that "reason" constitutes the structure of things or that it is the impelling force in human behavior and history. Marx is a rationalist in that he believes that rational or scientific method is the only method that can be successfully employed wherever we seek understanding and control. It is in this sense that he is a true child of the enlightenment. There is nothing that cannot be scientifically investigated, nothing to which scientific method is irrelevant whether it be the stars in their courses or human beings entangled in their emotions. The determinants of human behavior may be as far from "reasonable" as one pleases, but it is only by the use of reason that we can discover the fact. Passion and faith may move mountains but who can say whether they will set them down at the right place? They are not by themselves expressions of reason but after they are submitted to critical analysis and their historic causes and consequences investigated, they may become reasonable.

The charge that Marx and Marxism suffer from too much rationalism seems peculiar when one recalls that only a generation ago they were criticized for being much too sentimental. As everyone knows who follows the day by day activity of Marxist groups, it is marked more by zealotry than intelligence, more by narrow organizational loyalty than cool appraisal of events. Slander is a weapon more often employed than argument, and hate the ruling emotion. One may justifiably expect more of Marxist groups but it is doubtful whether these unlovely qualities are uniquely characteristic of them alone. It was not because they lacked enthusiasm that Marxists lost out to Fascists in Europe. It was partly because they lacked the courage to act boldly at the height of their power, partly because their doctrines were inflexible, and their specific practices unintelligent.

As for Marx himself, his irascible personality is hardly reconciliable with the view that human beings do, or should, live "a reasoning life" if that is contrasted with a life of reason. His one chronic lapse into rationalism, in the exaggerated sense, seems to be his optimistic assurance that all workers could read *Capital*, and that anyone who read it without prejudice, would therewith be convinced. However, if to be rational means to be intelligent, then it is sufficient to remark that since genuine intelligence knows its own limits, it is absurd to charge that anyone can suffer from "too much intelligence."

The most conspicuous illustration of Marx's legitimate rationalism is to be found in his theory of social organization. He believed that under existing historic conditions society could be organized by an intelligent plan. One of the purposes of such planning would be to increase human security and liberate men from the manifold antisocial consequences which flow from those unplanned and unorganized economic activities that constitute what is metaphorically described as our present social "system." Marx can claim to have inherited the bequest of classic rationalism as expressed in the social insights of Plato and Aristotle with much greater justification than those of his critics who rant with mystic fervor about the Graeco-Roman Whole. For the harmonious organization of natural impulses under the control of reason which according to Plato and Aristotle are essential to the good life, is conditioned, according to Marx, by the harmonious organization of natural and economic resources under the rule of intelligence. To be intelligent means to plan. And an intelligently organized society is one which is socially planned. Since the profit "system" makes *social* planning impossible, the intelligently organized society must be one in which the profit motive in the major spheres of economic activity has been abolished.

One of the primary justifications of a planned society is its promise to achieve a social and personal *security* not realizable under regulated or unregulated capitalism. But as we have come increasingly to realize, there are various kinds of security, all compatible within limits, with a planned society. There is the security of a cooperative enterprise of free men; there is the security of an army machine; there is the security of a jail. No philosophy of a planned society is complete without an indication of what and whom we are planning for. We are, with good warrant, suspicious of those who speak of security, and *only* of security, for human beings can be secure and yet shackled—securely shackled. There is no wisdom in staking one's life and fortunes in a struggle for an abstract ideal of security unless we know something about the kind of men and women we hope to see developed, and the price that we may have to pay for that security. To these questions Marx replies with a theory of man which indicates that economic security is not the be-all and end-all of the good society but the conditioning framework for the activities of free, creative, critical, and adventuring human beings. This brings us to another fundamental principle of Marx's social philosophy which has been ignored by his critics and caricatured by many of his professed followers—Marx's humanism.

## 12. MARXIAN HUMANISM

Criticism of Marx's social philosophy has alternated between the charge of soulless materialism and demonic spiritualism. Familiarity with the early philosophy of Marx would dispel misconceptions of this kind. It is saturated with a Feuerbachianism which brims over with terms like "humanity" and "justice" and "brotherhood." His critique of Feuerbach sought to give these abstract terms a material content in the present historical period and not to deny the possibility of giving meaning to them. As a matter of fact, they pervade even his technical works in economic theory and are always in evidence when he makes a political appeal. I shall state three specific expressions of Marx's humanism. If they have an air of novelty, this only re-enforces the necessity of making sharper distinctions between Marx and contemporary Marxist movements.

(a) The first is Marx's recognition that property (not *capital*) and personality are indissolubly connected. Despite his rejection of the use which both Kant and Hegel make of their philosophy of property, he agrees with them that the possession of some property—articles of use and enjoyment—is necessary to the enjoyment of personality. There can be no effective freedom if we can call nothing our own. Without the possession of some things, whose nature and extent depend upon the historic period, the only personalities we can develop are those of saints or ascetics for whom the whole of life is a preparation for death. William James somewhere makes the same point in tracing the way in which our personalities extend to our clothes, books, and other personal effects.

The juridical essence of property is the right not so much to use as to exclude others from what we have. Consider the right of property, Marx argues, in the basic instruments of production in the modern historic period where the independent craftsman and journeyman are anachronisms. No one can reasonably claim that property in these things is necessary for the development of personality. They are not personal objects of use but impersonal instruments of social utility, operation of which provide the livelihood of the masses. The right of private property in instruments of production carries with it the power to exclude the masses from their use, a power exercised whenever business becomes unprofitable. Since this use is necessary to existence, such a right means power over the very lives of those who exist by using them. In other words, Marx recognized that power over things, more specifically the tools and resources of labor, means the power to hinder, thwart, and sometimes destroy human personality. It was this insight, together with the desire to free human beings from the arbitrary control which variations in the rate of profit exercised over them, that led him to his detailed studies of the nature and effects of capitalist accumulation. Before him, in the interests of human personality, men had fought for liberation from a secularly armed, *religious* authority. With the expansion of the productive forces of capitalism and the growth of enlightenment, men turned against the traditional forms of *political* despotism as incompatible with the "rights of man." It is as a phase of this struggle in the interests of human personality that we must understand Marx's proposal to end *economic tyranny*—a tyranny no less onerous for being, in the main, the unconscious result of unplanned economic behavior. He believed that it was possible by scientific husbandry and democratic control to provide abundance, freedom from economic care, for all members of the community.

(b) Another expression of Marx's humanism is to be found in his ideal of the *whole man*. Under conditions of modern life, there are two kinds of specialization—one freely chosen by individuals who seek appropriate outlets for their creative energy, and the other imposed upon man by the uncontrolled machine process and the necessity of earning a living. The second kind of specialization reduces man, so to speak, to a part of himself, it *depersonalizes* him, and leads him to think of his life as beginning just where his work ends. The individual thus finds his life segmentized so that there is no commerce between his desires and his deeds, his play and his labor, his ambition and his opportunities. The natural process of growth is replaced by accidental shifts of energy and interest which build no meaningful pattern. Sooner or later, the worker finds himself, when not unemployed and at loose ends, sunk into a mechanical routine whose monotony is punctuated by bursts of passion against whatever scapegoats convention, and those who interpret so-called public opinion, create for him. Or he lives in the dimension of make-believe which requires no active participation of any kind on his part.

Marx's ideal of the whole man entails a conception of labor which gratifies natural bent at the same time that it fulfills a social need. In this way what appears in our present social context as onerous drudgery is capable of acquiring a dignified status. Welcoming, as he does, the division of labor because it makes possible those levels of productivity in the absence of which there can be no equality of abundance, Marx is distrustful of the psychological effects of overspecializations of any kind, even those voluntarily acquired. An artist who can paint but cannot think, a thinker at home with abstractions but blind to color and deaf to sound, an engineer aware of the slightest flaw in steel and stone but insensitive to the subtle and complex character of human relationships, indeed, any individual who can do a particular job well and nothing else—all these for Marx are creatures who are only partly men.

It is patent that Marx was overly optimistic about the potentialities of creative achievement in men, both as individuals and as a collectivity. Always partial to the great classic ideals of antiquity, he adapted to an age of scientific technology the Greek conception of harmonious, all-around self-development. He does not, however, expect men to be revolutionized by doctrinal conversion or by education in a society which sharply separates school from life. In an early philosophic work, he writes, "By work man transforms nature," and adds in *Capital*, "By transforming nature [and society], man transforms himself." The process is gradual but neither automatic, inevitable, nor universal.

(c) A more striking expression of Marx's humanism, and one particularly noteworthy today in view of the Bolshevik-Leninist distortions of his meaning, is his *democratic* conception of social control. This constitutes an unambiguous answer to the question: What kind of security, what variety of socialism, did Marx think worth planning for? Marx envisaged the active participation of all members of the community to a point where the vocation of professional politicians would disappear—a rather naïve hope but one which bears testimony of his pervading faith in the democratic process. He refused to consider man merely as a producer, a living instrument employed to implement directives laid down for him from above, acquiescent to any sort of totalitarian rule if only it guaranteed him a minimum of creature comforts. The "producer" for Marx was also a user; and it was the decision of the user which ultimately determined the basic objectives of production. That was why Marx looked to the organization—the free organization—of producers and consumers to provide the effective political unit of the future.

Marx's objections to the "clerical socialism" of his day apply even more aptly to the national socialisms of our own day in Germany, Russia, and Italy. It is not only another form of economic servitude for the masses but a state of spiritual slavery. "But the proletariat," Marx confidently declares, "will not permit itself to be treated as canaille, it regards its courage, self-confidence, independence, and sense of personal dignity as more necessary than its daily bread." As a prediction, this has turned out to be tragically wrong; as a declaration of an ideal, it expresses what Marx believed, and what millions today still continue to believe, worth fighting and dying for.

Certain things follow at once from Marx's humanistic democracy. (i) Any criticism of existing democracy, no matter how imperfect, is justified only from the standpoint which seeks to extend the processes of democracy in personal, social, and political life or which seeks to bolster it against reaction. (ii) Socialism cannot be imposed upon the community from above by dictators who are always, so *they* claim, benevolent and wise, but who can be neither because of their fear of criticism and love of power. "The emancipation of the working class can only be accomplished by itself." (iii) Just as evident is it that the dictatorship of a minority political party which has a monopoly of all means of publication, education, housing, employment, and which, in effect, owns the instruments of production, is a police state not a socialist democracy. (iv) Under certain conditions, socialism without democracy—which is really no socialism at all—may be worse, much worse, than any capitalism that abides by the forms of political democracy.

Marx was a tough-minded realist. He anticipated stubborn opposition to the advance of the democratic process by an influential minority whose immediate interests, prestige, and posts of power would be adversely affected in the course of it. If it resorted to violence to nullify the popular mandate, it would be swept from its place by the iron broom of revolution. But, and he was always careful to make this clear, such action would require the support of the great majority of the community; it would not be the work of a minority of self-delegated saviors, or a putsch, or the private creation of one political party.

Like all the revolutionists of the nineteenth century, Marx thought of the revolution as a progressive historical event. Beneath the cross-currents of the political struggle, he saw in the socialist revolution a profoundly conserving force rather than a destructive one. It conserved, first of all, the great technical achievements of capitalism. These were to be used, in peace and not merely in war, to their full capacity, as a foundation upon which to build the structure of a new economy of human welfare. It preserved, even where reinterpretation might be undertaken, the cumulative cultural wealth of the past, carefully treasuring everything of genuine beauty and truth in the arts and sciences of the recent and remote past. The vicious nonsense of "the Bolshevization of culture," one of the most far-reaching and fateful slogans of the Russian Revolution, would have been set down by him as nothing more than a form of militant barbarism. Thirdly, the revolution was conceived by him as something which would preserve and extend the civil rights and liberties which had been won during the Protestant Reformation and French Revolution and which Marx regarded as an essential portion of the bequest of the past. Greater intellectual and cultural freedom, as well as a larger area of independence in personal life, were to be fortified by removing the economic restraints which previous religious and political revolutions had left untouched.

All this provides us with a triple criterion by which to determine, in any given case, whether a revolution has a genuine socialist content or whether it marks merely the change by which a group of lean bureaucrats replaces the fat. First, is the standard of living of the great masses of people higher than their standard of living under the most highly developed capitalism? Second, is the level of cultural activity and creation higher, or at least more inclusive, than what has hitherto been the rule under capitalism? Third, do the citizens of the community enjoy *at least* as much freedom of thought, speech, and action, as much freedom to criticize and disagree, as they possessed under the most enlightened of capitalism? Unless it be the case that in respect to all three of these questions, the answer is emphatically in the affirmative, the socialist revolution, as Marx conceived it, has not been achieved.

## 13. MEANS AND ENDS

If we evaluate the validity of Marx's ideas in the light of predictions which follow from them, we reach some interesting conclusions. Insofar as they bear upon what may be called the instrumental presuppositions of socialism—the economic structure of the new society which emerged within the shell of the old—they are, by and large, true. Insofar as they bear upon the question as to whether the generous social and political ideals of socialism would, as a matter of fact, be realized within this new institutional framework, they are almost completely false. Insofar as the failure of these ideals to be realized reflects upon their adequacy as leading principles of social life, judgment must be suspended.

Consider to what extent the following, more or less explicit, predictions of Marx and his followers have been realized: the concentration and centralization of capital and economic power, the ever closer alliance between government and economy, the development of rationalization of industry, the place of technological engineering, the mechanization of agriculture, the contraction of the free market and the growth of monopolies—in short, the features of what we know as corporate economy. Let us make no mistake about it. Despite local variations, the fundamental tendency of economic development shows substantially the same pattern in England, France, and the United States as in Germany, Russia, Italy, and Japan.

Consider, on the other hand, the poignant disparity between the predictions about the political, social, and cultural ideals, which were to be realized within the new economy, and what we find in sober fact. If we chart the situation as it exists today in all countries, we discover that there exists an inverse relation between the degree of integration of economic life and the degree of democracy in social and political life. There is both irony and pathos in a situation in which socialists of many countries look back with nostalgia to the freedoms of the capitalistic democracies they had once considered their mortal enemy.

The means of socialism, its economic instrumentalities, have proved not to be integral with the ends of socialism, as most Marxists have hitherto considered them. Obviously, the political methods of Marxism have also been found wanting, for reasons already discussed.

What, then, are we to conclude? Our conclusions will satisfy neither those who have already written autopsies of Marxism nor those doctrinal diehards who would count history well lost provided they did not have to declare Marxism wrong.

Our first conclusion is that the failure of socialist ideals to develop within the economic framework which makes them possible is, in the main, due to *the failure of men*. Not "the dialectic," whatever that is, not the level of productive forces, not the "laws" of the class struggle, are responsible but men. The debacle of Marxism represents a colossal *moral failure*—a failure of intelligence and courage. The lack of a positive moral philosophy among all the Marxist movements of the world and the substitution of organizational piety for a genuinely scientific study of the problems of social change, has revenged itself upon them.

Marxism as a movement is dying, and in many countries is already dead. Yet there is a living kernel in the thought and ideas it failed to develop. As a program of scientific activity in behalf of socialist ideals, fortified by the lessons of experience, rearmed with deeper moral and psychological insights, and prepared to learn what it really means to be scientific, these ideas still constitute a promising social philosophy. Embraced by the labor movement, farmers, professional groups, and their allies, whether under the name of Marxism, or as is more likely, under another name, it may once again become a living force. If no "Marxist" movement arises, these ideas will undoubtedly fructify political and social research; but as a program of action, it will be remembered only as an historical possibility, as something that "might have been," and take its place beside the great ghostly IFS of history. For the history that has already been made in its name has been made by its counterfeits—German Social-Democracy and Russian Bolshevism.

If a "Marxist" movement, as here understood, i.e., an organized activity to achieve, by applied intelligence, economic security, political freedom, and opportunities for cultural development in an essentially socialized economy, does not arise, then we must conclude that democracy as a way of life is incompatible with the structure of modern economy.

We cannot resign ourselves to this conclusion until several more efforts have been made in the coming generation.

[1940]

## NOTES

1. *Selected Works*, vol. 10, English ed., pp. 80 if. [italics in original].
2. Ibid., vol. 9, pp. 105, 121, 181–82.
3. Ibid., vol. 9, p. 842 [my italics].
4. Karl Marx, Introduction to *Critique of Political Economy* (Chicago: Kerr & Company, 1904), 269.
5. Gaetano Mosca, *The Ruling Classes*; Vilfredo Pareto, *Mind and Society*, esp. vol. 4; Robert Michels, *Political Parties*; Max Nomad, *Apostles of Revolution*.

6. Compare my *John Dewey: An Intellectual Portrait,* chap. 7 (New York: John Day, 1939).

7. In the United States, a *Fortune* poll indicates that most American workers believe that Henry Ford, the arch-opponent of labor unions, has done more for them than their own trade-union leaders.

# 7

# KARL MARX
# VERSUS
# THE COMMUNIST MOVEMENT

There is a double paradox in the expression "Karl Marx versus the Communist Movement." It results from the natural but unfortunate identification of Marx with the multitudinous varieties of Marxism offering their ideological wares today in his name. Currently there are almost as many types and kinds of Marxists in Europe, Asia, the Americas, and even Africa claiming the legacy of Marx as Christian cults professing fidelity to the authentic teachings of Christ. Logically, with respect to both historical figures, although their self-characterized disciples cannot all be right in their doctrinal interpretations, they may very well all be wrong or at least partial and inadequate.

The other kernel of the paradox is that although Marx described the ideal society that was coming on the wings of history as "communist," Communist societies as they exist everywhere today are in marked variance to the ideals that inspired his social vision and heroic personal commitment. The man who concluded the preface to his *magnum opus* with a defiant line from Dante, "Follow your own course and let people talk," would have come to a violent and inglorious end in any Communist country of the world whether it be China, Cuba, or the Soviet Union.

One may protest that freedom as the right and power of the individual to determine his own life may have been Marx's *personal* ideal, but that the kind of society he envisaged for the future was one in which

Sidney Hook, "Myth and Fact in the Marxist Theory of Revolution and Violence," *Journal of the History of Ideas* 34, no. 2 (1973): 271–80. © Journal of the History of Ideas, Inc. Reprinted with the permission of The Johns Hopkins University Press.

such freedom did not exist. His favorite slogan may have been "Doubt everything," but his classless society of the future was one in which the coordinated activities of its members would make effective doubt and its public expression irrelevant if not dangerous. There are many scholars who are convinced that Marx's projected ideal of a Communist society was one in which there would be no room for genuine individuality at all. Far from there being a variety of projects among which individuals would be able to choose, society would be ordered in such a way that there would be no more variation among its citizens than among the leaves of a multibranching tree or the bees in a hive. Society would function without dissension or conflict because its members would have been shaped by its institutions to coexist in functional harmony. In other words, the end of history would be a benign totalitarianism in which every person would know his place and no person would be out of place.

If one could imagine modern Communist societies ever solving their problems of legitimacy and productivity and the myriad of other endemic problems that breed hostility within and between them, this might be the upshot of their development. But there is overwhelming evidence that this was not Marx's ideal. Although he was reluctant to describe in any detail what the classless society of the future would be like, he says enough to indicate that it would be quite different from the benign totalitarianism some critics attribute to him or from any of the current varieties of malignant totalitarianism in Communist countries today. This can be established without reference to his early manuscripts, in which Marx was not yet a Marxist. It is implicit in the writings of his mature years.

These writings show how Marx conceives of the individual whom he regards as free. He is contrasted with the typical wage worker under capitalism who, although legally and politically free, is constrained by the necessity of earning his living from enjoying what Marx calls true freedom. In a striking passage Marx suggests that the worker's real life begins only when his working life is over.

> The worker who for twelve hours works, spins, drills, turns, builds, shovels, breaks stones, carries loads, etc.—does he consider this twelve hours' weaving, spinning, drilling, turning, building, shovelling, stone-hauling as a manifestation of his life, as life? On the contrary, life begins for him where this activity ceases, at the table, in the public house, in bed. The twelve hours labor has no meaning for him as weaving, spinning, drilling, etc., but as earnings which bring him to the table, to the

public house, into bed. If the silkworm were to spin in order to continue its existence as a caterpillar, it would be a complete wage-worker.[1]

The true realm of freedom for human beings is one in which the exertion of energy is directed by goals autonomously chosen by themselves, and not dictated by any other person's will or the necessities of the market. The first prerequisites for this state of affairs are an economy of abundance and superabundance and, for most people, the shortening of the working day. But these are not sufficient, for what Marx is saying is that with respect to the most important values of life, a man's work must be meaningful to him, not as a means to leisure or to the wherewithal on which his other pursuits depend, but as a way of fulfilling himself. For the free man work is not a curse but a vocation or calling in which he realizes his desirable potentials. There have always been a few fortunate human beings for whom earning a living is a satisfactory way of living one's life, but until now that has not been the human estate. Marx sought to generalize this ideal of work as a personal need as well as a fulfillment in the unrealistic expectation that the development of science and technology would not only abolish material want but all other scarcities as well. In such a situation every human being is viewed as a potential source of some creative thought or action.

Marx goes even further and lapses into a utopianism more extreme than any of the projections of his great predecessors. Influenced by the Greek ideal of the harmonious all-round developed personality and repelled by the extremes of specialization imposed by industrial society, he decries the division of labor. He suggests that any kind of professionalization is a deplorable one-sidedness that limits the powers of growth in other areas of human interest that are equally legitimate and worthy of cultivation.

The starting point of Marx's criticism of the effects of excessive specialization of labor under capitalism is legitimate enough, and from *The Communist Manifesto* to *Capital* he inveighs fiercely against it. The development of productive forces

mutilate the laborer into a fragment of a man, degrade him to the level of an appendage to a machine, destroy every remnant of charm in his work and turn it into hated toil; they estrange him from the intellectual potentialities of the labor process . . . they transform his lifetime into working-time, and drag his wife and child beneath the wheels of the juggernaut of capital.[2]

Whatever may have been true for the early days of capitalism, as a description today of the actual conditions of work for the overwhelming majority of wage earners this would be far from the mark. The excessive specialization of labor is a consequence of industrial society rather than of capitalism. Under nationalized industries, whether in capitalist or socialist economies, the assembly line still operates. The legitimate disapproval of excesses in the division of labor leads Marx into an unqualified denunciation of the principle of division of labor that takes him beyond the confines of common sense. But—and this is the relevant point—his very exaggeration indicates how he conceives of the individual.

The following passage is from *die deutsche Ideologie*, but the attack upon the division of labor, albeit recognized as a necessary evil in the development of capitalism, runs through all of Marx's writings:

> For as soon as the division of labor comes into being, each man has a particular, exclusive sphere of activity, which is forced upon him and from which he cannot escape. He is a hunter, a fisherman, a shepherd, or a critical critic [the reference here is to Bruno Bauer and his circle], and must remain so if he does not want to lose his means of livelihood; whereas in communist society, where no one has one exclusive sphere of activity but each can become accomplished in any branch he wishes, society regulates the general production and thus makes it possible for me to do one thing today and another tomorrow, to hunt in the morning, fish in the afternoon, rear cattle in the evening, criticize after dinner, just as I have a mind, without ever becoming hunter, fisherman, shepherd, or critic.[3]

We are trying to establish what Marx means by human freedom and individuality, not whether his conceptions are valid. I submit that this passage is sufficient to destroy completely the views of those who attribute to him the notion that he conceives of man in his ideal society as a creature in a beehive or as a leaf almost indistinguishable from other leaves on a tree. Marx's man had the individuality of a Leonardo da Vinci, capable of becoming accomplished in any branch of knowledge or skill he wishes, and free to turn from one accomplishment to another day by day. Such a man would be unfit for any totalitarian society and would certainly be barred from the enlightened totalitarianism of the Platonic Republic.

Taken literally such a man would be as rare as a Leonardo, and the notion that he could be *everyman* is an absurdity. It runs counter to the well-attested insight of Goethe and Charles Feirce that the secret of great achievement lies in limitation, and that when an ordinary man tries his hand at everything he is not likely to do anything of great significance. All we need to do to show its bizarre character is to recast Marx's schedule of activities in terms of modern vocations and avocations "to perform brain surgery in the morning, engage in nuclear research in the afternoon, do some gene splicing in the evening, and conduct a symphony after dinner, just as I have a mind to, without ever becoming a brain surgeon, or nuclear physicist, or geneticist, or conductor." Not even the Greek freeman, whose physical needs were supplied by slaves, had that degree of versatility. Marx's citizen of the future was certainly an individual, but his mode of life suggests the hopeless amateurism of a British squire. Capitalism did not create the brutalized "man with a hoe." Marx may have been justified in writing of "the idiocy of rural life" in 1847, but no one familiar with the mode of existence of the small farmer today—even in Tuscany—despite his precarious economic future, can properly characterize it in the same way.

When we inquire what kind of society would nurture and sustain an association of such individuals, all of whom are as different as they choose to be, it becomes clear that it is a society of anarchism wishfully imputed by Marx to the objective processes of history. By anarchism Marx meant more than a social organization characterized by the absence of state power of any kind. In more positive terms, anarchism, which is interchangeable with the highest phase of Communism as described in his *Critique of the Gotha Program*, is a community of harmonious self-determined individuals whose association gives rise naturally to forms of accepted authority and legitimacy without the presence of any coercive institutions whatsoever. That Marx could believe in the viability of such a society testifies to his faith not only in the perfectability of man but in a secular millenarianism as extreme as any of his great utopian predecessors. Marx was amused by the fantasies of a Fourier, who expected the applied science of the future to transform the seas into potable lemonade, but he was serious about the possibility of transforming human beings into creatures of an angelic nature by modifying their social institutions, despite the empirical evidence that geniuses from Leonardo to Marx himself were conspicuously lacking in those traits that made for harmonious relations with others. It was not the ideals of man professed by the utopians of the past or their vision of a harmonious community of persons with which Marx took issue, but only with the methods they advocated to achieve them.

Another feature of Marx's thought that should dispel the myth that he had no conception of genuine individuality is his impatience with egalitarianism. To him the belief in the moral and political equality of all members of society no more entailed that they would receive the same treatment, goods, offices, and rewards than the belief that everyone is morally entitled to medical care implied that everyone is to receive the same treatment regardless of his or her ailment. Parents know that it is possible to love their children equally without treating them identically. It is more legitimate to criticize Marx's ideal for its unrealistic assumption that an entire community can be organized by the same loving relationship that exists in a family, bound together by ties of affection, than to conflate his ideal with the organizing principle or discipline that binds an army. Marx's impatience with egalitarianism expresses itself in his rejection of the view that even the introduction of a uniform principle of distribution or reward for services or labor under socialism will result in equality. That is to say, even when private ownership in the instruments of social production has been abolished and the socialist state that has replaced the employers undertakes to treat everyone by the same principle or standard, equality will not result. Different individuals will end up with more or less than others by virtue of their natural inequalities. As Marx puts it, "they would not be different individuals if they were not unequal." The same holds true in the golden future in which individuals are rewarded, not according to their labor time or what they produce, but according to their needs. Needs, once we go beyond the basic needs of food, clothing, and shelter, are so variable and elastic that they could hardly be used to define self-identity. Not only is Marx's ideal community one of a vast plurality of different persons, it is also one in which the personalities of its denizens are not fixed.

That Marx apparently sees no problem in conceiving of this multitude of individuals voluntarily coordinating their activities as "associated producers rationally regulating their intercourse with nature" and each other, a complex planned society in which interlocking schedules for the movement of vast numbers of men and materials must mesh, is a mystery. In the absence of any coercive power, what will make things happen and guarantee the cornucopia of universal abundance once the rational will of men and women does not manifest itself? These are troublesome questions not only for Marx; they face any anarchist view that imagines that the administration of things can ever replace the administration of human beings who unlike bees in a hive or leaves on a tree, have purposes that are often at cross purposes with each other.

Only a naive person would believe that modern transportation in our crowded cities and express highways can flow safely and expeditiously without traffic rules. It is hardly less naive to believe that all that is required, once traffic rules are established, is the presence of someone to direct the flow of traffic. To be sure, such persons do not require the badge of authority to exercise their task. But unless they have at their call the power of a coercive authority to arrest drunken drivers and other alleged lawbreakers, and courts to determine their guilt or innocence, before long the transportation system would be in chaos.

What is distinctive about Marx is not the ideal of a cooperative commonwealth of freedom-loving individuals for whom private property in the instruments of social production does not exist. This was the common coin of many socialist and anarchist groups of his day. He differentiated himself from them, first, by his theory of social change that tried to spell out the objective historical conditions that had to be fulfilled before such a society could become a realistic possibility; and second, by his views about the means and methods to be followed in the struggle to actualize it. Although Marx's writings are neither clear nor consistent, the general drift of his meaning can be discovered when considered in their historical context.

Failure to take into account the historical context of Marx's thought and a too literal reading of his text sometimes makes nonsense of his meaning. It has led to the strange view that because for Marx ethical judgments are not completely autonomous of social and economic facts and tendencies, that therefore Marx had no moral theory. This accounts for his repudiation of any attempt to justify socialism on the basis of principles of justice or humanity. It is granted—indeed, it is sometimes insisted upon—that the overwhelming motivation for the support of Marx's proposals in the West is rooted in feelings and judgments that the inequalities of distribution under capitalism are unjust. But this is taken to be evidence of Marx's confusion and incoherence on the subject of morality and the relation between the factual and the normative.

For Marx morality is natural, social, and, at its best, rational. He differs from both Kant and Hegel. For Kant morality is ultimately independent of any empirical consequences. It expresses imperatives that transcend the facts of nature and human nature. "Let justice prevail though the heavens fall" is a Kantian dictum that Marx's position rejects as fanatical. There is something wrong with a conception of justice that results not only in the destruction of human life but in all the other moral values associated with the possibility of intelligent social life. On the other hand, partly as a response to the formalistic and nonnatural elements in Kant's stark opposition between the empirical and the ideal, Hegel elaborated a doctrine that, despite its obscurities and ambiguities, identified the actual or real with the ideal or what ought to be. The brutal upshot of this view is that whatever is, is right, or with respect to history, "Die Weltgeschichte ist das Weltgericht."

When Marx abandoned Hegelian idealism he unfortunately retained some of the Hegelian terminology. Although his writings are pervaded by passionate ethical judgments, he never developed a systematic ethical theory. His impatience with do-gooders and those preaching either the doctrine of love or salvation by violence as solutions to the social problem led him to deny that his condemnation of the evils of capitalism was based on any judgment of its injustice. Sometimes it resulted in his writing sentences that seem downright silly if the historic context of moral judgment is disregarded. For example, in trying to explain the differences in the schemes of distribution between the lower and higher stages of Communism, he declares: "Right can never be higher than the economic structure of and the cultural development of society conditioned by it." Taken literally, this means that there can be no rational justification for urging support of a social system like that of socialism or even of the welfare state with a more equitable system of distribution while the capitalist economy is functioning which would cut the nerve of agitation for a better society. This position would make unintelligible the meaning of the term "higher" when Marx speaks of "right" as higher or lower. If the concept of right can never be differentiated from a specific economic structure, what independent meaning can be given it? The higher right would simply reflect the higher economic structure. But unless "the higher economic" structure already involved an implicit value or moral judgment, all Marx would be saying is that every economic structure has a different concept of right, whether it be a primitive cannibalistic society that lives by war and in which all captives are owned and eaten in common, an Asiatic despotism, a slave society, or a feudal, or capitalist, or socialist society. We could not morally order such societies. Under such circumstances what sense would it make for those living in a slave society morally to condemn it? On what grounds could we morally approve the revolt of Spartacus, or the leaders of the Peasant Wars, or of the Paris Commune who sought to overthrow the economic structure under which they lived, in the light of moral ideals different from those that prevailed at the time?

Yet, despite Marx's unfortunate formulation, what he is saying makes sense—even common sense. This may be conveyed in the form of a parable. Suppose two castaways find themselves the only survivors on an island. After making a survey of its resources, A proposes that they dig a well for water. B refuses in the expectation that their luck will turn and rain or rescue will come in time. The digging is difficult and toilsome for A, aggravated by B's mockery of his efforts. Neither rain nor succor arrives, but at the point of utter exhaustion after several days, A opens up a seam of gushing water. B by this time is parched and requests some of the water. Would it be right for A to deny it to him? Since there is no alternative supply and B cannot survive without water, A's refusal to share some of the water would be tantamount to a sentence of death, a punishment whose severity seems disproportionate to B's thoughtlessness and irresponsibility. Since the water is so plentiful, most of it beyond any possible use by A, running out into the sand, it would be unjust to deprive B of any share of it.

Change the material condition of the problem. Suppose as a consequence of his labor, A finds an amount of water sufficient to keep only one person alive. Would it be wrong for him to deny B a share of it? Certainly not. We might praise him for his generosity or saintliness if he does share the water with B. But we could not justifiably condemn him if he refused to assume these roles.

What is the difference in the applicability of these two principles of distribution? Obviously the difference in supply. If any good or service is as plentiful and costless as air, we do not need any principle of distribution. Marx assumed that would be the case with respect to all human needs in a world of unlimited energy. We have seen how utopian such an assumption is. There will always be relative scarcities, if only with respect to temporal priority in the consumption of what is ultimately universally distributed. And with respect to the awards of honor, prizes, recognition—the very situation is defined in terms of scarcity. Not everyone can come in first.

We cannot do without some ethical principles. The fact that they are applied differently in different historical situations where material conditions are varied does not gainsay their validity. It is clear that Marx recognizes several ethical principles—not only the absence of needless suffering, but dignity, self-respect, intellectual independence, and the right to individual self-fulfillment—i.e., the development of one's desirable potential abilities. He does not seek to reduce them to each other, but assumes that in a rational, cooperative, socialized society mankind has the best possibility of realizing them. Although democracy was for him a political concept that was to be introduced wherever it was absent in any modern society and extended to other areas in societies in which it was present, when we bear in mind his concept of individual freedom, it is not reading a foreign element into his thought to say that for him the functioning of an authentic socialist society could be characterized as democracy as a way of life.

But how can such a faith be reconciled with advocacy of "the dictatorship of the proletariat?" This phrase, employed by Marx three or four times in the course of millions of words, fell into desuetude in the international socialist movement after his death and was revived by Lenin and his followers shortly before they seized power in Russia in October 1917. The meaning of the phrase is hotly contested for it combines political and economic connotations. A clue to Marx's meaning is that he contrasts "the dictatorship of the proletariat," not with "the democratic rule of the proletariat," but with "the dictatorship of the bourgeoisie." The latter exists whenever the conflict of economic interests between the working dass and its employers—which follows from the economic structure of class society—is systematically resolved in favor of the employers. According to Marx and Engels, this is the case regardless of whether the political system of capitalist society is autocratic or democratic, monarchical or republican. Whether it was England and the United States, imperial Germany, or czarist Russia, the dictatorship of the bourgeoisie operated.

The socialist revolution that exemplifies "the dictatorship of the proletariat" is transitional until it abolishes all classes. Marx's conception of class is narrowly defined in terms of the role men play in the mode of economic production. Once production is socialized, then by definition, since ownership is vested in the entire community, economic classes no longer exist. Marx apparently assumed that any other conception of class would not carry with it the possibility of exploitation, great disparities in standards of living, and conflicts over the distribution of social wealth—assumptions shattered in every country today whose economy is collectivized. Presumably an orthodox Marxist would argue in Marx's defense that this outcome, the emergence of "a new class" or a "privileged bureaucracy," was to be expected because the objective conditions of genuine social equality were lacking in the countries in which collectivism had been introduced and that they were therefore unripe and unready for

Socialism. This is precisely what Karl Kautsky and the leading Social Democratic followers of Marx maintained in contradistinction to the Bolshevik-Leninist-Stalinist view. However, even if in the light of historical development one grants that Marx's vision of socialism as a cooperative commonwealth of free and socially equal individuals was transformed into a totalitarian despotism by the Bolshevik-Leninist disregard of Marx's principle of historical materialism, this would not be a confirmation of that principle. For although it would explain why Socialism or Communism, even in its first phase, failed in Russia and the other underdeveloped countries in which it had been introduced, it would not explain the attempt to introduce it, and the peculiar economy—neither capitalist nor socialist—and totalitarian culture that resulted from it.

But how was it possible for the Bolshevik-Leninists who began their political careers convinced that they were the executors of the Marxist legacy to end up as the chief executioner of its theories and ideals? How was it that, intent upon liberating the working class from the yoke of capitalist society, they fastened an even more oppressive yoke on the workers and, in the judgment of some erstwhile sympathizers, discredited the entire idea of socialism in our time? Perhaps the single most important explanation lay in the transformation of that unfortunate phrase of Marx, "the dictatorship of the proletariat"—unfortunate in that Marx's meaning could have been expressed without the use of the term "dictatorship"—into the dictatorship of the Communist Party *over* the proletariat and all other classes.

According to Marx and Engels, revolution can be violent or peaceful depending upon the presence of democratic political possibilities, but whether peaceful or not, the socialist revolution must be democratic. At the time of the *Communist Manifesto* there were no realistic possibilities in view of the severe restrictions on suffrage that profound social change could be introduced through parliamentary means. Indeed the *Manifesto* indicates that among the first things that would be done after the revolution would be to introduce democratic institutions. Nonetheless both Marx and Engels assumed that revolutionary action even under oppressive or narrowly restrictive political institutions would have the support of the majority of the population behind it, and that it could justifiably be considered democratic. (The empirical evidence, however, that the working class actually constituted a majority of the population was lacking. It was based on an extrapolation of certain economic tendencies of capitalist development.) Subsequently, Marx and Engels, as is well known, anticipated the possibility that socialism could be introduced peacefully by parliamentary means in countries like England, the United States, and Holland. Toward the end of his life Engels explicitly declared that "the dictatorship of the proletariat" could express itself under the political form of the bourgeois parliamentary republic.

Marx and Engels and their followers disassociated themselves strongly from men like Blanqui and Bakunin on two grounds. The first was the latter's failure to recognize the controlling importance of the objective economic-social situation as providing a necessary condition for a successful political revolution. The second was their undisguised elitism. For Marx "the emancipation of the working class can be achieved only by the working class." This is of central significance in distinguishing between Marx's conception of revolution and the Leninist-Stalinist (Bolshevik) view. *There is not a line in Marx's writings that states or implies that "the dictatorship of the proletariat" must be exercised through "the dictatorship of the Communist Party."*

For Marx the concept of dictatorship, as we have seen, is primarily social and economic. The "dictatorship of the bourgeoisie" refers to the fact that the rule of the bourgeoisie is to its own economic advantage and to the economic disadvantage of the working class. But the dictatorship of the bourgeoisie could be exercised either through democratic or nondemocratic political forms. For Lenin, on the other hand, "dictatorship" is primarily a political concept. "Dictatorship," he tells us, "is rule based directly upon force and unrestricted by any laws." It is really unmitigated *Faustrecht*. Whereas for Marx and Engels "the dictatorship of the proletariat" could be established through peaceful parliamentary victory, for Lenin "the revolutionary dictatorship of the proletariat is rule won and maintained by the use of violence by the proletariat against the bourgeoisie, rule that is unrestricted by any laws."[4]

In contradistinction to Marx and Engels, Lenin proceeds to interpret the "dictatorship of the proletariat" as viable only through the dictatorship of the Communist Party, which constitutes a small minority of the population many of whose members are not even proletarians. Although Marx and Engels' interpretation of the Paris Commune of 1871 as a socialist revolution is extremely dubious, nonetheless they both refer to it as an exemplification of "the dictatorship of the proletariat" in which there was no dictatorship of any political party whatsoever. The followers of Blanqui seemed to be most numerous, than the followers of Proudhon, while the partisans of Marx and Engels, whose chief spokesman was Leo

Frankel, were miniscular. Actually there was no basic socialist content whatsoever to the reforms of the Paris Commune. No industries were socialized. The abolition of night work for bakers was no more socialist than the abolition of child labor and other "bourgeois" reforms. The real achievements of the Paris Commune, whose launching Marx disapproved, was the extension of democratic processes and principles, most of which could be implemented in a nonsocialist economy. The Leninist view that the Russian socialist revolution of October 1917 is a continuation or fulfillment of the heritage of the Paris Commune is sheer myth.

Lenin makes no bones about the fact that "the dictatorship of the proletariat" is exercised through "the dictatorship of the Communist Party." In his pamphlet on *The Infantile Sickness of Left Communism*, he states: "Not a single important political or organizational question is decided by any state institution in our republic without the guiding instructions of the Central Committee of the Party." And Stalin, here as elsewhere when he touches on doctrinal matters, echoes his teacher:

> Here in the Soviet Union, in the land of the dictatorship of the proletariat, the fact that not a single important political or organizational question is decided by our Soviet and other mass organizations without directions from the Party must be regarded as the highest expression of the leading role of the Party. *In this sense* it could be said that the dictatorship of the proletariat is in essence the "dictatorship of its vanguard," "the dictatorship" of its Party, as the main guiding force of the proletariat.[5]

If, as Lenin declares, "dictatorship is rule based directly upon force and unrestricted by any laws," the dictatorship of the Party entails that it may very well be a dictatorship, not *of* the proletariat, but *over* the proletariat as well as over others.

Aware of the enormity of this transformation of the concept of the "dictatorship of the proletariat" into the "the dictatorship of the Communist Party," Lenin and other Bolshevik leaders adopted several semantic devices to conceal their abandonment of the democratic component of the Marxist theory. In the early years the exigencies of the struggle for power led them to a forthrightness of utterance that becomes qualified in subsequent apologetic rationalizations when faced by critics invoking Marx's democratic principles.

Nothing signifies the non-Marxist undemocratic stance of Bolshevik-Leninism more clearly than Lenin's writings on the Constituent Assembly. Referring to his thesis on the Constituent Assembly, Lenin observes:

> My thesis says clearly and repeatedly that the interests of the revolution
> are higher than the formal rights of the Constituent Assembly. The
> formal democratic point of view is precisely the point of view of the
> bourgeois democrat who refuses to admit that the interests of the pro-
> letariat and of the proletarian class struggle are supreme.[6]

The plain meaning of this declaration exposes as a hypocritical
rationalization the pretexts Lenin offers for forcibly dispersing the Constituent Assembly after the Bolsheviks' miserable showing in the elections (19 percent) and after the Social Revolutionary and Menshevik
majority refused to accept Lenin's ultimatum to yield power to the Bolsheviks. Justifying his refusal to accept the legitimacy of the Constituent
Assembly, Lenin claims that although elections to the Constituent
Assembly had been held *after* the Bolsheviks seized power in October,
the mood or sentiment of the masses had changed by early January and
that in reality they favored the Bolsheviks.[7] Rosa Luxemburg, in sharply
criticizing Lenin's view, retorted that if this were so, the Bolsheviks could
have called for new elections without disputing the legitimacy of the
Constituent Assembly, particularly since in their propaganda against
Kerensky they had agitated so fiercely for the convocation of the Constituent Assembly.

In the light, however, of Lenin's thesis on the Constituent Assembly
cited above, his *ex post facto* talk about improper lists and unrepresen-
tative elections is revealed as a feeble and irrelevant cover-up. Assume
that the election on the basis of new lists had been as democratic as
Lenin had desired. If, as he unwaveringly claims, "the interests of the
proletariat and the proletarian class struggle are supreme," what difference would it have made to Lenin if the new electoral results showed that
the Russian masses had even more completely repudiated the Bolsheviks
than they did on the basis of the old lists? Would Lenin have recognized
the sovereignty of the Constituent Assembly? Certainly not! For if, as he
insists, "the interests of the proletariat," as interpreted by the Bolsheviks, of course, are "supreme," Lenin would have felt justified by his
political philosophy to take power against the Constituent Assembly
even if it had an overwhelming mandate from the masses—provided he
could get away with it.

If there is any doubt about this, an analysis of Lenin's article "On
Slogans" will confirm it.[8] When Lenin seeks excuses to ban the Constituent Assembly, he bases himself on the authority of the Soviets. But
in July 1917 when his article "On Slogans" was published he repudiates

the slogan "All Power to the Soviets" because the Soviets "are dommated by the Social Revolutionary and Menshevik parties."[9] In January, having seized power and already begun the terror, and after having acquired a majority in the Soviets of Petrograd and Moscow, the slogan "All Power to the Soviets" is restored and used as a foil and excuse to prorogue the Constituent Assembly. In every case what is decisive for Lenin is the question of *power*, not the question of democracy, formal or concrete, or representation, authentic or not, viz., whether the Bolshevik Party has a likely prospect of seizing and retaining power.

Lenin and Stalin explicitly disavow Marx's belief that socialism could be legally and peacefully achieved through the democratic political process in countries like England and the United States. Further, the conditions of affiliation to the Third International drawn up by Lenin imposed on *every* Communist Party of the world, the organization of illegal cadres and the resort to armed insurrection in the conquest of political power in all countries, including "the most free in the world." Even ambiguity on this point was not tolerated except as a linguistic maneuver to disarm the political enemy and to win suffrance to organize the seizure of power. The Russian road to power became the paradigm for all Communist Parties of the world under the discipline of the Third International. This may be illustrated in the programmatic declaration of William Z. Foster, head of the Communist Party of the United States, at a time when it enjoyed complete legality and freedom of propaganda:

> Even before the seizure of power, the workers will organize the Red Guard. Later on this loosely constructed body becomes developed into a firmly-knit, well-disciplined Red Army. The leader of the revolution in all its stages is the Communist Party. . . . Under the dictatorship all the capitalist parties—Republican, Democratic, Progressive, Socialist, etc.,will be liquidated, the Communist Party functioning alone as the party of the toiling masses. Likewise will be dissolved all other organizations that are political props of bourgeois rule, including Chambers of Commerce, employers' associations, rotary clubs, American Legion, Y.M.C.A. and such fraternal orders as the Masons, Odd Fellows, Elks, Knights of Columbus, etc.[10]

Under Khrushchev's rule the Leninist dogma of the inevitability of war between the Communist world and the Western world was abandoned, although the inevitability of world Communist victory was still proclaimed. But the insistence upon the view that the triumph and rule

196 SIDNEY HOOK ON PRAGMATISM, DEMOCRACY, AND FREEDOM

of the revolution could be achieved only through "the dictatorship of the party" was retained. It was asserted that the Communist Party in a "coalition" with other parties might come to power peacefully, but only if the Communist Party exercised leadership, which meant at least control of the Ministry of the Interior (police).

An analysis of the concept of "the dictatorship of the party" in official Communist literature (as well as the historical evidence) will show that even where Communist Parties, either alone or in formal coalition, come to power peacefully, their rule is based upon continuous exercise of force and violence. For, to repeat, the very meaning of "dictatorship," in the words of Lenin, "is rule based directly upon force and unrestricted by any laws." This dictatorship is directed not only against overt hostile elements seeking to restore the overthrown economic and social order, but against any dissenting thought in art, literature, science, and philosophy of which the Central Committee of the Communist Party disapproves.

With some variations, depending upon a number of historical and national factors, all Communist states that profess to be inspired by Leninist doctrine follow the Russian Soviet pattern, which is demonstrably incompatible with Marx's and Engels' commitment to socialist democracy and their criticism of elitist rule. These Communist views have remained unaffected by the Sino-Soviet split and by the emergence of "polycentrism."

Naturally, in democratic Western countries where there are large Communist Parties (and/or dissident Communist groups critical of the Leninist tradition) engaged in the parliamentary political process, attempts have been made to soften and tone down the harsh features of Leninist principles according to which "the dictatorship of the proletariat" results in the terror of a Communist Party dictatorship of varying degrees of intensity over the proletariat and all other groups of the population until the advent of the classless society. In these countries some theoretical spokesmen of Communism tend to blur the difference between the Marxist views on revolution, including the possibility of a peaceful transition to socialism through a multiparty democratic political process, and the Communist-Leninist position.

The lineaments of that position not long ago were authoritatively restated by the Institute of Marxism-Leninism of the Central Committee of the Communist Party of the Soviet Union, and reprinted in the Soviet official theoretical journal *Kommunist* (No. 3, 1972) under the title "Falsifiers of the Theory of Scientific Communism and their Bankruptcy." It is directed against Communist dissidents, characterized as "modern revisionists," who envisage the transition from capitalism to socialism as a process of "evolution" or "reform" or "renovation," and who believe that "the dictatorship of the proletariat" is possible without the dictatorship or leadership (a euphemism for dictatorship) of the Communist Party. The article declares:

> We know the numerous statements in which V. I. Lenin developed the basic Marxist thesis that the dictatorship of the proletariat is inconceivable without the leadership of the Communist Party. Practical experience has shown that even the existence of a multiparty system does not refute the necessity of such leadership. The Communist Party is the vanguard of the working class, its most conscious, organized and unified part. Only under the leadership of the Party can the working class implement its dictatorship over the defeated exploiting classes.

As if to leave no doubt that the Leninist line applies not only to the seizure of political power but to its exercise after the Communist Party has come to power, the article concludes:

> The grave consequences of any attempt to depart from the Marxist-Leninist teaching on the leading role of the Party and to renounce Leninist organizational principles are well illustrated by the events of 1968 in Czechoslovakia.

Although Marx's views on revolution, violence, and democracy are quite different from those identified as Bolshevik-Leninist, they suffer from certain basic difficulties, some of which have already been adverted to and others developed in subsequent chapters. Most of them flow from the failure clearly to recognize the primacy of political freedom in relation to all other desirable social and cultural freedoms, and the consequent underestimation of the possibility of modifying the economic structure of society by political democratic means.

Whatever the inadequacies of Marx's theory of revolution are, his commitment to a *scientific* or rational method of achieving a nonexploitative society permits—actually it should encourage—a modification of his specific views on political strategy in the light of historical evidence and shifting social forces. Marx was not born a socialist and certainly not a Marxist. What was distinctive about his theories concerning how socialism—which *au fond* was an extension of democracy to a way of life—was to be achieved have largely been disproved by historical events.

History, alas!, has been guilty of lese-Marxism. Marx underestimated the capacity of capitalist societies to raise the standard of living of its population, including even the longevity of the working class; he underestimated the growth and intensity of nationalism; he was mistaken in interpreting all forms of coercion and exploitation as flowing from private ownership of the social means of production; he ignored the prospect of bureaucratic forms of collectivism; and the very possibility of war between collectivist economies, illustrated in the nuclear threat of Communist Russia against Communist China, was inconceivable to him by definition. As we have seen, he shared the naïveté of anarchist thinkers in believing that the state would disappear with universal collectivism, and that "the administration of things" could ever completely replace administration by men and women and the possibility of its abuse. He underestimated the role of personality in history, and although he contributed profoundly to our understanding of the determining influence, direct and indirect, of the mode of economic production on many aspects of culture, he exaggerated the degree of its determination and its "inevitability" and "necessity." That is why those who have learned most from Marx, if faithful to his own commitment to the scientific, rational method, should no more consider themselves "Marxists" today than modern biologists should consider themselves "Darwinians" or modern physicists "Newtonians." "Marxism" today signifies an ideology in Marx's original sense of that term, suggestive more of a religious than of a strictly scientific or rational outlook on society.

In speaking of Marx's failure to do justice to personality in history, one may cite the life and work of Lenin, the greatest revisionist of Marx, as decisive evidence. The Russian Revolution of October 1917 has been regarded as among the most influential events, and some have even characterized it as *the* most influential event because of its consequences upon world history. Yet it is incontestable that if Lenin had not lived there would in all likelihood have been no Russian October Revolution.[11] Among the fateful consequences of the October Revolution under Lenin's guidance was the creation of the Communist International, which organized Communist Parties in most of the countries of Europe, Asia, and America. Its chief accomplishment was to split the European working class in the face of threats of social and political reaction.

It has been argued by some that the October Revolution was responsible for reforms introduced in non-Communist countries and that the development of the Welfare State was primarily motivated out of fear of domestic Communist revolution abetted by the armed intervention of the Red Army. It would be very hard to establish such a thesis. The history of political and social reform in Western Europe and America was impressive long before the Russian Revolution, and was primarily the result of indigenous class struggles that resulted in the extension of the democratic ethos to economic and social life. The New Deal in the United States, for example, as well as the emergence of the Welfare State in Great Britain, were in no way undertaken to meet any danger of a domestic Communist revolution.

It is far closer to the truth to assert that rather than inspiring democratic social reforms in the Western world, the Bolshevik Revolution and the operation of the Communist International were largely responsible for the rise of Fascism in Italy and Nazism in Germany. They not only weakened the democratic structure of pre-Mussolini Italy and Weimar Germany by splitting the working class, but by their activities, including abortive attempts at insurrection, they enlarged the mass base and support for the demagogic propaganda of the forces of social reaction. It is not unlikely that if there had been no October Revolution and attempts by the Communist International, serving as the instrument of the Kremlin, to organize revolutions in western Europe, there would have been no victory of Fascism in Italy and of Hitlerism in Germany. It may be difficult to predict in detail what the history of western Europe would have been if Lenin had not succeeded in overthrowing Kerensky's regime and destroying the democratic Constituent Assembly. In the light of what actually did occur as a consequence of the rule of Bolshevism—Fascism and Nazism—it is hard to see what could have been worse.

It remains to ask what light this analysis casts on identifying contemporary expressions of Marxism with respect to revolutionary thought and action. A position, of course, may be morally sound or justifiable regardless of whether it is Marxist or not. The question I pose here is this: what are the criteria for determining the truth of the claim of any party program or activity, independently of its own labels, to be Marxist? For example, on the above analysis, any movement based on the ideas of Herbert Marcuse is clearly non-Marxist. This follows not only from his repudiation of the working class as unfit for the role and honor of carrier of the socialist idea, but because of his undisguised elitism and unabashed justification of forcible repression of ideas, persons, or institutions that are not "progressive" according to his lights. Here Marcuse is a faithful Leninist.

Where socialist parties, alone or in alliance with others, come to power through the democratic political process, the crucial question is whether or not they permit freedom of political propaganda to parties that reject their program, and in the event of an electoral defeat, relinquish the reins of government to those who have won the support of the majority. Any political party, regardless of what it calls itself, that holds on to power by refusing to conduct free elections or to abide by their consequences is not Marxist.

The theory of Marxism makes no claim that the working masses are always right or even aware of what is to their best interests. At any definite time a Marxist party may know better than the masses what their best interests are. But this knowledge does not give it any right to impose upon the masses a program in opposition to their wishes and will. Indeed, this is integral to the very meaning of "democracy" in any political context.

In envisaging the democratic road to political power, Marx and Engels were realistic in considering the possibility of an antidemocratic revolt to defeat the will of the majority. This possibility has led some Leninists to justify the seizure of power without the support of the majority of the population, and when in power, to repress parties and individuals who dissent from the socialist program, and even from the Leninist version of that program, on the pretext that they *may* revolt. But such rationalizations are transparent evidence that they have no faith in the democratic process.

In dealing with children or mental incompetents, it is sometimes necessary, and therefore justifiable, to act in behalf of their genuine interests even when it runs against their wishes and will. What Marx would have thought of such procedure with respect to the proletariat or working class may be inferred from his declaration that this class "regards its courage, self-confidence, independence and sense of personal dignity as more necessary than its daily bread."[12] Marx may have been wrong in believing this, but it is not wrong that he believed it.

Mistaken as Marx's historical theories and economic predictions may have been or turn out to be, and regardless of the crimes and infamies committed in his name in the Soviet and Chinese Gulag Archipelagos, a critical but objective assessment of his ideas justifies including him in the calendar of fighters for human freedom. Hegel would not have recognized his progeny in Marx nor Marx in Lenin. The intellectual sins, like all sins of the fathers, should not be visited on the heads of their children. There is even less warrant for attributing the sins of the children to their fathers, especially when there is strong doubt of their legitimacy.

[1973]

## NOTES

1. "Wage Labor and Capital," *Collected Works,* vol. 9, p. 203.
2. *Capital,* vol. 1, p. 645
3. *Collected Works,* vol. 5, p. 275.
4. *Selected Works* [Moscow 1951], vol. 2, pt II, p. 41 if.
5. *Foundations of Leninism* [Moscow 1934], chap. 8.
6. *Selected Works,* p. 78.
7. Ibid., p. 81
8. *Selected Works,* p. 87 ff.
9. Ibid., p. 95
10. *Towards Soviet America* (New York: Coward-McCann, 1932), 275.
11. Compare my *The Hero in History: A Study in Limitation and Possibility* (New York: John Day, 1943).
12. *Gesamtausgabe,* Abt. I, Bd.6, p. 278.

# 8
# THE CULT OF REVOLUTION

The theme of this chapter concerns a disturbing phenomenon in the recent cultural and political life of the United States but not only of the United States. Although it is more muted elsewhere, signs of it are apparent in other industrial countries of the West. I refer to the emergence of a revolutionary political perspective encouraging deliberate episodic resorts to violence in hopes of precipitating consequences, including reprisals, that will increase the potential of revolutionary change and the ultimate likelihood of its success. These episodes sometimes evoke justifications for violence in the guise of explanations, penned by intellectual sympathizers, who maintain that those who initiate the violence are really the victims of society, not the aggressors. When the aggression is so bestial and unprovoked that it cannot be regarded as a defensive action, the bold claim is made that ethically crimes of the weak against the strong must be judged in a different light from other crimes.

To some extent this shift to a revolutionary stance has been facilitated by the climate of opinion of our time, and by the very idioms in which we discourse about change. During the nineteenth century the term "evolution" was extended from biology, the field of its primary application, not only to all the arts and sciences but to the universe itself. Sometimes the historical approach itself was carelessly identified with

From *Revolution, Reform, and Social Justice—Studies in the Theory and Practice of Marxism* (New York: New York University Press, 1975). Reprinted by permission of the Estate of Sidney Hook.

the evolutionary approach. By the end of the century the term "evolution," independently of a specific context, was so vague that despite its vogue it had little cognitive significance.

In the twentieth century a similar fate has overtaken the term "revolution." Never has there been a century in which judging by its literature have so many revolutions occurred in so many societies and nations, and in so many diverse disciplines and fields of thought. In no previous century has so large a proportion of books been published which flaunt the term, "revolution" in their titles. The word "revolution" has become the shibboleth of our era, the attention-getter, the quickest way to capture the ear of an audience. It has become so fashionable that even theologians have sought by means of it to breathe fresh life into the dry bones of their dogma. One theologian apparently more convinced of God's omnipresence than of his omnipotence assures us that: "Not even God can escape radical thought today." According to him, God is not dead, despite Nietzsche. He has come alive. "He is the God of Revolution." Small wonder then that the verbal counters of other periods— "reform," "reason," "compromise," "gradual or evolutionary progress"— are currently at a discount.

Sometimes this invocation of revolution seems comical in its juxtaposition of the serious and the trivial, and confusion of blood and ink. Here is a book on education, picked up almost at random, which tells us "it took only a few men and women to start three of the greatest revolutions of our time, in America, in France, in Russia. Who among us doubts that we are witnessing the beginning of the Fourth Revolution? *And who among us will not play his part?*" One wonders what the revolution means to this writer, in whose part he is playing a self-conscious role, since he approvingly quotes Burke in condemnation of the French Revolution and also assures us that "revolutions have occurred which do not change institutions." Instead of proclaiming stirring and spine-tingling revolutionary educational changes, alas! he turns out to be a pedagogical paper tiger, high on rhetoric. "The liberal arts colleges, with the dawning of the Fourth Revolution, must find a new democratic purpose, and it is hard to see how that purpose will be all that different from that of the old normal schools although teaching styles, curriculum, and level of profundity will assuredly be different."[1]

It would be a mistaken linguistic purism to object to the proliferation of usages of the term "revolution" provided that we keep their contexts clear; and a futile intellectual exercise to attempt to discover some nuclear meaning common to all usages. I shall be talking about social and political revolution in the modified Marxist sense in which it designates a *fundamental change in the power relations of classes within society* effected through economic controls. I say in the "modified" Marxist sense because Marx's theory of classes and class conflicts is much too narrow and cannot do justice to what Pareto, Mosca, and Michels prophetically saw long before the victory of any Marxist-led revolution, viz., that even when the mode of production is socialized, classes and bitter class struggles are still possible. From this it would follow that a classless society is a Utopian myth. The difference between reform and revolution on this view becomes one of degree, between small-scale and large-scale changes designed to eliminate the evils and lacks of existing society. So long as the mode of political decision remains democratic, the *ideal* of social revolution can be regarded as a large-scale reform, and historically all genuinely Social-Democratic parties function as reform parties. Where Communist parties, whether oriented toward Moscow or Peking, despite their rhetoric, genuinely participate in the political life of a nation (and drop their role as Fifth Columnists) they, too, despite themselves will gradually become reform parties and accommodate their ideal of revolution to the democratic process. So far there is no evidence that any Communist party has truly committed itself to the preservation of all the political rights of those opposed to its program in the event that it comes to power. To guarantee that other political groups in a socialist society, including those who peacefully oppose socialism, will enjoy the freedoms of the Bill of Rights, invoked by Communist parties when they have not yet acquired power, is to repudiate the Leninist version of Marxism. So far as I am aware no Communist party has done so. Politically the heritage of Lenin has remained sacrosanct among all Communist parties.

Revolution as a "cult," as I shall use the term, as distinct from revolution as an ideal, is the position that rejects the processes of democratic social change, as hopelessly ineffective or deceptive or both, and makes a fetish of various forms of opposition ranging from passive uncivil disobedience to open violence. Those who have accepted this cult—or violent revolutionary faith—are often critical of the political position of official Communist parties, even when they declare themselves as still sympathetic with their ideology, and accuse them of betraying the authentic social revolution conceived as a total transformation of traditional, social, economic, political, and cultural institutions. The leaders of the cult are disaffected intellectuals of the Western world whose followers are other intellectuals, would-be intellectuals, militant students, and certain politically conscious elements of marginal or minority groups. Among them are Sartre in France and Marcuse in the U.S. and the late Ché Guevara, whose writings have an appeal to erstwhile social reformers disillusioned with the rate of social progress or outraged by some institutional practice of injustice toward some nationality or race that stubbornly refuses to yield to the corrective measures of legislation. Their influence has been mediated mainly through adult student leaders of the New Left.

There are several paradoxical features about the resurgence of the revolutionary myth among intellectuals of the Western world, whose influence the public media of the market economy they so scornfully condemn have helped spread out of all proportion to their numbers. The basic paradox is that as the welfare state moves to ever higher and more inclusive levels of social reform, even to the consideration of an annual guaranteed wage for every family, that would in effect wipe out traditional poverty, and to the progressive elimination of electoral discriminations, thus increasing the potential political power of the masses, the attacks on the system which makes this progress possible mount in frequency and ferocity. This paradox is accentuated by the fact that the commitment among student leaders of the New Left to a position of revolutionary opposition grows at a time when the likelihood of *successful* revolutionary uprisings in advanced industrial countries is extremely small, and when the costs of any attempts at such action would be catastrophically high.

Nonetheless the cult of revolution, even when the term "revolution" is not expressly invoked, flourishes above ground even more than underground. Its rhetoric has become chic and fashionable. Those who broke with the authoritarian regimes of the past used "to go to the people." Today those who denounce the welfare state or "the system," whose nature they cannot adequately analyze with the tired concepts of Marxist orthodoxy, proclaim they are "joining the resistance." To join the resistance is something quite different from going to the people—for "the people," whether the blue collar working class or the white collar lower middle class, seem to have little stomach and some revulsion both for violent revolution and revolutionists. Even the traditional parties of revolution—the Communist parties of the West, despite the existence of their underground apparatus, shun this extremist propaganda of the word and especially the terrorist propaganda of the deed with which the revolutionary rhetoric is occasionally punctuated. For in their experience such words and actions have been associated with the work of *agents-provocateurs* and irresponsible anarchists, long since read out of the organized workers' movement by Marx and his followers.

The failure of classical Marxist theory to interpret and predict historical events may be attributed chiefly to two factors. First, the phenomenon of nationalism which in crucial situations overrode considerations of class interest; and second, the relative material prosperity of the major capitalist countries attributable in a considerable degree to the influence of the democratic political process in redistributing wealth. In consequence, the economy of welfare states obeys neither the equations of doom of Marx's *Capital* nor those of equilibrium that hold for a perfectly free market. Those for whom Marxism was a scientific theory and practice of achieving a classless society, and therefore refutable by events, abandoned its apocalyptic doctrines according to which the increasing misery of the masses would culminate in the act of revolutionary overthrow. In general this is the development followed by Social-Democratic movements and parties. If the objective presuppositions of revolution were lacking, the revolutionary attempt itself must be condemned as adventurous and suicidal. And there is, in a sense, a Marxist wisdom in this dying grasp of renunciation of Marxist eschatology—in this refusal to transform the scientific predictions, refuted by historical events, into an ideology which in principle is beyond empirical refutation. These Social-Democratic movements in good conscience and good logic have become people's parties for social reform. And it is safe to predict that to the extent that Communist parties in the West become organizationally independent of Moscow and Peking and sincerely practice what they currently profess, a willingness to submit to the arbitrament of the democratic political process, they, too, in effect will ultimately become parties of social reform.

As the Marxist ideal of revolution fades today, it is being replaced by the "cult of revolution" among the small but influential groups in the West that are identified as the New Left in whose eyes even the Communist parties are already hopelessly reformist. And by the "cult of revolution," to repeat, I mean the attitude which rejects the existing system no matter what its political form as inherently repressive. It repudiates principled reliance upon the democratic and judicial process even for the redress of specific grievances, especially of those regarded as acutely and overwhelmingly evil, whether it be war or minority repression. And although it *says* on occasion that it will employ all means to transform society, peaceful if possible and violent if necessary, it leaves little doubt that it believes peaceful means are not possible, that violence of one kind or another is inescapable, and that immediate resort to violence is imperative.

The cult of revolution has various roots. They not only feed the blossoms of its rhetoric but its violent fruit. The longest and strangest of its tap roots grew out of the writings of those who, having revised Marx's theory and ideal of revolution, still wish to be considered his dialectical successors and heirs. Marx had proclaimed that the emancipation of the working class can be the work only of the working class. Marcuse who typifies the current revolutionary revisionism is dismayed by the decision of the working classes, through their political parties and trade unions, to emancipate themselves gradually and peacefully, even if militantly, by integration into the welfare society. He is even fearful that the proletariat and its allies, if they dissociate themselves from those who today make a cult of revolution, "may well become, in part at least, the mass basis of a neo-Fascist regime."[2]

According to Marcuse, the organized working class, and even all but the poorest sections of the unorganized working class, have betrayed their historical mission. They have preferred to luxuriate in the shoddy goods and the vapid leisure time excitements that modern capitalism makes possible rather than risk their comforts by heroic revolutionary action. Nonetheless Marcuse still clings to the view that he is within the Marxist canon, a position made even more odd by his neo-Freudian notion that under Communism human beings will be free of all class-infected "civilizing" restraints upon natural sexual impulse. Theoretically, however, despite his reaffirmed allegiance to the Marxian dialectic method, Marcuse's is a dialectic of retreat to the standpoint of the early Marx, which is a standpoint that Marx himself repudiated as an abstract, unhistorical moralism expressed as a fetishism of human nature, the Feuerbachian *Gattungswesen* which functions as an absolute norm, the true self from which the historical self has been alienated.

There are many devotees of the cult of violence whose intellectual origins are not Marxist. Disheartened by the gap which is ever present between our social ideals and their imperfect fulfillment, they are prepared on high moral ground to support violent action against the system. They tell us that we must finally make an end to all human oppression and exploitation including that of women by men and of students by their teachers. When they realize that this has eschatological overtones, they sometimes moderate their language. The revolution is then justified as necessary to *reduce* "oppression, exploitation, and alienation." But if that is our aim then there is no moral difference between the reformer and the revolutionist. Every reformer is in favor of this reduction but insists on translating these grandiose abstractions into concrete goals. We can then measure the extent and pace of progress toward them. If poverty diminishes as real wages increase together with more adequate social insurance, pensions, and opportunities to participate significantly in decisions affecting one's life, the natural response of the reformer is: why not more of the same, why not continue on the same course?

The cultists of revolution are impatient with this historical progressivist and reformist perspective. They come down hard on it, irritated all the more by its seeming air of reasonableness. There are two generic criticisms made of the reformers. The first is that the progress is spurious despite all the quantitative indices which show that real wages have increased and living conditions improved. Comparison is made not between the past and the present but between the relative incomes of the extremely wealthy in the present and the average working-class income. Even if the workers in the present are much better off than workers in the past, compared to the income of the extremely wealthy in the present they are worse off. Or alternately, attention is focused upon an extreme instance of utter deprivation and an inference is drawn about the entire system which permits such an unmitigated evil to occur. How valid are these critical responses to the reformist approach?

Semantically, the expressions "better off than before" or "worse off than before" are usually employed in comparisons made between the states of the *same* person or group in the present and the past, not in comparison with the states of different persons and groups. If with respect to one's health it is said, "He is better off this year than last year since he was ill only for ten days and not five months," it would be extremely odd to hear in response: "Not at all—he is worse off than he was last year since there have been others who have been ill for only five days." Or with respect to knowledge, if I say of John: "He is better off than he was last year—he knows so much more this year as measured by all the tests," it would be a plain abuse of language for someone to retort: "Not at all, he is worse off, he really knows less than last year because his friends know far more than he does." John's relative standing this year may be worse than last year's despite the improvement in his knowledge and understanding. But the precise point at issue is whether the relative standing has any bearing or effect on the positive improvement made.

Except as a desperate move in an argument to save a theory, we do not make this relative judgment when discussing improvements in the standards of living of a specific person or group—granting the legitimacy of such inquiries for other purposes, e.g., tax and fiscal policies. Tell a man who was quite familiar with hunger pangs in the past but can now eat to repletion on nutritious fare that he is worse off than before because some others can eat and overeat more often and more expensively, and he will feel he is being made sport of. What is true of individuals is true of groups. Compared with the state of affairs less than a century ago the longevity of the American people has increased and infant mortality decreased, both in spectacular fashion. The fact that the current records in Scandinavia are better shows only that there is still room for improvement, not that the improvement is unreal.

In one sense, of course, poverty is a relative term but not in the sense in which the Gospels mistakenly assures us "For ye have the poor always with you" (Matthew 26:11). In the Biblical sense, poverty could be wiped out in short order in the industrialized countries of the West. The sense in which poverty is "relative" involves questions of justice where that is defined simply in terms of equality. If my real wages double but the wages of others (whom I judge as no better qualified or worthy) quadruple, I may regard this as unjust but not as worsening my lot. Where there is no question of physical need and deprivation or suppression of basic human freedoms or punishment for criminal actions, the desire for justice, if defined in terms of equality, may express resentment or envy of the better fortunes of others, deserved or undeserved. It may show poverty of spirit, not physical poverty. "A hut is a hut," observes Marx, "but build a [mansion] beside it and it becomes a hovel."[3] This is a profound psychological observation, not an economic truth. And even as a psychological truth it is historically conditioned although the insight remains. A hut with all modern conveniences, heated in winter and air-conditioned in summer, overlooking a couple of acres and a pleasant view does not become a hovel no matter what is built beside it. Does a mansion, in turn, become a hovel when a palace is built beside it? The absurdity of conceiving of poverty only in relative terms is apparent in the fact that in a community of oil-sheiks, all of whom are millionaires, we would have to refer to those whose income was only one million as "poor."

When this first response to the case for reform is shattered by the avalanche of incontrovertible facts concerning improvements in the standard of living, the revolutionist shifts ground. He argues that the improvement is only temporary. His confidence that it is only temporary sometimes derives from an expectation of an economic earthquake or catastrophe that will level society. Even if we grant that possibility it would constitute no more of an argument against reforms than the possibility of a real earthquake against building houses. At this point a further shift occurs. The cultist of revolution contends that the reformist outlook makes for ethical and psychological complacency, for a self-congratulatory fixation upon the distance society has come from the darkest days of the past rather than upon the distance yet to go. Without denying the possibility that the very success of reform may undermine its spirit or *élan*, psychologically this seems unlikely. At any rate, what does the historical record of the last two centuries show?

Some writers have suggested that the history of health care for the masses be taken as a paradigm of the progress of social reform. They argue that once the social responsibility of the community for the health of its citizens is recognized, every achievement becomes the basis for an eager and more daring advance on the frontier of the yet to be accomplished. With some justification it may be objected that this is a special case bound up with the growth of scientific knowledge and not comparable to the history of social and political progress that involves fiercer conflicts than over the distribution of tax funds. Let us then examine the history of electoral reforms, of civil rights, labor unionism, welfare legislation, and public support of education in democratic countries. Do they show patterns of expansion or of the exhaustion we should find if the cultist of revolution were right? To be sure, the pattern of expansion shows some resting on plateaus and even some setbacks induced by the pace and success of the reforms and sometimes by resistance and backlash to violence that has accompanied demands for reform. But in every respect there has been a large net gain. This by no means guarantees continued gains but it places a heavy burden of proof upon those who would urge another course.

Psychologically, there is even less reason to believe that awareness of historical gain reinforces complacency. The natural momentum of a successful reform opens up possibilities whose existence may not have been suspected before the reform was introduced. Sometimes it generates a buoyant mood that the *Zeitgeist*, if not the cosmos, is on the side of the reformer. It is this mood that everything has become possible, that the gains won are natural and irreversible, that makes so dangerous the frustration of the popular expectation for more progress. The paradox of rising expectations shows that hope does not wither but flares with success. Far from making reformers complacent, awareness of how far one has come may even strengthen the resolution to continue in situations where grave injustices and needless suffering still exist.

The cult of revolution sometimes develops out of a consuming rage against a specific evil that looms so large that it blots out everything else. This is typified by the observation of one academic devotee of the cult: "Revolutionary violence in Sweden or Canada would be quite unjustified. . . . Rhodesia and the United States are something else again." Since Sweden, Canada, and the United States are capitalist welfare societies of approximately equal living standards for the working population, since no reference is made to the possibility of justified revolutionary violence in the Soviet Union or Mainland China, and since the political system of the United States is more like that of Canada and Sweden, while that of Rhodesia resembles the dictatorships of Russia and China, the coupling of the United States and Rhodesia obviously indicates that the author is referring to "racism" in the United States which he believes can be eliminated only by revolutionary violence. In passing, it should be noted that there are some cultists of revolution that do not draw the line at Canada. There are French revolutionary nationalists in Canada who are as *enragés* about their grievances as American Black Panthers. But from the point of view of a citizen opposed to any form of invidious racial discrimination what shall we say to this bland blanket justification of revolutionary violence?

First, it could only be made by someone insensitive to the tremendous progress in race relations that has been made in the last two decades *without* revolutionary violence, a progress much greater materially, socially, and educationally than was achieved by four years of the most violent civil war in human history up to that time and which resulted in a change in the legal status of the Negro but not his genuine political enfranchisement in former slave-holding states. Second, it overlooks the suicidal character of any attempt to tie the movement for *further* reduction of racial discrimination to a movement of revolutionary violence. This was understood by the NAACP, the largest and most representative of all Negro organizations, from its very founding, and reluctantly and belatedly grasped even by the Black Panthers. Third, anyone capable of a cool look at history should realize that neither racism nor nationalism would be destroyed even if a minority despite the odds against it succeeded in putting down a majority by force. At best the character and direction of the repressive nationalism and racism would be reversed.

The ways in which a social evil is attacked may in the long run breed consequences that are as bad or worse than the evil that spurred the original opposition. When minorities that suffer injustices at the hands of a majority in politically democratic societies reject existing legislative and judicial mechanisms instead of using them, and invoke the slogan "all power to the people," they are really invoking lynch law. When individuals join the so-called revolutionary resistance because of the presumed injustice of the draft or a war, they seem unaware that they may be committing themselves to the support of a wider draft or a more protracted war if by some historical fluke their revolutionary action was victorious.

Not all cultists of revolution exempt Sweden as a possible locus of revolutionary violence. Jan Myrdal, the Maoist son of a Social-Democratic father, protests that reforms are not adequate because "We have not solved the problem of the alienation of the individual." Whatever the problem of alienation is, there is not the slightest reason to believe that if it should be solved, about which there can be legitimate doubt, it will be solved by violent revolution rather than by reform unless the liquidation of multitudes is considered one form of solution. But, as we shall see, this talk about alienation reveals some significant facets of the cult of revolution and some of its moral pretensions.

The ideologists of the cult of revolution usually reply to their critics by trying to force upon them a position of either absolute pacifism or of absolute opposition to revolution under any conceivable circumstance. But it is not necessary to adopt the position of the absolute pacifist to oppose the cult of revolution any more than principled opposition to lying or deception entails that a person must always tell the truth regardless of consequences. Opposition to violence may sometimes necessitate a violent defense against those who resort to it. There is nothing inconsistent here. Morally to equate the two is like equating the violence of the thug with the violence of the victim who defends himself against the thug or with the force used by an arresting police officer. Of course one can easily *conceive* of historical situations in which a revolution would be justifiable as the lesser evil. But speculative possibilities are here irrelevant. Only a fanatic would justify revolutionary action in a specific situation on the basis of the merely *conceivable*. For the political issue is always of a specific time and place, here and now. Past revolutions may or may not have been justified: future revolutions may or may not be. They have no bearing on our responsibility in the present.

Another interesting aspect of the thought of present-day cultists of revolution is that they also claim to be principled believers in democracy. And yet they consistently overlook the fundamental difference between the resort to revolutionary violence in order to *establish* the processes of political democracy in whose absence the just and peaceful settlement of grievances is not feasible, and the resort to revolutionary violence in a democracy to transform it. To an ethical absolutist it may make little difference whether one is revolting against a tyrant who refuses to accept representative institutions or whether one is revolting against the alleged tyranny of the democratic majority. To the democrat, however, there is a fundamental difference. His decision whether or not to engage in revolution against the tyranny of the despot is largely prudential but, as a democrat living in a democracy, if he rejects the decisions of an *unenlightened* majority, he is in principle bound to appeal not to violence but to an *enlightened* majority. When he rejects that appeal to the enlightened majority on the Platonic ground that most human beings are either too stupid or vicious to be entrusted with self-government, he has rejected the democratic process. The cultist of revolution instead of admitting that *he* has abandoned his faith in democracy wants to eat his cake and have it, too. He denies that the existing democratic political system is truly democratic, denounces it as formal, pseudo, bourgeois, or with whatever deprecatory adjective comes to mind. He then defines democracy in vague and grandiose terms as a community in which individuals enjoy complete autonomy, self-determination, and freedom. When these terms are rendered meaningful, it turns out that no earthly community could possibly exemplify them. And so ignoring the necessity of determining whether any given society is more or less democratic in its basic institutions—which always defines our concrete choice—he can condemn *all* existing political democracies, praise—indeed cooperate with their totalitarian foes—and still proclaim himself as the only true and authentic democrat.

It is at this point that present-day cultists like Marcuse reveal that despite their insistence upon the authenticity of their democratic faith, they are really in direct line with the original totalitarian traditions of Bolshevik-Leninism from which they seek to differentiate themselves. The Leninists contrasted "the wishes and will of the masses" and the "real interests of the masses." They then claimed to know these real interests better than the masses themselves, and in their light oppose and correct the expressed wishes and will of the masses, and punish them for the form they took.

What was shamefaced in the Leninist revision of Marx is open in Marcuse who declares that "the Marxian concept of a revolution, carried by the majority of the exploited masses, is overtaken by the historical development."[4] The working masses are to be replaced by the middle-class student intelligentsia, allied with the ghetto population and other discontented groups on the margin of society—all of whom together do not constitute a majority of the producers, still less, as Marx claimed for the workers, a majority of the population. Together with aid from Third World revolutionists, this is the composite group that replaces the working classes which history has found wanting.

And why have the working classes been found wanting by the cultists of revolution? Because they have been corrupted by the affluence of the welfare society. They have been infected with consumerism. They desire the housing, the schooling, the clothing, the leisure and entertainment, the automobiles, the swimming pools, and holiday jaunts abroad which until now have been the monopoly largely of the prosperous middle classes. Marcuse and his academic disciples—revolutionists with tenure!—are not mollified by the absence of mass hunger among the workers. They are not reconciled to the attempts by guaranteed family income and other reforms to wipe out hunger everywhere. They are not happy that Marx was proved wrong about the mass pauperization of the working class. They are actually repelled by the spectacle of mass satisfaction, by the acquisition of personal property, by the fact that having acquired a vested interest in things, the workers resent losing them through the violence inspired by calls for revolution. For all his rhetoric about universal freedom and self-determination as sanctifying revolutionary overthrow, what Marcuse finds really offensive are the lifestyles, the patterns of values and choices both of the majority of the population and the majority of the working class.

Nothing reveals so starkly the elitist, undemocratic bias of the New Left cult of the revolution. There is something snobbish as well as hypocritical in the spectacle of middle-class intellectuals, cradled in security and comfort, luxuriating in a standard of living dependent upon the intensive use of the latest technological refinements, hectoring the masses for aspiring to the same material benefits that most of these intellectuals are loath to surrender. To be sure, the masses enjoy their leisure differently and in the contemptuous eyes of their liberators, vulgarly. But the fact that the masses are blamed for their choice, for acquiring artificial and inflated needs, shows that they are *not* being coerced. One may disapprove of their hierarchy of values and the way they choose to spend their leisure. But they are no less free in selecting their lifestyles, within limits of course, than their would-be liberators.

Marcuse denies this as a liberal evasion of the facts of social coercion. He insists that the masses are being seduced by carrots where previously they had been driven by sticks—and *both* are forms of coercion.

This equation between carrots and sticks as equal forces of repression preventing the liberation of the masses is central to the political theology of the priests of the revolutionary cult. But I make bold to proclaim in opposition that the difference between the carrot and the stick—or the gun!—in eliciting consent is the key to the whole culture complex we call civilization when we use the word normatively. It may be compared to the difference between seduction and rape which that genial anthropologist, Goldenweiser, in a *jeu d'esprit* once declared marked the moral basis of civilized family life. After all where adults are concerned seduction involves an offering of carrots in the generic sense of the term. It is an exchange of sorts, conscious and risky but always undertaken in anticipation of what are believed genuine values. To be seduced is to be induced. True, we are sometimes induced by invalid arguments—the remedy is to learn to reason better. True, we may be induced by false and glittering promises—the remedy is the cultivation of skepticism, reliance on the argument from Missouri, the plain man's critical empiricism. Except in certain extreme or limiting cases—induced behavior is not morally comparable to physically coerced behavior—to the violence that brutally overrides one's consciousness and reduces the human being to the status of an animal or unfeeling thing.

The cultists of revolution have written off the class that Marx had hailed as the carrier of progressive social change.

We cannot, however, doubt for a moment that the same arrogance that would dictate to the working masses how they must live to save themselves and society would be turned against the new carriers of the revolution, the ghetto inhabitants and the New Left students, if they were to come to terms with the political forces of the environment and entered into the coalition politics of the pluralist society. They, too, would be denounced for permitting themselves to be "co-opted by the Establishment."

Actually, there was a period in the past when Marcuse doubted that the black ghetto population in the United States would and could assume the burden of revolutionary redemption. He was prepared then to condemn even their right to choose if they were to choose wrongly. This was

during the years that preceded ghetto violence in which the black population was making great gains in breaking down the institutionalized
prejudices of the past. At that time Marcuse dismissed the civil rights
movement among the American Negroes as inconsequential on the
ground that they were using their new electoral freedom pretty much as
their corrupted white fellow citizens and that they were succumbing to
the same consumer-oriented blandishments of the affluent society. He
was then asked which state of affairs he considered more desirable—one
in which Negroes remained deprived of the civil rights and freedom possessed by white citizens or one in which they used these rights to choose
wrongly from *his* point of view. He replied without evasion that he would
rather they had no freedom to choose than that they choose to become
integrated in the corporate affluent, technological culture that had "corrupted" the organized labor movement.[5] Autonomous choice or genuine
self-determination on this view is present only when it conforms to the
values of the revolutionary elite—all other values are "prejudices." Being
wrong means disagreeing with Marcuse and the workers have no right to
be wrong. Naturally this paternalism is not likely to have a mass appeal.

One refreshing feature of this elitism and paternalism is that it is so
undisguised not only in Marcuse but in Sartre and in the writings of Ché
Guevara, whom they both admired, as a spokesman for the Cuban Revolution when it was free from bureaucratic deformations. Sartre admits
that the so-called dictatorship of the proletariat in the Soviet Union
which he had so passionately defended is and always was a dictatorship
*for* and *over* the proletariat. Ché Guevara, one of the key figures in the
cult of revolution, in justifying "the avoidance of the commonplaces of
bourgeois democracy," by which he means free elections and a legally
recognized opposition party, in the Cuban long march to libertarian
socialism frankly contrasts the roles of the privileged vanguard and the
masses. Members of the vanguard, in virtue of their superior insight, are
"qualitatively different from the masses who see only by halves and must
be subjected to incentives and pressures of some intensity: it is the dictatorship of the proletariat being exercised not only upon the defeated
class but also individually upon the victorious class." The reason that
free democratic choice cannot be permitted to individuals is that it may
interfere with the revolutionary aspiration "to see man freed from alienation." Guevara spells out what this involves with a Latin clarity that
reveals more than the Teutonic circumlocutions of Marcuse. But they
mean the same thing. For the revolution to succeed, he tells us,

involves the necessity of a series of mechanisms, the revolutionary institutions. The concept of institutionalization fits in with the images of the
multitudes marching toward a future as that of a harmonic unit of
canals, steps, well-oiled apparatuses that make the march possible, *that*
*permit the natural selection of those who are destined to march in the*
*vanguard and who dispense reward and punishments to those who*
*fulfil their duty or act against the society under construction.*[6]

Neither Marcuse nor Sartre are so devoid of a sense of the political
realities in the industrial societies of the West as to urge immediate
action to achieve the power that the working class has refused to seize.
There is no revolutionary situation. But until that auspicious moment
arrives, the revolutionary opposition must be one of constant preparation—not only "radical enlightenment in theory and practice but development of cadres and nuclei for the struggle."

The devotees of the cult of revolution consider themselves neither
romantics nor Utopians. Nonetheless they are far from having a realistic
view of the effect of their doctrines *today* in the surcharged atmosphere
of violence that prevails almost everywhere. The cultists of revolution
can *inspire* reckless and extreme action; but they have no means of
restraining or disciplining it. After all, despite Lenin, there are no firm
criteria of an objective revolutionary situation—they depend very much
on the fevered consciousness of street crowds and the audacity of the
"cadres and nuclei" that are being primed and educated for revolutionary
action. There was no objective revolutionary situation in France when
the students launched their rebellion in 1968. Yet in the heated climate
of the times, it was a near thing. Had it succeeded in sparking a revolution, the existence of an objective revolutionary situation would have
been retroactively inferred. After the rioting fizzled out, Sartre and Marcuse condemned not the student rebels for their precipitate action and
adventurism but the French Communist Party and the French trade
unions for betraying the student movement. Despite a certain ambiguity
in their judgment, their chief criticism of the students' rebellion was *not*
that their uprising was undertaken but that it was not thought through
and adequately prepared for. But this refers to a subjective, not objective
component. The moral is: try again but harder! The constant willingness
is presupposed; and the readiness is not so much a function of the social-
economic situation but of proper organization.

As the world is constituted today the traditional Leninist conception
of a revolutionary situation no longer appears valid in face of the trigger

readiness of so many groups to resort to violence and terrorism to enforce nonnegotiable demands. It should be noted that it did not apply to the Cuban Revolution. That was launched, Ché Guevara to the contrary, not as a socialist revolution to free man from his alienation but to restore simple democratic political freedoms, and conduct the free elections Batista had banned, and which Castro has never held.

In pure logic a social revolution engineered by a minority may be nonviolent but where the liberation of society is to be carried out by "repressive tolerance," to use Marcuse's phrase, the resort to revolutionary violence and terror necessarily becomes the order of the day when the moment to strike arrives. An affluent society has enormous latent powers of resistance. It must therefore be taken by surprise. The cultists of revolution must be on the lookout, really on the lurk, for opportunities to head and guide spontaneous outbursts of violence directed against the system. They cannot reasonably expect victory by any one act but hope through a series of acts that generate a continued chaos to ride to success. Despite their occasional disclaimers, in their hearts they cannot condemn any violence that erupts against the system. For not only do they regard the instigators of violence as victims, they nourish the wild hope that the whole fabric of society may catch fire from the eruption. When violence fails, the odium of the failure must therefore always be placed on those who have put it down not on those who have initiated it.

The espousal of revolutionary overthrow of the existing social and political system does not take place in a vacuum. In the United States, incitements to violence are no longer prosecuted, and even many acts of violence go unpunished. The very system denounced as repressive by the cultists of revolution gives them a platform and an audience through its public media, in quest for the sensational and extreme, which they could never reach by their own means, or command in virtue of the intrinsic merit of their ideas.

It would be absurd to attribute to the cultists of revolution primary responsibility for the tidal wave of violence that has engulfed almost all areas of American life in recent years. But it is not absurd to attribute to them, in a considerable degree, the growing acceptance of domestic violence, its social and intellectual respectability in American society. At the time of the ghetto riots one of the chief theoretical organs of the New Left with a wide circulation in the universities not only carried an illustration of a Molotov cocktail but instructions on how to make one. What is perhaps more serious, the glorification of "the creative function of violence," and the rationalizations to which it has given rise, has lamed the critical functions of our colleges and universities in dealing with the violent excesses of the student movement. Even Marcuse has shrunk from the spectacle of organized violence in the university which has given him a haven and protection from the fury of those who would turn his own principle of repressive tolerance against him and treat him as he himself advocates that others be treated. If, as he believes, the university is an integral part of the beaurocratized Establishment, and its destruction contributes to the radicalization of the student young, so necessary if the social revolution is to have a chance of success, the Cohen-Bendits and other leaders of extremist students are not altogether wrong in taxing Marcuse at this point with inconsistency.

There are some who regard concern with the verbal hysteria of violence as itself an hysterical expression of a fear that takes the shadow for the substance of danger. It is only *actions*, they say, that we need trouble ourselves about, and the social causes out of which they grow. The rest is ideology or mythology that functions as a rationalization for behavior that is *not* determined by ideas or words. This is a half truth. One would have imagined that the effects of mythological beliefs about race in our century would have taught us what practical effects ideas, even mistaken ideas, can have. Not only have ideas consequences, words have consequences, too. Auden may have been right when he wrote: "Poetry makes nothing happen" but he can hardly believe it of prose, even bad prose. Were Hitler's ranting speeches without effect?

All political movements have their peripheries of the psychotic and semipsychotic. That is why the terrorism of the word often inspires a terrorism of the deed for which the wordmongers of terror are responsible even when they find it politic to disavow the deeds. More dangerous is the growing tendency of cultists of violence to portray those who have been guilty of crimes of murder, assault, and theft as political prisoners, to glorify criminal elements in the population as revolutionaries, and to hail their prison revolts as part of the movement toward liberation. Where criminal violence can be interpreted by malefactors as a blow for collective freedom, it provides absolution in advance for the most callous kind of inhumanities. The thief becomes a freedom-looter who does not steal property but liberates it. If he kills in the course of his piecemeal expropriation of the oppressor, it is no longer murder but a symbolic act of protest against the systematic injustices of society. The revolutionary exploitation of prison violence since the outbreak at Attica, New York, has become more pronounced. In the long run it is self-defeating in any civilized society to link revolutionary movements with prison breaks by hard criminal offenders. But its short run impact may be a greater surge of violence, and inescapable counterviolence.

It has long been noted by students of crowd behavior that few individuals when alone commit, or are even tempted to commit, the bestial acts they find themselves doing as members of a lynch mob. The reason for this is in part that the mob is united by a common passion or idea that takes the individual out of himself. When the individual member of a crowd is caught up in violence, he tends to think of himself as a disinterested even an unselfish agent of a collective will. The inhibiting bonds of existing moral tradition are loosened not out of naked self-interest but by the authority of a cause which ennobles every vicious desire and impulse hitherto suppressed. That is why violence in behalf of an ideology or cause is apt to take more horrible form than ordinary criminal violence. This is not to equate crime with revolution. It explains only why the violence that results from the cult of violence is often so much worse than the violence of ordinary crime.

In their reflective moments the cultists of revolutionary violence insist that they, too, detest violence and desire to eliminate it from human life. To oppose violence, they admit, is not so much a sign of one's humanity as of one's sanity. It is intrinsically evil but when its use is necessary to avoid a much greater evil or promote a very great shared good, it is morally justified. Again, one can agree with these abstract considerations but if adduced to justify revolutionary resistance today they are completely question-begging. Most of those who talk this way are completely and avowedly ignorant of what the costs of revolution would be, and they refuse to examine carefully the human costs of the revolutions of our time. Instead they fall back on general considerations to present a persuasive case in justification of revolutionary violence. Before concluding discussion of the cult of revolution, some cautions are in order that may be overlooked when fear and revulsion grip the community after some unspeakable atrocity has been committed by the self-denominated "vanguard" of liberated humanity.

There are two great dangers. One is that the genuine evils and injustices of society which have spurred idealistic fanatics into a mad impatience will remain unmet even after the violence is put down, or that if they are being met, they are not being seen as met. One of the reasons why the cult of revolution has fallen on deaf ears among the workers in Western democratic countries is that they have had visible and continuing evidence of the relative improvement of their estate. But the economic improvement is still insufficient and uneven, and acute problems, in some countries racial, in others religious, cut across class lines. *The ineptitude of the language and barbarity of the methods used by revolutionary cultists should not blind us to the existence of these problems and the moral necessity of grappling with them in order to expand the area of human freedom.* There are some who claim that the true "permanent revolution" is to be found not in any self-proclaimed revolutionary state today but in the processes of continuous democratic social reform. I think it is a confusing use of the term "revolution." At any rate democratic welfare states do not guarantee this permanent revolution. They only make it possible.

The second danger posed by the phenomenon of violence is that the methods used to counteract, suppress, and punish those who initiate it may themselves be so extreme and indiscriminate as to awaken sympathy and support among elements of the population not previously infected by the contagion of violence. The problem is extremely difficult. It has never arisen in the past in the same fashion that exists today.

The *forms* of violence we find today, whether they are assassinations, kidnappings, fire-bombing of innocent civilians, the seizure of hostages, even self-immolation are an old story. What is new is the strategy of violence of urban guerrillas in many countries who hope by senseless acts of terror (like the murder of kidnapped hostages who may not even be citizens of the country) to provoke measures of repression that by falling on guilty and innocent alike tend to discredit those who are defenders of public order.

This strategy has been described by Carlos Marighella, one of the ideologists of Brazilian terrorism, in frankest terms.

> "It is necessary," he says, "to turn political crisis [always at hand in some countries] into armed conflict by performing violent actions that will force those in power to transform the political situation in the country into a military [or police] situation. That will alienate the masses who from then on will revolt against the army and police and blame *them* for this state of things."[7]

This strategy can be very effective when implemented by suicidal acts of terrorism and atrocity. It makes it all the more essential that the guardians of public order act intelligently, and even when they have to react firmly against extreme provocation, do so in a civilized way. In crisis situations this may appear as a counsel of perfection to those whose lives are at stake on the firing line. But these crisis situations must be prepared for in advance. This is a lesson that applies just as much to violent campus disruption and prison revolt as to hit and run tactics of political terror. All the appropriate resources of the community must be brought to bear on the situation with vigor and promptness, with the promise of justice but rarely, if ever, of amnesty. And when force must be deployed, it should never be excessive.

[1973]

## NOTES

1. Donald Bigelow, *The Liberal Arts and Teacher Education*—A Confrontation (Lincoln: University of Nebraska Press, 1970), pp. xxxiv, xiv.

2. Herbert Marcuse,"Re-examination of the 'Concept of Revolution,'" *New Left Review* (July–August 1969).

3. I am aware that in the quotation from Marx, he used the term "palace" instead of "mansion" which I use to make my point clearer.

4. Marcuse, "Re-examination of the 'Concept of Revolution.' "

5. This public response was made at the Conference on The Idea of the Future at Rutgers University, New Brunswick, New Jersey, June 1965 to the question posed by the author.

6. Ché Guevara,"Man and Socialism in Cuba," translated by Zimmerman, in *All We Are Saying,* ed. Arthur Lothstein (New York: Putnam, 1979), 365 [my italics].

7. Quoted by Robert Moss in "Urban Guerillas in Latin America," *Conflict Studies* (October 1970): 7 [my italics].

# III
## DEMOCRATIC THEORY

# 9

# NATURALISM
# AND DEMOCRACY

## I

In the famous third chapter of his *Four Stages of Greek Religion* Gilbert Murray characterizes the period from 300 B.C.E. through the first century of the Christian era as marked by a "failure of nerve." This failure of nerve exhibited itself in "a rise of asceticism, of mysticism, in a sense, of pessimism; a loss of self-confidence, of hope in this life and of faith in normal human efforts; a despair of patient inquiry, a cry for infallible revelation; an indifference to the welfare of the state, a conversion of the soul to God."

A survey of the cultural tendencies of our times shows many signs pointing to a new failure of nerve in Western civilization. The revival of the doctrine of the original depravity of human nature; prophecies of doom for Western culture, no matter who wins the war or peace; the search for a center of value that transcends human interest; the mystical apotheosis of "the leader"; contempt for all social programs and philosophies, because of the obvious failure of some of them; violent attacks against secularism; posturing about the cultivation of spiritual purity; a concern with mystery rather than problems and the belief that myth and mysteries are modes of knowledge—these are only some of the secondary evidences of the new failure of nerve.

From *Naturalism and the Human Spirit*, ed. Y. H. Krikorian (New York: Columbia University Press, 1944). Reprinted by permission of the Estate of Sidney Hook.

The primary evidence of the new failure of nerve is to be found in an attitude which accompanies all the movements and views listed in the previous paragraph and many others as well. It exhibits itself as a loss of confidence in scientific method and in varied quests for a "knowledge" and "truth" which are uniquely different from those won by the processes of scientific inquiry. Often, with no great regard for consistency, these uniquely different truths are regarded as "superior" to the common garden variety of science and good sense. This distrust of scientific method is often concealed by statements to the effect that science, of course, has a certain validity in its proper place and sphere, that only the pretensions of scientific philosophy—naturalism, empiricism, positivism—are being criticized. Yet it is not to the actual procedures of scientific inquiry that such critics go to correct this or that formulation of scientific philosophy; rather do they invoke the claims of some rival method to give us knowledge of what is beyond the competence of scientific method. Occasionally they boldly assert that their substitute method gives a more reliable and complete knowledge even of the matters that the sciences report. What an eloquent revelation is contained in Reinhold Niebuhr's words, "Science which is only science cannot be scientifically accurate."

Distrust of scientific method is transformed into open hostility whenever some privileged "private" truth pleads for exemption from the tests set up to safeguard the intelligence from illusion. The pleas for exemption take many forms. They are rarely direct and aboveboard. Usually they are presented as corollaries of special *theories* of knowledge, being, or experience. There are some who interpret science and discursive knowledge generally as merely a method of confirming what we *already* know, in a dim but sure way, by other modes of experience. If the methods of scientific inquiry do not yield this confirmation, they are held to be at fault; some other way must be found of validating and communicating primal wisdom. Others maintain that scientific method can give us only partial truths, which become less partial, not by subjecting them to more careful scientific scrutiny, but by incorporating them into a theological or metaphysical system. Still others openly declare it to be axiomatic that every experience, every feeling and motion, directly reports a truth that cannot be warranted and does not need to be warranted by experiment or inference.

These, bluntly put, are gateways to intellectual and moral irresponsibility. But of the view that every mode of experience gives direct authentic knowledge it would, perhaps, be more accurate to say that it carries us far beyond the gateways. For frequently it is a defense of willful obscurantism. It starts from the assumption that *every* experience gives us an authentic report of the objective world instead of material for judgment. It makes our viscera an organ of knowledge. It justifies every passionate prejudice by asserting that if only we feel deeply enough about anything, our feeling must declare some truth about the object which provokes it that is just as legitimate as the considered judgment which discovers the root of the feeling in a personal aberration. After all, is it not the case that every heresy-hunting bigot and hallucinated fanatic is convinced that there is a truth in the feelings, visions, and, passions that run riot within him? Hitler is not the only one for whom questions of evidence are incidental when they are not dismissed as impertinent. If the voice of feeling cannot be mistaken, every difference would be an invitation to battle, every insane mind could set itself up as a prophet. It is not only as a defense against the marginally sane that we need the safeguards of critical, scientific method. Every vested interest in social life, every inequitable privilege, every "truth" promulgated as a national, class, or racial truth likewise denies the competence of scientific inquiry to evaluate its claims. Nor are our own normal selves free from the tendency to mistake intensity of the feeling or conviction with which beliefs are held as indubitable evidence of their validity.

Sometimes the demand that the revelations of feeling, intuition, and emotion meet scientific canons of evidence is rejected as an arbitrary legislative decree concerning what visions are permissible and what may or may not exist. The complaint is made that such demand impoverishes the imaginative resources and chokes off the vision, without which there is no growth of new knowledge, but at most a blind fooling with canons and methods. As far as seeing visions and winning new truths are concerned, such an interpretation is nothing short of grotesque. The essential point, where the question of knowledge or truth arises, is whether we have seen a vision or been a victim of a delusion; or, to avoid the appearance of question-begging, whether we have beheld a trustworthy or untrustworthy vision. Some people claim to see things that we know are not there. If seeing were believing, men could be perpetually duped.

The intelligent demand for evidence need not paralyze the pioneers of truth who catch glimpses of what may until then be undreamed of. For the sciences themselves do not demand complete or exact confirmation of an hypothesis to begin with, but only enough to institute further inquiries; and the history of science is sufficient evidence that the discipline of its method, far from being a bar against the discovery of new truths, is a positive aid in acquiring them. As for decreeing what does or can *exist*, there is nothing in scientific method that *forbids* anything to exist. It concerns itself only with the responsibility of the assertions that proclaim the existence of anything. It does not jeer at the mystical swoon of rapture; it only denies the mystic's retrospective cognitive claims for which no evidence is offered except the fact of the trance.

Scientific method does not entail any metaphysical theory of existence, and certainly not metaphysical materialism. The attack upon scientific method, in order to be free to believe whatever voice speaks to us, is really a flight from responsibility. This is the dominant characteristic of the failure of nerve.

## II

The causes of the failure of nerve in our time are multiple and obvious. Economic crises, world war, a bad peace, tragically inept statesmanship, the tidal wave of fascism tell the story of the twentieth century. It is important not to ignore or minimize this. The "arguments" of those who have been panicked into embracing refurbished varieties of transcendental consolation may be met a thousand times over. But not until a stable, democratic, freedom- and welfare-planning economy is built out of what is left of our world can we legitimately hope that these cultural reversions will subside from epidemic to episodic proportions. Until then we must strive to prevent emotional hysteria from infecting those who still cling to the principles of rational experiment and analysis, as the only reliable instruments for riding out and mastering the cultural and social chaos of our age.

It is characteristic of the tendencies hostile to scientific method that they reject the view that the breakdown of capitalism and the rise of fascism are due primarily to a conjunction of material factors. Rather do they attribute the crisis of our culture to a specific faith or philosophy rooted in scientific method. They allege that the bankruptcy of Western European civilization is the direct result of the bankruptcy of the positivist and naturalistic spirit which, sprouting from seeds scattered during the Renaissance, came to full flower in our own time. They assert that science and the scientific attitude pervaded every sphere of culture and experience, that all truth-claims and values were submitted to them for final arbitration, and that they were employed not so much to reinterpret as to deny the existence of human intelligence, courage, and dignity.[1]

No empirical evidence is offered for these extreme statements or for the fantastic conclusion that modern ills are the consequence of our attempt to live by scientific theory and practice On the contrary, a scientific analysis of modern history—and I am assuming that history is an empirical discipline—reveals that the chief causes of our maladjustments and suicidal conflicts are to be found precisely in those areas of social life in which *the rationale of scientific method has not been persistently employed*. Where is the evidence that any state ever attempted to meet scientifically the challenge of poverty, unemployment, the distribution of raw materials, the impact of technology either in government or in industry? The belief that we have grappled with these problems in a rational and scientific spirit is a myth. The principles which have controlled our response to basic social problems have been drawn in the main from outworn traditions hostile or indifferent to the ethics and the logic of scientific inquiry. It is only by courtesy that we can call them principles at all. Drift and improvisation have been the rule. Enthusiasm for the bare *results* of the physical sciences—which undoubtedly did reach a high pitch in the nineteenth century—does not betoken an acceptance of a scientific or experimental philosophy of life in which all values are tested by their causes and consequences. The cry that a set of "laboratory techniques" cannot determine the basic values in a philosophy of life betrays the literary man's illusion that the laboratory procedures of the natural sciences are the be-all and end-all of scientific method instead of restricted applications of it in special fields. Wisdom is counterposed to knowledge as if it were a superior organ or faculty or method instead of a variety of knowledge, namely, knowledge of the nature, origin, and careers of human values.

Perhaps the most malicious expression of the attack upon naturalism in contemporary American thought is the attempt to prove that a consistent naturalist or positivist cannot in principle accept the philosophy of democracy. Sometimes it is even charged that naturalists and positivists constitute the philosophical fifth column of Western civilization and that their doctrines have paved the way for the triumph of totalitarianism. Usually this charge is coupled with the assertion that the philosophy of democracy *must* be based upon the specific dogmas of one or another theologic-metaphysical school.

The bulk of this essay will be devoted to the analysis of the demo-cratic faith in order to discover whether it necessarily rests upon theo-logical or metaphysical truths or whether an adequate justification of democracy can be made from a naturalistic standpoint.

A few preliminary remarks are necessary in order to indicate in what sense the term "naturalism" is to be understood. Despite the variety of specific doctrines which naturalists have professed from Democritus to Dewey, what unites them all is the wholehearted acceptance of scientific method as the only reliable way of reaching truths about the world of nature, society, and man. The differences between naturalists in the his-tory of thought can easily be explained in terms of (1) varying historical conceptions of what fields and problems are amenable to scientific treat-ment and (2) progressive refinements in the methods of inquiry them-selves. All their differences can in principle be resolved by appealing to the *method* to which they give common allegiance, except for those tem-peramental differences of emphasis and selective bias which no natu-ralist claims to be an avenue to truth. The least common denominator of all historic naturalisms, therefore, is not so much a set of specific doc-trines as the method of scientific or rational empiricism.

Naturalism is opposed to all known forms of supernaturalism, not because it rules out a priori what may or may not exist, but because no plausible evidence has been found to warrant belief in the entities and powers to which supernatural status has been attributed. The existence of God, immortality, disembodied spirits, cosmic purpose and design, as these have been customarily interpreted by the great institutional reli-gions, are denied by naturalists for the same generic reasons that they deny the existence of fairies, elves, and leprechauns. There are other conceptions of God, to be sure, and provided they are not self-contradic-tory in meaning, the naturalist is prepared in principle to consider their claims to validity. All he asks is that the conception be sufficiently defi-nite to make possible specific inferences of the determinate conditions—the *how*, *when*, and *where* of His operation. The trouble with most con-ceptions of God which differ from the conventional ones is that either they are so vague that no one can tell what they mean or else they des-ignate something in experience for which a perfectly suitable term already exists.

I do not see that anything is gained by blinking the fact that the nat-uralist denies the existence of supernatural powers. Nor need he pass as an agnostic except in those situations in which the weight of evidence is equally balanced and he suspends judgment until such time as more evidence is available. But if he is faithful to his method, he must assert that for every traditional conception of God, the weight of evidence so far is decidedly in the negative. So long as no self-contradictory notions are advanced, he will not rule out the abstract logical possibility that angelic creatures push the planets any more than that there exists a gingerbread castle on the other side of the moon. All he demands is the presence of sufficient precision of meaning to make it possible to test, let us say—taking an illustration disputed by the doctrinal findings of past naturalisms—the existence of extrasensory perception. The possibility of extrasensory perception cannot be ruled out a priori. Here, as elsewhere, the naturalist must follow the preponderance of scientific evidence. He therefore welcomes those who talk about the experiential evidence for religious beliefs as distinct from those who begin with mystery and end in mystery. He only asks to be given an opportunity to examine the evidence and to evaluate it by the same general canons which have led to the great triumphs of knowledge in the past. It is natural in this case, as in the case of extrasensory perception, that he should scrutinize with great care reports which if true would lead him radically to modify some of his earlier generalizations. The unusual must clear a higher hurdle of credibility than the usual. But only on its first jump. Unfortunately, for all their talk of appeal to experience, direct or indirect, religious experientialists dare not appeal to any experience of sufficiently determinate character to permit of definite tests. There is a certain wisdom in this reluctance. For if experience can confirm a belief, it can also invalidate it. But to most supernaturalists this is an inadmissible possibility. We therefore find that the kind of experience to which reference is made is not only unique but also uniquely self-authenticating. Those who are not blessed by the experiences are regarded as blind or deaf or worse! But is it not odd that those who worship Zeus on the ground of a unique experience should deny to others the right to worship Odin on the ground of a different unique experience?

I have deliberately sharpened the antisupernatural doctrinal conclusions of naturalism in order to meet squarely the challenge to naturalism to find a consistent and rational defense of democratic belief on the basis of scientific method.

# III

The successful defense of democracy does not rest primarily upon the analysis of its nature and presuppositions. Nonetheless, some clarification of the meaning of democracy, of the ground upon which we hold it and of the procedure by which we arrive at conclusions for the class of problems and decisions of this kind is necessary if our choice to defend democracy is to be intelligent. Insofar as intelligent choice makes a difference to events, analysis is not without ultimate bearing upon conduct. Particularly today, when the allegiances of large numbers have become unhinged and even larger numbers are more certain of what they want to believe than of the reasons for their belief, the answers to our questions may be of some practical moment. It is noteworthy that in an age not conspicuous for its appeal to reason, few will give assent to doctrines which they admit to be demonstrably false or out of line with verifiable fact.

Perhaps more dangerous to democracy than arguments against it is the feeling that analysis or reflection is irrelevant to those "beliefs" for which we are prepared to suffer, to fight, and sometimes to die. They are then regarded either as automatic consequences of conditioning—social or biological—or as sacred commands from a divine source, or as the irresistible cry of conscience. Once the rational nerve of belief is paralyzed, action may still be vigorous in behalf of expressed goals, but it cannot be intelligent. For whatever else intelligence is, it is sensitiveness to, and awareness of, the presence of *alternate means* which in fact determine the realized content of the goals we profess. Belief without reasons blinds us to the presence of alternate means. That is why the action it inspires is so often self-defeating. There are many causes in history of which we can say that they have been betrayed by their own successes.

# IV

It is hard to separate a discussion of democracy from a discussion of its philosophical presuppositions, for the nature of democracy is itself often in dispute. In addition, the meaning of the word "presuppositions" is not univocal. Its customary usage includes "consequences" and "implications," as well as "assumptions." What I propose to do, therefore, in order to facilitate the joining of issues, is to ask and answer three generic questions. The first is: What is democracy? The second is: What are the grounds or reasons on which we can justify our belief in democracy? The third is: Are there any facts of a cosmic, historical, or psychological kind which stand in the way of our acceptance of democracy, that is, which make democracy an impracticable ideal? It is apparent that the last two questions are related, since if any ideal is demonstrably impracticable—in a sense other than completely realizable, for no ideal can be completely realized—this would have some bearing upon its desirability or upon the grounds of our choice.

# V

Any adequate description of the nature of democracy must at the very least do justice to customary usage, which distinguishes between democratic and nondemocratic societies and between historic phases within any one society, regarded as more or less democratic with relation to each other. Although for propaganda purposes even totalitarian states claim to be democratic "in a higher sense," their canonic writings recognize the differences between the structure of these states and those considered democratic in a less esoteric sense. This is often betrayed in the adjectives prefixed to the latter, such as "so-called," "alleged," "parliamentary," or "bourgeois." Germany and Russia and Italy are not democratic states; England and the United States are. And when historians examine the development of English and American society they unanimously acknowledge, although they evaluate the fact differently, that these societies were less democratic, when property, racial, or religious qualifications were set for citizenship than they are today, when these qualifications have been eliminated or reduced.

What principle is expressed in these customary distinctions? The principle may be stated in various ways, but for our purposes we may say that a democratic state is one in which the basic decisions of government rest upon the freely given consent of the governed.[2] This obviously is only a beginning. For as soon as we begin to investigate the conditions which must be present before we grant that a state lives up to this principle, we are carried beyond the sphere of political considerations into the domain of ethics. Thus, if information has been withheld or withdrawn before consent is assessed; if the opposition is muzzled or suppressed so that consent is as unanimous as a totalitarian plebiscite; or if economic sanctions are threatened against a section of the community in the event that consent takes one form or another, we declare that the "spirit" or "logic" or "rationale" of democracy is absent from its political forms. If birth does not give divine right, neither do numbers. We are all acquainted with situations in which we say that a political democracy has traduced its own ideals. Whenever we criticize existing states which conform to the political definition of democracy on the ground that they are not democratic enough; whenever we point out that Athenian democracy was limited only to free men or that in some parts of the American South it is limited only to white men, or that in some countries it is limited only to men, we are invoking a broader principle of democracy as a controlling reference in our judgments of comparison. This principle is an ethical one.

What is this principle of ethical democracy? It is the principle of equality—an equality, not of status or origin, but of opportunity, relevant functions, and social participation. The enormous literature and bitter controversy which center around the concept of equality indicate that it is only a little less ambiguous than the concept of democracy. It is necessary, therefore, to block it off from some current notions before developing the argument.

1. The principle of equality is not a *description* of fact about men's physical or intellectual natures. It is a *prescription* or policy for treating men.

2. It is not a prescription for treating men in identical ways who are unequal in their physical or intellectual nature. It is a policy of equality of concern or consideration for men whose different needs may require differential treatment.

3. It is not a mechanical policy of equal opportunity for everyone at any time and in all respects. A musical genius is entitled to greater opportunities to develop his musical talents than someone who is tone deaf. It is equality of opportunity for all individuals to develop whatever personal and socially desirable talents they possess and to make whatever unique contributions their capacities permit.

4. It is not a demand for absolute uniformity of living conditions or even for arithmetically equal compensation for socially useful work. It demands that when the productive forces of a society makes possible the gratification of basic human needs (which are, of course, historical variables), no one should be deprived of necessities in order to provide others with luxuries.

5. It is not a policy of restricting the freedom of being different or

becoming different. It is a policy of *encouraging* the freedom to be different, restricting only that exercise of freedom which converts talents or possessions into a monopoly that frustrates the emergence of other free personalities.

6. It is not a demand that all people be leaders or that none should be. It does demand that the career of leadership, like all other careers, be open to all whose natural or acquired talents qualify them; that everyone have a say in the process of selecting leaders; that the initiative of leaders operate within a framework of basic laws; and that these laws in turn ultimately rest upon the freely given consent of the persons who constitute the community.

7. It does not make the assumption of sentimental humanitarianism that all men are naturally good. It does assume that men, treated as equals in a community of persons, may become better. The emphasis upon respect for the personality of all individuals, the attitude which treats the personality, not as something fixed, but as a growing, developing pattern, is unique to the philosophy of democracy.

What I have been trying to show is that the logic of the democrat's position compels him to go beyond the limited conception of political democracy—the equality of freedom—to a broader attitude extending to those other phases of social existence that bear upon the effective exercise of equality of freedom. This in fact has been the historical tendency observable wherever democratic principies and programs are permitted to operate. Perhaps the synoptic phrase "social equality," whose connotations encompass political, educational, and economic democracy, may be taken as the most appropriate expression of the meaning of democracy in the broadest sense.

It is clear that the principle of equality, like any principle of justice, cannot by itself determine what is specifically right or good in each concrete case. But whatever the right is discovered to be, from the point of view of democracy it is the result of an analysis which considers equally the needs of all the persons involved in the situation; and, furthermore, whatever the good is, it becomes better to the extent that it is shared among other members of the community. It is also clear that in concrete situations there will be conflicts between various demands for equality and that in negotiating these conflicts the methods of intelligence are indispensable for a functioning democracy. If "naturalism" and "scientific empiricism" be generic terms for the philosophic attitude which submits *all* claims of fact and value to test by experience, then scientific empiricism as a philosophy is more congenial to a democratic than to an antidemocratic community, for it brings into the open light of criticism the interests in which moral values and social institutions are rooted.[3] *Empiricism so conceived is commitment to a procedure, not to a theory of metaphysics.*

In this brief account of the nature of democracy as a way of life I have not aimed at an exhaustive analysis of the *forms* in which it may be expressed, but have tried to indicate the basic ideals which are involved in the customary usage of the term and in the implications of that usage.

# VI

We now come to the problem which is of primary concern to philosophers. What are the grounds upon which acceptance of democracy in contradistinction to other modes of social life can be justified? So far as I can see, there are four generic types of justification which have been or can be offered.

The first asserts that the rational foundation of democratic belief consists in a set of supernatural religious truths in the sense that there can be no intelligent ground for choosing between democracy and other forms of society which does not logically commit us to some kind of theology.

The second asserts the same thing about metaphysics understood as a theory of "reality." Usually these two approaches go hand in hand.

The third maintains that the choice of democracy is a nonrational preference rooted in the constitution of our natures and brought to flower by nurture and education.

The fourth affirms that the belief in democracy is an hypothesis controlled by the same general pattern of inquiry which we apply to any scientific hypothesis, but referring to different subject matter, that is, our evaluations.

1. *Democracy and religion.*—Does democracy as a way of life rest upon belief in supernatural religious truths in the sense that if the latter are denied, the former must necessarily be denied? It is becoming increasingly fashionable to maintain this. Were historical considerations relevant here, I think it could be conclusively established that the great institutional religions, with the possible exception of some forms of Protestantism, have tended in fact to support theocratic forms of government. Nor is this surprising if the Kingdom of Heaven be taken as a model

or inspiration for the Kingdom of Earth. Whoever heard of a democratically organized Paradise? Walt Whitman in heaven would meet with the same fate as Lucifer, but for different reasons. Not only is the notion of a democratically organized heaven blasphemous, but the proposal to reform along democratic lines a hierarchically organized church would lead to excommunication. If we examine the actual behavior which has been sanctified by the maxim: "Render unto Caesar what is Caesar's and to God what is God's," we will discover that historical, institutional religion has always been able to adapt itself to any form of government or society which will tolerate its existence.

But our concern is not with historical questions, fascinating as they are, but with the logic of the position. We must consequently rephrase the question to read: Does belief in democracy logically rest upon any theological propositions in the sense that the denial of the second entails the denial of the first? And for this discussion I shall take as illustrative of theological propositions the two cardinal propositions of natural theology, namely, "God exists" and "Man has an immortal soul." To assert that whoever has no grounds for affirming the existence of God and immortality has no grounds for affirming the validity of democracy is to claim that the former are at least necessary conditions of the latter. I shall argue that they constitute neither necessary nor sufficient conditions.

a) Before examining this claim, let us note the tremendous risk it involves. Were those who advance it ever compelled to admit that these theological propositions are indemonstrable or false, they would have to surrender their belief in democracy. But this, I submit, very few of them are prepared to do. They would search for other reasons and grounds. Like those who would make the validity of moral judgments dependent upon the existence of God and immortality, the theological defenders of democracy shift from a problem in which, although difficult, it is possible to reach an agreement on the basis of some empirical evidence, to one in which the nature of the terms and sphere of discourse makes such agreement much more difficult. Confirmed democrats, it seems to me, are much more convinced of the validity of the democratic ideal than they are of the theological propositions upon which it presumably depends. They would no more exonerate from the obligation of accepting the democratic ideal an atheist or agnostic who pleads that he has no reason to believe in God and the hereafter than they would exempt him from the obligation of living honestly.

b) Aside from the difficulties of establishing God's existence, how can we get from the fact of his existence to the desirability of the democratic way of life? None of the attributes of God, save the moral attributes, can serve as a premise justifying one way of life rather than another. And if the moral attributes of God can serve as premises, necessary or sufficient, for the democratic way of life, it is only because *we* regard them as worthy, that is, as truly moral. Obviously any theology which makes God's power the justification or source of his goodness is worse than useless for purposes of deriving democracy. The attribution of moral qualities to God is an expression of what we think his qualities ought to be. And this is a problem of precisely the same order as that which we are called upon to answer when we ask for the grounds of our democratic allegiance.

c) The situation is the same if we grant that human beings have immortal souls. In what way is this a necessary or sufficient presupposition of democracy? The brotherhood of man may be a theological fact as it is a biological fact, but what makes it wrong for Cain to kill his brother Abel and right, under certain circumstances, for us to kill Cain is a moral principle which can no more be derived from theology than from biology—unless, of course, the moral principle is one of the premises of our theological (or biological) system. In this case we are no further along than we were when we raised the question about the democratic way of life. In passing it should be observed that belief in the immortality of the soul can be, and has been, used (in the Hindu doctrines of *samtra* and *karma*) to sanctify the tightest system of antidemocratic social stratification the world has ever seen.[4]

2. *Democracy and metaphysics.*—The problem of the metaphysical foundation of democracy is more difficult because of varying conceptions of metaphysics. By "metaphysics" I shall understand the discipline designated by the term "ontology" or any theory of "being *überhaupt.*" The evidence seems to me to be overwhelming that there is a definite historical connection between the social movements of a period and its dominant metaphysical teachings; furthermore, I am prepared to defend as a historically true proposition that systems of idealistic metaphysics, because of the semiofficial roles they have played in their respective culures, have been more generally employed to bolster antidemocratic social movements than systems of empirical or materialistic metaphysics. Whether there is *always* an intrinsic personal or psychological relation between a philosopher's metaphysics and his ethics or politics is a more difficult question, but one which seems to me to require an answer in the negative. More germane to our present concern is my con-

tention that there is no necessary logical connection between a theory of being or becoming and any particular theory of ethics or politics. Stated more accurately, it seems to me demonstrable that no system of metaphysics *univocally* determines a system of ethics or politics. There may be certain facts about man and nature which might have a bearing upon our judgment about what social system is of the highest worth, but, as I shall argue later, these are facts concerning which the empirical sciences are qualified to report without benefit of metaphysics.

Two species of metaphysics are most often invoked in behalf of democracy. One asserts that the value of democracy or the values from which it may be derived are "grounded in reality," a phrase which is interpreted to mean that the universe "justifies" or "guarantees" both the validity and the ultimate supremacy of basic human ideals. I must confess that it is difficult for me to understand this view except as a shamefaced kind of theology. However that may be, there is no agreed-upon denotation of *the* universe. There are many universes. Nor is there any one basic human ideal, but there are many human ideals which are often in conflict with one another, even though they all invoke the universe as ground of their validity and as a guaranty of their triumph. Finally, and most important, no matter what character the universe is alleged to have, no matter what the nature of the far-off event toward which it is moving, no matter who wins or loses, nothing logically compelling in the way of judgment follows unless *we* have already morally evaluated the character of events. For most metaphysicians the very word "reality" is an implicit value term. To be sure, history may be conceived as a struggle between the Prince of Darkness and the Prince of Light, but the latter is so named because he carries *our* moral flag.

The second metaphysical view to which resort is often made is at the same time a kind of rejoinder to our position. It distinguishes between a metaphysical realm of being and a metaphysical realm of values and grounds the democratic way of life in the latter. Just as the spectrum of colors is there to be beheld by all who are not color blind and would still be there even if man's ancestors had climbed no higher than the mole in the tree of evolution, so the spectrum of values is there to be beheld by all who are not value blind and would still be there even if human beings had never existed at all. The view that colors would still be there even if human beings had no eyes is not without its difficulties. But they do not begin to compare in difficulty with the view that values are essentially unrelated to an evaluator and his interests. Santayana has quite aptly remarked of this doctrine that there is much sense in saying that whiskey "is pervaded as it were, by an inherent intoxication, and stands dead drunk in its bottle."

The subject is vast, but it is enough to show that this view is question-begging in precisely the same way as other theological and metaphysical derivations. The existence of these absolute norms is presumably certified or authenticated at some point by an act of immediate intuition. If the testimony of the intuition is construed not merely from what individuals *say* they intuit but also from the conduct that flows from their intuition—and conduct counts more in any moral scheme than mere words—then it is clear that individuals intuit or "see" *different* values. The "great" visions are not all compatible with one another in what they command, not to mention the visions that we do not call great. Which visions are the authentic ones? Prior to every conclusion that these are the objective values of all eternity, or even of all time and existence, is the assumption that *this* is the trustworthy seer. In a dispute between two men, one of whom asserts that the other is color blind and the other that the first is "just seeing things," there are definite ways of determining who is right. In a dispute between two seers whose immediate intuitions report conflicting news about the nature and hierarchy of absolute values, there is no rational way of reaching a consensus. The true prophet cannot be distinguished from the false by invoking absolute values whose validity depends upon a prior assumption of the reliability of prophetic testimony. The complacency with which some writers have cut the Gordian knot by introducing reference to the intuitions of "the best people" or "the most cultured people" or "the saving remnant" is evidence either of parochialism or of snobbery.

The record of human error and cruelty shows what ghastly consequences often result from the conviction that one's moral insight cannot possibly be wrong and that it needs no further justification than its own incandescent purity. No more than a solipsist can make plausible on his own assumptions the existence of another solipsist, can an absolutist find a rightful place for another absolutist who disagrees with him. Absolutists face each other over an abyss which cannot be bridged even by their weapons of war.

3. *Democracy and preferences.*—The view that an acceptance of democracy is an expression of a preference does not carry us far until the kind of preference is indicated. A preference may express a passing whim or a deep natural bent; it may be impulsive or reflective. Preferences are

rooted in our natures. Their forms, occasions, and objects are supplied by education, that is, broadly speaking, by social habits and intelligence. But either our natures can be changed, or the educators can be re-educated. If neither is possible, then the fact of moral choice becomes unintelligible. If we can offer no justification of a preference except that it is ours, obviously no point of intellectual or moral issue is raised; nor, a fortiori, can any be settled by the trial of arms. If we offer a justification of a preference, it will take one of the generic forms already discussed or about to be discussed.

4. *Democracy as a hypothesis.*—When democracy is taken strictly as a form of political government, its superiority over other forms of government can be established to the extent to which it achieves more security, freedom, and cooperative diversity than any of its alternatives. If we test the workings of political democracy by Paul's scheme of virtues or by Nietzsche's, we may perhaps reach another conclusion. So long as there is no dispute about observable effects and so long as we raise no question about the moral ideals by which we evaluate these effects, we have clear sailing.

But, as has already been made plain, by democracy as a way of life we mean a way of organizing human relationships which embodies a certain complex of moral ideals. Can these ideals be treated as hypotheses? The conventional reply has always been that no moral principle can be regarded as a hypothesis, for we must already have certain knowledge of what is good before we can evaluate the consequences of acting upon it. If any position is question-begging, surely this seems to be.

Were this a symposium on value theory, I would devote all my time to developing the general theory of moral ideals as hypotheses. But here I can only barely indicate that the notion is not viciously circular. A moral ideal is a prescription to act in a certain situation or class of situations in determinate ways that will organize the human needs and wants involved so as to fulfill a set of other values which are postulated as binding in relation to the problem in hand. No more than in other cases of inquiry do we start with an empty head. The cluster of values we bring to the situation is the result of prior experience and reflection. *They are not arbitrarily postulated.* The consequences of acting upon the hypothesis may lead us to challenge a postulated or assumed value. This in turn can become the subject of a similar investigation. Terminal values are always related to specific contexts; there is no absolute terminal value which is either self-evident or beyond the necessity of justifying itself if its credentials are challenged. There is no vicious infinite regress involved if we take our problems concretely and one at a time. Nor is the procedure narrowly circular. For if after a long history of raising and solving moral problems we postulate as a value in solving a later problem a value which had itself to be certified in an earlier problem, this would testify to the presence of a fruitful set of systematically related values in the structure of our moral behavior. New values would emerge or be discovered in the course of our attempt to act upon our ideals and from the necessity of mediating the conflict between the postulated values as they bear on concrete human needs in specific situations.

I should like, however, to make the general position take form out of the discussion of the theme before us. That theme is: *Why should we treat individuals of unequal talents and endowments as persons who are equally entitled to relevant consideration and care?* Short of a treatise, I can state only the reasons, without amplification of the concrete needs of the social situation which democracy seeks to meet and the institutional practices by which it must meet them.

1. This method of treating human beings is more successful than any other in evoking a maximum of creative, voluntary effort from all members of the community. Properly implemented, it gives all persons a stake in the community and elicits a maximum of intelligent loyalty.

2. It enlarges the scope of our experience by enabling us to acquire insight into the needs, drives, and aspirations of others. Learning to understand how life is organized by other centers of experience is both a challenge and a discipline for our imagination. In aiding the growth of others, we aid our own growth.

3. The willingness to understand another man's point of view without necessarily surrendering to it makes it more likely that different points of view may negotiate their differences and learn to live peacefully with one another. A democratic community cannot be free from strife in a world where inequalities will always exist, but its ethics, when intelligently acted upon, makes more likely the diminution of strife or its transference to socially harmless forms than is the case when its principle of equality is denied. The consequences are less toadying, less fear, and less duplicity in the equalitarian community than there are in the nonequalitarian society.

4. In nurturing the capacities of each individual so that they may come to their greatest fulfillment we can best share our existing stores of truth and beauty and uncover new dimensions in these realms. How can anyone dedicated to the values of science and art  consistently oppose a

policy which maximizes the possibility of the discovery and widest dispersion of scientific truths and artistic meanings?

5. Regard for the potentialities of all individuals makes for less cruelty of man toward man, especially where cruelty is the result of blindness to, or ignorance of, the needs of others. A community organized along democratic lines is guilty of cruelty only at those points where it has failed to live up to its own ideals. A totalitarian community is systematically insensitive to the personal needs not only of members of the outlawed scapegoat group but also of the majority of its subjects who are excluded from policy-making discussions. At best, there is no way of determining these personal needs except by the interpretation of the dictator and his experts who act on the fateful dogma that they know the true interests of their subjects better than the subjects themselves. At worst, the dictator assumes not only that, he speaks for his subjects but that in some mystic way he feels and thinks for them too. Despite the great limitations—limitations from the point of view of their own ideals—under which the nineteenth- and twentieth-century democracies of the Western world suffered, I think it is indisputable, on the evidence, that by and large their social life, insofar as this was the consequence of policy, displayed less cruelty than the social life of any other historical period.

6. Reasonableness of conclusions, where attitudes and interests conflict, depends upon the degree of mutual consultation and free intellectual communication between the principals involved. The democratic way of life makes possible the widest forms of mutual consultation and communication. Conclusions reached by these processes have a quality that can never be found where conclusions are imposed by force or authority—even if they are our own. Let me illustrate what I mean by taking as an example an enterprise represented by a community of scholars, let us say the American Philosophical Association. Who among us, desirous as we may be of the possibility of philosophical agreement, would forego the methods of public discussion, criticism, argument, and rejoinder for a philosophical consensus imposed by a Gestapo or a G.P.U., even if by a strange quirk of affairs it was *our* philosophic position that the goon squads of orthodoxy sought to make the way of salvation? Who among us, knowing that outside the threshold of our meetings there stood an individual of foreign country, color, or faith, capable of making a contribution to our deliberations, would not open the door to him? These are not rhetorical questions framed to discover philosophical fifth columnists. They are designed to show that the procedures of critical dis-

cussion and discovery, which are preeminently exhibited in the work of a scientific community, take for granted that national, racial, or religious origins are irrelevant to the logic of the method by which reasonable conclusions are reached. Democracy as a way of life differs from its alternatives in that it makes possible the extension of this method of reaching reasonable conclusions from the fields of professional science and philosophy to all areas of human experience in which genuine problems arise.

There are other grounds that may be offered in justification of democracy as the most adequate social philosophy for our times. Every one of them, like the foregoing, postulates implicitly or explicitly values or desiderata. But I repeat: these postulates are ultimate only for the problem in hand. They may require justification. When we undertake such justification, we have undertaken a new inquiry into a new problem. Much is assumed on the basis of previously tested evidence: nothing is logically begged.

There are two important consequences of approaching democracy in this way. The first is that we avoid the temptation, which is rapidly gaining vogue, of making democracy absolutely valid in and for itself. There are many today who write as if they believe that democracy should prevail even though the heavens fall and say in so many words that "to question the validity of democracy is to disbelieve in it"[5] and that we can meet the blind fanatical faith of fascism only with a faith in democracy which is at least just as fanatical. This temptation, it seems to me, must be avoided because by counterposing subrational dogma to subrational dogma, we prepare the ground for an acceptance of a "might makes right" morality. Secondly, those who make of democracy an absolute value, which requires no justification but its inherent rightness, tend to identify this absolute democracy with whatever particular democratic *status quo* exists. On the other hand, the natural tendency of those who cannot distinguish between social philosophies on the ground of their inherent rightness is to test a social philosophy by the social institutions in which it is embodied. They are, therefore, more attentive to the actual workings and effects of democracy, more historical minded, and less likely to gloss over existing imperfections.

To those who say that human beings will not fight wholeheartedly except for certainties, and emphatically not for a hypothesis which is only probable, the reply must be made that this empirical proposition is highly dubious. Men have fought and do fight vigorously for causes on the basis of preponderant evidence. Vigorous action, indeed, is only desirable in troubled situations when we have first decided what *is* intelligent action. And intelligent action does not result when we assume that our ideas or ideals simply cannot be wrong. That both intelligence and resoluteness are compatible is clear in fields as far apart as military science and medicine. Once it is decided that the chances of one military action are relatively better than another or once it is decided that an operation gives a patient a better chance of surviving than no operation, wisdom demands that the best warranted alternative be pursued with all our heart and all our soul. Let us remember that when we are called upon to fight for democracy we are not asked to fight for an ideal which has just been proposed as a *merely possible* valid ideal for our times; we already have considerable evidence in its behalf, the weight of which, unfortunately too often, is properly evaluated by some critics only when democracy is lost or imperiled. We have every reason to believe that we are fighting for a truth, and sometimes it is necessary to fight for it even though the fighting doesn't make it true. But in contradistinction to others who fight for their truths, we are prepared to establish to reasonable men that democracy is the better alternative. But not all men are reasonable, it will be objected. This brings us to the theme of our final section.

## VII

We now turn to the question, Is democracy feasible? We can imagine someone who has accepted the tentative ends by which we evaluate ways of life criticizing us as follows: "If only the assertions made in the previous section could be established as true, the case for democracy would be convincing. But the nature of man as we know him, of history as scientifically understood, and of the larger world we live in precludes the possibility of ever achieving democracy. It runs counter to the facts. Although you may still choose to live or to die for democracy, the attempt to realize it, like any attempt to realize an ideal which has no natural basis, will be a ghastly failure. Its natural consequences will be worse than the evils it sets out to cure, and it will subvert the very ideals to which you have appealed in your argument. Democracy is an infirmity of noble but innocent minds who have never understood the world. It is not an intelligent option."

I have to consider briefly three types of objection to the feasibility of the democratic ideal.

1. The first is based upon the alleged psychological impossibility of democracy. It maintains that democracy is too good for men who are essentially evil, fallen creatures, dominated by the lust for power, property, and self. In less theological form it asserts that democracy makes too high a call upon human intelligence and disinterestedness.

It is true that the psychological nature of man is quite relevant to our problem. If most human beings were idiots or infantile or permanently incapable of self-development, the democratic ideal could hardly be defended on plausible grounds. But there is no evidence that most human beings are such, and *an intelligent attempt to find out whether they are would require that equalization of social opportunity which is of the essence of democracy.* Even without such an experiment, if we surrender the utopian expectation of the complete realization of the democratic ideal and bear in mind that the forms of democracy may be direct as well as indirect and that democracy is compatible with the delegation of powers and responsibilities, the evidence at hand could hardly justify the belief either in universal cretinism or in man's permanent ineducability. Nor do we have to counter, with the assertion that men are *infinitely* perfectible to make our option for democracy reasonable. We require merely that they be sufficiently plastic, sufficiently capable of learning, improvement, and intelligent self-criticism, to choose responsibly between alternatives of action whenever—and here is the rub— they have alternatives of choice. It is only the democratic community which will systematically give them the alternatives of choice on basic decisions. It is not without significance that no free people has ever voluntarily relinquished its democratic forms in favor of a government which has openly proclaimed as its aim the establishment of a permanent dictatorship. Principled dictatorship, as distinct from those that come in through the unguarded doors of democracy, always triumph by usurpation. As low as the human estate is today, there is no reason to believe that human beings belong to a psychological species inferior to that of their ancestors. Although history is rich in human stupidities and lost opportunities, in the face of men's achievements in the arts and sciences it would be simply foolish to read history as nothing but the record of human error.

The theological doctrine of man's essentially evil nature metaphorically expresses the truth that he is always limited, always tempted, and never free from his animal origins. But, taken literally, it makes any kind of moral virtue inconceivable except by interposition of divine grace or mystery. Here, too, we do not have to counter with a contrary theological proposition that man is essentially good. He is neither one nor the other, but he becomes good or evil depending upon his society, his habits, and his intelligence.

2. The most powerful arguments against the feasibility of democracy, strangely enough, have been neglected by most social philosophers. These are developed in the writings of Gaetano Mosca, Vilfredo Pareto, and Roberto Michels. Their common thesis, formulated on the basis of vast, detailed studies of political and social history, is that all historical change, whether reform or revolution, consists of the substitution of one ruling minority for another. This rule rests upon three pillars: vital myths which cement human relationships and conceal differences of interest; fraud or manipulation which negotiates differences of interests; and force which ultimately settles differences of interest. The nature of social organization, they maintain, is such that democrats may be victorious, but democracy never. So it has been; so it is; and so it will be.

I have elsewhere tried to meet their arguments in detail.[6] But here I content myself with one consideration which points to the self-confessed inadequacy of their position. Despite this alleged law, every one of them admits, explicitly or implicitly, that some forms of society are better than others—and in every case it is the society which has a greater degree of democracy than the others. Thus Mosca, after maintaining the inescapability of minority rule, pays strong tribute to the superiority of parliamentary democracy over all other alternatives.[7]

Three basic errors, it seems to me, vitiate their conclusion. The first is that the amount of freedom and democracy in a society is determined by a law *already known*, or, as some would say today, by a historical wave. The truth is that the amount of freedom and democracy in the present and the future depends as much upon human willingness to fight for them as upon anything else. The second error is the belief, common not only to these thinkers but also to countless others, that human nature is unchangeable. Insofar as this is neither a proposition of biology or of theology nor a logical tautology, but refers to psychological and social traits, it can be shown to be false. The third is their confusion between an organizing principle and the individual members of the series organized. Since no identification is possible between the principle of democracy and any one member of the series, they go from the true conclusion that the principle is incompletely realized in any one case to the false conclusion that there are no degrees of realization in the series of cases.

3. The third class of objections to the feasibility of the democratic ideal is derived from alleged cosmic or physico-chemical laws which contain the equations of doom for man and all his works. Even granting the validity of such laws, they would hold no matter what society exists, and therefore they establish nothing about the relative superiority of one form of society over another. Such laws, as William James already pointed out in a definitive refutation of all views of this type, tell us about the *size* of "energy-rills," not their *significance*.[8]

# VIII

That the cosmic home of man limits his power, if not his dreams, is, of course, true. It is a perennial source of his humility before the intractabilities of things and the transient character of what he builds. But it is also true that this limitation is the source of his opportunities and a necessary condition for all achievement. From these truths we cannot infer that nature is the guarantor of man's ideals, certainly not of the democratic ideal. But neither is it the enemy of human ideals. Man's friends and enemies are other men. To forget this is to go from natural piety to superstition. The cosmic scene against which men live out their lives will not be affected by Hitler's victory or by his defeat. Democracy needs no cosmic support other than the *chance* to make good. That chance it has, because man is part of nature. To ask for more is unreasonable, even if it is not unworthy. The way in which man acts upon his chances is additional evidence of the objective possibilities and novelties of existence. Insofar as he is caught up in the flux of things, the intelligent democratic man honestly confronts the potentialities of existence, its futurities, its openness, its indeterminateness. He is free from the romantic madness which would seek to outlaw the truths of science and of the quaint conceit, permissible only as poetry, that nature is a democratic republic. He takes the world as science describes it. He employs his knowledge of the world to increase man's power over things, to decrease man's power over man, and to enlarge the fellowship of free and equal persons striving to achieve a more just and happier society.

[1944]

# NOTES

1. These contentions run through the *Proceedings of the Conference on Science, Philosophy, and Religion in Their Relation to the Democratic Way of Life*. The neo-Thomists are most vociferous in their promulgation. Other religious and metaphysical groups are now echoing them. See Hallowell, *Ethics* 3, no. 3 (1942): 337.

2. Although the chief terms in this statement are vague, they can be made more precise (see my *Reason, Social Myths, and Democracy* [New York: John Day, 1940], 285). On the basis of the analysis a set of important conditions is enumerated, in the absence of which democracy cannot exist; in addition, a set of conditions is described on the *presence* of which the effective functioning of democracy depends.

3. For further elaboration of the connections between empiricism and democracy see my "Metaphysics and Social Attitudes: A Reply," *Social Frontier* 4, no. 32 (February 1938): 153–58.

4. See Max Weber, *Religionssoziologie*, Tübingen, 1920, vol. 2, 119–20. The lot of the Hindu in this life is a consequence of his sins or virtues in a previous life. Therefore, he cannot complain about the injustice of any, "accident of birth" or station. But, no matter how unclean his caste, he has the hope that, by exemplary observance of the caste rituals and cheerful acceptance of his present lot, he may improve his social position in the next cycle of rebirth.

5. James Feibleman, *Positive Democracy* (Chapel Hill: University of North Carolina Press, 1940), 124: "Democracy requires the same unconscious belief in its rationality as does science. To question the validity of democracy is to disbelieve in it, for we must not even be aware of our belief if it is to be profound enough to mean anything."

6. *Reason, Social Myths, and Democracy*, chap. 7.

7. Gaetano Mosca, *The Ruling Classes*, Eng. trans. by H. D. Kahn; New York and London: McGraw-Hill, 1939), 256.

8. See his reply to Henry Adams, who tried to draw social and historical implications from the second law of thermodynamics (*The Letters of William James*, Henry James, ed. [Boston: Atlantic Monthly Press, 1920], vol. 2, 344–47).

# 10

# THE PHILOSOPHICAL HERITAGE OF THE ATLANTIC DEMOCRACIES

ncreasingly in recent years I have been struck by the frequency with
which practitioners of the arts and sciences have turned to philosophy
to supply some basic formula or comprehensive scheme of values to solve
the world's ills. This faith in the role of philosophy, whether well founded
or not, is a sign of cultural quickening, testifying to a belief in the power of
ideas even among those who are always talking about *the concrete*—which
has been called the most deceptive abstraction in our language. It is a faith
that should recall philosophy to its perennial mission. For modern professional philosophers have not been overmuch concerned with the great
questions of value and value conflict, whose critical study constitutes the
distinctive subject matter of philosophy in the grand tradition.

Nonetheless many of the tasks assigned to philosophers already pre-
determine the issues which we rely on philosophers to illuminate with
clarity and wisdom. They are asked to develop a philosophy that will make
for peace among nations, safeguard democracy, preserve the classical tradition, reinforce religious belief and practice, diminish the divorce rate,
justify free enterprise, or strengthen the United Nations. Any philosopher
today can find an audience if his book is advertised as a contribution to
world unity. All he need do is to tack a chapter of inspirational platitudes
on to his pet epistemology or metaphysic. But he has not proceeded in a

From *Political Power and Personal Freedom: Critical Studies in Democracy, Communism, and Civil Rights* (New York: Criterion Books, 1959).

philosophical way unless among other things he has asked whether world unity is desirable if it involves the existence of a totalitarian police state on a world scale. After all, if peace is the be-all and end-all of human life we should have surrendered to Hitler long ago or, in the light of the development of nuclear weapons, capitulated to the Kremlin. The philosopher is distinguished from the ideologist in that he is not the hired man of some national or party interest, in that his primary allegiance is to the truth—hard as it may be to come by and unwelcome though it be when found. He has no special gifts for discovering or discerning values; but his critical training should equip him to see the implications of the values to which we commit ourselves, their alternatives, their relation to our needs, and to see the kind of evidence relevant to making those rational choices without which self-understanding is impossible.

Among the most fruitful subject matters for philosophical analysis are value conflicts both within our own tradition and between our tradition and other traditions. But a successful approach to them requires a degree of knowledge of social, political, and economic fact which few philosophers, as I have observed them, show. This explains in part why philosophers avoid such themes, and why, when they do not, they say such extraordinary things—such as the pronouncement of one American philosopher that the conflict between democracy and communism is essentially a conflict between pre-Kantian British epistemology and post-Kantian German epistemology, and that the future of world peace depends upon teaching the true theory (which happens to be his own) of the relation between perception, sense data, and scientific objects.

In any case the crisis of our time, of which the Communist crusade against the Western democracies, particularly the United States and England, is a part, challenges us to engage in a process of self-understanding. Let us explore the question of what remains valid in the heritage of the English speaking peoples without necessarily assuming that such validity is universal, or that its forms are either the sole or superior expression of the values they embody. The original language and inspiration of democracy was Greek, not English. And today other countries besides English speaking ones have as good a right to be considered democratic as their older sisters. There is no gene which determines political allegiance or behavior. The influence of democratic Anglo-American institutions on other countries is a consequence of historical rather than biological diffusion.

In the order of exposition rather than logic, an analysis of the Anglo-American heritage may seem more helpful to begin with than a discussion of the definition of democracy. But such an analysis is extremely difficult if this heritage is conceived in exclusively historical terms. I shall treat its historical aspects very briefly because it seems to me apparent that whenever we invoke tradition, especially to settle or recommend matters of policy, *we are not merely describing what the tradition is, but also prescribing what it should be.* Traditions are multiple, so much so that every departure from tradition is justified in terms of something selected from that same tradition. William of Ockham insisted he was only returning to Aristotle, Luther to basic Christianity, and Lenin to Marx. Few would deny that Hamilton and Jefferson are both part of the American tradition, as are Lincoln and Jefferson Davis, Huey Long and Roosevelt. In England the divergence is no less evident, whether we consider thinkers such as Hobbes and Locke, Carlyle and Mill, or such political figures as Cobden and Disraeli, Churchill and Morrison.

The histories of all peoples show sharp vicissitudes and great overturns. Traditions have resulted in part from civil wars, conquests, and revolutions. This indicates that no one can predict from a current tradition what its future will be. We are therefore rightly suspicious of anyone who speaks of *the* tradition of a country as if it gave a final patent of legitimacy. Finding a tradition is like finding an ancestor on a genealogical tree—we pass over the sinners as an alien strain and stop with someone who seems to us exemplary, the fount of our tradition.

In discussing what I regard as most valid in the tradition of the English speaking peoples, I am quite aware that other things besides those selected here are part of it. But beneath all the diversity, there is, it seems to me, a dominant tendency.

Three facets of the Anglo-American cultural tradition stand out as of prime significance. These are (1) the institutionalization of the principle of freely given consent; (2) the development of the experimental, empirical attitude—which, were it not for the inevitable misunderstandings that attend the phrase, I should like to call "the pragmatic temper"; and (3) the recognition of the worth of diversity, and the appreciation of the possibility of many different varieties of "excellence." All of these are obviously imperfectly realized, but I think it can be established that our culture has developed in these directions, and that they count for more than they do in other traditional cultures, such as, for example, the Chinese or Russian.

I have selected them for discussion because, among other reasons, they are under a heavy ordeal of fire from other—I will not say peoples, but governments; and because, although they are an indigenous part of our tradition, they can be broadened to become an integral part of human culture—of a world culture in which various national cultures may preserve their differences and still unite in coping with problems of common concern.

Of these three features obviously the most important is the experimental, empirical attitude. It is an attitude that assesses the truth of assertions and claims, both of fact and value, in terms of relevant results and consequences. It judges profession by performance. It looks upon principles as rules of action. Without eschewing abstractions—for no one can think without abstractions—it relates them to what is observed or observable in public experience. It does not denigrate appearances in behalf of a reality with a higher claim to truth; the appearances are always part of reality and the real is rational only to the extent that the appearances are, while a reality that makes no difference to appearances is a chimera. This attitude is tentative in its judgments but, because it makes judgments, it is not irresolute. It is initially skeptical of all large claims but, by admitting that some are better guides to conduct than others, it is not cynical. It is profane, commonsensical, open-minded about possibilities, but tough-minded about evidence.

This attitude seems to me to represent the dominant philosophic genius of the English speaking peoples—often misunderstood and scorned from without and attacked from within. The fanaticisms of political and social creeds emotionally based on *Weltanschauungen* are foreign to it—so foreign that it has difficulty in understanding them, for which it has sometimes paid heavily.

The wisdom of this attitude is most clearly apparent in the fact that it has developed a consensus of agreement on its basic political institutions without an *official* metaphysics or theology. Within the Anglo-American community are to be found groups and individuals who subscribe to mutually incompatible views on the nature of God, the universe, the origin of life, and its destiny. Yet all of them accept the values and mechanisms of the democratic way of life even when their respective theoretical justifications are unacceptable to each other. This is a fact of enormous significance on which is shattered the arrogant claim that no one can be a principled and consistent democrat unless he accepts some particular metaphysical or theological dogma.

That this working agreement can be achieved despite the multitudinous presuppositions from which the pattern of democratic living is

allegedly derived, suggests two conclusions. First, that logically no metaphysical or theological doctrine entails any specific form of social or political life. Accept any such doctrine you please! I believe it is demonstrable
that it is not a necessary condition of democracy, that individuals and
groups can be and actually have been good democrats without subscribing
to it. Nor is any such doctrine a sufficient condition because individuals
and groups can be found who sincerely believe it and disbelieve in democracy. I think it can be established that even in countries where official
metaphysical or theological views—as distinct from false scientific theories—are prescribed, these do not by themselves logically justify the dictatorial political and social practices which prevail. Such practices are
only imposed to further the material interests of whatever power groups
are in control or to jibe with the obsession of some dictator.

Why, then, do Protestants and Catholics, Jews, Gentiles, and Moham-
medans, theists and atheists, absolute idealists, solipsists and materialists
for all their differences accept the democratic procedures and institutions characteristic of Anglo-American culture? I suggest that when they
consciously and rationally do so it is because they reach their political
judgments by following the lead of empirical evidence, by observing the
consequences of these practices for weal and woe in their own lives and
that of the community, by adopting in principle, however inadequately,
the same generic approach by which they attempt to reach reliable conclusions about everyday problems of experience. That they do not often
consciously and rationally evaluate political and social affairs is another
matter; I am speaking of the way they proceed when they do. We may not
agree with their judgments. We may be impatient with their slovenliness
or unwillingness to evaluate what the empirical consequences of proposals are, and in determining what is responsible for what. But our argument with the community—if we are socialists, single taxers, free-money
men, New Dealers, or anti-New Dealers—doesn't turn on metaphysical
considerations but on empirical fact. Such-and-such a proposal—we
say—will have these determinate observable consequences. No political
principle is so sacred that, when it leads to unendurable practical consequences, it will not be overthrown. And there is much less difference
among men as to what is endurable or not endurable than there is about
the first principles of metaphysics or theology.

The quest for a philosophical theory of man is irrelevant to the quest
for peace and a just social order—so long as it does not deny those
empirical traits of man we take note of in our everyday transactions.

When it fails to take note of these traits it is worse than irrelevant—it becomes misleading, an obstacle to further inquiry. Man may be conceived of as a soul inhabiting a tenement of clay—so long as it is admitted that the activity of the soul is a function of the organization of a body in a society. Man may be conceived of as a machine—so long as it is granted that he is a thinking, feeling machine. He may be considered a complex of sense data, just so long as the order of connection between different complexes of sense data is not reduced to a sense datum. He may be thought of as a complex of electrons or as a handful of salts in a solution of water—so long as he is also recognized as a creature who makes choices. No matter what our view here, the decisive question still remains to be settled, viz., whether these visiting souls or thinking machines or colonies of sense data or electro-chemical systems should or should not organize themselves democratically. And the considerations that bear on this question are usually of an entirely different order from those that incline us to one or another philosophy of man.

Second, we may note that the empirical temper of the Anglo-Amencan tradition is perhaps most focally in evidence in its refusal to be bound by, or even to believe in, *all* the logical implications of its theoretical propositions about social and political life. The purely logical implications of any assertion are always greater than those we draw, and especially more complex than those we intend. The context of any proposition is a situation, a problem, a difficulty which cannot be expressed in that proposition. In consequence there is almost always some disparity between the formal meaning of propositions considered independently of the situation they are formulated to resolve and what we really mean by them. This makes us particularly attentive to what is done in the name of principles rather than to what is said or written, to the public behavior to which they lead rather than to the personal emotional overtones they arouse. What is sometimes referred to as English and American indifference to principle is not really indifference but rather a realization that more than one principle usually applies, and that principles are to be interpreted as operating guides to actions. Depending on the case, now one, now another of the principles receives the greater weight—a process often called bungling or blundering through. If the British wanted socialism only, in the conventional sense, they could easily achieve it by a series of neatly planned and ruthlessly executed Draconian decrees. If they wanted freedom at any price, they could slip back to the economy of rust and rot of the thirties. Since they want both socialism *and* freedom, they must make compromises that for various reasons offend doctrinaires in different camps.

By and large our tendency is to judge our politicians, not by their party programs, but by the concrete actions taken in their names. And when we look abroad at the "new democracies" in Russia and Eastern Europe, at the "organic democracies" of Spain and, until yesterday, Argentina we naturally, to their great irritation, pay more attention to their reigns of terror and bloodshed than to the propagandistic documents and speeches with which their apologists regale us.

There are, to be sure, intellectual circles in both England and America who believe that the proper approach to political fact in *other* countries is through ideological analysis. A few American philosophers—whom one would expect to be watchdogs of our critical tradition—have publicly detected a family likeness between Anglo-American democracy and Soviet Communism, on the ground that the slogans and official documents of Soviet ideology sound very much like our own. What is especially mystifying about this particular piece of political innocence is that these philosophers would rightfully repudiate the notion that, because the dictatorships of Spain and Portugal profess to base themselves upon a belief in "the brotherhood of man under the fatherhood of God" and in "the infinite worth and dignity of the individual soul," this makes them members of the same political family as the Anglo-American democracies where the same phrases are also current. Franco is judged by what he does, but the man in the Kremlin by what he says—and even this is carefully picked over to reinforce the impression that he is a democrat merely speaking with a Russian accent. When it is pointed out that there is all the difference in the world between the formal implications of these propaganda statements and the tragic facts in the case, the inevitable retort is, "Perhaps so, but we aren't perfect either—there is a discrepancy between *our* ideals and practices, too." That such discrepancies if we disapprove of them can be, and have been, progressively reduced by the exercise of our rights of criticism and opposition under our functioning Bill of Rights—which is conspicuously not true in Soviet Russia in which absolutely no opposition is permitted—is dismissed as a trivial consideration, although it is surely the essence of the matter. Apparently, both countries are democracies, differing only in degree.

It was not so long ago that Hitler accused English and American public opinion of hypocrisy for protesting against the extermination of the Jews while discriminating against colored people. Did that silence us? Those who protested against Hitler's practices were certainly not those who defended or practiced discrimination in their own country. The status of the colored people has been slowly but steadily improving since their emancipation—even though they have far to go to achieve political and social equality. But the fact is that the number of individuals destroyed or sentenced to living deaths in the concentration camps of the Communist countries of the world is greater than the whole Negro population of the United States. We are morally responsible for our own imperfections, but they do not extenuate others' crimes. Even sentimentalists understand that, although we are not free of blame when crime is rampant in our community, this does not put us on the same plane as those who commit murder or militate against our moral right—no, our moral duty—to denounce and restrain those guilty of murder. And a state—at least in the Anglo-American moral tradition—can be just as guilty of murder as an individual.

To claim that the Atlantic democracies and Soviet Russia are equally democracies, differing only in degree, is to debauch our language—unless when we hear the claim we remind ourselves that the difference between life and death is also in a sense a matter of degree. The situation reminds me of the plea of a notorious thief and confidence man who cheerfully admitted his guilt in passing himself off as an ordained minister. He argued, however, that since no man is morally perfect—the very claim would betoken immodesty and lack of perfection—there was after all only a difference in degree of virtue between himself and the honest pastor whom he had defrauded. When official apologists of the Russian regime talk this way, it is noteworthy that they forget one of their favorite Hegelian dicta: a difference in degree may make a difference in kind.

In truth, without an empirical approach to meaning and truth there is a great danger of our never arriving at a common denotative reference to what we are talking about—of debasing our whole intellectual currency, of so confusing rational discourse about freedom of the press, economic democracy, national self-determination, free and unfettered elections, that nothing will appear clear but the logic of the iron fist. The best defense against this kind of semantic corruption is the experimental, empirical temper of mind which historically, although far from exclusively, has been associated with Anglo-American culture from Yorkshire to Missouri.

The institutionalization of freely given consent is the second notable facet in the culture of the English speaking peoples. Critics within and without our culture (with the exception of lineal descendants of Plato and Thrasymachus) do not question the validity of the ideal of freely given consent, but dispute the extent to which it pervades our political and social institutions. But since our task is to examine our uncriticized assumptions we may ask: why is freely given consent better than coercion? Where rules, laws, and plans rest upon freely given consent there is less friction, less fear, and more abundant opportunity for a more abundant life for more people. It is not necessary to labor the point. In almost every area of human relationships where decisions affecting others must be taken, freely given consent enhances the quality of the goals for which the decisions are made, as well as facilitating the execution of these same decisions.

It is obvious that freely given consent is no guarantee of just or wise decisions. But so long as that consent can be granted, withheld, or periodically renewed, there is a greater likelihood that the consequences of our policies will be considered. That is why it is better to accept a foolish decision of a democratic community—provided we are able to agitate against it—than to insist on our dose of wisdom, about which we may be wrong anyhow. The risks in accepting decisions that rest, directly or indirectly, upon freely given consent are far fewer than the risks involved in the only alternatives—anarchy and despotism.

The acceptance of the principle of freely given consent as a binding rule of social life entails certain beliefs about the empirical nature of man. The two most important are: first, that men are responsible; and second, that they are sufficiently rational to know when and where the shoe pinches and when and where not. No one would advocate democracy in an insane asylum or in an institution for the feeble-minded, except possibly an inmate.

Are these empirical beliefs true? I believe they are. But because the evidence is difficult to assess, a certain element of faith—of reasonable faith, since it is not arbitrary—enters into our allegiance to the ways of democracy.

The best way to test this faith, if the historical evidence seems uncertain, is to state the conditions under which freely given consent is most widely achieved. What are these conditions? When is consent free—when is it not? It is not enough that I have a choice. The man who pokes a pistol in my ribs and says, "Your money or your life," may argue that I have a choice, but he cannot decently claim that it was a free one. The presence of physical constraint, the threat of concentration camps for dissenters and their families, which attend elections and plebiscites in totalitarian countries, makes a grotesque mockery of the claims of such governments to be based on consent.

Coercion, of course, may take other than physical forms. There are few things to which a starving man will not consent. Even in the absence of physical and economic coercion, consent is not free if it is bound or blinded by ignorance. I am not speaking now of our inevitable ignorance, of the absence of knowledge because there is no knowledge, which is part of the human estate; such coercion is an aspect of the coercion of the natural scene—it can be mitigated but never entirely removed. I am speaking of the ignorance of what *is* or *could* be known, of the ignorance of other points of view and policies and the reasons therefor, which is engendered when all sources of information and inquiry are controlled by the state.

These considerations are elementary but decisive. From them we can derive the justification of the freedoms of the Bill of Rights—political democracy—of "economic democracy," and above all, because it is an infallible index of the presence of others, the legal right of opposition. Whatever limits are set to such opposition must depend on rules or laws which are themselves derived through the self-corrective procedures of democracy. The more nearly we approach these conditions, the more reliable becomes the test of our assumption that men are sufficiently reasonable and responsible to achieve their purposes better, and to compose their differences more peacefully, by the method of free consent than by any other method.

The acceptance of the principle of consent does *not* imply that the individuals from whom consent is derived are isolated, atomic centers of interest whose existence as fully developed persons is prior to the social order or state which arises out of contract or agreement. The social relationships into which all human beings are born are as essential to their natures as their biological endowments. Personality is a cultural achievement, not a precondition of culture. But from this it does not follow that we can draw an equation between the individual and the social, and legitimately speak of the social good or public welfare as if it were more than the good and welfare of you, of me, and our neighbors. The origin of social and political institutions is logically and morally irrelevant to their present functions. And in evaluating this function individuals are primary, and their judgment, imperfect as it is, must be regarded as supreme. Whoever denies this still speaks as an individual for other individual interests, no matter whether he speaks in the name of the general will, the state, the nation, a class, or a party. The state as an instrument, if it is to serve human interests adequately, has positive functions to perform, and not merely the negative ones of preserving domestic order. But insofar as the state rests upon consent, individual persons morally and collectively are just as much its master as they are of any other instrumentality of their will. This, it seems to me, represents the abiding insight of John Locke, who had more to do with formulating the principles that express the political traditions of Anglo-American culture than any other thinker. None of the strictures by his current detractors affect his wisdom on this point.

Consent is rarely if ever unanimous. There are losers as well as victors in every legislative battle, and the dissent of the former is usually more vehement than the assent of the latter. This raises the difficult problem of minority rights and majority rule in governments that profess to be based on freely given consent. Minorities can be and have been oppressed by majorities as well as by despots. The traditional doctrine, according to which all human beings possess absolute and inalienable rights which can never be abridged by any agency of government, is more coherent as an emotion than as a doctrine. Its meaning is ambiguous: and when not ambiguous, false. It is a very uncertain guide to action. For in most political situations a claim to one alleged absolute right conflicts with a claim to another alleged absolute right. There is no method by which we can measure degrees of absoluteness or establish the priority of absolutes in relation to each other. More important, it is doubtful whether anyone really believes in absolute rights that are unqualifiedly valid no matter what the consequences of their exercise upon social life. Every right in the Bill of Rights is subject to qualification and abridgment if its practice results in widespread misery and public danger.

Sometimes it is argued that, because democracies cannot guarantee absolute rights in all circumstances, and because totalitarian governments do not recognize them at all, that there is in principle no difference between the two kinds of states. This overlooks an all-important distinction. In a democracy, the abridgment of the Bill of Rights, whether for good or bad, is a crisis phenomenon of limited duration, and depends on the processes of consent, if not for its initiation then for its continuation. In a dictatorship the abridgment of any bill of rights is systematic, rather than episodic, and depends upon the arbitrary decree of a small minority. The dictatorship of the proletariat in the Soviet Union which, according to Stalin, is "substantially the dictatorship of the Communist

Party" is supposed to be transitional; but who determines when the transition is over—the Russian people or their rulers? Officially, Soviet Russia boasts of being a classless society; but the state instead of withering away has become stronger.

How then does a minority have redress for its grievances in a democracy? If it is given a hearing according to the rules and conditions that truly permit freely given consent, the majority may override what the minority believes to be its just claims. There is always the possibility of resort to revolution. This may have moral sanction but it entails abandonment of the theory of democratic consent according to which no minority is justified in using force to impose on the majority its conception of the true, the good, and the honorable. Such revolutionists may be good men, even saints, but they cannot be called democrats.

Short of this, however, there is the possibility of compromise, or integration of conflicting interests. In order to avoid the greater evil of civil war, we yield to the lesser evil of enduring what seems to us an unjust majority decision, in the hope that continued political education will lead to a reversal of majority judgment. This is the wisdom of Socrates rather than of John Brown: in a dictatorship the only appeal from Philip drunk is to Philip sober; in a democracy the appeal from an unenlightened majority is to an enlightened one. Justice Felix Frankfurter has put this admirably in one of his opinions: "Where all the effective means of inducing political changes are left free from interference, education in the abandonment of foolish legislation is itself a training in liberty." The English speaking peoples have learned this at a great cost, but they have learned it and it is now part of their tradition. The one great exception to this in the United States (but *not* in England) is "government by judiciary" which resides in the power of the U.S. Supreme Court Justices to nullify Congressional legislation.

No democracy can long survive in which majority decisions are consistently foolish or aimed at destroying minorities as well as defeating them. A majority is made up of individuals whose differences are not canceled out by their unity on certain questions. In virtue of these differences some may find themselves in a minority in respect to other questions when the wheel of history makes its next turn. The precedents established by unjust majority decisions may ultimately affect members of the leading group as well as those of the minority.

The causes of injustice are many. Among them two seem to me the most insidious—the interpretation of rules of equality as if they applied only to individuals in identical positions, and an insensitiveness and unimaginativeness to the experiences of others. We may conclude from this that the survival of democracy depends not only upon a faith in human educability, not only on commitment to continuous programs of public education for its citizens, but on the development of an attitude which appreciates and encourages differences instead of merely tolerating them. This brings us to the third and final facet of the heritage of the English speaking world.

That diversity of experience, direct or vicarious, is immediately enjoyable, few will be inclined to deny. It safeguards us against provincialism, and against the tyranny of the familiar whose hold may sometimes be so strong as to incapacitate us from making the new responses necessary for survival. Diversity in modes of experience freshens and refreshens the human spirit. Every new discovery is a triumph of variation over repetition.

Natural as human joy in diversity may be, so is human fear and dislike of diversity—and we know enough about ourselves to realize that both of these emotions can be experienced together. There are plausible reasons for believing that our fears prove most stubborn in the presence of differences which we suspect threaten in some way our existence, our uniqueness, our *conatus sui persevare*. Most of the time these suspicions are false; most differences are compatible with, not exclusive of, each other. Growth toward maturity consists largely in learning to appreciate differences, learning to understand them when we cannot appreciate them, and at the very least learning to live with them when we cannot understand them. Whenever we are challenged by the presence of differences, the task of intelligence is to find a way by which those differences that can enrich our lives may be distinguished from those that would destroy them. It is hard to tell which is the more foolish belief— that all differences threaten our life or that none of them do.

In the field of culture and politics, the traditions and present tendencies of the English speaking countries come closer to achieving a reasonable, practical solution of the problem of cultural unity and difference than any other dominant tradition. We have heard a good deal in recent years about the necessity for a basically unified culture to produce that community of taste, judgment, and ideals without which, so it is asserted, social life is in a state of potential civil war. Most of the discussion has been *a priori* and disregards patent fact. That a common religion or language or origin is not a *sufficient* condition for peace is evidenced by the

Spanish insurrection—and our own Civil War which occurred at a time when the States of the Union were in many respects much more homogeneous culturally than they are today. That it is not a *necessary* condition is revealed in the histories of Switzerland and of Canada, and in the greater part of the period of American national existence.

Whatever cultural differences exist in the community, and whatever our feeling toward them, they do not constitute a threat to a common life in society unless these differences are accompanied by *practices* which deny the right of differences to others, which fail to recognize the equality of all attitudes that accept a *common method* of negotiating differences. It seems to me that it is this emphasis upon method as more important than any specific result, as a way of insuring progress without anarchy, which underlies all three facets of our heritage—the empirical temper, the democratic attitude, and our cultural pluralism.

Ignazio Silone, the Italian novelist, has said that men must agree on a certain number of fundamental positions—on what is good or evil, true or false—in order not to massacre each other. I believe it is more accurate to say that they must agree on a basic method of reaching the truth or testing the good, rather than upon any *particular* truth or good. For so long as they agree on this method, all other differences about specific truths or goods are in principle resolvable.

There is an exact analogue to this in our political life. In a democracy, no matter what our political faith or beliefs may be, so long as we sincerely accept the basic rules of the game, so long as we are willing to abide by the consequences of the free give-and-take of critical debate, we may legitimately hold and practice any notion or doctrine we please. Our differences may reveal valuable insights and truths which we have missed, and would continue to miss, if no one were permitted to play under the rules unless he accepted our version of the true and desirable to begin with.

The same analogue holds for the even vaster region of cultural differences. We permit—or should permit—each group to preserve and develop its own cultural ways provided it does not attempt to impose its specific, exclusive pattern upon others, provided it leaves its individual members free to choose among the diversities of tradition which compete with each other.

It should be obvious that what is called cultural or ethnic democracy is no more possible without political democracy than is "economic democracy." This has been denied by those who point to Soviet Russia as a model of cultural and ethnic democracy. The principle and practice of Soviet Russia decrees that "culture must be socialist in content and national in form"; but the only national differences that are recognized are primarily those of language. The separation of content from form is a myth. No opportunity for the free development of the culture of the constituent Republics exists, precisely because what is called the socialist *content* of their culture, from art and music to astronomy and zoology, is prescribed for them by the Kremlin. Without the right to develop responses that are critical or even hostile to the reigning cultural dogmas (and this involves the freedom of the press together with other political freedoms) "ethnic democracy" is another deceptive phrase. What we have is ethnic equality, which in the Soviet Union turns out to be little more than the freedom to praise Stalin or any of his successors and the party line in many different languages (including the Scandinavian but not Hebrew).

The upshot of all this is that what is required to live prosperously and peacefully together is not a fixed common doctrine or a fixed body of truths, but a common method or set of rules under which we can live with our differences—mitigate, integrate, transcend them if we wish, or let them alone if *that* is our wish. We cannot make absolutes of doctrines, tastes, or principles without inviting the evils of fanaticism.

Nonetheless, there must be one working absolute on which there can be no compromise, about which we must be fanatical: the rules of the game, by which we settle differences. Whoever plays outside the rules, whoever tries to write his own rules, has given a clear declaration in advance that he proposes to interpret differences as *ipso facto* evidence of hostility. He has in effect declared war which can be avoided only if we knuckle under to any arbitrary demand. There is no inconsistency whatsoever in being intolerant of those who show intolerance. In fact, tolerance of the actively intolerant is not only intellectually stultifying, but is practical complicity in the crimes of intolerance.

The method of the empirical temper, of the democratic process, of cultural pluralism is open-minded but not tender-minded. It is a perpetual invitation to sit down in the face of differences and reason together, to consider the evidence, explore alternative proposals, assess the consequences, and let the decision rest—when matters of human concern are at stake—with the consent of those affected by the proposals.

This method does not guarantee results, not even the results of agreement. Values are relative to human interests and, although objective, may genuinely conflict. The conflict *may* be so deep that resolution is impossible *even* if we agree to negotiate. The assumption that in any particular case agreement on conflicting interests and values can be won rests upon the faith (or bet) that men are sufficiently alike to work out ways of becoming *more* alike, or sufficiently alike to agree on the permissible limits of being different.

We must not confuse an objective morality with a universal morality. Between a human being and a tiger on the prowl, there is no ground for agreement. But it does not follow that human values are not objective because they cannot be shared in this situation. The error of those who would forego the use of a critical method to reach ethical truths is the assumption *in advance* that in every conflict between two men or two groups one is human and another merely a tiger in disguise.

The qualities I have selected have not always been characteristic of the tradition of the English speaking peoples: they have become so. Some aspects already have been, and more of them may become, part of the traditions of other peoples and cultures. It was on its way to becoming the settled tradition of Western Europe until the First World War (which should never have been fought) prepared the ground for Lenin, Trotsky, and Stalin, and Mussolini, Hitler, and Franco. If the democratic tradition were to be combined with the welfare economy of democratic socialism, it might establish itself elsewhere, not only in Europe, but in the East. We undoubtedly have much to learn from Indian and Chinese wisdom, but the Sikhs, Moslems, and Hindus can also learn a little from us about religious freedom and toleration, and the Chinese about the processes of representative government.

Democracy is a way of life that outside of its own territories challenges no other way of life except in the urgencies of self-defense. Unfortunately, its existence has been threatened all along the line, first by Hitlerism and now by Soviet Communism. Whoever believed that Nazi expansionism constituted a threat to the survival of democratic institutions must conclude by the same logic and the same type of evidence that Soviet Communism represents today an even greater threat to our survival, because the potential opposition to totalitarianism is now much weaker in consequence of World War II, and because the Soviet government commands a fifth column in democratic countries stronger than anything Hitler or Franco ever imagined possible.

Here is not the place to outline in detail how this formidable crusade against what is permanently valid in the tradition of the English speaking peoples is to be met. Suffice it to say that, necessary as it is to build a decent social order and remedy injustices in our own countries to prevent totalitarianism from spreading for internal reasons, this would no more be sufficient to stop the march of Communism than social reforms in England and France were sufficient to stop Hitler.

The immediate desideratum is to conduct our foreign and domestic affairs so that more and more peoples of the world *voluntarily* associate themselves in a world union in which, on the basis of primary allegiance to democratic processes, the widest development of cultural diversity is encouraged.

The first step toward such a world union of democracies would be Federal Union among the Atlantic democracies. But this would be only a first step, and it raises the question of what nations are to be regarded as democratic. Here we must go beyond the heritage of the Anglo-American community.

[1959]

# 11

## CONFLICTS IN
## WAYS OF BELIEF

W̱e are living in an age of troubles. All the commonplaces of dire prediction made during the last generation have come true, often to the surprise of those who uttered them. Literally hundreds of millions are under fire from shot and shell. Other millions are stumbling over highways and bypaths toward mirages of refuge and safety. With bated breath the rest of the world seems to be living from one news broadcast to another.

### 1. BELIEF AND ACTION

At such a time it might appear that there is room in human consciousness only for questions of bare survival, not for questions of justification, direction, and value. To endure, to struggle, to survive this seems to be the ultimate answer to all questions that may reasonably be asked. But human beings are peculiar animals who, even when they fight for survival, fight best when they know why or believe they know why. This is the testimony of all recorded history. There never was a mass movement that markedly changed the course of events whose individual members were not inspired by some belief. The belief may be part of an ethos—an integrated complex of social values which determines the station and

267

duties of the individual. It may be a myth about this world or the next accompanied by a hope for greater felicity on earth or in heaven. Or it may be a sense of resentment against inequality rationalized as a demand for justice.

It is an interesting fact, however, that social action is the mother of inspiration and not, as is usually imagined, its offspring. The *causes* of a movement are rarely, if ever, to be found in its inspiring beliefs and doctrines. But the *results* of a movement cannot be explained without reference to them.

For they determine the ways of action, the human energies that are tapped in the course of it, and those ultimate decisions which often lead human beings to embrace death rather than survival. Indeed, it is hard to find a man who willingly fights only for survival. Else why should he risk death in the struggle for it? A man can almost always purchase his life if he is prepared to pay enough for it.

Even the fighting man, then, cannot be indifferent to why men fight and how they think. His emphasis upon morale is in part an acknowledgment of this. It was no less a military figure than Napoleon who said: "Wars are won by those who think clearly and calmly and act vigorously and promptly."

It is therefore not merely wrong but senseless, even in the darkest hour, to call for a moratorium on thought and to cry out for action, or in ponderous solemnity to appeal for serious thought as if it were an alternative to action. Not only are thinking and acting natural to man, but to some degree they are both present wherever there is conscious behavior. If we bear in mind that to refrain from doing something, to stand and wait on any specific occasion, is just as much an action, *because it has consequences*, as to throw oneself into the thick of things—then we will realize that men always act. There is no wisdom in saying men *must* act. They always do. The point at issue is: *What* shall they enact and *how*? Similarly, thinking, in the broadest sense of the term, is a process which is always involved in conscious action and cannot be stopped at command. Here, too, the question is not whether we shall or shall not think but *what* to think and *how*—clearly or confusedly, with images or ideas, drawing conclusions from our fears and hopes or from evidence and argument.

Thinking is one of the instruments of survival. It is also an integral part of that form of self-justifying enjoyment which we may call understanding. The test of understanding is always control, but there are as many forms of control as there are generic types of things to be known.

And not all of them are concerned with survival. There are many people who have an irrepressible urge to find out why things *have* happened even if it is doubtful whether they will ever have the occasion to use their knowledge to some purpose in the future. Strength permitting, even the dying are eager to know what they are dying of.

## 2. CHOICE AND BELIEF

The ways of belief, then, are important. It is no exaggeration to maintain that there are few things in our time which are more important in their bearing upon questions of social survival. For in the field of social and political behavior, errors in belief are costlier than anywhere else. This is a lesson which has not yet been sufficiently learned in America despite the evidence for it piling up all over the world. Many are busy with politics but few are really serious about their political ideas. Social allegiances, even among self-designated intellectuals, wax and wane with fashion; they are functions of mood rather than considered argument. In an era of social stability, where the effects of differences in political and social ideas are negligible, they may be indulgently regarded as private conceits. But today, whether an individual is aware of it or not, he is staking his head—and the heads of others—on his ideas. They are loaded and can no longer be safely fooled with. In a world where everyone must be armed with ideas, it is well to look to our weapons.

But what shall we believe? The beginning of wisdom is to remember that we do not have to ask this question about everything at once. We are in possession of beliefs of varying degrees of reliability; and, when a specific problem of belief arises, we can take some initial steps in answering it by checking our tentative answers against what we already know or assume we know. This does not take us far. Unfamiliar situations are always cropping up. The cherished beliefs of yesterday may have to be revised. Everything now becomes subordinate to the question: What *method* shall we follow in developing new beliefs and testing the old? For it is clear that no matter what belief we come to regard as valid, the evidence of its validity will depend in part, at least, upon the method which has been followed in reaching it.

If the validity of beliefs depends upon the methods of reaching them, what does the validity of these methods depend upon? In some quarters it is argued that the choice of methods of reaching beliefs represents an arbitrary decision. It needs no justification because no justification can be given. Its validity cannot be established without begging the question, since, in testing it, we would have to appeal to the very method which was undergoing test. Fundamental decisions concerning the methods to be used in reaching conclusions, it is argued, are therefore on all fours with each other. One may be more popular, or simpler, or older than the others, but no one of them is more "valid" than any other.

Even if this were granted, it would not diminish the importance of understanding these various modes of reaching beliefs. Since we live in a world where different people make different choices, and since, whether we like it or not, these choices have consequences which affect us, elementary caution dictates that we give them some study.

The weakness of the view that our fundamental ways of deriving beliefs depend upon a basic decision is not in calling attention to the fact that some decision or resolution is involved. It is rather to be found in its suggestion that the decisions in the nature of the case must be arbitrary, and that the choices they express are never influenced by what we can observe about the specific beliefs and practices to which they give rise and for which they are *presumably* responsible. If we take as our point of departure the empirical occasions on which men discuss the question of the relative validity of different methods of denying beliefs, we find that everyone defends his choice as in some sense "better" than others. An individual who asserts that one way of thinking is better than another does not mean merely that it is *his* way. For any other way, were he to adopt it, would be his way. Nor does he ever intend to be understood as saying, "I have no reasons for this decision or choice." No matter how he expresses the "reasons" for his choice of a method, *insofar as he urges its acceptance upon others*, they amount to a claim that the adoption of this method will enable us to control or anticipate the future more adequately than the competing methods. "Fundamental" decisions may be intelligent or unintelligent—they are not always, or merely, arbitrary.

Charles Peirce recognizes this in his assumption that the conflicting methods of iteration or tenacity, authority, apriorism or plausible intuition, and science, are all methods of fixing belief.[1] It is in the light, then, of their efficacy in fixing beliefs that they are evaluated. I believe that a more accurate designation of the aim of these methods, insofar as they are in *recognized* conflict with each other, is not the fixation of belief but the adjustment of beliefs, not so much the stability of beliefs but, as Peirce himself suggests, their reliability in settling doubt. But the sign of their reliability is the relative success with which they can predict the future.

Ways of belief are "fundamental" only in respect to the specific beliefs which they help come to birth. They are not fundamental if by that is meant that there is no getting around them, or that they need not or cannot be checked by something else. This conclusion is in line with what we observe when people tell us that they are making a "fundamental decision" whether it is a decision to take one's life, to abandon faith in democracy, to join a church or a political party, to take a wife or put one aside, or to think differently. Granted sanity, the decision never is made in the blue. There is always a controlling context, a specific problem, and a nucleus of difficulties. Rightly or wrongly, certain things are expected to follow from the decision. Some justifications are offered, or, at the least, reasons are advanced for rejecting alternatives.

The notion that there *must* be some fundamental belief from which all other beliefs, so to speak, hang, a belief which supports all others but itself needs no support, is a plausible error. Once we insist upon reducing the situation which evokes the "fundamental decision" to its concrete elements, the decision turns out to be a "conclusion," and like all conclusions depends upon something else. The bogey of an infinite regress is laid when we realize that although one problem always involves others, it does not involve all problems, and that it is possible to settle problems even when the answers suggest new problems.

All this may seem very abstract and far removed from the kind of decisions we have to make about democracy and totalitarianism, war and peace. If anyone is of this impression, let him ask himself how *he* justifies his belief or disbelief in democracy, or his acceptance or rejection of scientific method as contrasted with its alternatives. I venture to predict that he will discover his procedure to be something like this. He approaches the problem of evaluation with a determinate store of knowledge, and a number of preferences or valuations. He knows, or more accurately, he unquestioningly assumes (i) that he is in possession of certain "truths" or "facts," (ii) that the problems to which these truths or facts are answers have been solved in the past by employing certain methods, and (iii) that certain "goods" or "values" like health, wealth, friendship, loyalty, truth, honor, intelligence are desirable. These are immediately brought to the resolution of the problem. Insofar as he can envisage the consequences of carrying out the belief or beliefs in question, he evaluates them as "better" or "worse," more adequate or less

adequate. At any point, what he assumed to be knowledge may be criticized as an unwarranted assertion, and what he took as a reasonable
preference or value, dismissed as a prejudice. This sets another specific
problem which is resolved *in the same way.* The process may be theoretically unending, but it is not viciously circular. Actually, however, it
has its stopping points wherever sufficient evidence has accumulated to
meet the specific difficulties which provoked the inquiry.

It is in the light of a procedure of this kind that the method of scientific inquiry shows itself to be more adequate than any formulated alternative in anticipating the future. We can use scientific method and be
wrong about the future but not so often wrong as by using other methods.
And no matter how wrong we are, since scientific method is self-corrective, we become less and less wrong as we continue its practice.

An examination of the counterstatements of those who deny that scientific method is the most effective method of deriving reliable beliefs
about the future reveals flagrant inconsistencies, large but unsubstanti-
ated claims, and gross misconceptions of the nature of science. They
cannot indicate any definite connection between their generic way of
belief and their *specific* beliefs in particular situations. They either
assert an infallibility, which is conspicuously absent in practice, or when
they acknowledge their fallibility cannot explain how, on their own
premises, it is possible. In revising their specific beliefs, they often fall
back upon crudely empirical scientific methods.

Take as an extreme illustration of a way of belief differing from that
of science, one of Hitler's famous pronouncements, made after the military reoccupation of the Rhineland: "I go my way with the assurance of
a somnambulist—the way which Providence has sent me."[2] There is no
reason to doubt the subjective sincerity of this statement. It can be
matched with similar expressions of this peculiar form of mysticism from
his writings and those of his circle. But various things can be noted.
Despite his somnambulistic assurance in the ways of Providence, Hitler
finds it necessary to denounce the methods of science and reason as
inadequate. He does not entertain for a moment the possible validity of
conclusions reached by the somnambulistic assurances of others. He
cannot show in any manner whatsoever how his specific statements and
actions follow from his mystical way of "thought." On the contrary, once
we grasp his objectives, disapprove of them as we may, we can explain
his successes in achieving them as a result, in part, of a shrewd and scientific method of evaluation, preparation, and action. Whoever is

responsible for Hitler's successes, does not act as a somnambulist. Even in a country whose rulers aim to prevent their subjects from thinking scientifically, there is always one group which must think scientifically in order to carry out this aim successfully.

## 3. DEMOCRACY AND SCIENTIFIC METHOD

There is common agreement that democracy as a way of life can flourish only when differences of opinion can be negotiated by free, critical discussion in which those who at any time, and on any question, are a minority, may become the majority, provided they abide by democratic processes. It is also acknowledged that the intelligence of decisions made by the majority depends upon the extent to which it considers alternatives of action and the available evidence for each. In brief, it depends upon whether those who participate in social and political affairs are guided by habits of scientific thought or are swayed by passion, blind tradition, and irrelevant "authorities." This is not to say that scientific methods and practices are not employed to implement the goals of totalitarian states. German military strategy is nothing if not highly scientific, and the Russian system of domestic espionage is the most scientific that has ever been devised. But there is no room in a totalitarian culture for the scientific approach, with its critical probing of alternatives, when questions arise concerning the social ends and values which guide major national policies.

It is extremely difficult for the more notorious rivals and substitutes of intelligence to make headway in a democracy unless conditions have degenerated to a point where they have produced a psychosis of mass despair. The methods of somnambulistic intuition and personal authority have no plausibility in ordinary times. For in ordinary times, it is usually drift and improvisation, that is to say, no method at all, which rules.

Today we are not living in ordinary times. Nor, fortunately, have we in America as yet reached a state of mass despair. But time is short and a host of domestic and foreign problems press upon us which must be solved quickly and intelligently. We are now awake to the fact that more fundamental than armament, as essential as that is, is ideological rearmament—a rearmament of method rather than a doctrine. How are we to solve our problems and by what methods?

In all fields of inquiry, the recognition of a problem is tantamount to an invitation to use scientific method in its resolution. But this is far from being the case in the field of social and political action. Before scientific method can be successfully used, there must be the desire to use it. How to induce that desire is a tremendously complex problem of persuasion and education. The most convincing features to Americans of the educational process on this point are the consequences of following alternative methods—intuition and authority in Germany, Russia, and Italy; drift and improvisation in England and France.

But even the desire to follow scientific method is by itself not sufficient. If it is an intelligent desire, and if our actions are to realize its great promise, it must be based upon knowledge of what scientific method is and the ability to distinguish between its name and its substance.

Here we are confronted by a genuine difficulty. There is an imposing variety of ways of thought, actually opposed to the ways of science, which nonetheless pretend to represent the last word in scientific reflection. Just as recent years have witnessed the emergence of totalitarian groups which profess an exaggerated allegiance to democracy, so we can observe ways of thinking, incompatible with scientific method, that piously invoke its name. No exact analogy or correlation is intended, of course, between these two phenomena. Confusion, not duplicity, accounts for identifying as scientific, ways of belief which are primarily metaphysical or religious. But "science" like "democracy" is often a catchword; and it is precisely because of honest confusion that the detection of spurious scientific methods of thinking is so difficult.

[1940]

## NOTES

1. *Collected Papers,* vol. 5, p. 223.
2. Broadcast from Munich, March 14, 1936.

# 12

# THE DEMOCRATIC
# WAY OF LIFE

The greatest tribute to democracy as an ideal of social life is unwittingly paid to it in the *apologias* of the dictators of the modern world—Hitler, Stalin, and Mussolini. For all of them insist in the shrillest tones that the regimes they control are actually, despite appearances, democracies "in a higher sense." For example, Mussolini in a public address delivered at Berlin in September 1987, proclaimed that "the greatest and soundest democracies which exist in the world today are Italy and Germany"; while Stalin, after the worst blood purge in history, praises the constitution that bears his name—a constitution that openly provides (in Section 126) for the control of all socio-political institutions by the minority Communist Party—as the most democratic in all history. And here in America, due to the needs of the foreign policy of the various dictatorships, their partisans now wrap up their program of blood and steel in the American flag and make a great verbal play about being defenders of American democracy. Thus, in a letter to the *New York Times* (July 20, 1938) Mr. Fritz Kuhn speaks of Americans who have become members of his German *Bund* (Nazis) "because of their faith in its devotion to the institutions of the United States." With even greater fanfare the American Communist Party has proclaimed its love of democracy to the death on the assumption that Americans neither read nor have memories. Both pronouncements merely reflect the necessities of foreign policy of Germany and Russia respectively.

---

Originally published as "Democracy as a Way of Life," *Southern Review* 4 (summer 1938): 46–57. Reprinted by permission of the Estate of Sidney Hook.

That the greatest enemies of democracy should feel compelled to render demagogic lip-allegiance to it is an eloquent sign of the inherent plausibility of democratic ideals to the modern mind, and of their universal appeal. But that its enemies, apparently with some success, should have the audacity to flaunt the principles they have so outrageously betrayed in practice, is just as eloquent a sign that these principles are ambiguous. Agreement where there is no clarity merely cloaks differences; it does not settle them. Sooner or later it breeds confusion and confusion breeds distrust. In the end there grows up a venemous rancor which is so intent upon destroying the enemy that it is blind to what the real differences are.

The analysis of the concept of democracy is not merely, then, a theoretical problem for the academician. The ordinary man who says he believes in democracy must clearly understand what he means by it. Otherwise the genuine issues that divide men will be lost in the welter of emotive words which demagogues skillfully evoke to conceal their true intentions. There is such a thing as the ethics of words. And of all the words in our political vocabulary none is in greater need of precise analysis and scrupulous use than "democracy."

Anyone can use a word as a sign for any idea provided he makes adequately clear what be means by it. For example, if a man says, "By democracy I mean a government in which the name of the ruler begins with a D," we can smile at his peculiar definition and pass on. We need not dispute his usage if he always accompanies it with a parenthetical explanation of what he understands by the term. However, if he introduces the term into a political discussion without stating explicitly the special meaning it has for him, we have every scientific and moral right to object. For where words of a certain kind are already in use, to employ them as signs of new meanings without posting, so to speak, a clear public notice, is to be guilty of a form of counterfeit. New verbal signs can always be found for new meanings.

Democracy is a term which has customarily been associated with certain *historical* practices and with certain writings in the history of culture. Instead of beginning with arbitrary nominal definitions, it would be preferable to describe and critically evaluate the growth of democracy in Western Europe from its origins in the Greek city (slave) states to the present. But this could only be essayed in a systematic treatise.

The third alternative—one which we shall here follow—is to begin with a definition which formally is acceptable to most people who distinguish democracy from other forms of political organization, and which is in consonance with at least traditional American usage. We shall then indicate what it implies as far as the structure of other present-day social institutions is concerned, what techniques of settling differences it commits us to, and what fundamental ethical values are presupposed. In this way we shall combine the advantages of an analytical and "contemporary-historical" treatment.

## 1. THE DEFINITION EXPLORED

A democratic society is one where the government rests upon the freely given consent of the governed. Some ambiguity attaches to every term in this preliminary definition. The least ambiguous is the term "governed." By "the governed" is meant those adult participating members of the community, with their dependents, whose way of life is affected by what the government does or leaves undone. By "the government" is primarily intended the law-and-policy-making agencies, legislative, executive, and judicial, whose activities control the life of the community. In the first instance, then, government is a political concept; but in certain circumstances it may refer to social and economic organizations whose policies affect the lives of a large number of individuals. In saying that the government rests upon the "consent" of the governed, it is meant that at certain fixed periods its policies are submitted to the governed for approval or disapproval. By "freely given" consent of the governed is meant that no coercion, direct or indirect, is brought to bear upon the governed to elicit their approval or disapproval. A government that "rests upon" the freely given consent of the governed is one which *in fact* abides by the expression of this approval or disapproval.

A direct consequence of this definition may be that there is no complete democracy anywhere in the world. This no more prevents our employing the term intelligently and making comparative evaluation than the fact that no one is "perfectly healthy" prevents us from making the concept "health" basic to medical theory and practice. There is no absolutely fat man, but we can easily tell whether one man is fatter than another. So long as our definition enables us to order existing communities in a series of greater or less democracy, our definition is adequate.

If a democratic government rests upon the freely given consent of the governed, then it cannot be present where institutional arrangements—

whether political or nonpolitical—obviously obstruct the registering or the implementing of the common consent. We do not have to settle any metaphysical questions about the nature of freedom in order to be able to tell when consent is not free. A plebiscite or election which is held at the point of a bayonet, or in which one can only vote "Yes," or in which no opposition candidates are permitted, obviously does not express freely given consent. These are only the crudest violations of the democratic ideal but they are sufficient to make the pretense that the present-day regimes in Italy, Russia, and Germany are democratic sound almost obscene.

There are less obvious but no less effective ways of coercively influencing the expression of consent. A threat, for example, to deprive the governed of their jobs or means of livelihood, by a group which has the power to do so, would undermine a democracy even if its name were retained. In fact, every overt form of economic pressure, since it is experienced directly by the individual and since so many other phases of his life are dependent upon economic security, is an overt challenge to democracy. Where the political forms of democracy function within a society in which economic controls are not subject to political control, there is always a standing threat to democracy. For in such a society the possibility exists that economic pressure may strongly influence the expression of consent. Where it cannot influence the expression of consent, it may subvert or prevent its execution. This is particularly true in modern societies in which social instruments of production, necessary for the livelihood of many, are privately owned by the few. A political democracy cannot function properly where differences in economic power are so great that one group can determine the weal or woe of another by nonpolitical means. Genuine political democracy, therefore, entails the right of the governed, through their representatives, to control economic policy. In this sense, it might be said that where there is no economic democracy—a phrase which will be explained later—there can be no genuine and widespread political democracy. The exact degree of economic control necessary to political democracy will vary with changing conditions. It is clear that today modern economic organization plays such a dominant role in social life that political democracy cannot be implemented if it is unable to control economic policy.

A further consequence of "freely given consent" is the absence of a monopoly of education where education includes all agencies of cultural transmission, especially the press. Important as is the majority principle for a democracy, the expression of consent by the majority is not free if it is deprived of access to sources of information, if it can read *only* the official interpretation, if it can hear *only* one voice in classroom, pulpit, and radio—if, in short, all critical opposition is branded as treason to be extirpated by heresy trials, by re-education in concentration camps, and by execution squads. The individual has no more freedom of action when his mind is deliberately tied by ignorance than when his hands are tied with rope. The very dependence of modern man upon the printed word, greater than ever before in history, makes the public right to critical dissent all the more necessary if common consent is to be free. Not many years ago this would have been a commonplace. Today apologists have so muddied the waters of truth that its reaffirmation must be stressed.

## 2. POSITIVE CONDITIONS FOR DEMOCRACY

So far we have been considering conditions in the absence of which democracy cannot exist. But the effective working of a democracy demands the presence of a number of other conditions. Among these, the active participation of the governed in the processes of government is primary.

By active participation is meant not the attempt to do the specific work of officials but free discussion and consultation on public policies, and voluntary co-operation in the execution of mandates reached through the democratic process. Where the governed feel that they have no stake in the government, indifference results. And political indifference may be called the dry-rot of democracy. "The food of feeling," as Mill well says, "is action. . . . Let a person have nothing to do for his country, and he will not care for it."

The country or community, however, is never a homogeneous whole. There may be common interests, but the conceptions of the common interest are never common. Nor in this world can all interests ever in fact be common. If they were, government would be a mere administrative detail. The variety of interests that is always to be found makes necessary that no interest be excluded from voicing its demands, even though these demands may, in the process of democratic deliberation, be compromised or rejected. The only historical alternative to the participation of the masses in the processes of government is the ancient, artful, and uncertain technique of "bread and circuses." That the modern bread is smeared with oleomargarine and the modern circuses are cinematic makes no essential difference. Such a technique conceals differences and trouble centers; whereas the methods of participation and consultation uncover them, articulate new social needs, and suggest instrumentalities for handling them. The wisest policy cannot succeed in face of popular indifference or hostility. Even those who believe that the professionally wise men or experts must do the governing exclude at their own peril those whom they would govern from their counsels.

Another requirement for the effective working of democracy is the presence of mechanisms which permit prompt action, through delegated authority, in crucial situations. What constitutes a crucial situation and what specific administrative mechanisms are best adapted to meet it cannot be settled in advance. But it is clear that there is nothing incompatible with democracy in freely delegating specific functions to authority provided that at a certain fixed time an accounting is made to the governed who alone have the prerogative of renewing or abrogating the grant of authority.

Today the very existence of democracy depends upon its ability to act decisively in its own defense. Effective defense against a foreign totalitarian enemy may require extraordinary and exceptional measures of coordination and control. Some fear that this is the road to totalitarianism. It *may* be. But the alternative is *certain* totalitarianism. So long as democratic communities are threatened by totalitarian states, they must make provision, openly and after discussion, for delegation of authority to responsible individuals to undertake technical defense in a crisis.

That such grants of authority may be abused goes without saying. It may even be acknowledged that there is no absolute guarantee against the risks of usurpation. But unless these risks are sometimes taken, democratic government may be destroyed by evils whose urgency will not wait until the close of prolonged debate. Common sense recognizes this in case of flood and plague. Flood and plague have their social analogues. *But whatever the crisis may be, the recognition that it is a crisis must come from the governed or their delegated representatives; grants of power must be renewed democratically; and the governed cannot, without destroying their democracy, proclaim that the crisis is permanent.*

The fact that the preservation of democracy sometimes demands the delegation of far-reaching authority, and the fact that the possession of such authority may corrupt those who wield it, reinforces another positive requirement of democracy. To understand this requirement we must take note of the psychological effects of holding power, and the historical evidence which indicates that many democratic organizations, sooner or later, become instruments of a minority group which, identifying its own special interests with the interests of the organization as a whole, keeps power by fraud, myth, and force. Taken literally, Lord Acton's maxim, "Power always corrupts and absolute power corrupts absolutely," is an exaggeration. But there is sufficient truth in it to give us pause when we are about to invest individuals or groups with great power, even temporarily. Similarly, Robert Michels's "iron law of oligarchy," according to which democrats may be victorious but democracy never, goes beyond the data he has assembled. But no one can read his powerful case studies and the data presented by other writers like Pareto, Machajaski, and Nomad without realizing how plausible Michels's induction is. And when we add to this the degeneration, under our very eyes, of the Russian Revolution—a revolution which began avowedly as a workers' democracy, developed into the dictatorship of the Communist Party *over* the proletariat, and finally took form as the bloody rule of a camarilla that has piled up more corpses in a few years than did the Roman emperors in as many centuries of Christian persecution—the lesson is driven home with sickening force.

This lesson is that a positive requirement of a working democracy is an intelligent distrust of its leadership, a skepticism, stubborn but not blind, of all demands for the enlargement of power, and an emphasis upon critical method in every phase of education and social life. This skepticism, like other forms of vigilance, may often seem irritating to leaders who are convinced of their good intentions. The skepticism, however, is not of their intentions but of the objective consequences of their power. Where skepticism is replaced by uncritical enthusiasm and the many-faceted deifications which our complex society makes possible, a fertile emotional soil for dictatorship has been prepared. The most convincing aspect of Plato's analysis of the cycle of political decay in the eighth Book of his *Republic* is the transition from a hero-worshiping democracy to an absolute tyranny.

Another positive requirement of democracy we have already referred to as economic democracy. By economic democracy is meant the power of the community, organized as producers and consumers, to determine the basic question of the objectives of economic development. Such economic democracy presupposes some form of social ownership and planning; but whether the economy is to be organized in a single unit or several, whether it is to be highly centralized or not, are experimental questions. There are two criteria to decide such questions. One is the extent to which a specific form of economic organization or ownership makes possible an abundance of goods and services for the greatest number, without which formal political democracy is necessarily limited in its functions, if not actually endangered. The other is the extent to which a specific form of economic organization preserves and strengthens the conditions of the democratic process already described.

Certain kinds of economic planning may give the security of a jail—in which, in exchange for freedom, the inmates are given food, clothing, and shelter of sorts. But any type of planned society which does not provide for the freest criticism, for diversity, for creative individuality, for catholicity of taste, cannot ever guarantee real security. In such a society the "security" is conditional upon accepting arbitrary bureaucratic decree as the law of life. This is conspicuously true wherever the instruments of promotion are socialized by a nondemocratic state. When Stalin tells us that "the dictatorship of the proletariat is *substantially* the dictatorship of the [Communist] Party," he is telling us that the Russian worker can purchase a problematic security only insofar as he accepts this Party dictatorship.[1]

The upshot, then, of our analysis is that just as political democracy is incomplete without some form of economic democracy, so there can be no genuine economic democracy without political democracy. Some may call this socialism. But it is certainly not the "socialism" of either Hitler or Stalin. Nor, despite the fears of frightened tories, of Roosevelt.

## 3. THE ARGUMENT AGAINST DEMOCRACY

Our discussion would be incomplete if we did not consider the chief objections which have been urged against democracy by some of the outstanding thinkers of the past and present. Most of these objections are variants of two fundamental arguments—practical and theoretical.

The practical argument, from the time of Plato down, stresses the imperfections in the actual working of democracy. It draws up a detailed indictment of the blundering inefficiencies of democracies, the influence of demagogy and prejudice in the formulation of their policies, and the operation of certain political mechanisms which place the power of selection of the rulers of the community, actually, in the hands of a minority. And from this largely accurate description of the way in which democracies do in fact work, it is concluded that democracy must be scrapped for another alternative.

The description may he granted without justifying the conclusion. For unless we know the precise nature of the alternative and how *it* works out in practice, we may legitimately reply that the cure for the evils of democracy is better democracy. This is not a catch phrase. For by better democracy is meant the realization of the conditions and requirements already outlined—or, at the very least, the struggle for them.

And what are the alternatives to democracy with all its imperfections? All alternatives turn out upon analysis to involve some form of benevolent despotism—whether a personal or a class or a party despotism. Now the fatal objection to a benevolent despotism of any sort—aside from the fact that people with different interests have different ideas of what constitutes benevolence—is that no one knows how long the despotism will remain benevolent, not even the despot himself. We may appeal from Philip drunk to Philip sober, but who is to keep Philip sober?

Not a single benevolent act of a despot recorded in history but can be matched with scores of malevolent acts. For every guilty man a dictator spares there are thousands of innocent men he dooms. The *ideal* benevolent despotism is a mere figment of the imagination; and even as an ideal, it is no more promising than *ideal* democracy. Moreover, it is wrong to compare the ideal form of benevolent despotism with the actual practice of democracy. If we intelligently compare the practices of both, whether in antiquity or in the modern world, the lovers of democracy need not fear the outcome.

The second type of argument against democracy, the theoretical, is really presupposed by the first. It holds that, the ultimate end of government being human welfare, only those having the best knowledge and highest intelligence are qualified for the difficult pursuit of discovering the nature of human welfare. Since the problems of government are largely administrative, demanding knowledge and intelligence, and since an effective democracy presupposes the possession of both knowledge and intelligence by the majority of the population, which even the lover of democracy must admit is rarely the case, democracy must be rejected. Plato put the nub of the argument in a metaphor: Who would propose that, setting out on a perilous journey, we should *elect* the pilot of the ship? And yet the pilot of the ship of state has a task infinitely more difficult, and the course of the vessel is beset by many more perils. What rhyme or reason exists, therefore, for electing him? Or as Santayana, a direct lineal descendant of Plato in political philosophy, put it, "It is knowledge and knowledge only that may rule by divine right."

Space permits only a brief indication of the Achilles-heel of this argument. While there may be experts in knowledge of fact, there are no experts in wisdom of policy. Ultimate welfare presupposes that there is an "ultimate good." But a conclave of philosophers gathered together to determine the nature of the ultimate good would resemble nothing so much as the Tower of Babel. Wisdom of policy depends upon knowledge of one's interests. It is true that some men are not clear as to what their own interests are. But it is arrant presumption for other men to pretend to them that they know what their interests "really" are, or what they should be. A parent dealing with children may sometimes be justified in asserting that he knows better than they what their real interests are; but any ruler who justifies his abrogation of democratic control by proclaiming that he knows what the real interests of the governed are better than they do themselves is therewith telling them that they are no more responsible than children. Besides oppressing them, he is insulting them, for he envisages their childhood as perpetual. It is not accidental that we call dictatorial government paternal. In paternal government, however, there is more authority than affection. The paternal ruler often takes his political children for guinea pigs upon whom he can try peculiar experiments. Their peculiarity lies in the fact that, whatever their outcome, the present generation of guinea pigs never recovers.

True, there may be no wisdom in electing a pilot or a cobbler. But in the last analysis, as even Plato was compelled to recognize, it is the user and not the maker who is the best judge of work done. Who wears the shoe knows best where it pinches. On this homely truth every theoretical attack on democracy founders.

## 4. THE VALUES AND METHOD OF DEMOCRACY

And democracy is more than a pattern of institutional behavior. Democracy is an affirmation of certain attitudes and values which are more important than any particular set of institutions, because those attitudes and values must serve as the sensitive directing controls of institutional change.

Every mechanism of democratic government has a critical point at which it may run wild. It may be formally perfect but actually murderous. For example, the principle of majority rule is a necessary condition of a working democracy. But a majority can oppress a minority. Numbers, even less than knowledge, give divine right, or immunity from folly. A government resting upon the consent of the majority may not therewith be good government—as the tragic history of the oppression of minorities testifies. To the lessons of that history no one can be indifferent; for every member of the community is part of a minority at some point or on some issue. The persecution of the Jews during the last two thousand years is sufficient evidence that political forms by themselves are no safeguards for a minority—even when it is innocent, unarmed, and culturally creative.

It is helpful but hardly sufficient to insist that democratic communities must provide for self-government by voluntary organized minorities on all questions which concern the minority rather than the community at large. It is not sufficient because minorities are often in opposition on communal issues, and the very willingness to extend autonomy on "local" issues is contingent upon acceptance of the values of democracy as a way of life.

Now there are three related values which are central to democracy as a way of life.

The first is found in many variant formulations, but common to them all is the belief that every individual should be regarded as possessing intrinsic worth or dignity. The social corollary of this recognition is that equal opportunities of development should be provided for the realization of individual talents and capacities. To believe in the equality of opportunities does not mean to believe in the equality of talents. But it does carry with it a recognition that, under conditions of modern technology, marked inequalities in the distribution of wealth or in standards of living are prejudicial to equal opportunities of development. If it is absurd to ask that identical technical opportunities be accorded the artist and the engineer, the machinist and the administrator, it is not absurd to expect that their living conditions be approximately the same. The ideal of equality is not something to be mechanically applied. But it must function as a regulative principle of distribution. Otherwise endemic conflicts, latent in all human associations, take such acute forms that they imperil the very existence of democracy.

The belief in the equal right of all members of the community to develop their personalities must be complemented by a belief in the value of difference, variety, uniqueness. In a democracy differences of interest and achievements must not be merely suffered, they must be encouraged. The healthy zest arising from the conflict and interchange of ideas and personal tastes in a free society is a much more fruitful source of new and significant experiences than the peace of dull, dead uniformity. Of course there are limits to difference as there are to specialization. For however different people are, they live in a common world, they must communicate in a common language, and accept the common constraints which safeguard the species from extinction. In nondemocratic societies this fact that men are always bound in some way by the necessities of living together is used as a premise for constructing vast techniques of repression to choke off differences in almost every way. In democratic societies, however, the same prime fact must serve rather as a condition for enlarging the scope of variation, free play, growth, and experiment.

No matter what the values are to which a democracy is committed, situations will arise in which these values conflict or are challenged by still other values. A decision made in one situation does not necessarily stand for all other situations. The ultimate commitment of a democracy, then, must be a faith in some method by which these conflicts are resolved. Since the method must be the test of all values, it would not be inaccurate to call it the basic value in the democratic way of life. This method is the method of intelligence, of critical scientific inquiry. In a democracy it must be directed to all issues, to all conflicts, if democracy is not to succumb to the dangers which threaten it from both within and without. It is not mere chance that the greatest philosopher of experimental empiricism—John Dewey—is also the greatest philosopher of democracy.

To say that the method of intelligence is essential to the democratic process seems like worrying a commonplace. But not when it is realized how revolutionary the impact would be of giving the method of intelligence institutional force in education, economics, law, and politics. Policies would be treated as hypotheses, not as dogmas; customary practices as generalizations, not as God-given truths. A generation trained in schools where emphasis was placed upon method, method, and still more method, could hardly be swayed by current high-pressured propaganda. The very liberties granted by free institutions in a democracy provide opportunities for special interests to forge powerful instruments to undermine it. The most insidious of all devices for overthrowing democratic institutions is to acquire protective coloration by hypocritical espousal of democracy, to occupy strategic posts, and to open the gates after the Trojan horse is safely within the city. There is no protection against this save the critically armed mind which is immune to rhetoric and parades, and which does *not* give the fanatic a tolerant kind of credit for being sincere in his belief that the end justifies any means.

Those who believe in democracy must distinguish intelligently and act resolutely. First of all, they must distinguish between honest opposition *within* the framework of the democratic process and the opposition, subsidized and controlled by the totalitarian enemies of democracy, which is a form of treason to everything democrats hold dear. Opposition of the first kind, no matter how mistaken, must be tolerated, if for no other reason than that we cannot be sure that it is not we who are mistaken. Opposition of the second kind, no matter what protective coloration it wears—and it will usually be found wrapped up in counterfeit symbols of patriotism or in recently acquired vestments of the Bill of Rights—must be swiftly dealt with if democracy is to survive.

Minorities know that the majority may be tyrannical. The tyranny of the mass flows from its insensitiveness to the consequences of means and methods, not only for the minority but for itself. An insistence upon evidence, relevance, and deliberation is not incompatible with action; it is incompatible only with blind action. The method of intelligence cuts under the fanaticisms which make a fetish of ends, by stressing the conditions and consequences of their use. It both uncovers and enforces responsibilities in social life. It, and it alone, can distinguish between social conflicts which are negotiable and those which are irreconcilable, and the degree of each. Where conflicts are negotiable, it approaches social problems as difficulties to be solved by experiment and analysis, not as battles to be fought out in the heat of blood lust.

What alternative method can be embraced by a society which permits and encourages plural values and plural associations? The more intelligence is liberated in a democratic community, the greater its control of nature and the sources of wealth; the greater its control of nature, the greater possibility of diversifying interests, values, and associations; the greater diversification, the more necessary the function of intelligence to mediate, integrate, and harmonize.

[1938]

# NOTE

1. The quotation is from a speech of Stalin. Compare his *Leninism* (New York: International Publishers, 1928), page 33. That the dictatorship of the Party is not a specifically Russian doctrine but an integral part of the Leninist (not Marxist) theory is clear from the "Theses and Resolutions" of the Communist International. Compare also, for the American variant, the following passage from William Z. Foster's *Towards Soviet America* (New York: Coward-McCann, 1932): "Under the [proletarian] dictatorship, all the capitalistic parties Progressive, Socialist [*sic*] functioning alone as the Party of the toiling masses" (page 275). And yet the Communist Party has such a profound contempt for the Intelligence of the American public, and of its own members, that it publicly proclaims itself as the heir of the traditions of Jefferson!

# 13

# THE ETHICS
# OF CONTROVERSY

**D**emocratic society cannot exist without free discussion. One of its basic assumptions is that truth of fact and wisdom of policy can be more readily achieved through the lively interchange of ideas and opinions than by unchallengeable edicts on the part of a self-perpetuating elite—whether of theologians or philosophers or politicians or even scientific experts. Throughout history, controversy and spirited differences have always marked the deliberations of communities of free men. Their pooled judgments, expressed in public decisions, always reflect the criticism of healthy opposition.

But if democratic society cannot exist without free discussion, some kinds of discussion tend to undermine democratic society. Political life, of course, is not a game; yet, it has certain implicit ground rules which must be observed if freely delegated government by majority is not to degenerate into the tyranny of the mob, or the dictatorship of faction.

In a democratic society, what is morally permissible and impermissible in public controversy follows from the commitment to permit all sectional, class, and individual interests to express themselves openly and honestly before reaching a consensus of agreement on measures that seek to further the common welfare.

As natural creatures, men have needs and interests whose specific form depends upon the times and society in which they live. Conflicts of interest,

Reprinted with permission from *The New Leader* of February 1, 1954.

conflicts of judgment concerning these interests and the best methods of fulfilling them are inescapable in a world of limited resources and fallible intelligence. The democratic process is the best method so far devised by which these conflicts of interest and judgment may be resolved without repression or violence. Discussion is the lifeblood of the democratic process, and, wherever discussion flourishes, controversy is sure to arise.

Certain methods of controversy, however, poison instead of refresh the lifeblood of democracy. They are characterized by the fact that they do not desire to establish the truth or to approximate it as closely as conditions permit. They seek to discredit persons rather than to consider problems. They ignore or suppress relevant evidence. They aim to create a mood of refusal to listen to views challenging some favored or dominant notions. Instead of exposing, confronting, reconciling, or negotiating the conflicts of interest and opinion, one interest is fanatically identified with the common interest, and one opinion with the loyal opinion.

The cumulative effect of such practices is to generate an atmosphere in which the self-corrective procedures of democracy cannot operate. Fact rarely catches up with rumor. Opponents legitimately at odds with each other within the framework of the democratic system are pictured as enemies of the democratic system itself. The reciprocal esteem which citizens of a democratic community should feel for each other, even in disagreement, is replaced by mutual contempt and hate. Instead of being used as an instrument to explore fresh possibilities in the quest for solutions, intelligence becomes a tool to secure only a narrow partisan advantage. Even the liberal mind, by focusing too intently on achievement of immediate objectives without concern for methods, risks becoming transformed into the crafty mind. Most dispiriting of all, some who recognize and denounce morally objectionable techniques of controversy when practiced by others often use them themselves, thus adding hypocrisy to confusion and forgetting that those who blandly lie in a good cause must continue to lie to avoid being found out.

The abuses of free discussion are legion. Short of criminal libel and incitement to, or advocacy of, violence in a situation of clear and present danger, they should not be the subject of legal restraints. For, just as soon as legal restraints are adopted against the various forms of deliberate untruth, malicious and scurrilous exaggeration, venomous insinuation, and outright fabrication, they become weapons to curb honest error and to hamper the spontaneous expression of free minds. In the last analysis, only self-discipline can prevent the level of public discussion from sinking below the safety-line of democratic health. The restraints entailed by good form in discussion are, therefore, more than a matter of good manners: They are a matter of good public morals.

In a world of universal literacy in which everyone is within earshot of a radio, words have become more potent social forces than ever before. No one can write the history of the Weimar Republic or the Kerensky regime or even of modern France without recognizing the extent to which whispering campaigns, calumniation of public figures, and ill-founded accusations against political opponents undermined civic morale and destroyed mutual confidence.

Totalitarian practices in controversy are at least consistent with totalitarian theory. Both Bolshevik and Fascist doctrine deny that there is, or can be, any such thing as "fair" or "classless" or even "objective" discussion of issues. Truth is identified with partisan interest. This serves as a premise to justify the wildest slander against those whom totalitarians oppose, if only it furthers the interest of the party or race. Hitler exhausted the vocabulary of abuse against the leaders of other political groups. Lenin was amazingly frank in justifying the use of poisoned weapons of controversy even against other working-class groups.

A few years before the Russian Revolution, Lenin was tried in a kind of Court of Honor set up by the Social Democratic party (one of whose factions he headed) for using morally impermissible polemical methods. He was charged with impugning the integrity of party members and thus confusing the Russian workers. Lenin defiantly stood his ground and admitted that the tone of his words and their formulation were

> calculated to evoke in the reader hatred, aversion and contempt. . . . Such a formulation is calculated not to convince, but to break up the ranks of an opponent, not to correct the mistakes of an opponent, but to destroy him, to wipe his organization off the face of the earth. This formulation is indeed of such a nature as to evoke the worst thoughts, the worst *suspicions* about the opponents, and indeed, *as contrasted with formulation that convinces and corrects*, it "carries confusion into the ranks of the proletariat."[1]

Only toward members of a *united party* (that is, when they agreed with him or his faction in the Central Committee) did Lenin admit that such methods were morally impermissible. But against all others such methods were mandatory. "Against *such* political enemies I conducted and . . . *shall always* conduct a fight of extermination."[2]

When political feelings run high in democratic communities, many who are firmly opposed to communism and fascism employ techniques of disputation which bear the hallmarks of totalitarian polemics. Anyone who studies the totalitarian press and the proceedings of demonstration trials will find certain recurrent patterns of accusation that show up with alarming frequency in countries this side of the Iron Curtain. One of the most familiar is the systematic confusion between what constitutes evidence of the *consequences* of an action or policy with what constitutes evidence of its *intent*.

No *moral* judgment can be passed upon any individual human action without an appraisal of its intent. Consequences *alone* cannot be a fair test of intentions. A common procedure in Soviet and satellite countries is to charge that the consequences of a policy have been disastrous (the charge is rarely proved), and then to take the alleged disastrous consequences as sufficient proof of the presence of an intention to bring them about. This "justifies" the secret police in torturing the defendant to confess to an intention which has already been objectively established by the consequences. In effect, an accident becomes a crime; ignorance is indistinguishable from treason, and error a form of sabotage. The Bolshevik concept of "objective counterrevolutionary" guilt, inferred not only from the presumed consequences of a man's actions but from his membership in a family or class and other *nonvoluntary* forms of association, led to the liquidation of millions.

Recent political argument in the United States seems to show that, in the heat of controversy, the most elementary distinctions have been overlooked. From the true proposition that policies can be intelligently tested only by their consequences, the false proposition is drawn that the consequences alone are the conclusive test of the intent or motives behind the policies. A bad result is deemed proof of a wicked purpose (particularly if one's political opponents are responsible for the decision), and a good result is proof of good will (particularly if one's political friends initiated it). This summarizes many pages of discussion today.

In nonpolitical contexts, the crudity and cruelty of such simplistic criticism is easily recognized and universally repudiated. It would be tantamount to charging a surgeon whose patient had died under the knife with murder or a general of a defeated army with being in the service of the enemy.

It would be preposterous to equate the systematic employment of poisoned instruments of controversy in totalitarian countries with the serious abuses of discussion in free cultures; for, in the former, a single minority party has a total monopoly of the power of denunciation and defamation. But the presence of intellectually dishonest techniques of argument in a free culture, even when they are employed by many parties in the peaceful struggle for political power, is a disquieting phenomenon. It is a betrayal of the spirit of the democratic process even when it abides by its legal forms.

Several books and many articles have been written which persuasively argue that *if* someone had set out to serve the Communist cause, he *would have* advocated certain policies and behaved in certain ways. Evidence is then presented that some individuals *did* advocate these policies and behave in these ways. This is then considered conclusive proof that he did set out to serve the Communist cause. No further inquiry is deemed necessary to determine the independent facts about his memberships, activities, and other data relevant to his intentions or purposes. It is overlooked that, just as the same conclusion can be reached from different premises, so the same policy may be advocated for two entirely different, and sometimes incompatible, sets of motives. A member of the Communist party, for example, may advocate unilateral disarmament for the United States. But so may an absolute pacifist, in the belief that the Kremlin will kiss the other cheek instead of slapping it. The first should not be eligible for government employment, certainly not in a sensitive post; the second, however, may be eligible, and, if ineligible, only on grounds relevant to his competence which have nothing to do with his loyalty.

One of Senator McCarthy's favorite techniques of argument is to insinuate that, since a policy has been followed by the Kremlin, or approved by the Kremlin, anyone else who advocated such a policy is therewith suspect of being a Soviet agent. Unfortunately, some of those who are critical of Senator McCarthy's methods do not hesitate to use some of his techniques of argument against those who disagree with them: Because Senator McCarthy says that the Communist party is a conspiracy, therefore anyone who says that the Communist party is a conspiracy is suspect of McCarthyism. But what makes a thing true is not who says it, but the evidence for it; the evidence that the Communist party is a conspiratorial movement, and not like other American political parties, is by now overwhelming.

The intellectual circles of the country have a responsibility for teaching, and living up to, the highest standards of vigorous controversy.

But there are signs even here of infection by the virus of partisanship. One occasionally hears members of the learned professions substitute abuse for logical analysis and, unable to meet argument or evidence for some positions of which they disapprove, inveigh against the presumed "unconscious" of those who uphold them. When the methods of the marketplace—and of the black marketplace—invade the academy, the intellectual life of a country is debased.

The ground rules of controversy in a democracy are simple, and their reaffirmation may sound like truisms. They *are* truisms. But when denied or violated, truisms become very important. That their reaffirmation is necessary is an indication of how low political discussion has sunk. Among these rules are:

1. Nothing and no one is immune from criticism.
2. Everyone involved in a controversy has an intellectual responsibility to inform himself of the available facts.
3. Criticism should be directed first to policies, and against persons only when they are responsible for policies, and against their motives or purposes only when there is some independent evidence of their character.
4. Because certain words are legally permissible, they are not therefore morally permissible.
5. *Before* impugning an opponent's motives, even when they legitimately may be impugned, answer his arguments.
6. Do not treat an opponent of a policy as if he were therefore a personal enemy or an enemy of the country or a concealed enemy of democracy.
7. Since a good cause may be defended by bad arguments, after answering the bad arguments for another's position present positive evidence for your own.
8. Do not hesitate to admit lack of knowledge or to suspend judgment if evidence is not decisive either way.
9. Only in pure logic and mathematics, not in human affairs, can one demonstrate that something is strictly impossible. Because something is logically possible, it is not therefore probable. "It is not impossible" is a preface to an irrelevant statement about human affairs. The question is always one of the balance of probabilities. And the evidence for probabilities must include more than abstract possibilities.

10. The cardinal sin, when we are looking for truth of fact or wisdom of policy, is refusal to discuss, or action which blocks discussion.

These ground rules express *in nuce* the logic and ethics of scientific inquiry. From one point of view, science may be considered as a field of continuing controversy which leaves behind it not burning hatreds, but vast accumulations of knowledge. It is not necessary to deny the vast differences between the *subject-matters* of the natural sciences and the disciplines concerned with human affairs to recognize that, if the spirit of scientific inquiry were brought to bear on most questions of politics, American democracy would be both wiser and more secure.

[1954]

## NOTES

1. V. I. Lenin, *Selected Works* (New York: International Publishers, 1943), vol. 3: 490 [italics mine].
2. Ibid. p. 491 [Lenin' Italics].

# 14

# THE DEGRADATION
# OF THE WORD

In one of the early dialogues, *The Phaedrus*, Plato relates a charming myth about the Egyptian God, Thamus, who sat in judgment upon the creations of Theuth, polymath and inventor of the art of writing. Theuth pleads for the dissemination of letters among the Egyptians on the ground that they are a kind of medicine for memory and wisdom. But Thamus sternly rejects the plea. "For this invention of yours," Plato makes him say, "will produce forgetfulness in the minds of those who learn it, by causing them to neglect their memory, inasmuch as, from their confidence in writing, they will recollect by the external aid of foreign symbols, and not by the internal use of their own faculties."

Plato's myths are often expressions of dramatic irony suggesting different meanings hard to reconcile by those who forget the poet in the system maker. Classical scholars may dispute concerning which meaning is the one Plato really intended, but we may enjoy them all.

One of the simple yet profound truths suggested by this Platonic myth is the danger of mechanical literacy to the life of intelligence. We all know that the ability to read is not the same as the ability to think. But can it ever be that an ability to read is an obstacle to thinking? To suggest that it can be and, at the same time, to admit that the ability to read is a natural good, sounds like a paradox. And yet we are all familiar with situations in which goods and values seem, in a manner of speaking,

Reprinted with permission from *The New Leader* of January 27, 1945.

to turn into bads and disvalues. Goods and values in our experience come in clusters, not separately. Whatever may be the immediate quality of a specific good or value, its validity or worth depends upon its relations to other goods and values. One of the ways by which we check the worth of a good or value in a concrete situation is by its effects on the family of goods and values to which it belongs. Friendship without generosity, justice without sympathy, strength without sensitivity, courage without intelligence, do not lose their meanings but their validity as desirable ends. Moral insight consists in knowledge of the way in which goods and values are related to each other. Sometimes the relationships are obvious and at hand; sometimes they are obscure and surprising.

One of the interesting aspects of literacy as a natural good—and we are beginning to see that this is true for a great many other natural goods—is that its "goodness" is organically related to *human freedoms*. By human freedom we mean here rights found in a libertarian society where democratic institutions make it possible for individuals to criticize their governing agencies. Where there is no human freedom in this sense, literacy may not be a blessing but what the Egyptian God, Thamus, feared it would be.

The reason for this is not hard to see. In a totalitarian society, whose tyranny as distinct from the past requires a mass base, literacy can and has been used as an instrument of consolidating the power of the minority. Through universal literacy under a monopoly of power, words and slogans reach into the mind of every man. There is no escaping them. They root out the very recalcitrance of silence. They supply a continual and unvarying stimulus to all who cannot keep their eyes shut. "Thinking" becomes a conditioned response to words, and "thought" is completed by providing the appropriate words to the opening cue. The unconscious processes are "educated." This education reaches its triumph when the right response from the point of view of those who control the propaganda seems to their victims to be an expression of uncoerced first nature. Without the challenge and the stimulus provoked by open criticism of word by word, to read means to acquire the habit of credulity. It is to rely on external symbols, not "on the internal use of their own faculties."

An unfailing argument in the arsenal of defenders of totalitarianism is the increase in literacy which has taken place under dictatorial rule. The argument has been made for Japan, Germany, most frequently for Russia, and least frequently for Italy—and most recently for Venezuela. Those who argue about the percentages of increase to indicate that they are not as great as claimed miss the main point. Grant the apologists of totalitarianism all their claims; it still remains true that where only what the government approves can be read, literacy may become an effective means for the mental enslavement of the people.

The skepticism and shrewdness of the illiterate European peasant has probably been exaggerated. Tolstoy and other novelists idealized their portraits of the peasant type. But the kernel of truth behind the legend is the reliance the peasant placed upon the deliverances of his own experience as evidential signs of what he was told. His data were crude, limited, but strictly verifiable. He was ignorant and could easily be misled. But when he counted his bruises and pains he could recognize that he had been misled. It is said that some Russian peasants were so illiterate that they disbelieved the existence of remotely distant countries and suspected that wars against them were government inventions designed to increase taxes and recruit their sons for forced labor. But such deep distrust was really a demand for evidence. The range of evidence was limited by the horizon of his interest and feelings. Even his superstitions testify to his "vulgar" empiricism. He knew exactly what to expect in the hereafter. (One is tempted to describe him as living according to the faith of the popular semanticists who lump together all abstractions as untrustworthy, without distinguishing between those that can lead us at some point to definite observation tests and those that cannot.) The result was that the peasant was often fooled. *But he didn't fool himself.*

In a free society, where words do not come from one center and men are exposed to the clash of conflicting doctrines, it is *possible* for the individual to employ abstractions of high order and relate them to experience as a test. *But in an unfree society there is a tendency for literacy to corrupt the natural pragmatism of the human mind.* The illiterate peasant knew when he was hungry; he knew when and where his boots—when he had any—pinched. He knew that the knout which lashed him was not wielded by his hand, and that it was not *his* will which moved the officials of the state to imprison and deport him. Teach him to read, but let him read nothing except what the dictatorship approves; give him schooling, but only according to the party line; subject him to a sustained barrage of slogans—and lo and behold! he can be led to deny the evidence of his own senses. His hunger is now a subjective illusion. The boots he hasn't got are on order for when the $n$th five-year plan is finished. And as for the boots he has: they don't really pinch, nothing wrong with them—it is merely that his *feet* are defective, and therefore not properly molded to the perfect shoe the factory has sold him. His feet are the real saboteurs. He himself is the state which deprives him of freedom, because, forsooth, he is a worker and the state is a worker's state. And if the secret police find it necessary to shoot him, they are merely carrying out the sentence of his own judgment—which Rousseau, Hegel, and the commissar-philosopher Mitin all teach.

Totalitarian countries are not the only breeding grounds of metaphysical syntheses which wipe out empirical differences. But by imposing literacy, they can see to it that no one escapes their influence. And by monopolizing the use of words, they prevent the conflict of metaphysical systems with each other, and the conflict between all of them and scientific philosophy, which safeguards the intelligence in democratic culture.

I am not, of course, making a plea for illiteracy. I am on the side of Theuth, not of Thamus. But even in a democracy, literacy is not enough for the intelligent performance of the duties of citizenship unless it is accompanied by the critical training in the use and analysis of language which our schools only too often fail to give. A few years ago there was an outcry against the few educators who called for a vigorous program of critical analysis in our educational institutions. They were taxed with being skeptics who robbed youth of its faith, philosophical fifth columnists who subverted the simple pieties toward God and a decent foreign policy: all because they maintained that literacy which was not the gateway to intellectual sophistication, an ability to read without a developed sense of what constitutes evidence, a failure to distinguish between a definition, and a hypothesis and the consequent inability to apply the proper criteria in considering them—that these softened the minds of Americans for the onslaught of domestic and foreign propaganda.

One of the most popular techniques of undermining free society is the *degradation of the word*. Intellectually, this marks our era just as much as the "new failure of nerve." The comparatively recent spectacle of the head of a large American news service seriously accepting the claim of a Russian propaganda sheet that Russia enjoys a free press, the instance a few years ago of a Town Hall audience leaving unchallenged the plea by a professional propagandist that Russia is entitled to a third of Poland because the London Polish government was undemocratic, is some evidence of how far the degradation of the word went during and just after the end of World War II.

Or consider the argument that no state is completely democratic! The United States is in some respects undemocratic: the USSR is in some respects democratic: therefore they are both democracies, differing merely in degree. The same line of argument would also have proved Germany and the United States both democracies, differing merely in degree—a conclusion violently opposed by those who at the same time accepted the sequence in the first sentence. The same line of argument would prove that the United States and the USSR are both dictatorships; this might be accepted by some muddled apologists because it would remove the odium of totalitarianism from Russia. This same line of argument would prove that since no one can be perfectly good, and since Hitler was kind to animals, there was only a mere difference in degree of goodness between Hitler and Eugene Debs. This argument would be indignantly repudiated, by those who would applaud its analogue, were Stalin's name or that of his successor to be substituted for Debs.

There is no quick remedy for uneducated literacy. The schools by themselves cannot solve the problem, for at bottom it is an aspect of deeper social and political problems. But the schools can do something— how much cannot be known until they reorganize their curriculums on every level to educate for critical intelligence. The very least we can expect from them in a society still democratic is that they recognize the problem. Everybody wants the schools to educate students so that they will not be ensnared by the other fellow's illusions. At this point perhaps the schools can attempt to implement what everybody agrees on, and then press on to the conclusions that follow from an illusionless method.

But in the last decade the degradation of the word has sunk to even lower depths. The use of the slogan of "peace" by the Kremlin regime at the very time it inspired the Korean invasion seemed to indicate that the Communist chieftains were intent upon substantiating the actuality of Orwell's account of intellectual life in *1984*. The mystery is not that the Communist "peace partisans" could regard a war initiated by their ideological fellows-in-arms as a method of waging peace, but that this was also believed by some on this side of the Iron Curtain. And these believers included not only those who had given no evidence of intellectual sophistication, but also eminent men in the arts and sciences who in their own field have a keen sense for the unproved and falsely inferred. Something more is at work than the "degradation of the word"—there is a receptivity, a need, a positive willingness to believe, despite the apparent evidence which destroys illusions.

I wish to safeguard myself against the charge made by an editorial writer on the *Washington Post* that these ironical observations are an argument against literacy and that in effect I am rewriting Marx's revolutionary manifesto to conclude with the warning: "Workers of the

World, don't read or write, you will lose your brains!" The simple point is not that these reflections are an argument against literacy, but merely that literacy is not an argument *for* totalitarianism even if in the end totalitarianism cannot succeed in reconditioning the human mind to wipe out the difference between the true and false.

A closer examination of the record of totalitarian countries reveals that it is difficult to condition the human mind to ignore completely the evidence of experience and the senses. Much indeed can be accomplished, but after a few Barmecidean feasts the clamor of the senses, physical and mental, makes itself heard. This is especially true if knowledge of the different thoughtways of free countries can percolate the barriers totalitarian countries throw up around themselves.

We have additional evidence that a generation of students brought up under the severe ideological indoctrination of Marxist-Leninism can challenge much that it has been taught to repeat without question. Although this critical postrevolutionary generation has expressed itself most openly in satellite countries where the unquenchable fires of nationalism burn through ideological pretense, there is even in the Soviet Union some critical questioning which increases in volume as the pitch of terror is slightly lessened. There is a tendency to magnify human intellectual resistance to totalitarian conditioning when we are confronted with heroic cases of those who cling to their own integrity. There is also a tendency to magnify human suggestibility and ability to believe what is false when we see or hear crowds acclaiming the executioner of their own liberties. Undoubtedly there is a genetic factor at work which accounts in part for the diverse reactions of individuals similarly situated socially to the techniques of unintellectual persuasion. Each one can recall some incident which renews his faith in what seems the natural curiosity, perversity, or cantankerousness of man. The question one must ask, however, is how general and sustained such a reaction can be. An unforgettable experience during the Communist blockade of Berlin in August, 1948, illustrates the point.

I met a young Red Army lieutenant, born and nurtured under the Stalin regime, who had deserted to our side. Naturally I was eager to find out why he had broken. He told me that his hostility to the Soviet regime had anteceded the war and that he had seized the first opportunity to escape. It appeared from his account that he had been a student in a technical institute and was taking the prescribed course in Marxist-Leninism. His instructor was laying down the orthodox line on historical materialism, and had asserted that the mode of economic production in any culture uniquely determines the political system in that culture. In the most innocent way, this young man asked why different political forms of government weren't compatible with the same economic base. He pointed to the capitalist system in Italy which existed first with democratic then dictatorial forms. The instructor, unable to give him a satisfactory answer, then tried to talk the student down, to ridicule him, and finally to charge him with revisionism, mechanism, formalism, Menshevik idealism, and other heresies the young man didn't understand. That young man in his own way had discovered for himself the distinction between necessary and sufficient conditions, and he clung to it even when he was expelled from the Young Communist League for refusing to yield. He narrowly escaped the charge of counterrevolutionary Trotskyism, but he was always under suspicion, and his hatred of the regime grew apace.

I expressed wonder that a purely intellectual difficulty should have had such fateful consequences. Men are rational animals, but not that rational. But his answer was very revealing (even though it sounded as if he had been reading Karl Jaspers).

"If I had been asked," he replied, "to say that two plus two is five I would not have cared—everyone knows it's four and this truth did not particularly concern me. But if I had denied my notion about the relation between economics and politics, it would have been like renouncing a piece of myself. *You see, I had thought this out for myself.*"

He uttered this last sentence with emphasis. What he was telling me was that he had risked his life for the sake of his creative and critical integrity. It was not the abstract truth he was struggling for, but his dignity and self-respect as a person.

Can we rely altogether upon the indestructibility of this natural impulse to speak truth, to distinguish, to argue, to contradict, to find out, to do things alone, or differently, or privately? Perhaps in the long run. But the opposite is also true in the long run: terror is a great persuader even though it is not omnipotent. And a terror which can use modern technology to change the mind and self is more often successful than unsuccessful in persuading the subjects to be changed. That is why it seems to me that, honor the heroes of intellectual resistance as we should, we cannot expect, independently of what the free peoples themselves do, that their example will necessarily inspire their fellow subjects. For one thing the "example" is rarely known, and totalitarian dictators sometimes organize their own opposition in order to be able to deal effectively with it in good time.

We cannot rely only upon the rare chance of a distinguished spirit to see through and resist the degradation of the word. We must find ways of reaching the citizens of totalitarian countries so that at the very least the knowledge of the examples is not lost.

[1945]

# IV

## DEMOCRATIC PRACTICE

# 15

## DEMOCRACY AND SOCIAL PROTEST

### NEITHER BLIND OBEDIENCE
### NOR UNCIVIL DISOBEDIENCE

I n times of moral crisis what has been accepted as commonplace truth sometimes appears questionable and problematic. We have all been nurtured in the humanistic belief that in a democracy citizens are free to disagree with a law but that so long as it remains in force they have a *prima facie* obligation to obey it. The belief is justified on the ground that this procedure enables us to escape the twin evils of tyranny and anarchy. Tyranny is avoided by virtue of the freedom and power of dissent to win the uncoerced consent of the community. Anarchy is avoided by reliance on due process, the recognition that there is a right way to correct a wrong, and a wrong way to secure a right. To the extent that anything is demonstrable in human affairs, we have held that democracy as a political system is not viable if members systematically refuse to obey laws whose wisdom or morality they dispute.

Nonetheless, during the past decade of tension and turmoil in American life there has developed a mass phenomenon of civil disobedience even among those who profess devotion to democratic ideals and institutions. This phenomenon has assumed a character similar to a tidal wave which has not yet reached its crest. It has swept from the field of race relations to the campuses of some universities, subtly altering the connotation of the term "academic." It is being systematically developed as an instrument for influencing foreign policy. It is leaving its mark on popular culture. I am told it is not only a theme of comic books but that children in our more sophisticated families no longer resort to tantrums in defying parental discipline—they go limp!

More seriously, in the wake of civil disobedience there has occasionally developed *uncivil* disobedience, sometimes as a natural psychological development, and often because of the failure of law enforcement agencies especially in the South to respect and defend legitimate expressions of social protest. The line between civil and uncivil disobedience is not only an uncertain and wavering one in practice, it has become so in theory. A recent prophet of the philosophy of the absurd in recommending civil disobedience as a form of creative disorder in a democracy cited Shay's Rebellion as an illustration. This Rebellion was uncivil to the point of bloodshed. Indeed, some of the techniques of protesting American involvement in Vietnam have departed so far from traditional ways of civil disobedience as to make it likely that they are inspired by the same confusion between civil and uncivil disobedience.

All this has made focal the perennial problems of the nature and limits of the citizen's obligation to obey the law, of the relation between the authority of conscience and the authority of the state, of the rights and duties of a democratic moral man in an immoral democratic society. The classical writings on these questions—Socrates's argument in the *Crito*; the confrontation between Antigone and Creon in Sophocles's *Antigone*; the writings of Rousseau, Thoreau, Garrison, Tolstoy, Gandhi, and their critics—have acquired a burning relevance to the political condition of man today. I propose briefly to clarify some of these problems.

To begin with I wish to stress the point that there is no problem concerning "social protest" as such in a democracy. Our Bill of Rights was adopted not only to make protest possible but to encourage it. The political logic, the very ethos of any democracy that professes to rest, no matter how indirectly, upon freely given consent *requires* that social protest be permitted—and not only permitted but *protected* from interference by those opposed to the protest, which means protected by agencies of law enforcement.

Not social protest but *illegal* social protest constitutes our problem. It raises the question: "When, if ever, is illegal protest justified in a democratic society?" It is of the first importance to bear in mind that we are raising the question as principled democrats and humanists in a democratic society. To urge that illegal social protests motivated by exalted ideals are sanctified in a democratic society by precedents like the Boston

Tea Party is a lapse into political illiteracy. Such actions occurred in societies in which those affected by unjust laws had no power peacefully to change them. As a democrat, I am in favor of any social protest, legal or illegal, peaceful or violent, in any nondemocratic society that is likely to free human beings from oppression or lessen the pitch of such oppression, without exposing them to serious risks of greater evils at the time.

Further, many actions dubbed civilly disobedient by local authorities, strictly speaking, are not such at all. An action launched in violation of a local law or ordinance, and undertaken to test it, on the ground that the law itself violates state or federal law, or launched in violation of a state law in the sincerely held belief that the state law outrages the Constitution, the supreme law of the land, is not civilly disobedient. In large measure the early sympathy with which the original sit-ins were received, especially the Freedom Rides, marches, and demonstrations that flouted local Southern laws, was due to the conviction that they were constitutionally justified, in accordance with the heritage of freedom, enshrined in the Amendments and enjoyed in other regions of the country. Practically everything the marchers did was sanctioned by the phrase of the First Amendment which upholds "the right of the people peaceably to assemble and to petition the Government for a redress of grievances." Actions of this kind may be wise or unwise, timely or untimely, but they are not civilly disobedient.

They become civilly disobedient when they are in deliberate violation of laws that have been sustained by the highest legislative and judicial bodies of the nation, e.g., income tax laws, conscription laws, laws forbidding segregation in education, and discrimination in public accommodations and employment. Another class of examples consists of illegal social protest against local and state laws that clearly do not conflict with Federal Law. An act of civil disobedience is not only deliberate and nonviolent but public. Were it not public, it would be pointless and hard to distinguish from a criminally evasive action for personal gain.

Once we grasp the proper issue, the question is asked with deceptive clarity: "Are we under an obligation in a democratic community always to obey an unjust law?" To this question Abraham Lincoln is supposed to have made the classic answer in an eloquent address on "The Perpetuation of Our Political Institution," calling for absolute and religious obedience until the unjust law is repealed. Said Lincoln: "Bad laws if they exist should be repealed as soon as possible, still while they continue in force, they should be religiously observed." This sentiment was echoed by President Kennedy. Said Kennedy: "Americans are free to disagree with the law but not to disobey it. For in a government of laws, no man, however powerful or prominent, and no mob, however unruly or boisterous, is entitled to defy a court of law."

I said that this question is asked with deceptive clarity because Lincoln, judging by his other writings and the pragmatic cast of his basic philosophy, could never have subscribed to this absolutism or meant what he seemed literally to have said. Not only are we under no moral obligation *always* to obey unjust laws, we are under no moral obligation *always* to obey a just law. One can put it more strongly: sometimes it may be necessary in the interests of the greater good to violate a just or sensible law. A man who refused to violate a sensible traffic law if it were necessary to do so to avoid a probably fatal accident would be a moral idiot. There are other values in the world besides legality or even justice, and sometimes they may be of overriding concern and weight. Everyone can imagine some situation in which the violation of some existing law is the lesser moral evil, but this does not invalidate recognition of our obligation to obey just laws.

There is a difference between disobeying a law which one approves of in general but whose application in a specific case seems wrong, and disobeying a law in protest against the injustice of the law itself. In the latter case the disobedience is open and public; in the former, not. But if the grounds of disobedience in both cases are moral considerations, there is only a difference in degree between them. The rejection, therefore, of legal absolutism or the fetishism of legality—that one is never justified in violating any law in any circumstances—is a matter of common sense.

The implications drawn from this moral commonplace by some ritualistic liberals are clearly absurd. For they have substituted for the absolutism of law, something very close to the absolutism of individual conscience. Properly rejecting the view that the law, no matter how unjust, must be obeyed in all circumstances, they have taken the view that the law is to be obeyed only when the individual deems it just or when it does not outrage his conscience. Fantastic comparisons are made between those who do not act on the dictates of their conscience and those who accepted and obeyed Hitler's laws. These comparisons completely disregard the systems of law involved, the presence of alternatives of action, the differences in the behavior commanded, in degrees of complicity of guilt, in the moral costs and personal consequences of compliance, and other relevant matters.

It is commendable to recognize the primacy of morality to law, but unless we recognize the centrality of intelligence to morality we stumble with blind self-righteousness into moral disaster. Because, Kant to the contrary notwithstanding, it is not wrong sometimes to lie to save a human life, because it is not wrong sometimes to kill in defense to save many more from being killed, it does not follow that the moral principles: "Do not lie!" "Do not kill!" are invalid. When more than one valid principle bears on a problem of moral experience, the very fact of their conflict means that not all of them can hold unqualifiedly. One of them must be denied. The point is that such negation or violation entails upon us the obligation of justifying it, and moral justification is a matter of reasons not of conscience. The burden of proof rests on the person violating the rules. Normally, we don't have to justify telling the truth. We do have to justify *not* telling the truth. Similarly, with respect to the moral obligation of a democrat who breaches his political obligation to obey the laws of a democratic community. The resort to conscience is not enough. There must always be reasonable justification.

This is all the more true because just as we can, if challenged, give powerful reasons for the moral principle of truth-telling, so we can offer morally persuasive grounds for the obligation of a democrat to obey the laws of a democracy. The grounds are many and they can be amplified beyond the passing mention we give here. It is a matter of fairness, of not being a freeloader, i.e., profiting from the political system that one professes to reject or refuses to support, of social utility, of peace, or ordered progress, of redeeming an implicit commitment.

There is one point, however, which has a particular relevance to the claims of those who counterpose to legal absolutism the absolutism of conscience. There is the empirically observable tendency for public disobedience to law to spread from those who occupy high moral ground to those who dwell on low moral ground with consequent growth of disorder and insecurity.

Conscience by itself is not the measure of high or low moral ground. This is the work of reason. Where it functions properly the democratic process permits this resort to reason. If the man of conscience loses in the court of reason, why should he assume that the decision or the law is mistaken rather than the deliverances of his conscience?

The voice of conscience may sound loud and clear. But it may conflict at times not only with the law but with another man's conscience. Every conscientious objector to a law knows that at least one man's conscience is wrong, viz., the conscience of the man who asserts that *his* conscience tells him that he must not tolerate conscientious objectors. From this if he is reasonable he should conclude that when he hears the voice of conscience he is hearing not the voice of God, but the voice of a finite, limited man in this time and in this place, and that conscience is neither a special nor an infallible organ of apprehending moral truth, that conscience without conscientiousness, conscience which does not cap the process of critical reflective morality, is likely to be prejudice masquerading as a First Principle or a Mandate from Heaven.

The mark of an enlightened democracy is, as far as is possible with its security, to respect the religious commitment of a citizen who believes, on grounds of conscience or any other ground, that his relation to God involves duties superior to those arising from any human relation. It, therefore, exempts him from his duty as a citizen to protect his country. However, the mark of the genuine conscientious objector in a democracy who professes belief in a democracy as morally preferable to any realistic alternative at the time, is to respect the democratic process. He does not use his exemption as a political weapon to coerce where he has failed to convince or persuade. Having failed to influence national policy by rational means within the law, in the political processes open to him in a free society, he cannot justifiably try to defeat that policy by resorting to obstructive techniques outside the law *and still remain a democrat.*

It is one thing on grounds of conscience or religion to plead exemption from the duty of serving one's country when drafted. It is quite another to adopt harassing techniques to prevent others from volunteering or responding to the call of duty. It is one thing to oppose American involvement in Vietnam by teach-ins, petitions, electoral activity. It is quite another to attempt to stop troop trains: to take possession of the premises of draft boards where policies are not made; to urge recruits to sabotage their assignments and feign illness to win discharge. The first class of actions falls within the sphere of legitimate social protest; the second class is implicitly insurrectionary since it is directed against the authority of a democratic government which it seeks to overthrow not by argument and discussion but by resistance—albeit passive resistance.

Nonetheless since we have rejected legal absolutism we must face the possibility that in protest on ethical grounds individuals may refuse to obey some law which they regard as uncommonly immoral or uncommonly foolish. If they profess to be democrats, their behavior must scrupulously respect the following conditions:

*First, it must be truly nonviolent—peaceful not only in form but in actuality.* After all, the protesters are seeking to dramatize a great evil that the community allegedly has been unable to overcome because of complacency or moral weakness. Therefore, they must avoid the guilt of imposing hardship or harm on others who in the nature of the case can hardly be responsible for the situation under protest. Passive resistance should not be utilized merely as a safer or more effective strategy than active resistance in imposing their wills on others. And nonviolence must be judged by the consequences of the allegedly nonviolent action, not by whether physical force is dramatically employed. To cut off a person's food or water, or to deny him access to them, is an act of violence which, if prolonged, may be more cruel than cutting off his head. It is almost always counterproductive. Uncivil or violent disobedience evokes a fear in the general population of either an incipiently revolutionary movement directed against the existing political and legal system or of chaos and anarchy whose potential evils dwarf any existing one.

*Second, resort to civil disobedience is never morally legitimate where other methods of remedying the evil complained of are available.* Existing grievance procedures should be used. No grievance procedures were available to the southern Negroes. The courts often shared the prejudices of the community and offered no relief, not even minimal protection. But such procedures *are* available in the areas of industry and education. For example, where charges against students are being heard such procedures may result in the dismissal of the charges not the students. Or the faculty on appeal may decide to suspend the rules rather than the students. To jump the gun to civil disobedience in bypassing these procedures is telltale evidence that those who are calling the shots are after other game than preserving the rights of students. This was the case when students of the FSM [Free Speech Movement] at the University of California at Berkeley in 1964, in response to a request that four of their leaders appear for a hearing before the Faculty Committee on Student Conduct to answer charges that they had engaged in acts of illegal physical violence, seized possession of Sproul Hall, the administrative building.[1]

*Third, those who resort to civil disobedience are duty bound to accept the legal sanctions and punishments imposed by the laws.* Attempts to evade and escape them involve not only a betrayal of the community, but they erode the moral foundations of civil disobedience itself. Socrates's argument in the *Crito* is valid only on democratic premises. The rationale of the protesters is the hope that the pain and hurt and indignity they voluntarily accept will stir their fellow citizens to compassion, open their minds to second thoughts, and move them to undertake the necessary healing action. When however, we observe the heroics of defiance being followed by the dialectics of legal evasion, we question the sincerity of the action.

*Fourth, civil disobedience is unjustified if a major moral issue is not clearly at stake.* Differences about negotiable details that can easily be settled with a little patience should not be fanned into a blaze of illegal opposition.

*Fifth, where intelligent men of good will and character differ on large and complex moral issues discussion and agitation are more appropriate than civilly disobedient action.* Those who feel strongly about animal rights and regard the consumption of animal flesh as food as morally evil would have a just cause for civil disobedience if *their* freedom to obtain other food was threatened. They would have no moral right to resort to similar action to prevent their fellow citizens from consuming meat. Similarly, with fluoridation.

*Sixth, where civil disobedience is undertaken, there must be some rhyme and reason in the time, place, and targets selected.* If one is convinced, as I am not, that the Board of Education of New York City is remiss in its policy of desegregation, what is the point of dumping garbage on bridges to produce traffic jams that seriously discomfort commuters who have not the remotest connection with educational policies in New York? Such action can only obstruct the progress of desegregation in the communities of Long Island. Gandhi, who inspired the civil disobedience movement in the twentieth century, was a better tactician than many who invoke his name but ignore his teachings. When he organized his campaign of civil disobedience against the Salt Tax, he marched with his followers to the sea to make salt. He did not hold up food trains or tie up traffic.

*Finally, there is such a thing as historical timing.* Democrats who resort to civil disobedience must ask themselves whether the cumulative consequences of their action may in the existing climate of opinion undermine the peace and order on which the effective exercise of other human rights depend. This is a cost which one may be willing to pay but which must be taken into the reckoning.

These observations in the eyes of some defenders of the philosophy of civil disobedience are far from persuasive. They regard them as evading the political realities. The political realities, it is asserted, do not provide meaningful channels for the legitimate expression of dissent. The Establishment is too powerful or indifferent to be moved. Administrations are voted into office that are not bound by their election pledges. The right to form minority parties is hampered by unconstitutional voting laws. What does even "the right of the people to present petitions for the redress of grievances" amount to if it does not carry with it the right to have those petitions paid attention to, at least to have them read, if not acted upon?

No, the opposing argument runs on. Genuine progress does not come by enactment of laws, by appeals to the good will or conscience of one's fellow citizens, but only by obstructions which interfere with the functioning of the system itself, by actions whose nuisance value is so high that the Establishment finds it easier to be decent and yield to demands than to be obdurate and oppose them. The time comes, as one student leader of the civilly disobedient Berkeley students advised, "when it is necessary for you to throw your bodies upon the wheels and gears and levers and bring the machine to a grinding halt." When one objects that such obstruction, as a principle of political action, is almost sure to produce chaos, and that it is unnecessary and undesirable in a democracy, the retort is made: "Amen, if only this were a democracy, how glad we would be to stop!"

It is characteristic of those who argue this way to define the presence or absence of the democratic process by whether or not *they* get their political way, and not by the presence or absence of democratic institutional processes. The rules of the game exist to enable them to win and if they lose that's sufficient proof the game is rigged and dishonest. The sincerity with which the position is held is no evidence whatsoever of its coherence. The right to petition does not carry with it the right to be heard if that means successfully influencing those to whom it is addressed. What would they do if they received incompatible petitions from two different and hostile groups of petitioning citizens? The right of petition gives one a chance to persuade, and the persuasion must rest on the power of words, on the effective appeal to emotion, sympathy, reason, and logic. Petitions are weapons of criticism, and their failure does not justify appeal to the criticism of weapons. Some groups that have resorted both to civil and uncivil disobedience justify themselves by claiming that the authorities did not listen to their demands on the ground that their demands were not granted. This begs all the questions about the legitimacy and the cogency of the demands.

It is quite true that some local election laws do hamper minority groups in the organization of political parties; but there is always the right of appeal to the courts. Even if this fails there is a possibility of influencing other political parties. It is difficult, but so long as one is free to publish and speak it can be done. If a group is unsuccessful in moving a majority by the weapons of criticism, in a democracy it may resort to peaceful measures of obstruction, provided it is willing to accept punishment for its obstructionist behavior. But these objections are usually a preface to some form of elitism or moral snobbery which is incompatible with the very grounds given in defending the right of civil disobedience on the part of democrats in a democracy.

All of the seven considerations listed above are cautionary, not categorical. We have ruled out only two positions—blind obedience to any and all laws in a democracy, and unreflective violation of laws at the behest of individual consciences. Between these two obviously unacceptable extremes, there is a spectrum of views which shade into each other. Intelligent persons can differ on their application to specific situations. These differences will reflect different assessments of the historical mood of a culture, of the proper timing of protest and acquiescence, of the extent to which the procedures of democratic decision obtain in practice or are being violated and of what the most desirable emphasis and direction of our teaching should be in order to extend "the blessings of liberty" as we preserve "domestic tranquillity."

Without essaying the role of a prophet, here is my reading of the needs of the present. It seems to me that the Civil Rights Acts of 1964 and the Voting Acts of 1965 mark a watershed in the history of social and civil protest in the United States. Upon their enforcement a great many things we hold dear depend, especially those causes in behalf of which in the last decade so many movements of social protest were launched. We must recall that it was the emasculation of the 15th Amendment in the South which kept the Southern Negro in a state of virtual peonage. The prospect of enforcement of the new civil rights legislation is a function of many factors—most notably the law-abiding behavior of the hitherto recalcitrant elements in the southern white communities. Their *uncivil*, violent disobedience has proved unavailing. We need not fear this so much as that they will adopt the strategies and techniques of the civil disobedience itself in their opposition to long-delayed and decent legislation to make the ideals of American democracy a greater reality.

On the other hand, I think the movement of civil disobedience, as distinct from legal protest, in regions of the country in which Negroes have made slow but substantial advances are not likely to make new gains commensurate with the risks. Those risks are that what is begun as civil disobedience will be perverted by extremists into uncivil disobedience, and alienate large numbers who have firmly supported the cause of freedom.

One of the unintended consequences of the two world wars is that in many ways they strengthened the position of the Negroes and all other minorities in American political life. We do not need another, a third world war, to continue the process of liberation. We can do it in peace—without war and without civil war. The Civil Rights and Voting Acts of 1964 and 1965 are far in advance of the actual situation in the country where discrimination is so rife. Our present task is to bring home and reinforce popular consciousness of the fact that those who violate their provisions are violating the highest law of the land, and that their actions are outside the law. Therefore, our goal must *now* be to build up and strengthen a mood of respect for the law, for civil obedience to laws, even by those who deem them unwise or who opposed them in the past. Our hope is that those who abide by the laws outlawing segregation may learn not only to tolerate them but, in time, as their fruits develop, to accept them. To have the positive law on the side of right and justice is to have a powerful weapon that makes for voluntary compliance—but only if the *reasonableness* of the *prima facie* obligation to obey the law is recognized.

To one observer at least, that reasonableness is being more and more disregarded in this country. The current mood is one of growing indifference to and disregard of even the reasonable legalities. The year's headlines from New York to California tell the story. I am not referring to the crime rate which has made frightening strides, nor to the fact that some of our metropolitan centers have become dangerous jungles. I refer to a growing mood toward law generally, something comparable to the attitude toward the Volstead Act during the Prohibition era. The mood is more diffuse today. To be lawabiding in some circles is to be "a square."

In part, the community itself has been responsible for the emergence of this mood. This is especially true in those states which have failed to abolish the *unreasonable* legalities, particularly in the fields of marriage, divorce, birth control, sex behavior, therapeutic abortion, voluntary euthanasia, and other intrusions on the right of privacy. The failure to repeal foolish laws, which makes morally upright individuals legal offenders, tends to generate skepticism and indifference toward observing the reasonable legalities.

This mood must change if the promise of recent civil rights legislation is to be realized. Respect for law today can give momentum to the liberal upswing of the political and social pendulum in American life. In a democracy we cannot make an absolute of obedience to law or to anything else except "the moral obligation to be intelligent," but more than ever we must stress that dissent and opposition—the oxygen of free society—be combined with civic obedience, and that on moral grounds it express itself as legal dissent and legal opposition.

## ADDENDUM: SOME THESES ON THE NATURE AND SOURCES OF CONSCIENCE

1. The term "conscience" is used ambiguously:
   a) sometimes it refers to a power or faculty that enables a person to determine what his *duty* is;
   b) sometimes it refers to a distinctively moral sense that discloses the presence of good or bad in human conduct;
   c) sometimes it is identified as "a still, small voice" of regret, remorse, or guilt expressing a *negative* judgment on what has been done or is about to be done;
   d) infrequently it refers to an emotion or feeling of approval that allays anxiety over the rightness or wrongness of an action already performed or contemplated.

2. The objective reference of these terms, whether considered as a power, faculty, emotion, or disposition is a psychological reality.

3. Whatever its source or origin, the most important question we can ask about conscience is its moral authority.

4. This moral *authority* cannot be derived from the psychological experience itself. Seeing is not believing; nor is moral sight *ipso facto* warranted belief.

5. The moral authority of conscience cannot be derived from any religious source without obvious question-begging: If the voice of conscience is the voice of God, how can we know we have heard the genuine voice of God rather than the tempting, deceptive voice of

Satan without antecedent knowledge of the goodness or rightness of what God commands? For example, Feuerbach versus Kierkegaard: "Men build their gods in their own image."

6. The deliverances of conscience cannot all be infallible since every person who invokes his conscience must in principle believe that the deliverance of any other consciences declaring him to be an imposter is mistaken.

7. There are other reasons for doubting the moral authority of deliverances of conscience:
   a) The consciences of past generations led to actions which in the perspective of later times seemed needlessly cruel. "Thou shalt not permit a witch to live."
   b) The consciences of present generations rarely speak up in many kinds of situations in which conduct is clearly morally wrong. For example, customs, income tax, the imposition of unnecessary suffering on sentient creatures consumed as food (vegetarianism).
   c) The multiplicity of complex moral problems—housing patterns, bussing, punishment, the rights and limits of privacy—on which conscience speaks either not at all or with an uncertain voice.

8. There is no reason to invoke any transcendental or supernaturalistic element in accounting for the existence and operation of conscience.

9. Among the natural causes that enter into the development of conscience and the expression of its edicts are:
   a) the internalization through growth of habits of the norms of behavior of society, family, school, peer groups;
   b) fear of detection of violation of accepted norms and of consequent sanctions, physical and social.

10. Most explanations of the origin of conscience explain plausibly why conscience speaks whenever an action is proposed or committed that violates an accepted social norm. They do not explain when and why conscience will manifest itself by condemning what the social norm approves—
    a) Jeremiah, Socrates—John Brown
    b) What distinguishes the prophet from the crackpot?

11. Conscience acquires authority only as the outcome of conscien-
    tiousness, or conscientious reflection.
    a) Where the edict of conscience is taken as an unalterable moral
       datum, conscientiousness is merely rationalization, i.e., the quest
       for "good reasons" (rather than valid ones) and refusal to uncover
       the "real reasons" (actually "causes") of bias.

12. No genuine moral problem, therefore, in which good conflicts with
    good and right with right can be solved by reliance on conscience
    which in its immediacy can only reflect the strength of the initial
    dispositions associated with the conflict of values.

13. This analysis of conscience does not invalidate "conscientious
    objection" when it is an attitude toward a specific law resulting from
    the use of discriminating intelligence in tracing the consequences of
    the relative alternatives of action open to the moral agent.

14. This analysis of conscience calls into question the validity of any
    deliverance that claims to be final or ultimate or infallible, or
    "absolute," for example, absolute pacifism.

15. It recognizes as the overriding obligation of moral life the obligation
    to be intelligent (Erskine's phrase) and to take into account the con-
    sequences of individual action upon the public welfare or common
    good.

[1967]

## NOTE

1. See my "Second Thoughts on Berkeley," *Teachers College Record* 67
(October 1965), reprinted as an appendix in my *Academic Freedom and Academic Anarchy* (New York: Cowles, 1969).

# 16

# ARE THERE LIMITS TO FREEDOM OF EXPRESSION?

From the East to the West coast, from the Great Lakes to the Gulf, a spirit of unlawfulness lies like a brooding presence over the land. It has seeped into the very fabric of social and political life and burst into flame in areas where minorities, moving to break out of the patterns of segregation and discrimination, meet majorities resisting the pace and method of their movement. Hatemongers, black and white, are finding susceptible audiences. All this is developing in a period in which reliance upon democratic procedures of resolving conflicts has been weakened by open contempt for law and legal institutions. The spectacle of the late Michael Quill, with the television eyes of the country upon him, ripping to pieces a court injunction and cursing the judge who issued it, is a dramatic symbol of deeply felt attitudes.

Incitement to violence, civil and uncivil disobedience, wild threats against individuals, group libels, organized chants denouncing the chief magistrates of the nation as "murderers" and "assassins" have come to be regarded in certain quarters, even on some campuses, as normal methods of political dialogue. At no time in the twentieth century has expression in America been so uninhibited, so reckless, so inflammatory.

To those who believe that the First Amendment guarantees absolute freedom of expression to all members of the community, these unlovely

Originally published in *Book Week*, November 6, 1966. Reprinted by permission of the Estate of Sidney Hook.

phenomena are merely the price of a free society. But there are obvious difficulties with this absolutist position. The Constitution also provides that no one should be deprived of the right to life, liberty, and property without due process of law. What happens when freedom of expression imperils life, threatens a defendant's liberty, leads by malicious falsehood to loss of property, good name, or reputation? Obviously if there is more than one absolute right, and they conflict, as when speech prejudices a man's right to a fair trial or violates his right to privacy, one or both must be abridged. Which right is to yield to which, and when? Granting the strategic importance of freedom of expression in a democratic society, we must still face the problem, growing more acute in recent days, under what circumstances may speech, press, and assembly reasonably be curbed?

Professor Thomas I. Emerson of the Yale University Law School addresses himself to this problem in *Towards a General Theory of the First Amendment* (New York: Random House, 1968). He criticizes with vigor the chief general principles that have been previously advanced to distinguish expression which is constitutionally privileged from expression which is not. He rejects the "bad tendency" test that would limit expression if there are reasonable grounds for believing it would lead to substantial social evil. The "clear and present danger" test of justices Holmes and Brandeis, once hailed as a libertarian doctrine, is declared too vague and ambiguous to be of any practical use. The "*ad hoc* balancing test" which seeks to strike a judicial balance between interest in freedom of expression and other individual freedoms and social interests is ruled out as untenable, as affording little or no protection to free expression.

Emerson is also somewhat critical of "the absolute test," associated with Justice Black, because some of its formulations suggest that the First Amendment gives unqualified immunity to all expression. On the whole, however, he is very sympathetic to the absolute view; his own theory essays a restatement of the absolute test that would make it less vulnerable to criticism.

Professor Emerson believes that the only adequate theory that can guide us in applying the First Amendment to the troublesome problems is one based on a strict distinction between "expression" and "action." The upshot of his discussion is "if the theory of freedom of expression means anything, therefore, it requires that social control be directed toward the subsequent action." But if the reader takes this to mean that only actions are to be legally punishable while utterances, oral or written, remain immune, he will be mistaken. For Emerson concedes that certain threats, solicitations, insults, libels, obscenities, incitements, and so forth, may justifiably be punished by civil or even criminal sanctions. How is this apparent contradiction to be reconciled? Quite simply! By a process of semantic legislation. Whenever we have good reason to hold that certain expressions or forms of speech should be legally punishable—like a false charge that a judge has taken a bribe, or a leaflet to soldiers in wartime urging them to desert, or threats to a jury to convict a defendant, or a speech inciting a crowd to a lynching bee—we put quotation marks around the term expression and then classify this "expression" as an action. In other words, whenever speech is deemed legally actionable it becomes "speech," a type of action. Conversely, whenever we have good reasons to hold that certain actions, which some citizens regard as evil, like mass picketing or joining a subversive organization, should not be subject to legal restraint, we put quotation marks around the term action and classify "action" as an expression or form of speech.

The term abridgment is the object of the same semantic ploy. An employer is properly forbidden to distribute a statement to his employees, who are being polled on whether they want a union, to the effect that he may have to go out of business if a union is voted in. This is a clear and justifiable abridgment of his speech. Not so according to Emerson. It is not an abridgment but only an "abridgment" because his expression is "an expression," and therefore to be classified as an *action*.

This procedure seems to me to be an outrage both on common usage and common sense. The "clear and present danger" test, for all its difficulties, which are not as great as Emerson contends, is intellectually more forthright in recognizing that it is the use of certain *words* and *expressions* that is being punished because of their tendency to bring about "substantive evils Congress has a right to prevent." It does not pretend with brazen indifference to the ethics of words that when a speech is being punished, it is not speech but something else. It would be less bizarre to repudiate the strict distinction between expression and action, regard all expressions or acts of speech as forms of behavior or action, and employ various moral criteria to determine the degree of freedom these speech-acts should enjoy.

What Professor Emerson is proposing may be more apparent if we apply the same technique of redefinition to "freedom of religion." This is not discussed by him although it comes first in the First Amendment and is as "absolute" as the other provisions. The "free exercise of religion" was considered by the framers as every whit as important as freedom of expression. Nonetheless a man whose religious conscience justifies the practice of plural marriages, or human bloodletting, or refusal to permit administration of lifesaving drugs to his critically ill child may find himself in jail. Since the absolutists do not object to the laws that would send him to jail, they presumably must hold that he is not exercising his religion but only "religion," and that therefore his freedom of religion is not being abridged, but merely "abridged," that he is not a sincere martyr to his faith but a criminal masking his action under "religion"—thus adding insult to injury. The simple truth overlooked by both Justice Black and Professor Emerson is that the framers were too intelligent to be absolutists about freedom of religion, expression, or any other specific freedom.

It is not necessary to resort to desperate expedients of redefinition to honor the strategic or central importance of freedom of expression in a democratic society, and yet recognize that at certain times, places, and occasions, in the interest of preserving the whole cluster of freedoms essential to a functioning democracy, some expressions may have to be curbed. I do not believe that any one criterion or test can be found that will satisfy our reflective moral sense in all situations where some limit on expression is justified.

What Emerson pejoratively calls "*ad hoc* balancing" is not itself a criterion, like the clear and present danger test, but a process of weighing and weighting the relevant considerations, involving various criteria, of which reflective judgment must take note when right conflicts with right, good with good, and right with good. He himself is aware that one resorts to some balancing of rights and interests even in distinguishing between "expression" and expression. Every genuine *problem* of conflict of rights requires some balancing. That is why his objections, as well as those of Frantz and Meiklejohn, seem to me to lack cogency and to be based on misunderstanding. Intelligent balancing does not mean we must reopen all questions in considering all issues of conflict, that nothing is ever presumptively settled, and that the rights and interests balanced against each other are always of equal weight.

The notion that whatever balancing of rights is required, where the limits of freedom of expression are in question, has already been done by the framers of the Constitution is bad history, bad logic, and bad ethics. It is bad history because not only may the ends or values of the Preamble to the Constitution obviously conflict with each other—justice does not always ensure domestic tranquility—but because the rights enumerated to achieve them may conflict, a fact that could hardly have escaped the architects of the Constitution. It is bad logic because the very language of key sections of the Constitution, including the First Amendment, is not sufficiently precise to give determinate answers to many questions. It does not tell us what the limits of free expression are, nor even, as Court opinions show, what constitutes a religious establishment or religious freedom. It is bad ethics because it implies a willingness to be bound by the presumed mandate of persons who, however worthy, could not possibly have anticipated many of the conflicts of rights which arise over freedom of communication in an electronic age. If we eschewed balancing when rights conflict we would have to resort to the complicated and cumbersome process of amendment in the face of each fresh situation.

Ultimately all the arguments against the process of balancing turn out to be variations of the view that it is dangerous and perhaps ultimately disastrous to make exceptions to general rules. Emerson declares that "once the principle of governmental restriction is accepted for any purpose, it becomes difficult to establish a stopping place." Surely, even if this were true, it would be no argument against the use of police power or taxation that are also forms of restriction. But it is truer for some purposes than for others, and the degree of difficulty varies. After all, what is our intelligence for, if not to find appropriate stopping places? We do not have to do everything whole hog.

Freedom of expression is intrinsically and instrumentally so valuable in a good society that there is a presumption in its favor when it conflicts with other rights and interests. But presumptions are always rebuttable. There is no greater paradox here than in the realization that food is of central importance for life, but that sometimes in order to preserve life it is necessary to fast. Emerson is like the man who warns us that the fast may end in starvation. Nonetheless he willingly admits that despite the dangers of governmental regulation, where individuals need protection against *private* organizations, it may be a lesser evil. But he is extremely reluctant to recognize that sometimes it may also be a lesser evil in the area of public expression. In part this flows from a mistaken underestimate of the power of words to injure and incite to mob action, particularly in the present period. In part it seems to me the result of not stressing sufficiently that whenever the right of expression is properly limited, it is in behalf of other human rights, and not out of a fetishism of "law and order" as such. Like other ritualistic liberals, Professor Emerson fails to do justice to the position of realistic liberals like Justice Frankfurter, who do not share his absolutist prepossessions. When a community is threatened with the breakdown of law and order, we are told that "the remedy lies in using other means which will restore a basic consensus rather than in abandoning the system of free expression." But this is a false disjunction, and far from exhaustive. *Until* the consensus is established, what do we do? Specifically, what do we do about speech inciting to riot and violence? Suppose a consensus cannot be easily established? In such situations intelligence requires not "the abandonment of the system of free expression"—which no one proposes—but only its reasonable and temporary limitation. Despotism is not the only alternative to anarchy. Failure to appreciate this is one of the differentia of ritualistic liberalism as over against the realistic liberalism of Holmes, Brandeis, and Frankfurter.

The invariable response to any legislative proposal or judicial decision that limits freedom of expression, even if there are good and sufficient reasons to believe that it will incite violence, is that such a limitation will have a chilling effect on legitimate expressions of opinion. Reasonable attempts to curb the public distribution of hard-core pornography in the streets, it is sometimes argued, will have a chilling effect on the distribution of unpopular political and religious tracts. These are dogmatic a priori asseverations comparable to the objection against fluoridation on the ground that once we introduce even a minimal amount of a noneliminable poison like fluorides in our drinking water, we may end up by injecting massive doses of potassium cyanide into our reservoirs. A far better case can be made in such situations for the chilling effect of our failure to limit utterances that because they incite violence, in justice Holmes's words, "may have all the effect of force," on other human rights and freedoms.

[1966]

# 17

# THE WAR AGAINST
# THE DEMOCRATIC PROCESS

We are living in a time of great fear and confusion in our country. The fear and confusion are so profound that our very language has become infected with mischievous ambiguity. The disorders rampant in our cities and schools have brought the slogan of "Law and Order" to everyone's lips. But there is no agreement about what it means.

One looks behind the words to the motives of the persons using them. This remains true even when the slogan "Just Law and Civilized Order" is counterposed to it. "Justice for whom?" ask militant students with a sneer at liberal illusions.

"The only difference between civilized and uncivilized order," I have heard it said, "is the difference between the veteran cop and the raw recruit. Both wield clubs."

The relations between law and liberty and their place in a free society are complex questions, themes for perennial dialogue or discussion. Until recently we had thought that certain elementary truths could be accepted about law and freedom and democracy as a basis for understanding and improving our society. Among these truths are the propositions that if freedom is defined as the absence of restraint on our powers of action, then no freedom can be absolute; that one freedom limits another; that law creates and protects certain freedoms only by restricting certain other freedoms; that where freedoms conflict, the best

From *American Freedom and Academic Anarchy* (New York: Cowles Book Co., 1969).

hopes of rational and peaceful resolution are through the democratic process; and that, finally, the only alternatives to the democratic process are—as Lincoln put it when the nation faced the torment of civil war—anarchism, on the one hand, and despotism, the normal reaction to prolonged anarchy, on the other.

Today these truths have been put in dispute not only by the behavior of many of our citizens but by the justifications offered for this behavior. In the past we used to believe that we could turn for intellectual guidance to our colleges and universities as relatively disinterested centers of inquiry in these matters. Unfortunately, colleges and universities have themselves become embattled storm centers of controversy, not only about the presuppositions of the democratic process but about the nature and goals of the university.

A few years ago there was a movement in educational circles that advocated that the study of communism, fascism, and other forms of totalitarianism be incorporated into the curricula of our colleges, that we teach in a scholarly and objective fashion about the fighting faiths and subversive stratagems of the enemies of a free society. Judging by the nationwide behavior of student bodies, during the last election, in refusing to give a hearing to points of view they did not share, we have failed, for the most part, to teach our students properly even about the meaning of democracy.

Instead of the colleges and universities functioning as centers of enlightenment to a bewildered and distraught population, because of what has occurred on their campuses, they have become objects of revulsion and disgust to large numbers, and have strengthened the furies of backlash and reaction. There is little room for doubt that events at Berkeley as well as Watts contributed to changing the climate of political opinion in California. The riotous happenings at Columbia and other campuses definitely cast their shadows on the elections in 1968. The defeat of school-bond issues in many areas of the country, and more particularly in California, has been attributed by informed observers to the almost daily televised spectacles of campus confrontations and disorders.

That many of our students have not been properly taught the meaning of democracy is apparent in the reasons they sometimes offer for their disillusionment with the democratic process when they have failed to convince others of the validity of what they firmly believe to be true or right.

In extenuation of conduct that breaks out of the frame of academic civility or political due process, militant student leaders have been heard to say: "You advise us to rely on democratic processes when we have legitimate demands. But what's the use of resorting to such processes when it results only in frustration? We make demands that are good for the country, we talk, we even get a hearing but our proposals on the war or draft or military spending are not adopted. We are only invited to talk some more! We have learned that rocks and riots can make people listen to reason when arguments fail. When we put our bodies on the line, we get results."

This is, indeed, a very odd conception of the democratic process. The failure to convince others may indicate that the evidence or argument is not strong enough, or that even when it is valid one must learn how to be more persuasive, to wait a little longer and work a little harder. In some respects the democratic process is like the scientific process. Its validity does not depend upon any one specific outcome but on a whole series of decisions. It can't guarantee that any particular policy we passionately regard as valid will be adopted any more than the particular findings of a scientific inquiry will be true.

A guess may sometimes turn out to be right and the conclusion of a careful investigation wrong; an old wives' remedy may, on a rare occasion, work when scientific medicine fails. But no sensible person, therefore, discards scientific method. A democrat knows that a majority may sometimes be wrong. But he believes that in an open society where the processes of freely given consent operate, conflicts of interest can be more satisfactorily resolved by majority rule than by minority rule, and that he must therefore appeal from the decision of an unenlightened majority to the decision of an enlightened majority.

The assumption made in certain students' quarters today that what *they* want or believe desirable is what the majority of the electorate wants or believes desirable is very questionable in the light of reliable polls in the past on our policy in Vietnam, the draft, defense spending, and many other issues. On these matters the thinking of students has differed from that of the general population, as the election returns show.

Let us grant, for the moment, that the students are right and the others wrong. What follows? Surely not—if they are democrats—that they have a right to disrupt society. And surely not that they have a right to make the university the scapegoat for the mistakes of the majority. For even irresponsible fanatics must grant that the university is not responsible for American involvement in Vietnam, for the draft, for failure to enact proper legislation to solve problems of race and poverty. There is something contemptible in compensating for one's political weakness by taking it out on the university—that soft underbelly of society vulnerable to any violent thrust by minuscule groups.

Even if the university faculties supported the policies students opposed (in fact, they have been the chief critics of these policies), and even if society, so to speak, could be held up to ransom by demoralizing universities, this would not justify the strategy of student extremists, were they truly committed to democratic principles. Although they occasionally invoke these democratic principles, they are confused and ambiguous about them, except for members of one or another Communist faction for whom "the dictatorship of the party" is an expression of "socialist democracy."

No matter how convinced we are as democrats that we are right, this does not give us a mandate to impose what is right on the general population. Deny this and we surrender to the logic of totalitarianism. This elementary truth has been persistently ignored, and sometimes contested, by student rebels. They seem to be unaware of the elitism behind their imperious political attitudes.

They will agree it is wrong for any group convinced that smoking causes lung cancer to march on tobacco warehouses and fire them because the democratic majority refuses to outlaw the sale of cigarettes. They will scoff at those convinced of the harmful effect of alcohol on the nervous system who, outraged by the preferences of the majority for the joys of drink over the sobrieties of abstinence, act like disciples of Carry Nation. But they seem to expect the country to come to heel if its "intellectuals," among whom they include themselves, disapprove of some political policy. They have not the slightest compunction in disrupting voluntary ROTC courses or other curricular or extracurricular activities approved by a majority of their fellow students.

The elitism of student militants makes them knights of the double standard. They will cry out that the police or the military have no place on any educational campus. But they heartily approve of the use of bayonets to guarantee the enforcement of the court order to make it possible for black students to attend Central High School in Little Rock, Arkansas, and to enable James Meredith to enroll at the University of Mississippi. It is "democratic" for a minority, no matter how small, to defy the decisions of the majority if it disapproves of them. It is "undemocratic" for a segregationist minority, no matter how large, to do the same. It has to be the right minority. And who determines that?—The right minority, of course.

There are some additional misconceptions both of the democratic process and of the educational process that have contributed to current confusions and bid fair to confound them. Indeed, there is a real danger that unless they are exposed, they may inflame disorders both in school and society. The disconcerting thing is that these misconceptions are being circulated not by demagogues and rabble rousers, appealing to the vigilante spirit, but by members of the intellectual establishment—individuals in a position of influence and power both in the academy and judiciary.

It was said of Florence Nightingale that she began her great reforms of the hospitals of her day with the maxim that whatever hospitals accomplish, they should at least not become centers for the spread of disease. Similarly, it is not too much to expect that one who professes to live by the word of reason should not encourage propaganda by the deed, that educators not apologize for or extenuate violence on the campus, and that members of the judiciary not incite even indirectly to lawlessness.

The first misconception I wish to consider is the role of violence in a democratic society.

One of the standard responses made to the condemnation of violence by those who are more fearful of excessive law enforcement than of widespread violation of law is the equation of violence with force, and the contention that since force and the threat of force are natural, even essential, to any ordered society, violence is not a phenomenon that per se should provoke moral outrage. This overlooks the difference between violence and force. As long as law exists, force is potentially present. Otherwise, there can be no law enforcement. This is a truism.

Violence, however, is the *illegal* use of force. Those who resort to it in a democratic society while continuing to regard themselves as democrats call into question the processes of freely given consent on which laws ultimately rest. A democracy provides the mechanism by which grievances may be remedied, but the manner and form of remedying grievances cannot be determined only by those who suffer from them but by the community. Otherwise, the grievances of one group may be remedied by imposing greater grievances on another group.

We sometimes hear it said that those in position of governmental authority cannot consistently condemn violence because the government itself is engaged in violence. This is the sheerest nonsense ever when it is mouthed by eminent scholars. The government uses force, to be sure, but unless that use can be shown to be illegal—and in a democracy the existence of an independent judiciary makes it possible to do so—such force may be wise or unwise but it cannot properly be called violence. Furthermore, the government cannot be counterposed to the people in a democratic society unless it can be established that it has usurped or forfeited its authority.

The use of force by a democratic government may be immoral even when legal but as long as one remains a democrat he eschews violence against a democratic government to get it to reverse its course, and works through the political process that permits nonviolent civil disobedience as well as other forms of peaceful dissent.

We are accustomed to hear the Rapp Browns and Stokely Carmichaels say that "violence is as American as cherry pie," but one gets quite a turn when he hears Dr. Harvey Wheeler of the Center for the Study of Democratic Institutions characterize rioting as "an American way of life" and speak of its "creative uses." As the coauthor of *Fail-Safe*, a book that frightened large numbers of citizens unaware of the fact that it was based on a complete misunderstanding of the simplest facts of the American defense system, he now reveals a corresponding lack of understanding of the American political system.

"Direct action," he says, "the sort that now issues in violence too often [apparently there is no objection to its often issuing in violence], must be given fuller constitutional protection."[1] I am not concerned for the moment with the absurdity of a law that would make the violation of a law legal. This is comparable to speaking of a legal right, as distinct from the moral right, of revolution. What is irresponsible to the highest degree is the view that because something is allegedly American, whether "rioting" or "cherry pie," it is therefore good or acceptable.

"Violence is as American as cherry pie," but so is a lynching bee. Does this make it good? There are many things that are American that as democrats we should deplore from our earliest history to the present. What makes an action good or bad is not whether it is American or un-American, but its consequences for justice and human welfare. Lynch law on the American frontier sometimes resulted in justice but most times it did not.

And what does this talk about "direct action," for which constitutional protection is demanded, actually mean? Dr. Wheeler is saying that if students—impatient with the refusal of the faculty and/or administration to grant their demands—seize a building and bar access to classes by other students and teachers, thus bringing the university to a halt, they should have *legal* protection for their action. Presumably violence occurs only when attempts are made to prevent lawless students from preventing other students from carrying on their legitimate educational business—acquiring an education.

According to this view, if the faculty or students invite a speaker of whom some other students disapprove and these latter bar his access to the campus or shout him down, the disrupters should have legal protection against any disciplinary measures taken against them. I shall have more to say about "direct action" in a moment, but surely such student conduct goes far beyond the expression of orderly dissent and protest. It would be too much to demand that dissent and protest be reasoned or reasonable. But is it too much to ask that it be orderly and peaceful? Otherwise, it is as obvious as anything can be that this call for the constitutional protection of "direct action" is an invitation to chaos.

Suppose one group of students resorted to "direct action" against the "direct action" of another group of students. Since the law must be equitably enforced, it could not prevent any group from preventing those who would prevent others from carrying on. What we would have is a kind of academic Hobbesian war of all against all, with the police standing idly by as those in pursuit of the good, the true, and the beautiful pursue and decimate each other.

When anyone says that in a democratic society, in which the legal process has not broken down, persons should resort to "direct action" to get their way, he is using a calculatedly ambiguous expression to conceal the fact that he is advocating the use of violence. When anyone urges "direct action" on students in a university, in which due process cannot be strictly legal but must be interpreted as the use of rational procedures, he is urging the substitution of mob rule for the rule of reason.

After all, what is "direct action" as distinct from "indirect action"? It is action that shortcuts deliberation and consultation in order to produce confrontation. Even when passive, its consequences may be harmful to person and property. Union picketing is a right under the First Amendment only when it is *peaceful*. But direct action is not necessarily peaceful any more than resistance is. That is why it is a clear evasion, and further evidence of confusion, when Mr. Wheeler equates his new constitutional right to direct action with the demand that "We must have a new constitutional right to civil disobedience."

A constitutional right, like any legal right, is a claim made by an individual or group that the state must be ready to enforce. Presumably, then, Mr. Wheeler would have the state protect Southern racists standing in the doorway of integrated school buildings to prevent, by their show of direct action, Negro children from entering. How then could the law enforce the constitutional rights of these children? The law itself would suffer a breakdown from a new disease—legal schizophrenia.

It is a striking phenomenon that more has been written about civil disobedience in the last few years than in the entire period of American history that preceded it. But the nature of civil disobedience in the political democratic process has been radically misunderstood by many, and when these misunderstandings are applied to the academic world, the results border on the grotesque.

There are two fundamental misapprehensions about civil disobedience in general that have seriously misled many. The first is the assumption that each law in a democratic community posits as a legitimate question to every citizen whether to obey that law or to disobey it. What is overlooked is the fact that, except on rare occasions, the prior allegiance of the *democrat* is to the legitimacy of the process by which the law is adopted. There is always, to be sure, a moral right to reject the whole democratic process on revolutionary or counterrevolutionary grounds, but we are speaking of civil disobedience by *democrats* in a *democracy*.

The democrat cannot make an issue of obeying or not obeying *every* law without repudiating the principle of majority rule and the democratic process to which that rule is integral. It is only on a matter of the gravest moral importance that he will be civilly disobedient, and the limits of his civil disobedience, *if he wishes to remain a democrat and operate within the democratic system,* will be drawn at that point in which the consequences of civil disobedience threaten to destroy the democratic system. That is why there is presumption that a good citizen will obey the law that passes by majority vote of his fellow citizens or their representatives, even if he happens to be on the losing side. Else why have a vote?

The implicit obligation to the law, once the decision has been freely made after open discussion, is prima facie binding  It is also clear that despite this prima facie obligation, any democrat may find *some* decision so unjust that he publicly refuses to obey it and, confident he is not destroying the democratic system, accepts the legal consequences of his refusal. But he cannot make *every* law of which he disapproves, *every* vote that that has gone against him, a matter of conscientious brooding, of potential commitment to civil disobedience or defiance.

An analogy may make this clear. In the ethical universe of discourse and behavior, we assume that the truth must be told. But only a fanatic will assume that we must tell the truth all the time; and we can all conceive of circumstances in which, despite Kant, a moral man will tell a lie. Yet, if anyone therefore inferred that as a moral man he must *always* grapple with the option to speak the truth or not to speak the truth whenever a question is put to him, he would either be the victim of doubting mania or would be disclosing the fact that he was not so much a moral man as a confidence man. There is a prima facie obligation to speak the truth, even if in order to save a human life or a woman's honor (to use an old-fashioned phrase) one must lie.

The trouble with much of the literature on civil disobedience is that in recognizing that it is *sometimes* justifiable, it does not recognize the presumptive validity (not necessarily wisdom) to a democrat of laws passed by means of the democratic process. Whoever, like Thoreau, says that as an individual he will obey society's laws when he can benefit by it, but will not accept its laws when they limit his freedom of action or offend his conscience is a freeloader. The failure to recognize this point is evidenced in the remarks of a newly minted college president who says that to a democrat, every law should be seen not as a law of presumptive validity, but *"as a question."*

Because there are some laws—for example, those restricting a man's right to worship God according to his conscience or enforcing racial segregation—that are so unjust as to justify morally our civil disobedience, the inference is drawn "then that option should be open to every citizen with every law." By the same logic, we could say: "Because we may sometimes lie with a good conscience, let us always recognize the option about any question asked us—to lie or not to lie." I submit that this attitude would destroy the possibility of ordered democratic society as it would that of a moral community.

The second misconception of civil disobedience has far more dangerous fruits. The civilly disobedient democrat violates the law and accepts punishment in order to bear witness, to reeducate the majority by provoking them to second thoughts. Having failed to persuade his fellow citizens about the wisdom or justice of some measure by using all the methods open to him through the democratic process, he cannot honestly use civil disobedience as a strategy to prevent the majority of his fellow citizens from achieving their political ends.

A citizen may refuse to pay a tax he regards as morally objectionable and go to jail to bring about the repeal of the tax. But he has no right to prevent his neighbors from paying the tax. A student may refuse to take a course required of him and suffer the consequences. But he has no right to prevent other students who wish to take it from doing so. He may even go on strike and urge other students to join him but he has no right to prevent his fellow students from attending class if they so desire.

What I particularly wish to challenge is the application of the principles of civil disobedience to the university as fundamentally confused. The university is not a political community. Its business is not government but primarily the discovery, publication, and teaching of the truth. Its authority is based *not* on numbers or the rule of the majority, but on knowledge. Although it can function in a spirit of democracy, it cannot be organized on the principle of one man, one vote—or if it takes its educational mission seriously—of equal vote for student and faculty in the affairs of the mind or even with respect to organizational and curricular continuity.

The fact that a society is politically organized as a democracy does not entail that all its other institutions be so organized—its families, its orchestras, museums, theatres, churches, and professional guilds. I think that we may expect that all the institutions in a political democracy function in a *democratic spirit*, and by that I mean that all participants of any institution should be regarded as persons, should be heard, listened to, consulted with. But as we have already argued, the responsibility for decision cannot be shared equally without equating inexperience with experience, ignorance with expertise, childishness with maturity. The assumption of a political democracy is that each citizen's vote is as good as any other's. If we make the same assumption about universities, and define a citizen of that community as anyone who functions in any capacity on the campus, we may as well close up educational shop.

All this is denied, directly or indirectly, by the newly appointed President of Bryn Mawr College, Harris Wofford Jr., who in an address in the summer of 1968 to the American Bar Association in Philadelphia maintained that our chief danger in college and country has not been civil disobedience, but "undue obedience to law."

I leave to the victims of our riot-torn cities the proper rejoinder to this observation as it concerns them. I limit myself to the university. Why does Mr. Wofford believe that our students suffer from undue obedience and that they should be encouraged to accept "the theory and practice of civil disobedience"? He admits that "speech, lawful assembly, or peaceful petition for the redress of grievances are permitted in most of our colleges and universities." He asserts that "the right of students or faculties or visitors to advocate anything on our campuses—Nazism, Communism, sexual freedom, the legalization of marijuana, black supremacy, the war in Vietnam, the victory of the Vietcong—is generally accepted by academic administrators."

Surely this takes in a lot of ground. *Why isn't this enough?* Why, if students have the right to speech, which in effect means they can talk to faculty and administration about anything, and can make a reasonable case, do they need to be encouraged to resort to direct action? Speech means the possibility of communication. Reasonable speech means the likelihood that procedures can be established in which grievances can be heard and settled. What academic rules exist comparable to the Nazi laws against Jews and Alabama laws against Negroes, which, as Mr. Wofford claims, an "increasing number of our students feel a basic need to destroy"? Certainly not at Berkeley or Columbia!

Mr. Wofford fails to cite any. But with respect to both the community and the academy, he does say, "We need to develop a different and stronger dialectic than mere words and periodic elections." What can this mean when a thorny issue arises, but a resort to direct action that truly corrupts words by making them "mere," and defeating the popular will? What can this mean except a discreet invitation to resort to violence in order to get one's way after "mere" words have proved unavailing?

Mr. Wofford wants "to encourage civil disobedience and discourage violence." But having justified civil disobedience as a method of resisting or *preventing* the occurrence of what is regarded as evil, rather than as a self-sacrificial educational act of *teaching* what is evil, he is in effect countenancing student violence, although he sincerely believes he is not.

With respect to violence, he is the epitome of confusions. On the one hand, he says that "we should prosecute and punish violence and lesser crimes." On the other, he scorns using force to counter force, as if the arrest and prosecution of violence never required force. His confusion hides an actual ambivalence about violence. He would rather that the Columbia students had not forcibly held a college dean captive and burned a professor's research papers—the trespass and denial of other students' rights do not concern him. But more important than these actions, he tells us, is the fact that through them the students were communicating what they wanted. Here, indeed, lies the central issue. *The truth is that they communicated nothing that could not be, and had not previously been, communicated by words.*

To a liberal mind, nothing that was communicated by the words and actions of the students was of greater moment than their violation of the canons of academic decency and integrity. This point should be crystal clear. No matter what grievances the small group of Columbia students had, curricular or extracurricular, strictly educational or political, there was no warrant whatsoever for the violence, physical harassment, or obstruction to which they resorted. This is the issue that transcends everything else of significance. It is amazing how many relatively well-informed persons, including some faculty members, talk around it.

It is not startling, therefore, to discover that Mr. Wofford misstates or ignores the facts. For him, the issue at the center of the student uprising at Columbia was "student participation in the government of the university." Actually this was not one of their six demands. The most intransigent of their demands, even after the administration yielded on the construction of the gymnasium, was complete and total amnesty for all their depredations and violations of law. These students, Mr. Wofford to the contrary notwithstanding, were not being civilly disobedient. Not a single law they violated affected them. They were insurrectionists who had vowed either to transform the university into an instrument of their political interests or to destroy it. Their refusal to accept voluntarily the punishment a genuine conscientious objector would have proudly insisted upon is sufficient evidence that we are not dealing with disciples of Gandhi or Martin Luther King Jr.

In this connection, another important confusion gets in the way of understanding. There are some ritualistic liberals—Mr. Wofford among them—who make a sharp distinction between human rights and property rights, and profess relative unconcern about illegal interference with property rights, especially the lawless occupation of public premises. In some context this distinction between human rights and property rights may be illuminating, particularly in legislative decisions where the public interest sometimes conflicts with large vested interests in corporate property. But in the educational context it is misleading and specious.

Is the right to learn a human right or a property right? When a handful of students seize buildings at Berkeley or Columbia and prevent the great mass of other students from learning, is a property right or a human right being violated? If the right to learn is a human right, how can it be exercised if classrooms or libraries are blocked or burned?

When a teacher's or administrator's office is being occupied and vandalized, is this not a grave violation of his human right to exercise his profession, an arrogant abridgment of his freedom of movement? When his files are rifled and his letters destroyed or published, is not this the gravest violation of the personal right of privacy? Even if we do not agree with the Supreme Court justice who held that the most basic of all human rights is the right of privacy, surely it ranks high among personal rights. Are a professor's research notes, burned by the Columbia students, even when they represent ten years labor, merely a property right?

When the Nazi Storm Troopers burned the books of Socialist and Jewish professors, were they merely destroying some property rights? Actually, in basic political terms, the exercise of most human rights, especially civil rights, depends upon the possession of some property rights in things, particularly in the means and instruments of communication. Madison made much of this. It is an essential political truth recognized by Marx but not by many "vulgar Marxists."

The first thing totalitarian regimes do in depriving their subjects of civil freedom is to deprive them of those forms of private or personal property on which such freedom depends. A man's home is his property. When the law says his home is also his castle, it recognizes the extent to which his other freedoms or human rights depend upon this property right. Have I a *human* right to freedom of the press if I am *forcibly* deprived of my *property* rights to typewriter, mimeograph machine, printing plant, paper, and ink?

Actually the justification for some student sit-ins on the ground that only property rights, not human rights, are being violated is often hypocritical. For sometimes sit-ins have been justified to protect property even at the cost of human rights.

For example, at CCNY in 1967, students, by lying down in front of bulldozers, prevented the removal of some trees that were on the only ground available for the construction of necessary dormitories for new Negro students. Here was a conflict of values—ultimately, of human rights. After the petitions and arguments have been heard on both sides, by what right does any self-constituted group set itself up as the arbiter of the common good?

The decisions in matters of educational policy cannot always be taken by simple majority vote—even on matters exclusively affecting students—because sometimes a minority and the educational needs of that minority must be protected against a majority. In such cases, the instance of final decision should be the faculty, whose primary concern is the educational health and excellence of the institution. Of course, the faculty is not infallible, but because no one is infallible, it does not mean that all are equally qualified to decide.

It is this presumption—that whenever there is a conflict of values or judgment, only those who are prepared to defy the outcome of reasoned inquiry, if they disagree with it, have right on their side—that makes the apologies for student disorders sound so overridingly arrogant.

Mr. Wofford, for example, asserts that student sit-ins and strikes last year, whatever their excesses, were justified whenever colleges and universities refused to suspend classes on a particular day to give collective testimony against the Vietnam War. By what right does he assume that all have the same point of view either about the war or about how to discuss it? By what right does he or protesting students presume to dictate to teachers, some of whom have already given effective testimony one way or another as citizens against the war, that they should *not* hold classes, if in the judgment of these teachers such instruction is necessary?

There are plenty of occasions to discuss the war, but there is rarely enough time to cover the materials in the course. The almost unconscious assumption that Mr. Wofford and others make that the *outcome* they favor is much more important than the *due process of reaching it* is another crass illustration of their fetishism of antecedently held conclusions over the process of inquiry.

By now I hope I have made abundantly clear that the democratic spirit in institutions of higher education has its locus not in any specific mechanisms of voicing ideas, opinions, judgments, requests on any relevant matter of educational concern, but in the realities of participation. I know of few educational institutions in which participation of students in the discussion of issues is not welcomed—and where it is not, it seems to me to be elementary educational wisdom, as well as discretion on the part of the faculty, to see that the situation is remedied as soon as possible. But once it is present, there is no place for the violence and lawlessness that paralyzed Columbia University in the spring of 1968 and that is currently being prepared for other universities on the visitation list of the Students for Democratic Society and similar groups. And here let it be said that they do not represent most students, and in criticizing them we are not criticizing all students and all youth.

We have noted an understandable uneasiness about the presence of violence on university campuses on the part of Messrs. Wheeler and Wofford, betrayed by their ambiguous and inconsistent remarks about direct action. We must, however, consider finally a more forthright defense of violence in the academy, recently presented by, of all people, a leading figure in the Federal Judiciary, Judge Charles Wyzanski, Jr., apropos of his discussion of the Columbia imbroglio. Judge Wyzanski begins his discussion by expressing agreement with Harold Howe, II, former U.S. Commissioner of Education, that "the colleges were to blame, not the students, for what has been going on at Ohio State, Columbia, Boston University, Paris, and Italy."[2]

This is not an auspicious beginning. For to couple such disparate events and to imply that colleges at home and abroad are equally to blame, or are blameworthy in the same way, is to overlook the fact that European students revolted against conditions of squalor and material scarcities not found anywhere except, perhaps, in small denominational colleges in the South. On no important American college campus that has spawned violence have students suffered the material deprivations and the rigid authoritarian rules of the French and Italian university systems.

Furthermore, the statement that periodically comes from government bureaucrats, trying to act as mediators between embattled administrators and *enragé* students, that universities have brought their troubles on themselves by their ineptitude, can only be explained by the simplistic belief that where no one is free of guilt, all are equally guilty. The faults of administrators are many and real, but to equate them with the physical outrages, the bombings, and beatings that have occurred on American campuses as a preface to a pious disavowal of both sides is a sentimentalism that can thrive only as a result of carefully cultivated ignorance.

Judge Wyzanski goes on to speak of the specific situation at Columbia University. He says that "one can see how justified students were in resenting a proposed gymnasium that would have a separate entrance for Harlem residents." The word "separate" here, suggesting segregated facilities, is extremely misleading. First of all, the entrances were not separate, but *different*, one for Columbia students, white *and* black, and one for Harlem residents, blacks and a few whites. This was not a Jim Crow gym.

Secondly, the entrances were different because the building, which occupied less than two acres of stone outcropping not serviceable for anything else, had to be built on two levels. No one has been able to uncover a scintilla of discrimination in the business. Thirdly, whatever the wisdom of spending money on a gymnasium rather than on books, flowers, and music, the project was approved at one time or another by forty-four Harlem organizations and officials.

Let us grant that the students were justified in feeling resentment, although no poll was taken at the time to determine whether they wanted a new gymnasium; nor was a poll of Harlem residents taken to determine whether they preferred the existence of the stone outcropping in its barren uselessness to the presence of the gymnasium with its impressive, even if limited, facilities.

The pertinent question is not whether the students were justified in feeling resentment, but whether they were justified in expressing their resentment as they did. To mention just a few things, were they justified in (1) invading and seizing five university buildings, (2) holding an assistant dean captive and threatening him with violence, (3) pillaging the personal files of the president, (4) committing acts of arson, including the destruction of the research notes of a professor they disapproved of, the fruit of years of labor, (5) carrying out widespread vandalism costing in the neighborhood of $350,000, (6) destroying records, (7) publicly denouncing the dean of Columbia College before the assembled students, and other members of the administration and faculty, with some of the choicest gutter obscenities, and (8) to cite only one action symbolic of the practices of the gutter as well as its languages, spitting in the face of University Vice President David Truman, who, as Dean of Columbia College the previous year, had received a standing ovation from both students and faculty for opening up new lines of communication between the administration and student body?

Suppose for a moment that Judge Wyzanski were to make an important legal decision that some citizens of the community resented. This is not an unusual occurrence. What would we normally say if they expressed their resentment at Judge Wyzanski's decision in a manner comparable to the behavior of the resentful students toward the Columbia administrators? Would we content ourselves with saying that these citizens were justified in feeling resentment—as well they may!— and remain silent, as Judge Wyzanski has, about the horrendous method of expressing it? Would we say, as so many have, that these outraged citizens were trying "to communicate" something by making a shambles of the courtroom and disrupting its procedure? Grant that the dignity of the academic process cannot be compared to the awful majesty of the judicial process. But in either case, is not the basic or paramount issue, not the fact of the resentment, however justified, but the violent disruption of the educational or legal process? That this is no fanciful comparison is evidenced by the increasing number of incidents in which deliberations in our courts of justice have been hampered by organized groups massed to intimidate judge and jury.

There is something much worse—something that is a grave sign of hysteria of our times. Not only does Judge Wyzanski defend "black power," which he mistakenly identifies as merely one pressure group among others, thus overlooking its racist character, he also asserts that the Columbia students are not wrong in their concept of the legitimate scope of violence.

"I ask you to reflect carefully," he says, "about the Boston Tea Party, or John Brown and the raid on Harper's Ferry, or the sit-down strikers in the plants of General Motors. Every one of them is a violent, unlawful act, plainly unlawful. In the light of history, was it plainly futile? There are occasions on which an honest man, when he looks at history, must say that through violence, regrettable as it is, justice of a social kind has worked itself out."

Let us follow Judge Wyzanski's injunction and reflect carefully—wondering, as we do, whether he himself has reflected as carefully as he should have about the meaning and implication of his words in their present historical context. Is the appropriate question to ask about violence whether or not it was futile or successful? One would have thought the important question is, Was the violence morally justified and historically necessary?

If the question is—as Judge Wyzanski seems to think—whether violence is historically effective or futile, *then any violence that results in victory for those who use it would be justified*; and the more ruthlessly effective it would be, the more justified it would be. Mere might would determine right.

Surely this should give us pause! The only pause it gives Judge Wyzanski is the doubt whether we can always know in advance that violence will be as effective and as justified as "the three instances I have cited, the Boston Tea Party, John Brown's raid, and the General Motor sit-ins, and many others I might have mentioned [which] have shown that violence worked."

This bastardized pragmatism is prepared to bestow the crown of moral legitimacy on any violence that works—independently of the cost, the bloodshed, and the agony. Every lost cause may not necessarily be a wrong cause in this view, but every winning cause is a right one. And like the Boston Tea Party, which was also illegal, the violent actions of the Columbia rebels, according to Judge Wyzanski, were successful and therefore right. Coming from a judge on the Federal Bench, this pronouncement is both morally scandalous and juridically bizarre.

That violence sometimes works, no one disputes. That sometimes through violence justice of a sort has been done is also true. But the relevant question, in the context of student outbreaks, is whether violence was *necessary* to do justice, whether it did not result in greater injustices. Could not a Southern segregationist urging forcible resistance to federal directives he deems unjust also invoke the violence of the past as justification? After all, reference to the Boston Tea Party was not uncommon in the speeches of fire-eating secessionist hotheads on the eve of the Civil War.

Let us look at the comparison between the actions of the Columbia rebellion and the Boston Tea Party more closely. It is a comparison made often by the student apologists—by Mr. Wofford, of course. It was made by the students themselves, in appealing for a federal injunction against Columbia University's feeble efforts to hold disciplinary hearings on the lawless conduct of some of its students. Why was the Boston Tea Party justified?—Because at the time democratic process was not available to the colonists, because there were no means by which the colonists' grievances could be peacefully remedied. But what was justified in the *absence* of the forms of due process is not justified once they have been introduced.

The Columbia students had not been deprived of previously existing rights, had not been denied a hearing; all the remedies available to them had not been exhausted—despite the claim to the contrary on the ground that they had failed in a few efforts to get their way. One does not need to exonerate the Columbia administration from blunder and ineptitude and even with the easy after-the-event judgment of authoritarian tendencies, to deny that it functioned like the tyrannical English Crown. The administration was guilty more of a laissez-faire decentralization than of despotic centralism, guilty more of indifference and lack of sensitivity to student concerns than of oppression and cruelty. And what it was guilty of did not begin to compare in magnitude and gravity of offense to the violence to which it was subjected.

When the Columbia students played their card about being the descendants of the Boston Tea Party patriots, they proclaimed: "Had the Americans agreed that the rule of law, however despotic, must prevail; had the Americans not focused on fundamental principles, this country might still be a colony today."

Fortunately, it was not to Judge Wyzanski that this appeal was made but to a sober-minded brother-judge of the Southern District of the U.S.

District Court, Judge Marvin Frankel, who replied—in an opinion I recommend to Justice Wyzanski's careful consideration—that arguments of
this sort that invoke the Boston Tea Party are:

> at best useless [and at worst deeply pernicious] nonsense in courts of
> law. It is surely nonsense of the most literal kind to argue that a court of
> law should substitute "the rule of law" in favor of more "fundamental
> principles" of revolutionary action designed forcibly to oust govern-
> ments, courts, and all. But this self-contradictory sort of theory—all
> decked out in forms of law with thick papers, strings of precedents, and
> the rest—is ultimately at the heart of the plaintiff's case.

But it is not only from a legalistic or constitutional point of view that
this reference to the Boston Tea Party as a justification for violence is
altogether misconceived. Its invocation from a political and commonsense point of view is pernicious and irresponsible because it, in effect,
asserts that the political systems under which the colonists lived and
under which present-day American students and minority groups live are
substantially the same, which is demonstrably false.

Thus, in their foreword to *The Politics of Protest*, a report of the
National Commission of the Causes and Prevention of Violence, which
takes more than four hundred pages to say the same thing as Rapp
Brown, that "violence is as American as cherry pie," and with the same
misleading associations, i.e., that therefore it is as unobjectionable as
cherry pie, Grier and Cobb write:

> If the Boston Tea Party is viewed historically as a legitimate method of
> producing social change, then present-day militancy, whether by blacks
> or students, can claim a similar legitimacy.[3]

And why was John Brown's lunatic raid against innocent people justified?—Because the North won the Civil War? Who knows that but for
John Brown and direct-action fanatics, there may never have been a civil
war of such magnitude and intensity and bitter consequences. It was
John Brown and those with a mind-set like his on both sides who sent
glimmering Lincoln's project or hope that the slaves could be liberated by
purchase at a price considerably less than the cost of the Civil War.

Judge Wyzanski's reference to the General Motor sit-ins warrants
somewhat more extended consideration because it has become quite
fashionable to compare present-day university sit-ins and their accompa-

nying violence with the labor sit-ins at Flint, Detroit, and elsewhere during the 1930s. The comparison is usually a preface to a justification of the student action. Occasionally the reference is made in order to reassure the public. Student violence and lawlessness, it is said, are merely evidence of the growing pains of the American educational system as it matures into the twentieth century, just as the labor sit-ins were evidence of industry's coming of age.

This comparison overlooks several crucial differences that make the comparison extremely misleading.

First, the workers who sat in at General Motors and other factories made no demands unrelated to their industry and to its framework of possibility. They did not protest the stand or the absence of a stand by General Motors, or the U.S., on foreign policy, the Spanish Civil War, investments abroad, expansion in the city, the feeding of the hungry, or other issues that fall within the provenance of the federal, state, and local governments.

Second, they did not demand the abolition or restructuring of the entire industrial system in the way that SDS and its allies demand the revolutionary transformation or, more moderately, the restructuring of the university.

Third, the only issue the workers raised was recognition of their right to collective bargaining, which was already the law of the land. Students everywhere have won the right to student organization, and much more besides. A student organization is not and cannot be a trade union, but it enjoys many comparable privileges. For example, a student activity fee is automatically collected from all students and turned over to the student organization.

Fourth, there is an objective "antagonism" between the interests of the workers and of the General Motors Corporation in that no matter how much is produced, the more one party receives in wages, the less remains for profits or dividends, and vice versa. In the academic community there is a shared interest, a cooperative rather than antagonistic interest, on the part of both the faculty and the student body in the product of the educational process—the new knowledge, insights, and vision won. The more one produces, the more there is for all to enjoy. Educational values that are shared become not less by being divided but more; they grow more significant.

Fifth, the attitude of American industry toward union recognition—until the principle of collective bargaining was made the law of the land—was, on the whole, inflexible, hostile to change. Change in the institutions of American education, on the other hand, has been the law of its life. None of these changes, especially profound curricular revolutions, was brought about by violence or the threat of violence. *Valid* educational grievances invariably have been remedied by prolonged expressions of lawful dissent without violent confrontations. Whenever a sit-in has occurred on an American campus in recent years, the right to vigorous dissent and peaceful demonstration *had already been won.*

Sixth, the demands made by the workers were made by representatives of the great majority of the workers, and for the benefit of all of them. University sit-ins are undertaken by minuscule student groups. Some of their demands, such as equal power with the faculty to determine what the curriculum should be and who is to teach it, threaten the rights of their fellow students to get the best possible education. The sit-in that prevents other students from attending classes or denies them access to laboratories or libraries deprives them of their rights to *any* college education.

Seventh, the workers did not engage in acts of destruction and kept the machinery of the plants in apple-pie order. Student rebels have often engaged in costly acts of vandalism, including arson.

One could go on detailing other relevant differences, but enough has been said to indicate how far-fetched the comparison is. As in the use of metaphors, such historical comparisons are no substitute for a sober analysis of the situation created *today* by student lawlessness, administrative compliance, and faculty passivity and fearfulness manifested in failure to lay down in advance fair guidelines of permissible student activism and *to enforce them.*

The industrial sit-ins of the thirties may be adjudged right or wrong. They have little bearing on the question of academic confrontation today. The criteria by which we assess the justice of the one or the other are incommensurable.

What is objectionable in all of these comparisons is the assumption that the position of the Columbia students is assimilable to those of the oppressed American colonists, the enslaved Negroes, and exploited workers. The notion that students are the victims of academic imperialism, that they are a subject-class ground down by the lettered minions of the capitalist establishment for purposes of profit and power, is part of the juvenile literature of vulgar Marxism distributed by the Students for a Democratic Society.

It is difficult to believe that any seasoned mind shares these absurdities. At any rate, the SDS, as distinct from its academic and juridical advocates, is faithful at least to the logic of its absurdity. It declares that its purpose is to revolutionize society, to exploit the university as recruiting grounds for the revolutionary vanguard, and, failing that, to destroy the university. What makes altogether odd Judge Wyzanski's plea in extenuation for the Columbia student rebels is their own frank proclamation through the mouth of one of the SDS leaders (Paul Rockwell): "The issue of due process is secondary to the issue of [student] power."

How far we have come in the short period of time since the colleges sensibly, if belatedly, abandoned the notion that they stood *in loco parentis* to their students. How far we have departed from the notion that the university is a community of scholars, teachers, and students not in quest for power, but in quest for the truth wherever it can be found.

Actually, those who speak of student power do not speak for *all* the students but are comparatively a mere handful, whose actions rarely command the support of the majority. But modern political history should teach us not to underestimate the capacity of a small minority, whose chief virtues are courage, organizational skill, and daring, to manipulate thousands. Its position is fortified by the shrewd appraisal of the failure of nerve on the part of administrators, faculty, and moderate students to act intelligently and vigorously at the first outbreak of lawlessness.

Discussion, dialogue, orderly protest, eloquent dissent are always appropriate within the university. They should be encouraged and protected. But once the university yields to threats of force or intimidation, it recognizes a vested right to what has been illegitimately gained; the subsequent cancellation or negation of this right can be skillfully exploited by dissenting students to win the sympathy of the uninformed and uninvolved. Not everything can be negotiated. Student demands that weaken academic freedom and the self-respect of faculties cannot be taken as points to bargain over.

A faculty that respects itself must respect its students as persons. We treat individuals as persons when we hold them responsible for their conduct, when we avoid—in the absence of empirical evidence to the contrary—the assumption that they are creatures without intention, pushed out of their passivity by external forces completely beyond their control.

There are those who dismiss the entire concept of responsibility as meaningless on the ground that all causation is ultimately reducible to the influence of objective conditions on human behavior. But I know of no one who in considering human affairs can consistently exclude reference to responsibility from his talk and thought.

At the time of Little Rock, Arkansas, if someone had blamed the riotous behavior of the white racists against Negro woman and children altogether on the objective conditions in which they were nurtured, we would dismiss such an explanation as evasive apologetics. Not all people brought up under the same conditions rioted. Sometimes conditions do reduce men to the state of things. In that case moral judgment on human behavior becomes irrelevant. But whoever would explain away the assaults against academic due process as the result not of deliberate action, but primarily of the state of the world or nation, of the Vietnam War or the draft, has barred his own way to understanding the problems we face in attempting to extend human freedom under law both in schools and in society. Whatever the conditions are, as long as we are recognizably human, we are still responsible for our actions if the conditions permit alternative courses of conduct. Sometimes we are responsible for the conditions under which we act, too, but, of course, not in the same way and not to the same degree.

One sign of responsibility is the making of an intelligent response not only to events that have occurred, but to the possibilities of what might occur. The faculties and student bodies of this country can only measure up to their responsibilities by addressing themselves now, separately and cooperatively, to the problems of achieving the best liberal education possible under the imperfect conditions of American society. That is still their main function. Those who take it seriously are committed to a proposition that is justified by a variety of independent considerations, viz., that in a democratic culture there is *no* justification for the use of physical coercion or the threat of such coercion as a method of resolving differences in a university. Force—not violence—may sometimes have to be used to enforce the right against those who violate it. It never determines the right!

There remains to consider two observations about violence or the illegal use of force in a democratic society that have been very influential in recent thinking about the subject. It is sometimes said that peaceful reforms, even in democracies, are the result of fear of violence or the accommodating reaction to actual violence. Therefore it is wrong to condemn violence, whether riots, mutinies, seizure of buildings, arson, looting, even assassinations, if we wish to progress.

According to this view, a legitimate, if not the best, way to improve the conditions of the ghetto is to burn it down periodically, or the neighborhoods it adjoins; a legitimate, if not the best, way to reform and improve the universities is to seize them and build barricades. This is an opinion widely held today among militant Black Nationalists, extremist student radicals, and an assorted group of junior faculty members, newspaper columnists, and revolutionists of the pen who extenuate and sometimes openly encourage the strategy of violence. It is a dangerous view. But dangerous or not, is it true?

As a matter of fact, it is worse than false. It is thoroughly confused. First of all, it does not distinguish between the effect of *fear* that violence will break out if evils are not properly remedied, and the effect of the *actual* violence when it *has* broken out.

Fear of violence does have an influence upon willingness to reform conditions; and up to a point, it is altogether reasonable that it should have. To survive, a democracy must rest upon some shared values. Basic in any hierarchy of such values is a shared interest in survival. Where conditions are so oppressive that those who live under them are tempted to a revolt that may encompass our common doom, self-interest reinforces the weight of ideals and human sympathy in motivating the necessary reforms. If deficiency of imagination and moral feeling make me indifferent to the plague, the poverty, the crime that flourish beyond my narrow horizon, the realization that the diseases they carry may infect my own children will sting me into proper action. Under certain circumstances, therefore, a common fear may further cooperative effort.

It is a profound mistake, however, to assume that reforms, both past and present, necessarily depend upon the fear of violence. Vast social-welfare legislation for children, women, the aged, the sick and handicapped, the unemployed, tremendous advances in penal practices and in the defense and extension of civil rights, have been adopted in the absence of any credible threats of violence. Not a single landmark decision of the Supreme Court, including its outlawing of school segregation in 1954, was made under the threat of the gun, the mob, or fire. Numerous progressive measures in controversial fields such as marriage, divorce, and sexual relations owe their enactment to the growth of enlightenment, not to violence or the threat of violence.

Although the *fear* of violence is often a persuasive factor in expediting reforms, the same cannot be said of the *threat* of violence. Least persuasive of all is the brute outbreak or fact of violence that threatens the security of life and personal property. For the consequence of such violence is the generation of hysteria and panic among the victims, particularly when children and women are in the path of the violence.

Hysteria and panic are blind. They breed unreasoning, not intelligent, fear and hate. If enough people among the majority group are swept away by these emotions, a reaction sets in that makes reforms more difficult to achieve, not less. It can stop the movement toward reform and sometimes reverse it.

Whoever then calculates on the educational value of violence on the community, who anticipates that violence will strengthen the influence of moderates and facilitate reform, is taking a considerable risk. For it may provoke a backlash hardening opposition toward further reforms and support a counterviolence that, as it escalates, moves the conflict toward civil war, the cruelest of all forms of war.

There is not much point in discussing possibilities in the abstract. Each historic situation must be assessed in its own specific context. Since the Civil War, the greatest gains in the condition of the Negroes in the United States were made not in consequence of violence or the threat of violence but by the use of administrative and legal processes. The ghetto riots that periodically swept cities during the first four decades of this century brought no substantial reforms despite great losses of life.

Truman's Presidential decree outlawing segregation in the armed forces, the influential report of his Commission on Human Rights, the series of Court decisions opening up Southern universities to Negro students and outlawing discriminatory zoning laws and practices in public carriers and places, *Brown* v. *Board of Education of Topeka*, which reversed *Plessy* v. *Ferguson*, the great victories of the civil rights movement headed by Dr. Martin Luther King Jr.—all these were accomplished without violence.

On the other hand, urban Negro riots delayed the adoption of an open-housing law for years. Although the contrary has been claimed, there is no convincing reason to believe that riots in the black ghettoes brought positive gains to the black communities that could not have been achieved in other ways, and without the cost and suffering involved.

What is true for the relationship between violence and reform with respect to the black citizens of the United States is also true for the relationship between student violence and university reform. The important differences between these phenomena result from the interesting fact that student grievances were, in the main, unrelated to the structure of the university. It is true that reforms have been adopted on some campuses where violence was feared or actually erupted. But was this student violence necessary to achieve these reforms, assuming their desirability?

After all, the causes of student violence from Berkeley to the present were not sparked by failure to meet student demands for university reform. Such demands in most instances were not even formulated. The universities rushed to reform themselves in the expectation that they would head off further violence. There is no guarantee it will succeed. Had students demanded the restructuring of the university by persistent and peaceful demonstrations, there is good reason to believe that the reasonable proposals among their demands would have been accepted.

That student violence has often been counterproductive is evident in California. Here, because of popular reaction to campus rioting, the electorate has refused to approve measures for the extension of higher education. This means that because of their violence, radical student militants are largely responsible for depriving tens of thousands of qualified young men and women of the opportunity of a higher education or, at the least, of the possibility of such education under adequate facilities.

The punitive measures proposed both in Congress and in many state legislatures to meet the frightening manifestations of student disorders are another indication of the pervasiveness of the backlash against students as well as of its intensity. This confirms what public-opinion polls so strikingly showed, for legislators do not bestir themselves on these matters to the degree they have, without feeling the touch of the whip of outrage from home.

Actually no legislation is needed to preserve order on any university campus. The faculties have all the power necessary to cope with the lawlessness and violence of students. Where necessary, they can impose penalties, for good and sufficient reasons, ranging from a warning to expulsion. Every court of the country before which the power of faculties to distribute these punishments has been challenged has upheld their right to defend the integrity of the educational process from disruption. The great difficulty has been that until now, with some notable exceptions, faculties have been reluctant to exercise these powers. Most violations of codes of student conduct, even when very grave, have gone unpunished.

Student disruption and violence have already done enormous harm to American universities. But potentially they threaten to do even greater harm by provoking anti-intellectualist tendencies among the general citizenry, curtailing educational budgets, and worst of all, giving a pretext and color of reason for government intervention and control of matters that hitherto have developed in relative autonomy of the state. Where student groups in effect declare war against school, society, and government, the great likelihood is that others besides themselves will suffer in the ensuing battles.

Student radical activists and Black Nationalist militants have their defenders who exonerate them of responsibility for the reaction to their violence. The most eloquent of those who speak in their behalf is perhaps Tom Wicker, an editor and columnist of the *New York Times*.

Mr. Wicker denies that violence produces any significant backlash. Any controversial action, he tells us, is sure to produce some opposition. But he also argues that if there is a backlash to student and black-militant violence, the fault is not theirs: it merely reveals the bigots and reactionaries for what they really are. If they really were liberal or even decent people, they wouldn't react as they do.

Wicker concludes with the charge that those who reproach black militants and student extremists for their tactics of violence are giving them a choice merely between accepting the status quo or passively suffering the backlash.

The consequences of holding this position are momentous. For if one adheres to it, it justifies disregarding the probable reaction of the public to any tactic employed in behalf of a good cause. If anyone turns against the cause because of the character of the means used to fight for it, why, in Mr. Wicker's eyes that proves he didn't really believe in the good cause in the first place; he exposes himself as a hypocrite or reactionary.

To those, however, who judge a cause, among other things, by the means and tactics employed to realize it, Mr. Wicker's *apologia* will appear as the height of political irresponsibility. For indifference to or disregard of public reaction to the tactics used not only coarsens and blunts the moral sensibilities of those who fight in a good cause, so that they are prepared to use any means at hand to get their end, it guarantees the defeat of any good cause that needs allies and sympathizers for victory.

To do justice to Mr. Wicker's position, we must quote his own words:

> It is remarkable . . . that the suggestion is being seriously put forward that blacks and students somehow are responsible morally and tactically for the reaction they have provoked—ultimately, even, for Yorty—and therefore shouldn't have done what they have done, and certainly shouldn't do it again for fear of even worse consequences.
>
> This is sophistry; it is as if to say that prejudice and bigotry and hysteria are understandable and maybe even justified when the tactics of

protesting or disadvantaged parties become questionable, when they inconvenience or frighten people. . . .

It is as if to say to black militants, who are militant mainly because nonmilitant political action has availed them so little, particularly in cities like Los Angeles and Berkeley, that direct protest will avail them even less; they can choose either the status quo or white backlash.

The black kids who sat in, years ago, at Southern lunch counters heard the same argument. . . . Martin King heard the same argument at Selma. . . .

The truth of the matter is that the people of Los Angeles are responsible for Sam Yorty's re-election.

And those who reproach "militant" tactics have still to show that, for students and blacks, any other kind of action gets them even a hearing, much less action.[4]

Before analyzing this amazing passage, I wish to express my agreement with the only observation in it that is valid: "The truth is that the people of Los Angeles are responsible for Yorty's re-election"—not the social conditions under which they live. Excellent! Would that Mr. Wicker recognized that blacks and students are responsible for *their* actions, for their rioting, and violence, not the objective conditions he always cites when he explains their actions away, sometimes minimizing, sometimes justifying them. But to return to the passage. To begin with, Mr. Wicker is wrong about the historical facts. The peaceful sit-ins at Southern lunch counters produced no backlash. On the contrary, it was Southern violence in repressing these peaceful sit-ins that produced an upsurge of support for the Negro cause throughout the nation. It made all but the most vicious racists ashamed and angry at the tactics that were used against the demonstrators.

Dr. King achieved his great triumphs precisely because his protests were nonviolent. His tactics may have alienated a few, but they won over millions more. Any leader of a reform movement who scorns to reckon the public reaction to his tactics in considering their advisability is intellectually and morally bankrupt. For he is refusing to consider the very real possibility that his efforts and those of thousands he influences may be self-defeating. Mr. Wicker misstates the facts. The arson, the bombings, and the beatings at Berkeley, San Francisco State, and other campuses were not the tactics followed by those who sat in at Southern lunch counters. Nor were they the tactics followed or advocated by Dr. King. It is worse than sophistry to assimilate one to the other.

Mr. Wicker is wrong about the elementary facts of human psychology. When people are frightened by the spectacle of violence and arson, and in consequence vote to preserve the political status quo, rather than for a change they are sincerely convinced threatens them with greater evils, they are not therewith bigots and racists. They are only behaving as human beings, as Mr. Wicker himself would behave in any situation in which *he* was truly persuaded that these were the only choices. That many of those who voted for Mr. Yorty (like those who voted against the Police Review Board in New York City a few years ago) sincerely believed that this was their choice is incontestable. Reporters on the scene confirmed it.

If this belief was mistaken, as Mr. Wicker contends, is it not incumbent upon him to ask what caused this belief? By all accounts, it was the spectacle of violence by militant students and blacks that caused it, and the demagogic exploitation of that violence. Otherwise, we could not explain the numbers who voted in the Los Angeles local campaign (or, in New York, the defeat of the Police Review Board measure in normally liberal districts). Unless one can show that violent tactics are necessary, the normally intelligent leader condemns them because he is aware of their effects in mobilizing public opinion against his cause.

That is why student and Negro leaders who are *not* committed to revolution strongly condemn violence as inimical to reform. Those opposed to reform secretly hope that the tactics of violence will alienate the great majority. If there is no such thing as a backlash or it is of little effect, how does Mr. Wicker account for the fact that *agents-provocateurs* are sometimes hired to use tactics of violence to defeat reforms? Those student and black leaders who incite to violence are acting just as *agents-provocateurs* would act if they were seeking to discredit a cause or movement. If they were to succeed, Mr. Wicker presumably would condemn the majority repelled by this violence as reactionaries whose true colors have been revealed.

Mr. Wicker is all at sea about the educational scene. He implies that the Black Nationalist and white student extremists on campuses in California and elsewhere are being doomed by liberal critics of violence to a choice between the status quo and the backlash. Actually, there is no status quo. Changes are taking place all the time. But if there were a status quo and the backlash threatened to be worse than the status quo, and these were the only alternatives, common sense would impel one to defend the status quo. Even the Communists learned—too late—that the status quo of Weimar and the backlash threat of Hitler's rule, which they equally condemned with fine disdain, represented a choice between life with hope and death.

However, it is emphatically not true that the choice in education is between the status quo and the backlash of reaction. Mr. Wicker is obviously unfamiliar with the situation at the University of California at Berkeley, at Los Angeles, at San Fernando State, at Heywood State, and especially at San Francisco State, which loomed so large in the consciousness of so many voters. Many and important educational changes have been introduced in those institutions without violence. Educational agencies, academic mechanisms, and curriculum committees exist at every one of these institutions before which students can always get a hearing. Mr. Wicker's denial of this is a measure of his ignorance.

When he says that "those who reproach 'militant' [read "violent"] tactics have still to show that, for students and blacks, any other kind of action gets them even a hearing. . . ." he convicts himself of irresponsibility unless he can cite cases in which hearings have been denied them. The simple truth is that there has not been a single demand made by students and blacks for which they did not have a hearing or could not have had one if they had requested it.

Perhaps Mr. Wicker believes that the test of whether a student has been given a hearing is whether he gets what he demands, no matter what—even the right to hire and fire teachers, to determine the content of instruction, and to destroy academic freedom. If he believes this, it is evidence of an even greater irresponsibility.

Sober Negro leaders who have given a lifetime to the cause of racial justice, like Roy Wilkins, Bayard Rustin, A. Philip Randolph, and others, are profoundly concerned about the consequences the use of certain tactics may have on the struggle. They believe, with justification, that the view that progress depends upon urban and student riots, or that tactics should be chosen with no thought to a possible backlash, is practically an invitation to take the road of violence to the solution of the racial problem. But the road to violence will not solve racial problems unless it leads to the extermination of one or both races.

The Civil War in the United States saved the Union. It did not solve the racial problem. If there is no hope in the nonviolent methods of reform then there is no hope in any other available method. But the history of the last twenty-five years shows that there is hope in such nonviolent methods of reform, and that if gains commensurate with those made in the past are continued, by the end of the present century, a rough equality and justice between races will probably have been established.

The war against democratic process (and much more needs to be said) is also a war against academic freedom. But another war has been declared that more directly threatens academic freedom. This is the war against the university or against that concept of the university that grows out of the committment to academic freedom.

[1969]

## NOTES

1. *Saturday Review,* May 11, 1968.
2. *Saturday Review,* July 20, 1968.
3. *The Politics of Protest,* edited by J. H. Skolnick (New York: Ballantine, 1969).
4. *New York Times,* June 3, 1969.

# 18

# EDUCATION AND CREATIVE INTELLIGENCE

**I**t is related of William James that he began a course of lectures by reading to his class large extracts from Henry Sidgewick's "Lecture against Lecturing." I must confess that whenever I discourse about education I feel like discoursing about the futility of discourse about education—particularly the ends of education. How multiple, encompassing, and vague are the recommended ends of education! Education for citizenship, education for maturity and health, education for world and intercultural understanding, education for self-understanding, education for freedom, or loyalty, or peace, or vocation. Despite this plethora of apparently diverse principles, educational practices at any period, barring professional schools, do not exhibit a commensurate diversity. Most schools and colleges until recently have done pretty much the same thing after a while, despite what they said. The history of education, especially American education, leads one to the generalization that educational institutions respond more to social needs and pressures than to first principles. It would be extremely hazardous to guess *what* a college is teaching or *how* a college is teaching on the basis of knowledge of its declared objectives alone. This tempts us to the conclusions that the for-

Read in part at the 27th annual meeting, Eastern Association of College Deans, Atlantic City, New Jersey, November 26, 1955, and at the biennial conference, Association of Wisconsin State College Faculties, Eau Claire, Wisconsin, April 27, 1956. Reprinted by permission of Open Court Publishing Company, a division of Carus Publishing Company, Peru, Illinois, from *Education and the Taming of Power* by Sidney Hook, copyright © 1956 by Open Court Publishing (a division of Carus Publishing).

mulations of ends and principles represent obeisances colleges make to the traditional ways of talking about education or, when news of change or innovation is in the wind, to the current jargon of reform. They are not reliable guides to what actually goes on in the classroom.

Although we are tempted to such conclusions, we should resist them, for it would follow that educational ideas and principles are of slight importance because of no immediately perceptible effect. If this were so, it would be hard to explain the fear in which so many people stand of educational ideas, or at least of some ideas. It would be hard, for example, to explain the prolonged, organized, and systematic vendetta waged against the educational philosophy of John Dewey, among the molders of American public opinion—newspapers, mass periodicals, and some of the churches.

This fear of ideas may be exaggerated. It certainly exaggerated the extent to which Dewey's ideas made headway in higher education. But it is testimony to the fact that ideas *do* count and that when they do not, they *can* count, not perhaps immediately but in time. Ideas count not because needs and interests, impulse and passion, cease to operate when we think, but because, as visions of possibilities and plans of realizing them, ideas gradually affect our own conceptions of our needs and interests. In this way, they acquire the motor power to change the world. The difficulty is to know when we have ideas and when we are merely repeating catchwords that trigger not thought but only emotion. The difficulty is to know when our words make significant assertions or proposals of a kind that are relevant and testable and when they are vacuous abstractions functioning as slogans.

At first blush it seems as if all this is provided for in contemporary education. If one reads, or listens to, discussions about the purpose of education, he will find there is not lacking in the enumerated objectives reference to the importance of "critical thinking," "the cultivation of reason," and "the use of intelligence." But there is a number of puzzling things to account for. Is there any indisputable evidence that the college-bred or educated are more thoughtful about general social and human issues—about precisely those concerns which are crucial for the survival of democratic society—than those who are not college educated? How in fact do we *know* that we are educating for thinking? There are to be sure, some technical subjects like mathematics and physics which cannot be done at all except by thinking—and hard thinking. But these are just the disciplines from which there is no automatic transfer of thinking skills and habits to the field of social policy. The pronouncements of some of our greatest scientists on social issues, especially foreign policy, are certainly no more distinguished than those of lesser mortals, and are occasionally just as irresponsible.

Sometimes it is assumed that education in any academic discipline of an intellectually rigorous character necessarily makes for enlightened, i.e., liberal and humane, attitudes in social affairs. Education for intellectual training, in this view, is *ipso facto* education for freedom. Before assenting, we would do well to reflect upon the historical fact that the great milestones in the achievement of Western freedom and the recognition of the rights of man were not primarily the result of movements born in the great universities of Europe whose vocation was scholarship. In the Wilhelmine era, the universities of the German Empire were the Mecca of scholars everywhere. Yet they were hardly notorious for being either centers of social enlightenment or democratic infection. We owe the growth of freedom far more to the dissident churches and the labor and trade union movements than to the citadels of European learning. Indeed, to the extent that students and teachers were active in social affairs, aside from movements of national liberation, they gave leadership and support more often to reactionary causes than to liberal and democratic ones. European social-democracy was not born in the university.

In the United States, especially since World War I, the situation has been different. On the whole, the colleges and universities of this country, to the degree that they have had an influence on social affairs, have spoken for the *public* interest rather than a class interest. Nonetheless, that influence has been slight, mainly because of the absence of feudal traditions and of fixed physical and social frontiers and partly because of the role of demagogues in American political life, the distrust of ideas, "anti-intellectualism," and the absence of great ideas in the academies themselves.

With the emergence of the cold war, there developed a split in the attitudes of large sections of the general population on the one hand and, on the other, of members of colleges and universities and those associated with them in kindred pursuits. This split in attitudes was provoked by a whole cluster of issues posed by the conflict between the democratic and Communist worlds. Whatever differences in attitudes existed did not flow in the slightest from any sympathy toward Communism on the part of either group. It reflected different conceptions of the degree of danger and of the relevance and adequacy of different methods of combating

Communism, particularly as the cumulative consequences of defeat and retreat made themselves manifest. Popular emphasis has been on what we may call security in its multiple forms; academic emphasis has rightfully been on freedom, especially the freedoms that are imperiled in the quest for security. Both elements are integral to the question, for, although at points they conflict, it is also true that the exercise of certain freedoms contributes to security, while the conditions of freedom must themselves be properly secured. At first glance, it is hard to understand why this was not realized. Nonetheless, it is undeniable that suspicion, distrust, and vague resentment were stirred up against colleges and universities leading to such foolishness as special loyalty oaths, while in turn a countersentiment of being distrusted, harried, and even persecuted was voiced on occasion among some of the faculties of the country.

The fact that our education has not immunized our citizens against waves of irrationalism should be a cause of great concern to us as educators. To a considerable extent, the trouble has been that our thinking about social and political matters, not only popular thinking but our own academic thinking, has become sloganized. Attitudes crystallize around expressions like "the American way of life," "national security," "freedom," "loyalty," "progressive education," and "free enterprise," which then become semantic fetishes that short-circuit genuine thinking. Genuine, fruitful thinking presupposes an awareness of problems and, where they are urgent, concrete proposals to meet them. A problem in human affairs is more than a mere difficulty or obstacle which can be forced or hurdled by effort. It involves the recognition of the presence of incompatible or conflicting value-elements in a situation. It requires analysis of means, of concrete programs that strive to do justice to both value-elements, even though both cannot be realized in an unqualified form. It involves readiness to modify the specific ends-in-view with which we approach the problem in the light of the consequences of the means used. And whatever the solution, if there is a solution, it must involve reliance upon knowledge of relevant fact and, therefore, a willingness to inquire into the facts.

How much of our discussion of the multiple problems connected with freedom and security, at home and abroad, proceeds this way? The marketplace crying for security applauds any declaration and any measure designed to achieve it, independently of whether the declarations are followed up and whether the costs of the security measures in individual hardship and injustice are actually necessary. The academy, in the name of freedom, is eloquently and justifiably indignant about the abuses, hardships, and injustices of hastily contrived measures of security and of declarations which mislead us and others. Yet, it often gives the impression that there is no problem of security at all, only a synthetically concocted excitement about it; that the cold war is the result of bungling by Western statesmen, instead of a deliberately initiated move in the Communist strategy of expansion. But serious problems, like serious wounds left unattended, fester. Korea was a problem long before the U.S. withdrew her troops from it, and it is still a problem 150,000 casualties and 24 billion dollars later. But when thinking about it might have done some good, who thought about it? If those who are professionally concerned with ideas do not think about problems—problems that are sensed by ordinary citizens only as vague difficulties—then demagogues are sure to capitalize on public ignorance and frustrations. Happily, McCarthy was defeated, but not by the academy, not by the aroused intelligence of the country, but—by overreaching himself.

If in the abstract we define thinking as an affair of problem-solving, then in the concrete a great deal of our social and political discussion cannot be regarded as thinking, for it does not even reach the level of problem-facing but takes the form of the counterposition of slogans. Let us ask ourselves frankly: To what extent are the actual problems connected with the causes, spread, strategy, and threats of international Communism, and the defense of the free world against it, seriously studied as problems in our schools? The ironical truth is that far from being too much concerned with Communism, as the detractors of our schools charge, our institutions of learning concern themselves too little with its intelligent problematic study. The American Citizenship Committee of the American Bar Association once proposed that the study of the theory and practice of Communism be required in all secondary schools of the country. The recommendation was promptly voted down. This is significant; first, because the proposal came from educational laymen to professional educators who should have been the first to have given the subject curricular emphasis; second, because of some of the grounds offered for rejecting it. It was said that some students might be infected with what they study—a fear which no one took seriously—and, what was apparently the decisive point, that some teachers might have difficulties in their communities with local cultural vigilantes bitterly opposed to Communism.

What a commentary upon the educational scene! Communism is

rightfully declared to be one of the most formidable enemies of free institutions, and yet in many quarters there is reluctance to study *how* formidable it is, *what* makes it formidable, and *how* the formidable danger can be reduced. How often have we heard Jefferson quoted to the effect that if a people expected to remain free and at the same time ignorant in the modern world, it was expecting what never was or will be? Denunciations of Communism which are uniformed, even when uttered by those who love freedom, are merely virtuous slogans and as ineffective as incantations.

Even more disturbing is to observe evidences of sloganized thinking in educational circles. This expresses itself in fantastic exaggerations of the forces of intellectual repression outside the academy, underassessment of the realities of freedom within it, and a neglect of manifold opportunities to do the necessary work of thinking without asking anybody's permission. We hear slogans like "the black shadow of fear" and "the the reign of terror" which are supposed to exist in our colleges. Robert Hutchins with his characteristic flair for exaggerated inaccuracy claims that "everywhere in the U.S. university professors, whether or not they have tenure, are silenced by the general atmosphere of repression." Mr. Hutchins apparently can only hear the sound of his own voice.

It may be that we educators do not talk as much as we should, but we have talked more than we ever have in the past. The question is: What have we to say? My point is that we do not talk enough about problems, and the way we tend to talk seems ineffectual. As a kind of compensation for this ineffectuality, there is often heard in educational quarters a new slogan—the importance of nonconformism. It requires only a moment's reflection to see that the terms "conformity" and "nonconformity" are relational and that, unless one knows the what, why, and how of conformity or nonconformity, the terms are meaningless, more accurately emotive symbols communicating at best a mood.

On the other hand, if we define conformity merely as agreement of belief, we should have to say that scientific method is the most reliable method of achieving conformity, since it is the most reliable method of reaching agreement of belief. Who ever heard of a nonconformist mathematician as distinct from a metamathematician? If our language is silly enough, short-change artists and swindlers may soon call themselves arithmetical nonconformists. A man who professes a doctrine he does not believe may be called a conformist. Is he also a conformist if he sincerely believes it? Is he still a conformist if he has a good and sufficient reason for believing it? If you call such a person a conformist, too, the term has no intelligible opposite that can be fruitfully applied in making necessary distinctions.

The life of intelligence consists not in the mouthing of slogans, no matter how traditional or liberal, but in analysis, in Socratic questioning, in uncovering presuppositions, drawing implications, defining fields of relevance, and elaborating hypotheses which are testable and which promise to lead to fruitful conclusions. Men thinking never make a slogan of "nonconformism." Those who do make a slogan of it tend to defy larger groups in which they have no roots or intimate associations in order to keep favor or status in some smaller group to whose prejudices they themselves conform with far greater "fear and trembling" of intellectual deviation than the philistines they condemn. This is particularly true of the psychology not only of left-wing political sectarians, but of ritualistic liberals. Nonconformism with the democratic outlook of the majority of the community is *de rigueur*, but is compensated for by an intense desire to conform with the canonical orthodoxy of the left-wing or ritualistic group.

Unfortunately, sloganized thinking breaks out in places where we have a right to expect some intellectual sophistication. A few years ago, the New York City Regional Meeting for the White House Conference on Education recommended, as part of its very first point, that our schools "should help develop the art of dissent." What is commendable in dissent as such? Gerald L. K. Smith and William Z. Foster were both dissenters. What we require is neither assent nor dissent but independent judgment. It is just as idiotic to make a fetish of dissent as of assent.

The task of education is not to produce conformists or nonconformists, but intelligent men and women who will see through slogans and who will take responsible positions on current problems of importance, unafraid to agree or disagree with anybody. But a position is never responsibly taken, whether of agreement or disagreement, of conformity or nonconformity, unless it is based on knowledge of the relevant evidence in the case and on reflection of the consequences of alternative policies with respect to the evidence.

No society which seeks to meet the domestic or foreign problems with which it is beset can be indifferent to the intellectual character and level of the instruction given and received in its educational institutions. This is particularly true in a democracy like ours where each vote counts for one and no more than one and where the qualification for casting it, short of feeblemindedness or insanity, is not an intelligence test but a settled domicile and a minimum age. It is all the more true in a world of ever-growing technological, social, and economic complexity, where issues are rarely clear and never simple and on which experts frequently offer divided counsel.

Any pressure or threat, therefore, no matter what its source, no matter how sacred or patriotic its inspiration, which seeks to limit the free play of inquiry or exploration of possible alternatives and solutions to problems is, in the first instance, a grave blow to democratic society. In the most literal sense, it is a subversion of the assumption on which our society professedly rests. It abridges not a personal or selfish vested right of the teacher as a member of a professional guild but the civic right of all citizens to improve their chances of leading freer and more prosperous lives. It abridges it in much the same way as external interference with freedom of medical research is not merely an invasion of the physicians' sphere of competence but a deprivation of our chances to enjoy better health. This must be stressed, because, although it is obvious that where the health of the community is at stake the community must stand behind the physician, unfortunately it is far from obvious to many that where the wisdom of community decision is involved it is no less a community matter. That is why academic freedom is everybody's business and not only the professor's business.

In the natural sciences the lesson has been learned and the right of untrammeled inquiry largely won. It was not always thus, particularly when the physical cosmos was considered a moral cosmos. Even today when certain inquiries into problems of genetics seem to bear on social issues about which some persons feel strongly, we will hear hysterical outcries demanding the suppression of inquiry. On the whole, in democratic countries there is no political party-line or officially enforced church dogma which arrests the march of creative intelligence as it mounts from the earth and sea to the skies leaving behind awesome feats of engineering as its monuments. In social affairs, however, although it has some important technical achievements to its credit, like the institutions which make the life of a great modern city possible, creative intelligence lags far behind. It has not solved the social and human problems generated by the very triumphs it has won in bending material forces to human will. It has mastered the problems of production but not of full employment and equitable distribution, won our wars but not our peace, calculated to a nicety the logistics of human energy at work but failed as yet to make the work of most of mankind a significant and rewarding experience.

It is in the field of social problems and social conflict, broadly conceived, that our most pressing tasks lie. Not only must our creative intelligence devise the institutional patterns and procedures, the schemes and programs, to meet our own troubles, but it must also cope with the challenges of ancient cultures and peoples wakened to modernity by a touch of science and made feverish by a nationalism all the more virulent for being so long delayed. And, most difficult of all, we must work out techniques of persuasion to win the consent and cooperation of those affected by what we propose. Intelligence in human affairs, without infringing on the dignity of human beings or forgetting that persons are not raw materials, must show something of the same creative imagination and inventiveness in reconciling apparently incompatible ends, the same patience and willingness to experiment, which primitive man showed in solving the problems of how to get across a river without getting wet and his modern descendants, in learning to fly without breaking their necks.

The social and political problems of our age cannot be wished or prayed out of the world. They must be met somehow. The effect of scientific technology is to create new needs everywhere. Even in India where Gandhi's spirit is venerated, his way of life is not. Renunciation goes out of fashion among the masses when there really is something to renounce. Sooner or later institutions have to accustom themselves to the pressure of new needs which are historical variables and grow with the possibilities of their fulfillment. The question is not whether social changes will take place, but in what direction and by what means. Some of the groups that seek to curb or inhibit freedom of social inquiry are motivated by a professed fear of violent change or revolution. And yet the logic or illogic of suppression is that it tends to bring about the very things it fears. For, when habit or customary use and wont fail, as they do when social crises arise, only two alternatives of social control remain. The first is the method of creative intelligence whose life consists not in a quest for total solutions but in a series of measures of piecemeal change. The second is the violent method of reaction or revolution. If the scientific and experimental attitude in social studies is impugned or discouraged, if teachers are made to feel that the power relationships of society, which are in uneasy equilibrium anyhow, are beyond criticism, then the more successful the intimidation, the less likely are the chances for orderly and peaceful change. Those responsible for the change are failing, to adapt Erskine's phrase, in the moral obligation to be politically intelligent.

This assumes that morals and politics cannot be dissociated. Today our greatest moral problems are political problems. It also assumes that we can be intelligent about morals, i.e., intelligent in our judgment of values, as well as in our judgments of fact. These are large assumptions. Let us examine them.

To some readers the argument so far, may appear as an elaborate exercise in question-begging. Am I not taking too much for granted in assuming that intelligence, whether of the creative or garden variety, can do justice to complex social affairs, especially value-conflicts? Am I not underestimating the strength of the irrational in men? Is it not, to start with, an illusion that human beings, especially in the mass, are willing to be guided by their intelligence in human affairs, even if it is available? And is it available? Does not modern science itself show that intelligence is merely an instrument of the power drives, class interests, ego, and idiomaniacal strivings of the subconscious? Have not even rational philosophers, like Bertrand Russell, proclaimed that "reason has nothing whatever to do with the choice of ends"?

These raise very large issues which can only be touched upon briefly. Let us begin with anti-intellectualism. This is a very ambiguous expression. If one is opposed to anti-intellectualism, must one be in favor of intellectualism? Intellectualism, in scientific philosophic circles, is usually prefaced with the adjective "vicious." "Vicious" intellectualism, as Peirce and James and Dewey criticize it, is a mistaken theory of the way in which intelligence operates. And they recognize that there are vicious anti-intellectualisms too. The issue among most philosophers is not whether we should use our intelligence or reason, but, rather, what is the proper analysis of intelligence or reason.

Anti-intellectualism as an issue which concerns the citizen is not a philosophical doctrine about modes of reason but a question of the causes and consequences of the attitude of distrust toward rational, scientific inquiry whenever a momentous practical or political decision is in the offing. This is not the same as a distrust of intellectuals. For very often in the past, especially in labor groups, this distrust has been of the social status of the intellectual, not of his intellectual function. The history of human culture does not show that professional intellectuals have been overly sympathetic to the needs and aspirations of the common people. In the literature of social apologetics the people have been portrayed as beasts of burden and, when aroused, beasts of prey. There is, therefore, a healthy kernel in the popular distrust of the social position of the intellectual which reflects the time when, as a priest or lawyer, clerk or tax collector, he was on the periphery of the ruling group but not a member of it. Significantly enough, such distrust was never strong against the physician whose function usually took precedence to his status. Some of that latent distrust is revived whenever it is proposed that human affairs be administered by experts or a "brain trust," with its connotation that a favored few have a monopoly of intelligence, if not of virtue.

To the extent that anti-intellectualism, by a process of transference, is directed from the past position of intellectuals as poet laureates of the *status quo* to the function of free intelligence in social or political affairs, it is largely the result of the activity of "bad" intellectuals. The demagogue is usually an intellectual manqué or frustrated, sometimes an "armed Bohemian," but always power hungry, who exploits the fears and grievances of the community—fears and grievances which the community, including those whose professional function it is to think, have failed to resolve.

But can they be resolved by intelligence? Let us look at some of the considerations urged against the possibility of its use. And by intelligence in this context I mean reliance upon the rationale or pattern of scientific inquiry to reach a warranted conclusion about fact and policy, which is emphatically not the same thing as the use of scientific techniques varying from field to field. A neurosis, which cannot be put in a test tube, can still be studied scientifically.

A common objection today calls attention to the complexity, unmanageability, and unpredictability of the world, especially of the social scene. It speaks contemptuously of "the the optimistically drawn blueprints" and "plans" which seek to box humanly uncontrollable forces into their simple geometrical designs.

This objection can be put much more eloquently. But even if everything said about the limitations of intelligence were true, the conclusions would be a *non sequitur*. Granted that man is a finite, limited creature, temptable and fallible, what follows? How limited, how finite, how fallible is he—and how can we tell in advance of effort? How often has failure been redeemed by success? And, further, problems approached in a scientific spirit are not approached with blueprints but with hypotheses. Blueprints and detailed, definite plans mark a termination of a phase of inquiry and are scientifically subject to modification in the course of investigation and construction. To impose blueprints where the conditions of their application are absent, to force conclusions on facts, to insist on a plan irrespective of its consequences is precisely the opposite of the scientific attitude.

It is one thing to recommend intellectual humility, tentativeness, and a certain resignation to failure before the stubborn intractabilities of men and events. But it is quite another thing to speak with a Jove-like dogmatism about necessary limits of inquiry, thus making a claim that is belied by the profession of cosmic piety which prefaces such speech. We cannot be certain, this criticism tells us—a lesson scientific intelligence long since learned. We are then told of at least one thing that is certain—that we will fail.

There is not a single argument or consideration directed from this standpoint against the proposal to use scientific intelligence which does not, *mutatis mutandis,* hold for the field of medicine. The suffering we relieve today is no guarantee that we shall not suffer tomorrow from other, and perhaps, worse, diseases. Nor have we a guarantee that we will ever find a cure for cancer. But who, therefore, would stop the unremitting search for one? Of course, the social world is more complex than the biological and physical world, but this is no sure criterion of what exists within or without human power. Although we cannot plan the weather, we can plan to meet the social effects of the weather. If we can plan to defend ourselves in the eventuality of war, why are we foredoomed to failure in planning to meet changes in population, employment, migration, and price levels?

Another type of argument directed against the adequacy of creative intelligence to cope with the problems of men and society comes to the fore when we ask: "Very well, what should we put in its stead?" What is the third viable alternative to the methods of force and the methods of scientific intelligence? The answer comes in a thousand variations: tradition and history. The advocacy of scientific intelligence in social affairs is regarded as a continuation of that terrorism of Reason which in the past put the ax of criticism to the trees of tradition and threatened to transform the shady woods of human culture with its self-regulating ecology into an area of sandy desolation.

What is true in this charge is the insight, always relevant, that human beings cannot escape history when confronted by their problems. Indeed, in no area does intelligence start from scratch and, least of all, in social affairs. But history and tradition are taken as data when we are confronted by problems, not as solutions. Wise decisions take note of them not as the direct source of principles or ends, but as conditions which affect methods and means of carrying them out. The traditions and history of the South did not lead to the decision against segregation. If they spoke, they spoke for segregation. But its traditions and history are certainly relevant to the wise implementation of the decision. The very existence of acute social problems testifies to the fact that history and tradition are no longer sufficient to give the contentment and ordered satisfactions men require for their lives.

Those who invoke history as sacred usually do so to resist change. But since there never is one tradition—the American way of life, like the Greek way of life, is woven of many conflicting strands of thought and practice—and since history itself is a pattern of complex plural changes, anybody can read out of them ancestral blessings for any current venture. All history, including our own, is a record of revolution and civil war, as well as of evolution and peaceful cooperation. Logically, therefore, history cannot determine what we select from it as our guide. In addition, it should be apparent that some of the most difficult problems we face today arise from the conflict between cultures with different traditions and histories. We can recommend to each decent respect for the opinions and beliefs of the other. But we still must come to grips with the facts of objective conflict. To leave it to history alone is to leave it to war. There is no substitute for history but it is never sufficient.

There is also the view that any conception of creative intelligence which leaves God or the Creative Source of all intelligence out of our reckoning cannot provide a firm basis for social reconstruction and political wisdom. Any human plans not sanctioned by reference to the Divine Plan, it is said, invite disaster. It is unquestionable that there have been great religious revivals in our country, whose bearings on American education and culture have been marked. But what problems did they help solve? True, some years ago, Congress established for the use of its members a new prayer room. Who will contend that it had any effect on legislation? I shall not discuss here the substantive assertions according to which the foundations of a good society rest upon religious principles. It is a very complex problem. My only question in this connection is the relevance of theological belief to creative social intelligence. It seems to me demonstrable that the "truths" of theology are compatible with any social system. God can never be left out of account, because by definition He is everywhere. The pertinent observation here is that from the same religious premises diverse recommendations have been drawn in domestic as well as foreign policy. For example, one group is inspired by its religious affirmations to call for a moral crusade against Communist aggression. Another group, on the basis of the same religious affirmation, urges a counsel of accommodation, caution, and unilateral disarmament, emphasizing almost as much the shortcomings and imperfections of the victims of Communist aggression as the crime of the aggressor. Now moral crusades, as well as policies of appeasement (which do not, of course, exhaust the alternatives), have been justified on other and purely secular grounds. Therefore, irrespective of the truth or falsity of religious or theological assumptions, they are neither necessary nor sufficient conditions for the solution of any social or political problem whatsoever.

This brings us to the view that the processes of creative intelligence can operate only where ends are antecedently given. The role of intelligence, we are told, is merely to fashion means to achieve ends about which we cannot be wise. This flies in the face of a long philosophical tradition, from Socrates to John Dewey, which has taught that virtue consists precisely in being intelligent or wise about one's ends. Now, if no one can be reasonable about ends, if intelligence is mere cunning in the use of means, virtue as well as wisdom is a superfluous word. On this position, ends are wishes or preferences or commands. As expressions of desire they are all on the same moral level. They are neither desirable nor undesirable, because, presumably, one can be intelligent about how to kill and about how to avoid getting killed. But the decision whether to kill or not to kill is outside the province of intelligence.

If this theory were valid, the prospects both for education and democracy would be grim indeed. The whole position is based on a faulty psychology and a failure to note that, far from our ends (whether conceived as wishes, preferences, or desires) being fixed, our moral problem actually arises when ends conflict. Most people in difficulty do not know what their ends are. We commit ourselves to our ends often blindly or on the basis of authority, but sometimes on the basis of verifiable fact, more particularly on the basis of what it costs us to realize them. The more we are trained to assess evidence in any field in which we make a choice, the stronger become our habits of evaluation and the more often do we modify the ends chosen or substitute other ends for them.

Sometimes, those who deny that intelligence can modify ends stress the extent to which human beings are swayed in their choice of ends by sophisms, propaganda, and brass bands. This is only too true, but the significant admission here is that ends can be and are changed. If they are modifiable by bad and irrelevant argument, there is nothing that prevents them from being modifiable by good or relevant argument, providing the capacity for intelligent inquiry exists and provided there is a disposition to use that capacity. And it is precisely here that the educational agencies of a democracy have an enormous responsibility. They must teach not merely the facts, but how to test them, how to relate them to problems, and how they bear upon relevant alternatives. They must also stir imagination and sensibility in envisaging the effects of proposed modes of conduct on the human situation. In other words, they must develop the habits of intelligent choice and decision in personal and social affairs, in the relation of person to person and persons to groups. Passion and emotion, as such, are not the enemies of intelligence. But prejudice is. And prejudice is passion or emotion expressed or formed outside the context of inquiry. Hume and his modern followers to the contrary notwithstanding, reason or intelligence is not necessarily the slave of the passions, even though the passions are always present. For intelligence can govern, modify, frustrate, and find substitute equivalents for passion, and this role, when it is exercised, is more like that of master than slave.

I do not pretend to have established my position here but only the intellectually grounded right to hold the view that we can and do intelligently reflect on ends or goals. For the healthy functioning of a democracy depends upon the emergence of an informed public opinion, one capable of appraising conflicting policies and choosing wisely among them, i.e., being intelligent about ends although the means of execution may be entrusted to experts. If it were true that intelligence is incompetent or has no jurisdiction here, there is no way of distinguishing between the demagogue and the responsible leader. Every difference could become a provocation to a struggle, every struggle an incipient civil war. That social conflicts and class struggles are sometimes resolved by honest inquiry into their causes and consequences, and not by chicanery or physical force, suggests that we are dealing with a question involving not the *possibility* of using creative intelligence in human affairs, but with the question of its diffusion and degree.

This often gives rise to a shift of position. Granted, it is said, that ends are modifiable by intelligence. However, the capacity to use intelligence for that purpose is limited by nature. As society grows in complexity, the availability of intelligences able to settle difficult questions becomes less and less, leaving only an elite in a position truly to know what is for the best interests of society. But the assumption of democracy is that the majority of the electorate is sufficiently intelligent to determine what its best interests are and what are the best policies of furthering them. This is a fiction, so the allegation goes. Where the masses have power without knowledge, and without the intelligence requisite to acquiring and applying knowledge, they are a potential mob. Characteristically, emphasis is placed not on democratic process and participation, but on a type of constitutionality which keeps in check the unintelligent demands and desires of the masses, protecting them as much as the elite from the consequences of their own ignorance. The fear of the tyranny of the majority, about which we are hearing more and more, follows from the distrust of the intellectual capacities of the masses and the counterposition of the mob to the elite.

This tendency to think of the majority in a democracy as if it were a constant threat to the minority runs through the entire history of our country. In the main, this concern in the past with what a majority could do revolved around the fear for the safety of the institution of property. It was assumed that men's intelligence would be roughly measured by the amount of property they possessed, so that if those without property ever acquired the right of suffrage, they would immediately expropriate the propertied minority. This dread eventuality never occurred. The small property-holder used his suffrage in an attempt to prevent the large property-holder—Big Business—from expropriating him. But the fear of the majority remained. It often took the form of a desire to respect the civil rights of minorities. As a matter of fact, the legitimate rights of minorities have been more crassly abridged by other minorities than by majorities. But if it were true that the majority of men, in affairs of their common concern, were inherently and irremediably devoid of sufficient powers of intelligence to determine their interests and choose wisely from among ends, the basic assumption of democratic government would be rendered untenable. For that basic assumption, without denying differences in intellectual power among men, is committed to a belief in their educability. This was the source of the American faith in universal education, in the education of the masses at a time when, elsewhere in the world, education was a leisure-class privilege. No one put this faith more clearly than Thomas Jefferson, who wrote: "I know of no safe depository of the ultimate powers of the society but the people themselves, and if we think them not enlightened enough to exercise their control with a wholesome discretion, the remedy is not to take it from them, but to inform their discretion by education."

This does not mean that majorities are always right. Neither are minorities. It means, as Justice Frankfurter once put it, that the appeal from unenlightened majorities in a democracy must ultimately be made to enlightened majorities. It means that our reliance must ultimately rest not on vetoes or courts or any other mechanism which can be used just as well as an instrument of oppression as of defense of freedom, but on the liberal temper and rational spirit. This temper and spirit cannot be forged overnight to meet an emergency. It must develop in the course of the entire educational career of the student.

The essential proposition of the democratic faith is that men are sufficiently reasonable to discover, in the light of the evidence and the give-and-take of free discussion, a better way of solving their common problems than they can either through anarchy, on the one hand, or despotism, on the other. This proposition asserts a matter of fact. Is it true? It cannot be established as true by faith, but only by the same generic method of reasonable inquiry present wherever we seek to discover in any field which of two conflicting hypotheses is truer or more adequate. The evidence is not all in. Until the character of our education changes so that greater emphasis is placed upon the habits of reasonableness and creative intelligence, we may not be able to tell. Some evidence we have from our past history, but it is a mixed bag. Some evidence we have from social psychology, which suggests that, despite variations in native intelligence, in some fields consultation, discussion, mutual criticism, and committee thinking give better results than the pooled conclusions of individuals working independently of one another.

Not irrelevant to the argument is the evidence provided by the history of governments based upon elites, whether despotic or totalitarian. It may confirm Winston Churchill's observation that democracy is the worst possible form of government except all the others which have been tried.

Despite all the favorable evidence, our belief in democracy, which at bottom is a belief in the educability and reasonableness of man, involves a risk that in the future our creative intelligence may not rise to new occasions rapidly and effectively enough. We can fulfill our own responsibilities—by avoiding slogans, focusing on problems, keeping open the channels of free communication, putting our thoughts in order, and courageously defending them.

[1956]

# 19

# A CRITIQUE
# OF CONSERVATISM

**O**ne of the recurrent phenomena of social life is a periodic swing
in thought and attitudes between polar positions. In the arts the
movement is from order to revolt, from tradition to experiment, and back
again. In education the movement is from a curriculum of the tried and
true fundamentals to varied and individually oriented offerings, from the
discipline of method to the permissiveness of self-expression. In politics
and economics today we are experiencing, at least in ideologicial
emphasis, a reversion from the so-called welfare state to the liberal state
of a century ago, from government conceived as an instrument of social
progress and justice to government conceived merely as a watchman
upholding public order.

The significance and infectious influence of Proposition 13 is currently
being widely interpreted as a repudiation of the philosophy of the welfare
state, of the role and rule of Big Government, bureaucratic intervention into
the economy, overregulation, and overcentralization. And oddly enough,
almost everyone, including former opponents, seems to have become a partisan of Proposition 13, fiercely embattled against government intervention
in the economy except, of course, where one's special economic interests
are involved. *Herbert Spencer Redivavus* could well be the rallying cry of
the ideological spokesmen of the flight from the welfare state.

From *Marxism and Beyond* (Bowman and Littlefield, © 1983) "A Critique of Conservatism," by Sidney Hook, chap. 18, pp. 208–18. Reprinted with permission of the publisher.

376   SIDNEY HOOK ON PRAGMATISM, DEMOCRACY, AND FREEDOM

The most paradoxical feature of the current attack on the welfare state is that it is being conducted under the rallying cry of "freedom." Freedom has become the shibboleth of the libertarian movement and all the prophets of the market-enterprise system. To the extent that this commitment to freedom is sincere, then even Social Democrats, who put freedom first, must meet the challenge posed by this attempt to undermine the precarious achievements of the welfare state, which from our point of view has still far to go to meet the legitimate expectations of free men and women. To us the opposite of the welfare state today is the illfare state, indifferent to the remediable ills of its citizens.

To begin with, I for one wish to stress that I hold no brief for the present plethora of controls and regulations on current production and consumption. Many of them are unnecessary. Everyone can furnish his own illustration of bureaucractic ineptitude. As one who believes in the moral right to commit suicide, I myself see no need for a host of regulations and controls, provided things are properly labelled and identified, that would protect mature persons from the consequences of their own reflective decisions. Nor am I prepared to defend the whole complex of government supports and subsidies, many of which have been adopted at the bidding of special-interest groups who profit most from them. Here, an intelligent approach requires a case-by-case analysis and decision.

But the real target of the conservative and libertarian revival is not this or that particular government program or regulation. It is rather the whole policy of government intervention itself they wish to reverse.

It is one thing to introduce regulation of social and economic behavior in the interest of safety and informed risk. It is quite another thing to presume to dictate to citizens what their lifestyle should be on the basis of an arrogant and bureaucratic decision as to what is good for them. This is typified in the failure to distinguish between the regulations that prevent the distribution of drugs like thalidomide and those that would prevent the customary use of cyclamates and saccharin when these are properly labelled. Unfortunately socialism and even social democracy have been identified too much with wholesale regulation and control of human conduct and not enough with the expansion, the enrichment, and the varieties of personal freedom. Yet historically the socialist movement developed out of a protest against the indignities of an industrial system that tied workers to fixed schedules and modes of conduct whose deadening monotony was felt to be incompatible with natural growth and the spontaneity of freely selected vocation.

Common sense would indicate that in part a cost-benefit analysis be undertaken here as in all other situations in which we have to balance good against good when we cannot have both, or bad against worse when we must choose one or the other. But the so-called libertarian ideology rejects this approach because it assumes that the only alternative to existing bad regulation is necessarily no regulation rather than a better or worse regulation.

One would have thought that the regulations that were introduced after the thalidomide disaster to insure greater safety in drug use would meet with no principled opposition. But even with respect to these regulations, it has been argued that they are unacceptable because their restrictions resulted in a severe reduction in the development and marketing of new drugs that allegedly could have saved more lives than were blasted by the monstrous deformities of thalidomide-affected births. When those who hold this view are questioned, they point to the fact that in certain other countries new lifesaving drugs were used before they were adopted in this country. But they play down the fact that in every one of these countries, regulatory controls on the marketing of dangerous drugs exist, so that even if one accepted all the factual allegations made, this would be no argument for the abandonment of regulations on drugs but only for more intelligent regulations. To the opponents of regulation, the measure and content of freedom are determined not by specific consequences but by the degree to which the economy is free from any kind of direction or control. This in effect is to make a fetish of the free market, whereas for Social Democrats the economy is the means by which a whole cluster of other human freedoms are furthered.

Let us grant that one of the major functions of government, even the major function, is to protect freedom. Let us also grant on the basis of logic and historical experience that unlimited government is evil because it countenances no checks on its power to restrict freedom. This is an undeniable truth. But no less undeniable is the truth that the unlimited absence of government would be even more oppressive than unlimited government because that would spell anarchy—the rule of a thousand despots.

Those who speak of government, the agency of organized society, as if it were an inherent foe of human freedom seem to me guilty of a fundamental error. They assume that freedom exists in a state of nature, that it is a natural good that comes with the environment, and that it is surrendered when human beings are organized under laws which necessarily limit some freedom of action. Unless one defines freedom as the right and power to do anything one pleases—which no one can consistently do who becomes a victim of the cruel or malicious action of others—this view of freedom is a myth. There is no human freedom in *rerum natura*: it is an outcome of society, of a free society. Government and the state are not artificial accretions to the human estate. Long ago Aristotle recognized that the individual as a human being, as distinct from a biological organism, could not exist outside of society, that in such a situation he would have to be something more than man (divine) or less than man (animal).

To be sure, governments can be restrictive and oppressive, and of such governments we can say that they are best when they govern least. But it is just as true to say that sometimes government can protect freedoms and not merely threaten them, that sometimes government can expand freedoms rather than restrict them. Whatever freedoms or rights we deem desirable, including the right to privacy, the right "to be left alone," governments and laws are necessary to secure them in a world where others are intent upon violating them. Our own historical experience is evidence of that. It was not the operation of the market that extended and protected the civil rights of the Negroes in the South but the government, and the central government at that. It was not the operation of the market but of the government that guaranteed the rights of the American working class to collective bargaining. Since there can be no government without law, what is true for government is analytically true for law. In a sense *every* law, no matter how wise and enlightened, restricts someone's freedom. As Bentham put it, "every law is contrary to [someone's] liberty," i.e., it is contrary to the liberty or freedom of those who would do what the law forbids them to do and who would interfere with us in the exercise and enjoyment of our rights. The government or the law can only protect our liberty by depriving others of their freedom to act as they please. That is why it is simply false to argue that there is always an inherent opposition between law and freedom, and that the more we have one, the less we have of the other. Would any sensible person argue that the fewer the traffic laws, the greater the freedom motorists would enjoy in our crowded cities and highways to get to their destinations quickly and safely? And even if it were true for motorists, it would certainly not be true for pedestrians.

So long as human beings have conflicting desires, laws are inescapable, regulations are inescapable. Legislation is or should be the process by which we determine what kind of trade-offs we wish to make in the conflict of freedoms, and which are to be given priority.

But the real gravamen of the criticisms of the conservatives against the program of the welfare state is that by its interference with a free-market economy it necessarily limits, coerces, and ultimately destroys human freedom which can flourish only on the basis of a market economy. This is the burden of William Simon's bestselling *A Time for Truth*, enthusiastically endorsed in special introductions to the volume by the high priests of the free-market economy.

I propose that we take as our postulate the desirability of human freedom—which the free-market defenders also stress—and examine the bearings of the market economy on the freedom not only of those well-endowed with the goods of the world but of those who are not, on the freedom not only of the haves but of the have-nots. Is it true that all, or most, human beings are really free even in an ideally perfect market economy? No action is free unless it is uncoerced, unless it is based upon freely given consent. If I have no food or water or the wherewithal to live for myself and my family, how free am I to exchange my services in bargaining with someone else who has more than enough to live on? What alternatives have I to match his? In such bargaining situations, the individual who has more than he needs can command anything from me, including my freedom, for what sustains life. In an ideal free market, on paper everyone starts from scratch—everyone has equal means, equal needs, equal power. But in the real world, we do not start from scratch, there are great and growing disparities of power between those who have and those who have not that often make the notion of a fair and equal exchange a myth.

Suppose a man says to me: "Your money or your life"—and I give him my money. He is caught and pleads that I gave the money to him freely, that I *had* a choice. According to him, I could have saved my money at the cost of my life. Would anyone else say that I was a free agent? To say so would sound like a macabre joke. Now suppose I am without any means in the free market, and someone offers me work for a bare pittance under humiliating conditions—and there is no other work available or work I can do—am I really a free agent in that case? The situation is such that I am essentially faced with the objective ultimatum: "Your labor or your life," actually "Your labor or your life and the lives of your dependents." The coercion of hunger or the fear of hunger can be just as persuasive, although different, as the coercion of physical violence or its threat. The chief difference is that one is long drawn out, the other sudden and more immediately painful.

The basic point is incontrovertible. In any society, whether it possesses a market economy or a socialized economy, property is power. Whoever owns property has the power to exclude others from the use or possession of what is owned. Whoever owns property in the means of life which I must operate to earn a living—whether the property is owned by the state or an individual—has the legal right to exclude me from its use. Therefore property in things, especially in the social instruments of production, means power, power over human beings. In the very interest of the human freedom that upholders of the free market advocate, we Social Democrats contend that such power must be made socially and morally responsible to those who are affected by its exercise.

This is not the place to demonstrate in detail the multiple ways in which a market economy functions to affect the lives and freedom of those who contract to work within it. Take as a paradigm case the shutdown of a large plant in a community or town in which the plant or factory is the sole or chief supplier of employment. The individual worker in such situations is almost as helpless and unfree as he is in a natural castastrophe, with the normal expectations and lifestyle of himself and his family destroyed. The decision as to where to work, the conditions under which to work, and the rewards of work seem to be made by forces beyond his control. In the long run, the apologists of the free market argue, the individual will somewhere and somehow be able to find work again. But even if true, what happens until then? Even if true, who pays for the agony and costs of waiting for the market to stabilize itself? If we are to strengthen genuine freedom of choice and even approximate the quality of opportunity which the ideal market economy presupposes, we must do something to provide those who are thrown on the slag heap of the unemployed through no fault of their own, who are willing and able to work, with some alternative possibilities of existence.

After all, as a rule those who close down their enterprises because they are unprofitable, or not as profitable as other kinds of investment, have other means of existence at their disposal. In the very interest of freedom of choice, unemployment insurance and some kind of welfare payments to the victims of hazards beyond their control seem required to redress the bargaining balance. But this and similar government interventions into the economy are precisely what the high priests of the market economy deplore.

Let us openly admit that we share with the conservatives a fear of concentrated government power, but on the same grounds we are fearful of large concentrations of private property that can also have oppressive effects. Like them we seek the dispersion of power, but unlike them we seek to avert those gross inequalities of power that unduly influence the political process in these days of multiple mass communication. Even Thomas Jefferson, in the days in which the economy was mainly agricultural and rural, deplored extremes of wealth as subversive of the democratic spirit of a self-governing nation. The only way in which these extremes can be prevented today is through intelligent and equitable tax policy, through wiser and better government, not absence of government.

There are some concentrations of economic power that can be countered only by the power of government. It was none other than John Stuart Mill who proclaimed that "Society is fully entitled to abrogate or alter any particular right of property which on sufficient consideration it judges stands in the way of the public good." This recognizes that property is a human right but not all forms of it have the same weight and justification in the light of the public good.

The concept of the public good is a complex and difficult one, hard to define, except in terms of the reflective process in which we balance good against good and right against right. But without the existence and power of government, we could not peacefully determine or enforce the public good. Even those who would limit the power of government to that of watchman of the rules of the road, or to the exercise of police power, are committed to the notion of the public good.

Although it has been denied, I am prepared to show that even on the premises of the watchman theory of government, the public good requires some concern for public welfare, the extent of which depends on public resources. One form of this theory of the state and government professes a belief not only in equality before the law but in equality of opportunity, not equality of outcome. If we take equality of opportunity as an ideal, we must grant that so long as differences in family and home environment exist, as they always will, as well as extreme genetic variations in capacity, absolute or literal equality of opportunity is unattainable. But this is true of all ideals! That absolute health and wisdom are unattainable is no reason for not attempting to become healthier and wiser. The inability to establish absolute equality of opportunity is no justification for ceasing to move toward greater equality of opportunity. If democracy as a way of life implies an equality of concern for all members of the community to develop themselves to their full capacities as human beings, then it is obligatory on the democratic community to move toward greater equality of opportunity in all areas, especially education, housing, health, and employment, required for the development of the individual's best potential. That is why the American slogan of equality of opportunity is one of the most far-reaching principles ever enunciated and expressive of the ethics of Social Democracy. It is a premise for continuous social reform. And that is why the most influential school of thought in the conservative revival is abandoning the principle of equality of opportunity, and insisting that the only kind of equality which is compatible with a truly liberal society is one in which there is simply and only equality before the law.

In this view there is no such thing as "social justice" but only conflicting claims equally justified. Equality of opportunity is "a wholly illusory ideal." Justice is procedural, the impartial application of a rule or principle to all who fall under it regardless of the consequences of the rule.

There is one obvious and fatal flaw in any conception of justice that makes it merely procedural—the impartial application of a rule. It cannot distinguish between the just and unjust rules and cannot grasp the difference in significance between the statement that "justice consists in treating all persons in the same or relevantly similar circumstances equally" and the statement "justice consists in mistreating all persons in the same or relevantly similar circumstances equally." Equality is a necessary, but not a sufficient, condition of any intelligible theory of justice. Over and above formal legal equality, the just law must concern itself with the effects of law on human weal and woe. What modern-day conservatism fails to realize is that the pursuit of justice can be distinguished from, but ultimately not separated from, the pursuit of happiness or human welfare. No one in the world is really a self-made man or woman. When we consider what we owe to the community—our language without which there could be no thought, our skills that are dependent upon the cumulative traditions forged by generations of early pioneers, our knowledge most of which we have inherited, our safety, health, and even our goods possessed not only in virtue of our own efforts but because of the activities and forbearances of others—we become conscious of a debt that cannot be discharged if we are indifferent to the fate of our fellows. Concern for the public welfare does not require self-sacrifice but the wisdom of common sense that recognizes the obligation of unpaid debts and the dictates of enlightened self-interest.

As if this were not confusion enough, there has developed, out of inability to see how differences among men can be resolved by rational moral principles, a call for a return to transcendental religion. It is alleged that all our social problems and evils are a consequence of failure to grasp the supernatural truths concerning God's existence and his supreme goodness as well as power. The failure of moral nerve in the West and the cult of irresponsibility and hedonistic abandon, with all their degrading side effects, are attributed to the loss of religious faith. We are told that a politics oriented toward man and the fulfillment of his needs on this earth can end only in the worship of Caesar.

With the profoundest respect for the great moral figure of our time who has recently articulated this point of view, Aleksandr Solzhenitsyn, we must repudiate it on many grounds. First of all, it is irrelevant to the basic issues that divide the free world from its chief totalitarian enemy. Those issues are rooted in freedom of choice. In a free and open society, freedom of religion is central to be sure, but freedom of religion means not only the right to worship God according to one's conscience, but the right not to worship, the right to believe in one, many, or no Gods.

Second, it is historically false to assert that religious faith is necessarily on the side of a free human society. The totalitarianism of the Soviet Union and of the fascist states both in the past and present has had its religious defenders.

Third, it is logically false to make any kind of religious belief the basis of human morality because men build their gods in their own moral image. What makes an action good or bad is not any divine command but the intrinsic nature of the act and its consequences for human weal and woe. It is not true that morality logically depends on religion. It is the other way around. We must first know what the good is before we seek its alleged source.

Finally, to introduce religious faith as a necessary condition of a humane society is divisive. We can rally mankind around a program of autonomous human rights. In a world of conflicting religions in which Christians are a minority, in a world of conflicting faiths even among Christians, it is wishful thinking to expect agreement on any transcendental dogmas. If we can agree and unite on the basis of acceptance of universal human rights, we do not have to agree on their religious or philosophical justifications.

As Social Democrats we yield to none in the cause of freedom— whether moral or political. And we repudiate as unfounded, indeed untrue, the conservative view that we need the unconscious help either of a pure market economy or a Supreme Being to realize that freedom in our institutions. It is true that we cannot properly plan for an entire society. Nor can we rebuild any aspects of it without regard for human history and the limitations of human nature and power. It is true that human reason is neither all powerful nor infallible. But these truths are no grounds to forego the use of intelligence and the self-corrective methods of experience in trying to cope with the problems of our economy—the chief of which are to provide full employment at an adequate wage level, economic growth, and minimal inflation.

There are redefinitions of conservatism that go beyond the libertarian ideology of the free market and seek to enstate the varied traditions of Savigny, Hegel, Burke, and even the Church fathers and philosophers. We are confronted by a curious melange of insight, ambiguity, and prophetic utterance which despite its emphasis on history neglects the liberating effect in its time of the ideals of free enterprise on the encrusted privilege, cruel prejudice, hereditary squalor, and periodic purges of the underdogs of the past. They mock with justification the invisible hand of the market but substitute for it the Cunning of Reason, the compensatory rhythm of history, or the Hand of Providence and other obscurantist notions.

Burke's maxim, "Change is the means of our preservation," can be accepted even by antagonists in a death struggle—it all depends upon the nature, direction, and degree of change. The traditions of the past are multiple not unitary, authorities are usually conflicting, interests are not always common or shared. All too often conservatism is a way of doing nothing disguised by the consoling rationalization that whatever predicaments society faces are integral to the human condition. The paradox of some conservative traditions that fear reforms as a prelude, rather than as an alternative, to revolution is that the historical figures they venerate, whether it be the Richelieus and Talleyrands, the Disraelis and Metternichs, the Frederick the Seconds or Bismarcks, were movers and shakers of events—many of them of unhappy consequence—rather than servitors of the status quo.

The contrast between "conservatism" and "liberalism" today is not very instructive because these terms have been labels for varied and ambiguous positions. It is more illuminating to discuss *issues*, particularly when according to some conservatives ideas of any generality are considered abstractions applied mechanically to any situation regardless of its specificity and history. When a problem arises our quest should be not for *the* liberal or *the* conservative solution, but for one we consider the most intelligent under the circumstances evaluated in the light of the consequences of alternative courses of action on the preservation of a free society.

In furthering the ideals and institutions of a free society, choices must sometimes be made that require genuine sacrifices by the citizens of the community. For example, sufficient means may not be available to provide adequately both for the necessary defense and the public welfare. In such cases measures of economy may have to be adopted that result in genuine hardship. The regulating principle in such situations should be an approximate equality of sacrifice for all groups. No formula can be worked out in advance, and there will always be dissatisfaction with the results. But so long as these differences are submitted to the arbitrament of the democratic process there is hope that the considered judgment of the community will be accepted, that the unifying allegiance to the process will override other residual differences. These in turn become the subject for further discussion and possible remedial action.

The differences between conservatives and liberals, when the terms are reasonably construed, are family differences among adherents of a free society, defined as one whose institutions ultimately rest on the consent of those affected by their operations. When the security of a free society is threatened by aggressive totalitarianism, these differences must be temporarily subordinated to the common interest in its survival. There is always the danger that in the ever-present and sometimes heated struggles between conservatives and liberals, each group may come to fear the other more than their common enemy. If and when that happens, the darkness of what Marx called "Asiatic despotism," in modern dress to be sure, will descend upon our world.

[1983]

# V

## IN DEFENSE OF
## A FREE SOCIETY

# 20

# EDUCATION IN DEFENSE OF A FREE SOCIETY

A s we approach the bicentenary of the American Constitution, it seems to me fitting and fruitful to explore two related themes in the intellectual legacy of Thomas Jefferson, the first philosopher-statesman of the fledgling American republic to call himself a democrat. These themes are, first, his conception of a free self-governing society; and second, his faith in the processes of education to guide, strengthen, and defend this free self-governing society from the dangers—internal and external—that might threaten its survival. Since Jefferson's own time, discussion of the relation between democracy and education has not been absent from political discourse, but as a rule, it has been subordinated to narrow curricular issues. Periodically, however, the question becomes focal whenever we seek, as we are doing today, to rethink, revise, and reform the educational establishment of the nation.

Jefferson was not a systematic thinker and his rhetoric sometimes carried him beyond the bounds of good sense. A revolution every twenty years or so, which he advocated to nourish the tree of liberty, would have destroyed the American republic long before the Civil War came near to doing so. Nor were all elements of his thought consistent. Jefferson once wrote that man was "the only animal which devours its own kind." Yet in the very passage in which man is so characterized, he declared that "were it left to me to decide whether we should have a government

Reprinted from *Commentary*, July 1984, by permission; all rights reserved.

without newspapers or newspapers without government, I should not hesitate for a moment to prefer the latter." The case for a free press does not rest on such an absurd position, which overlooks the fact that in a state of anarchy, one without government, there would be no press at all. It would be destroyed by mob rule when it exercised its critical functions, as indeed happened during some stormy years of American history in various regions of the country. Of course, government is not a sufficient condition of a free press, but it is a necessary condition not only of press freedom but of any freedom. For how can any freedom be exercised unless those who would violate it are not free to do so?

Rhetorical excesses and logical inconsistencies apart, the most profound feature of Jefferson's political philosophy, and what all major political groups in American life today regard as possessing a perennially valid significance, is its emphasis on self-government. Self-government in Jefferson's conception has three central figures. It is based on freely given or uncoerced consent. Secondly, freely given consent entails the guaranteed right to *dissent*, to wit, the freedoms of speech, press, association, and assembly, and all other freedoms legitimately derived from them. It is this feature that distinguishes the Jeffersonian, or modern, conception of self-government from the ancient and transient democratic orders of the past which recognized no limits on government power, and treated opponents within the democratic system as enemies. Finally, given the recognition of the right to dissent, a *sine qua non* of a self-governing community is the principle of majority rule. In the absence of a consensus, rarely to be expected in the inescapable conflicts of human interests and opinions, this rule is the only way to reach orderly decision and effect a peaceful succession of government. Jefferson stressed this, as did many years later the uncompromising individualist, William James. "The first principle of republicanism," writes Jefferson, "is that the *lex majoris partis* is the fundamental law of every society of individuals of equal rights. To consider the will of society enunciated by a single vote, as sacred as if unanimous, is the first of all lessons in importance. This law, once disregarded, no other remains but the use of force."

Jefferson was acutely aware, as are we all, that majorities may go astray, be injudicious, and even be morally tyrannical within the letter of the law. For this he had only one remedy: not the rule of presumably enlightened minorities, but the education of experience. His not unreasonable assumption is that, given access to knowledge, most adult human beings are better judges of their own interests than are others.

However, to be able to learn effectively from their present experience, to make it available for their future experience, citizens should have access to education of the narrower kind—to schooling that develops the intellectual skills and imparts the relevant knowledge necessary to sustain a free society. The people themselves, Jefferson continually observes, are "the only safe depositories" of nonoppressive rightful government.

One may ask, of course, whether such government is not only safe, but whether it is sound, not only whether it is right, but whether it is good. Jefferson's reply indicates where he puts his faith: "To render them [the people] safe, their minds must be improved to a certain degree. This is indeed not all that is necessary though it be essentially necessary. An amendment of our Constitution must here come in aid of the public education. The influence on government must be shared by all the people."

How far we have come from the Jeffersonian faith that the people or their representatives are the only safe depositories of a free society is evidenced by current discussion of a constitutional convention. I am not a partisan of any particular measure advocated for the agenda of such a convention and I disapprove of most. But I am appalled at the reasons offered by some who oppose its convocation and who cry out in alarm that it will run amok and even abolish the Bill of Rights. No more flagrant contradiction of the Jeffersonian faith is imaginable than such a sentiment. It confidently predicts that measures threatening the foundations of a free society will not only be adopted by a majority of the delegates but also by three-quarters of our fifty states, and by both freely elected legislative assemblies in those states. If such a thing were to come to pass, it would certainly establish that a majority of citizens are either too obtuse or too vicious to be entrusted with selfgovernment. And if this were indeed true, as some philosophers from Plato to Santayana have asserted, why should anyone be in favor of a politically free society? The current state of civic education and behavior is indeed deplorable. But the situation is not so far gone as to make the case for a free society a lost cause.

Far from fearing a constitutional convention, I believe its convocation, timed for our bicentenary, could become the occasion for a great historic debate. Reviewing and interpreting the experience of two centuries, it might strike a more adequate balance among the branches of our government and clarify some central ambiguities in present constitutional provisions that sometimes generate dangerous deadlocks.

Jefferson, as we know, was in advance of his time. He provided the rationale for the systems of public education that developed in the

United States after his day, especially for instruction going beyond the fundamentals of literacy—reading, writing, and the arts of calculation. He even ventured on the outlines of a curriculum of studies, mainly based on science and history, to strengthen faith in a free society and safeguard it from the corruptions of human ambition and power.

Now suppose that, in the spirit of Jefferson, we wanted to devise an educational system that would indeed strengthen allegiance to our self-governing democratic society: how would we do this today? One possible way—consistent with Jefferson's own prescriptions—would be to modify our educational system so that its central emphasis became the detailed study of the sciences. But is there really any convincing reason to believe that this would result in an increase of support for a free, self-governing society? After all, the subject matter and techniques of the sciences can be mastered in any kind of society. Even though it is true that the greatest burgeoning and bursts of creative discovery in science have occurred during the last two centuries in modern democratic countries, it does not tax our imagination to conceive a world in which, once political freedom has been lost, the sciences become not only the organon of continuous inquiry into nature but also the instrument of enforcing a cruel and ruthless despotism over society. The domination man exercises over nature has often been used to fasten bonds of domination over other men.

To be sure, as John Dewey often pointed out, there is much in the process of scientific inquiry—its openness, sense of evidence, tentativeness, and cooperative intelligence—that when carried over into the discussion and practice of human affairs vitalizes the free society. But Dewey also never ceased to remind us that, desirable as it is to carry over scientific methods in the pursuit and testing of human ends, science and politics differ in several crucial respects. For one thing, not everyone is qualified to be a scientist or has a right to a scientific judgment, while all citizens of a free society are deemed qualified to participate in determining judgments of political policy. Deny this and one is committed to the view of government by experts, which is incompatible with the premises of a self-governing society. For those premises imply that on crucial questions of policy one does not have to be an expert to judge the work of experts or choose among their oft-conflicting proposals.

Further, scientists are united in one overriding interest—the interest in the pursuit of truth; human affairs, on the other hand, are a field of conflicting interests. The agreements scientists reach are ultimately determined by the compulsions of fact; in human affairs, even when there is agreement on facts, the resolution of differences may require tolerance and compromise of interests. In a free society, it may be necessary to forgo demands for the full measure of justified claims in order to preserve the *process* by which future claims may be peacefully negotiated. Science develops by the elimination of error. But the life of a free society consists not so much in the elimination of interests as in their reconciliation. In science, a wrong judgment loses all value as soon as it is shown to be wrong; in a democracy, even the interest which is outvoted has value. It must be respected in defeat if only because it has submitted itself to the arbitrament of argument and persuasion.

In short, a curriculum concentrating entirely on science could not be expected to achieve the aim Jefferson sought. Not that Jefferson himself was a simple-minded believer in the effect of science and science education on the moral estate of humanity. He called freedom "the first-born daughter of science"; yet he was aware that science could "produce the bitter fruits of tyranny and rapine." He never wavered in his belief that through the diffusion of scientific knowledge the human condition could be advanced. And if by the advance of the human condition we mean the material improvement of the human estate, the extension of longevity, and the increase of our power over nature, none can gainsay him. Yet even if we grant the dubious proposition that all knowledge is good, surely not all of it is relevant for our political purpose. Henry Adams to the contrary notwithstanding, no law of physics has any bearing on the justification for a free society. Einstein's theory overthrew Newton's, not the Declaration of Independence.

It is a commonplace but an important one that it is not science and technology that are fateful to man, but the uses to which they are put. When we speak of uses, we imply purposes and ends, goals and policies. We therewith find ourselves in the realm of values. The humanities, broadly speaking, are concerned with the exploration of this realm. Though Jefferson prescribed a mainly scientific course of study for the intellectual elite, a curriculum built on the humanities is roughly what he had in mind for the ordinary citizen, whose studies should, he thought, be chiefly historical. Might not such a curriculum today provide what the sciences cannot—a strengthened faith in a free self-governing society?

I wish to declare at once that regardless of how we answer this question, the humanities—primarily the disciplines of language and literature, history, art, and philosophy—should have a central place in the education of *any* society. For their subject matter is perennial and transcends, even when it touches on, the temporalities of politics.

The reasons for this are manifest and heralded in many ways from ancient days to the present. The study of the humanities nurtures an understanding and appreciation of the great and often unfamiliar visions and modes of life. Within any mode of life, they present "the problems of the human heart in conflict with itself" (William Faulkner). They therefore embrace but go beyond the dimensions of the political and ideological. They strike no consensus. They have no flag or creed, even when they celebrate ways of life and death fought under warring battle cries. They take us out of ourselves and enable us to see with the eyes and minds of others, just as we become aware of the reach and power of others in us. Define the humanities and limit their concerns for curricular purposes as one will, their cultivation leads to the permanent enrichment of the internal landscape of the mind in any clime or social station. For they provide an ever renewed source of delight, consolation, insight, sometimes hope.

Surely this is merit enough to justify the place of the humanities in any curriculum of liberal studies. Surely this justifies us in maintaining that their absence is the sign of a truncated, one-sided, and impoverished education—whatever other virtues such education may have.

Nonetheless, we cannot honestly maintain that the study of the humanities of itself generates allegiance to the free society. Two considerations prevent us from doing so. The first is the historical fact that the student population of Western Europe, who until recently were brought up in their *lycées* and *gymnasia* largely on classical studies, were certainly not noteworthy for their ardor and enthusiasm for free democratic societies. Indeed, not infrequently in countries like Spain, Italy, France, and Germany, it was students who provided the intellectual shock troops for antidemocratic movements.

There is a second troubling reason why we cannot maintain that an organic relationship exists between the humanist tradition in life and letters and commitment to the free or liberal society. This is the fact that many of the monumental writers of the past regarded the promise of democratic progress as a threat to the life of the mind and to the creative spirit, as the political gloss on the mechanisms that were leveling and standardizing culture and taste. No one can reasonably dispute the record. From the age of Plato to the present, the dominating figures in the humanistic disciplines have been critical of, sometimes even hostile to, the extension of political power to the masses, even when safeguards against the excesses of popular sovereignty have been adopted. In the nineteenth century, writers like Dickens, George Eliot, and Shelley were sympathetic to the advance of the democratic idea, but their influence was more than counterbalanced by Wordsworth, Balzac, Goethe, Dostoevsky, and many others. In our own time, such major literary figures as T. S. Eliot, Yeats, Pound, Faulkner, and D. H. Lawrence typify the distrust and suspicion of democratic society prevalent among the creative vanguard.

Why there should be this "adversary" relationship, as Lionel Trilling called it, between the sympathies and values of so many great humanists and the democratic tendencies of their culture, and why there should be a corresponding bias toward the aristocratic tradition, is hard to explain. A partial answer may lie in the greater receptivity among aristocratic classes to the novel and experimental than is generally found in the larger public. ("Nothing is so foreign to the plain man," observes Santayana, "as the corrupt desire for simplicity.") To this may be added the fact that where the people are sovereign they have sometimes been less tolerant of heresies that challenge accepted beliefs than have some benevolent despotisms, which under the mantle of a patronizing *Narrenfreiheit*, the freedom accorded to the court jester, sometimes sheltered purveyors of doctrines dangerous to the state.

Whatever the explanation, we cannot plausibly deny that the outstanding humanist figures have rarely been protagonists of the ordered freedoms we associate with democratic life and republican virtue in a self-governing society. The growth of such a society in the West owes more to the dissident, nonconformist religious sects, to the agitation and battles of the early trade unions and other manifestations of class struggle than to the classical humanist tradition. It was not a scholar inspired by Plato or Aristotle, Aquinas or Dante, or any figures of the Renaissance, but a spokesman of the Protestant Levellers who proclaimed that "the poorest he that is in England has a life to live as the greatest he," and therefore argued for the right "to choose those who are to make the laws for them to live under."

In pointing to the considerations that prevent us from making the easy inference that a liberal-arts education centered around the study of the humanities is integral to the existence and survival of a liberal society, I do not mean to suggest that there is a simple causal relation between curricular study and political behavior. A contemporary literary critic (George Steiner) has written in a tone of bitter discovery: "We know now that a man can read Goethe and Rilke in the evening, that he can play Bach and Schubert, and go to his day's work at Auschwitz in the morning." But he could have added that those who studied Euclid and Newton also built the crematoria at Auschwitz. And he undoubtedly is aware that those in previous times who led the massacres of innocents in their holy wars against heretics or infidels invoked the blessings of the God of love on their dedicated work. This is an old story. The face of evil can wear the mask of learning. The devil can play the role not only of a gentleman but of a scholar—but this does not make learning or manners evil or less desirable. The guilt of a criminal does not stain the means by which he commits or conceals his crime. As well maintain that the abuse of language is an argument for permanent silence.

Moreover, after one has said everything there is to be said to the contrary, there still remains at least some positive connection between the rationale of a free society and the great expressions of the human spirit in art and literaure. Regardless of their specific political orientation, these works are usually animated by a passion or vision of opposition to the customary. They move by challenging complacency. They are essentially nonconformist. To reach their mark they must disturb, upset, and sometimes frighten.

To the extent, then, that a free society thrives on diversity, the play and struggle of varied perspectives, the dialectic of confrontation, it *is* served by the humanities, just as in turn the free society often serves the humanities better than the authoritarian societies some humanists tend to favor. For a free society offers an unlimited theater for works of the spirit to develop, in contrast with authoritarian societies that always in some crucial area of the mind invoke the Augustinian dictum that "error has no rights," as a bar to further inquiry and experiment.

To be sure, free societies sometimes sin against the light of cultural freedom. But when they do, they are violating their own ethos. Conversely, some unfree societies may tolerate, even encourage, experiment and variation in some restricted area, but never in all the realms of the human spirit. I am struck by a story told about General de Gaulle. In refusing to endorse the arrest of Sartre for an infraction of the law, he is reputed to have said: "In a free society one does not arrest Voltaire." Sartre was no Voltaire, and he was to boot an apologist for Stalinism; but we know what his fate would have been as a dissident under a Stalinist regime.

I do not want to go beyond the modest claim that there is no essential or necessary hostility between the humanities and a free society, and that there need be no conflict between a love of the humanities and a commitment to liberal democracy. But I believe I have also shown that a curriculum concentrating on the humanities can no more be expected to achieve the Jeffersonian objective of strengthening faith in the free society than a curriculum based on the sciences.

I have brought up Jefferson's ideas about the relation between education and freedom not out of an academic concern with those ideas, but rather in the hope that examining them might yield some guidance in dealing with our urgent contemporary crisis. It is a crisis that threatens the very survival of a free, self-governing society in the United States. For it consists precisely of an eroding allegiance to the ideals of a free, self-governing society itself. It would require volumes to document the failure to abide by the democratic ethos in American life today. Restricting ourselves only to phenomena observable without enlisting batteries of research teams to report on them, we find: (1) the vehement assertion of rights and entitlements without the acceptance of corresponding duties and obligations; (2) the invocation of group rights to justify overriding the rights of individuals; (3) the growth of violence, and the tolerance of violence, in schools and local assemblies; (4) the open defiance of laws authorized by democratic process, and the indulgence of courts toward repeated and unrepentant violators; (5) the continued invasion by the courts themselves into the legislative process; (6) the loss of faith in the electorate as the ultimate custodian of its own freedom.

Each reflective observer can make his own list of the multiple threats from *within* our own society to the health, security, and civility of the processes of self-government. However conceived, they raise the question of whether we possess the basic social cohesion and solidarity today to survive the challenge to our society from *without*, particularly that posed by the global expansion of communism. Although there are different views of the immediacy and magnitude of the Communist threat to the free world, it is plain political folly to deny its existence. The map of the world from 1945 to the present bears witness to the fact that the policy of containment, initiated by President Truman alter the Baruch-Lilienthal and the Marshall Plan had been rejected by the Kremlin, does not contain.

The threat of Communist expansion is compounded by the fear that the defensive use of nuclear weapons will result in a nuclear holocaust. The artful, unremitting, and often unscrupulous propaganda by fanatical groups, exemplified by television programs like *The Day After* and by terrifying classroom scenarios on every level of our school system from a kindergarten to university, has generated a mood of fear not far removed from hysteria. The fallout from this sustained propaganda has often short-circuited reflection. It has led to the mistaken belief in some circles that we are confronted by the stark alternatives of unilateral disarmament or inevitable war, and to a disregard of the well-grounded position that an effective deterrent is the best way of preserving peace without sacrificing freedom. Clarity, however, requires recognition that to renounce in advance the retaliatory use of a deterrent is to proclaim in effect that we have no deterrent, thus inviting the very aggression the policy of deterrence was designed to discourage.

In our precarious world every policy has risks. What shall we risk for freedom? What shall we sacrifice for mere survival? If our nation were confronted by a nuclear ultimatum, would there be enough loyalty to a free society to generate the necessary resolution to cope with the threats without bluster or paralyzing panic? To many the answer seems doubtful, and this in itself is an alarming sign of the state of the national mind. Past generalizations about the American character are no guide, whether drawn from de Tocqueville, Whitman, or Lord Bryce.

What then must be done? Not long ago our President proposed and our Congress approved the organization of a National Endowment for Democracy to encourage the spread of democratic forces abroad. As welcome as such a program is, I submit that it is even more necessary to organize a National Endowment for Democracy at home. The first goal of such an endowment would be to develop programs to study the basic elements of a free society, and suggest them as required parts of instruction on every educational level.

Today it is widely agreed that fundamental educational reforms are needed to improve the levels of skill and literacy of American students so that they may cope with the present and future problems arising from multiple changes in our complex world. Agreeing with this proposition, I am suggesting that it is just as important to sharpen the students' understanding of a free society, its responsibilities and opportunities, the burdens and dangers it faces. Instead of relying primarily on the sciences and humanities to inspire loyalty to the processes of self-government, we should seek to develop that loyalty directly through honest inquiry into the functioning of a democratic community, by learning its history, celebrating its heroes, and noting its achievements. Integral to the inquiry would be the intensive study of the theory and practice of contemporary totalitarian societies, especially the fate of human rights in those areas where communism has triumphed.

The first retort to such a proposal is sure to be that it is just a variant of the propaganda and indoctrination we find so objectionable in Communist society. As to propaganda, Karl Jaspers somewhere says that the truth sometimes needs propaganda—a dark saying. I interpret it to mean that we require courage to defend the truth when challenged and the skills both to make it more persuasive and to combat its distortions. But as to indoctrination, the retort misses the basic difference between the open and closed society. This lies not in the presence or absence of indoctrination, but in the presence or absence of the critical, questioning spirit. Indoctrination is the process by which assent to belief is induced by nonrational means, and *all* education in *all* societies at home and in school *in the tender years* is based on it. The habits of character, hygiene, elementary sociality and morality are acquired by indoctrination and become the basis of all further learning. In a free society, however, such methods are, and always should be, accompanied by, and gradually become subordinate to, the methods of reflective, critical thought at every appropriate level. When students achieve greater maturity they are able to assess for themselves step by step the validity of the beliefs and the justifications of the habits in which they have been nurtured. A free society not only permits but encourages questioning, commensurate with the intellectual powers of students, as integral to learning.

In a closed society indoctrination induces assent by irrational as well as nonrational means, beyond the early years, and throughout the entire course of study in all except certain technical areas. It never permits a critical study of its first principles and the alternatives to them. The unfree society regards its subjects as in a permanent state of political childhood; it controls what they read and hear by a monopoly of all means of communication. The free society can live with honest doubt and with faith in itself short of certainty. Skeptical of perfect solutions, it eschews the quest for absolutes. In contrast with the closed society, it can live with the truth about itself.

I am not making the utopian claim that anything we do in the schools today will of itself redeem or rebuild our society. Continued institutional changes must be made to strengthen the stake of all groups in freedom. But of this I am convinced. In our pluralistic, multi-ethnic, uncoordinated society, no institutional changes of themselves will develop that bond of community we need to sustain our nation in times of crisis without a prolonged schooling in the history of our free society, its martyrology, and its national tradition. In the decades of mass immigration in the nineteenth and twentieth centuries that bond was largely forged by the American public school. What I propose is that our schools, reinforced by our colleges and universities, do the same job today in a more intelligent, critical, and sophisticated way.

There was a time when most Americans understood that the free, self-governing society bequeathed to them by Jefferson and the other founding fathers was the "last best hope on earth." If anything, the experience of the twentieth century, and especially of the past fifty years, should have made that truth even more evident than it was to Jefferson himself. During that period, our own society has been able to make gigantic strides in the direction of greater freedom, prosperity, and social justice, while its totalitarian enemies—first Nazi Germany and then the Soviet Union—have produced war and holocaust, economic misery, cultural starvation, and concentration camps. Yet in spite of that record, the paradox is that faith and belief in the principles of liberal democracy have declined in the United States. Unless that faith and that belief can be restored and revivified, liberal democracy will perish.

Jefferson thought that proper education was necessary to the birth and establishment of a free society. He would not have been surprised to discover that it is also necessary to its perpetuation, and indeed to its very survival.

[1984]

# 21

# THE PRINCIPLES AND PROBLEMS OF ACADEMIC FREEDOM

## ACCOUNTABILITY

In this day and age very few persons will be found who openly declare that they are opposed to academic freedom. But as is the case with the term "democracy," it would be extremely hazardous to predict the specific beliefs of those who profess democracy, particularly when prefaced with adjectives like "higher" or "directed" or simply "new" or "people's." Nonetheless, if we are careful, and are prepared to make relevant distinctions, I believe it is possible to clarify what academic freedom has meant in the history of higher education in the Western world, and particularly in the history of American higher education. Before we declare that academic freedom is present or absent or discuss its problem, we must begin a working definition.

I offer as a working definition of academic freedom the following: "Academic freedom is the freedom of professionally qualified persons to inquire or investigate, to discuss, publish, or teach the truth as they see it in the discipline of their competence subject to no religious or political control or authority, except the control of standards of professional ethics or the authority of the rational methods by which truths and conclusions are established in the disciplines  involved."

This definition is substantially the one elaborated in greater detail by

From *Contemporary Education* 58, no. 1 (fall 1986): 6–12. Reprinted by permission of the Estate of Sidney Hook.

Arthur O. Lovejoy who together with John Dewey founded the American Association of University Professors, the latter as President and the former as Secretary. At the time, 1915, academic freedom, as they defined it, could hardly be said to be recognized by most governing boards of American colleges and universities. Even in the '30s when I served as a member of the Council of AAUP its principles were far from being universally accepted. Today there is hardly a college and university in the country which does not proclaim its allegiance to those principles. Indeed the proclamation and acceptance of these principles have become commonplace. And like other commonplaces some of its implications are overlooked.

I want to begin by exploring some its implications. First, it is important to note that academic freedom is defined here not as the freedom to teach the truth but as the freedom to *seek* the truth. What is the difference? Isn't the truth important? Of course it is, but just as important is recognition of the fact that even if one believes in absolute truth, human recognition of the truth, however it be defined, varies, that many things once believed true are no longer accepted by competent inquirers as true, and some things considered false like the heliocentric hypothesis are now considered true. That is why we cannot accept without qualification the Augustinian dictum that error has no rights.

Secondly, academic freedom is a special right, it is *not*, much rhetoric to the contrary notwithstanding, a human right, or a civil right, or a constitutional right. It is the right of the professionally qualified teacher or researcher. What, one may ask, is the difference between a *special right* like academic freedom and these other rights—human, civil, or constitutional? To make a short answer—academic freedom is a right that must be *earned*. All these other rights we enjoy as members of the democratic community. They are our birthright as citizens; they do not have to be earned, and the community has an obligation to prevent others from denying or abridging them. The community and its law enforcing agencies in a democracy cannot arrogate to itself, except under carefully defined conditions, the power to limit the exercise of our human and constitutional rights. Freedom of speech gives anyone freedom to talk nonsense anytime, anywhere, barring for the moment, laws about public nuisance. But it does not give anyone the right to talk or teach nonsense in a university. One must, so to speak, be professionally qualified to talk nonsense in a university.

Of course, what may appear nonsense to you or the inexpert may turn out to be the latest or higher wisdom or knowledge. To some individuals the truths of non-Euclidian geometry, or the view that the simultaneity of two distant events is not absolute but relative to different frames of reference or current notions in cosmology, quantum physics, or genetic engineering, all appeared nonsensical to some when they were first enunciated.

Similarly, one can under the first amendment teach on the street or in one's home anyone who wants to be instructed. But he must be qualified to teach or engage in research before he can be permitted to teach in a university classroom or experiment in a laboratory. There are many problems connected with qualification some of which I shall discuss later. But we can't dispense with the principle of qualification without making a shambles of our educational system. The whole structure of our social life depends on the recognition of the indispensability of qualification as a necessary condition of professional performance. Every time we enter a hospital or clinic or entrust ourselves to a public conveyance, we stake our life on the assumption that some adequate tests of qualification have been conducted. And although going to a university is not so risky, no one who values his time or money would enter its classrooms unless he or she assumed that the teachers were qualified to teach their subject.

In this connection a certain feature of qualification must be mentioned which although not unique to university life is often misunderstood and productive of needless controversy. No institution, and certainly not a university, can function well if appointment to its staff conveys instant and permanent tenure. In the nature of the case there must be a probation period of varying length before full qualification can be established. When academic freedom is recognized, it holds for the probation period, too. The criteria that must be met before tenure is granted varies with different types of teaching. In those institutions where the greatest stress is placed on excellence of teaching, the criteria will be different from those in which excellence in research and quality of publication are given precedence. I shall not pursue this complex question here. Normally I have found that anyone who receives an appointment assumes that he or she is entitled to lifelong or permanent tenure if they conscientiously perform their duties. They are apt to be extremely suspicious of the grounds offered for their nonrenewal after the probation period.

It is at this point that cases allegedly involving breaches of academic freedom arise. For the grant of permanent tenure not only completes the rites of passage to full academic citizenship, it confers a lien on the university's future resources of almost three-quarters of a million dollars. No responsible faculty or administration can permit the grant of tenure to be taken as a matter of course. Every decision must be considered a major serious educational decision.

A third remarkable implication of academic freedom is that if one subscribes to it, one is committed to the belief that the professionally qualified person in pursuit of the truth, and abiding by the Canons of professional ethics, has a right to reach any conclusions that seem to him valid. This means he has what I have called the right to heresy in the field of his competence. This is a very momentous inference, for to those who disagree with him it means the right in good faith to be wrong. It means that an honest inquirer will be defended not only when he reaches a heresy that we agree with but a heresy with which we disagree. That is easily said but experience shows that often it depends on whose ox is being gored. In disciplines where controversy is rife, especially the social sciences and the humanities, this means that where academic freedom exists it will protect the right of a qualified teacher to reach conclusions that some will regard as Communist or Fascist or racist or irreligious or un-American.

There is another implication of academic freedom that is even more remarkable. I as a professor can stand on a public platform with my grocer, my butcher, my physician or lawyer. We all exercise our constitutional right of freedom of speech to advocate the same unpopular or heretical proposal. Select your own particular abomination as an illustration. Let us say voluntary euthanasia or the deportation of illegal aliens or curtailing social security. Every one of my fellow speakers may pay a very large price for the expression of their opinions. They may lose trade, or patients, or clients to a point where their very livelihood may be affected. I, however, to the extent that I have academic freedom claim and enjoy complete immunity from any institutional sanctions. Neither my salary nor my prospects of promotion can be affected. In a sense I am experiencing a privilege or freedom that comparatively few of my fellow citizens have. I am absolved of the normal costs of unpopularity and sometimes even of my defiance of convention. Coupled with the fact that once I acquire tenure, I cannot be deprived of it except by a long and arduous due process—rarely invoked in universities—this reinforces the exceptional nature of my vocational rights as contrasted with most other vocations and professions.

It is necessary to stand off and examine in perspective the remarkable character of the right to academic freedom. It is remarkable in that as distinct from what existed in any other period of human history, it involves not only the tolerance of intellectual heresy but its legal support. It is remarkable in that it offers safeguards in ways that are unprecedented, against the price or costs of intellectual heresies, and in that it has upheld the right of teachers to exercise their responsibilities of citizenship on the same terms as their neighbors without suffering academic sanctions. And it is remarkable above all because of its uniqueness in the long history of civilization, in its limited jurisdiction to certain areas of the Western and American world, and in the recency of its emergence in those areas.

There was no academic freedom in the ancient world, not even in democratic Athens as the death of Socrates attests. There was no academic freedom during the medieval synthesis, the Renaissance, the Reformation, or the Enlightenment. There was no academic freedom in colonial or revolutionary America or in England where instruction was largely in the hands of the clergy. Academic freedom was an un-American importation from Imperial Germany where it first took root in the University of Berlin in 1810 at a time, interestingly enough, when there was less political democracy in Prussia and the rest of Germany than in the United States or Great Britain. When I began teaching in the American University in 1927 academic freedom and faculty governance were in a very rudimentary state. Contracts were for one year with no legal presumption of renewal. The status of the faculty was little better than that of hired men in industry except that one's private life and public activity could more readily affect one's academic future than in other pursuits. Boards of Trustees often intervened directly into educational affairs. Gradually things improved, especially as members of the AAUP made their way up the administrative ladder. The turning point was the adoption of the AAUP'S Basic Statement of Principles not only by the Association of American Colleges and Universities but by forty-seven national professional organizations of scholars and teachers embracing almost the entire spectrum of the arts and sciences. By the end of the Second World War, the battle for academic freedom was essentially won although several problems on procedural matters remained to be clarified.

The very recency and rarity of academic freedom gives rise to the question: why should the community which either directly or indirectly through tax exemption underwrites the great costs of university education support the institution of academic freedom? There are many reasons but we can sum them all up in the statement: because it believes that it is to its own ultimate interest to do so. It believes that the discovery of new truths and the extension of the frontiers of knowledge are more effectively furthered by the presence of academic freedom than by its absence. It believes that fidelity to the mission of the university will result in the accumulation of bodies of reliable objective knowledge that may be used as guides or tests of policy by legislators and citizens. It gives relative autonomy to the university not for the pleasure and enjoyment of its teachers and researchers but for the good of society.

But it should be obvious that this precious right to academic freedom carries with it certain duties and responsibilities about which we unfortunately hear less and less. It is certainly true that academic freedom protects the expression of heresy but that does not mean that "anything goes" in the way of classroom or research behavior, that one is free to do or not do *anything* he or she pleases to do. The grant of academic freedom is based on the assumption that the mission of the university is to search for the truth, and therefore on the assumption that the professor or researcher is truly *seeking* to reach the truth or the best warranted conclusion on the available evidence. The assumption is that he or she is a free agent, not under orders from an outside group to indoctrinate or to cook his evidence, not bought, not a fanatic committed in advance of inquiry to a predetermined conclusion regardless of the evidence. In short, the assumption behind the grant of academic freedom is that the professor is a scholar not a propagandist, and this is the source of the duties and responsibilities correlative to the exercise of his freedom.

It is noteworthy but rarely acknowledged that the 1940 Basic Statement on Academic Freedom of the AAUP explicitly asserts that academic freedom "carries with it duties correlative with rights." It enumerates quite a few, e.g., "The teacher is entitled to freedom in the classroom in discussing his subject but he should be careful not to introduce into his teaching controversial matter which has no relation to his subject." (It seems to me that even if the matter is noncontroversial but has no relation to the subject, it does not belong in the classroom.) The duties enumerated in the AAUP statement are not confined to the teacher's behavior in the classroom. It reminds him that "As a man of learning and an education officer, he should remember that the public may judge his profession and his institution by his utterances. Hence he should at all times be accurate, should exercise appropriate restraint, should show respect for the opinions of others, and should make every effort to indicate that he is not an institutional spokesman." In a further statement in 1956, the AAUP adds:

The academic community has a duty to defend society and itself from subversion of the educational process by dishonest tactics, including political conspiracies to deceive students and lead them into acceptance of dogmas or false causes. Any member of the academic profession who has given reasonable evidence that he uses such tactics should be proceeded against forthwith, and should be expelled from his position if his guilt is established by rational procedure.

Similar sentiments are expressed in the famous declaration of the Graduate School of the New School for Social Research established by exiles from totalitarian countries.

The New School knows that no man can teach well, nor should he be permitted to teach at all, unless he is prepared "to follow the truth of scholarship wherever it may lead." No inquiry is ever made as to whether a lecturer's private views are conservative, liberal, or radical; orthodox or agnostic; views of the aristocrat or commoner. Jealously safeguarding this precious principle, the New School stoutly affirms that a member of any political party or group which asserts the right to dictate in matters of science or scientific opinion is not free to teach the truth and thereby is disqualified as a teacher.

Equally the New School holds that discrimination on grounds of race, religion or country of origin either among teachers or students runs counter to every profession of freedom and has no place in American education.[1]

It follows from this foregoing that the faculty which extends its *protection* to its members who exercise their right to academic freedom must also be *prepared* to discipline those who violate the duties and responsibilities of academic freedom. I have always held that there is no necessity for state legislatures or Congress to investigate where questions of professional ethics are involved, and that academic bodies are the best qualified to determine the fitness of their colleagues to teach and to give the benefit of due process to those charged with unfitness or violation of professional trust. It stands to reason that the unwillingness of a faculty to administer its own standards of objective scholarship and intellectual integrity, its indifference to what is taught, and how it is taught, or to whether anything at all is taught in its classes is both wrong and foolish. It will not only degrade the quality of the degrees it bestows and affect its scholarly standing, but sooner or later it will provoke community alarm and interference. In public institutions whose budget is underwritten by tax money, it is safe to predict that any academic scandal that seems to indicate laxity in the application of proper scholarly standards is sure to give rise to legislative investigation.

An illustration that has its amusing sides occurred in a western state college that shall here remain unidentified. In a course on human sexuality it was reported that a teacher was giving class credit to students for their accounts of their novel sex experiences and activity. You may have read of the hullabaloo that ensued when word of this reached the press. After considerable turmoil in which some state legislators were very vocal and emergency sessions of faculty and administrative committees were convoked, the trouble blew over because the instructor resigned. But it is significant that the faculty and administration had no notion of what was going on and made no provision for examining the quality and relevance of the instruction until the outside community clamor arose and the budgetary prospects of the college before the Legislative Committee became quite cloudy.

It seems to me that faculties should be very jealous of their scholarly reputations on teaching and research. Self-appraisal and self-criticism of their curricular offering should be an ongoing process. The enforcement of the statement about the responsibilities and duties of scholarship should not be treated as pious platitudes. They should be as vigorously enforced as the principles of academic freedom are defended. When that is done faculties can be prepared to stand up to any relevant legislative inquiry. They can with eloquent dignity point out that the legislature has the legal power to establish or not establish any educational institution, whether liberal or professional. But once that decision is made, then it is within the professional competence of the educators to operate and control that institution without let or hindrance from those not professionally qualified, including the legislators. For that is the meaning of academic freedom. And if the university faculties have lived up to their academic mission, they will ultimately win community support.

There are many other problems that remain to be explored that I cannot treat in short compass, particularly whether the exercise of a constitutional right by a teacher gives him automatic immunity from any academic sanctions, and what safeguards exist against the abuse of faculty power. But I want to conclude by pointing to what I regard as the central question bearing on the future of the university freedom, viz., whether the ideals of academic freedom I have sketched can be sustained. Today those ideals are not so much endangered by the traditional enemies of academic freedom, the church and state, but sometimes from within the university.

I have referred to the mission of the university as providing the context of academic freedom. I have defined that mission in terms of the pursuit of intellectual ends—discovery, clarification, criticism aimed at reaching the various modes of truth. But during the last decades a new conception of the university has emerged in some quarters which discards the traditional objective of scholarship and regards the university as primarily an agency of social change to effect political goals. This view is not satisfied to present programs to the democratic electorate for acceptance or rejection but insists on the right to use the classrooms for political purposes. Now to be sure, in the past the classroom and university have often been used for such political and religious purposes but according to the conception of academic freedom I have defended, this has been a lapse from the mission of the university and the ideal of objectivity. But the new view challenges the very conception of objective truth as a superstition. In effect it regards the university as an arena of struggle for conflicting political views, and refuses to recognize any distinction between the quest for objective truth and propaganda. It accepts whatever freedom it can acquire but refuses to recognize any responsibilities and duties. It proudly carries the bias and partisanship of the hustings and marketplace into the university which then becomes transformed into a battlefield of warring groups struggling for domination.

Let me offer a typical statement by a representative of this point of view:

> The social university is not primarily concerned with the abstract pursuit of scholarship, but with the utilization of knowledge obtained thru [sic] scholarship to obtain social change. Therefore it does not recognize the right of its members to do anything they wish under the name of academic freedom; instead it assumes that all its members are committed to social change. To give an example, a course in riot control would simply be declared out of place in such a university, while a course in methods of rioting might be perfectly appropriate.[2]

There are even more extreme statements of this position.

If such a view of the university prevailed or even achieved wide currency, I doubt whether any community would support its existence for long. Now in my view of academic freedom any qualified teacher has the freedom to say or write or advocate such a view of the university, but if he were to *act* on it and subordinate his teaching and research not to the controls of scholarship and evidence, he would be in violation of the duties and responsibilities of academic freedom. He or she should be held to account by their faculty peers. And if they lacked the courage to do so, both their institutions and the cause of academic freedom would suffer irreparable damage.

## ACCURACY IN ACADEMIA: CRITICISM

Unfortunately the politicalization of many American universities since the '60s and the introduction of some new disciplines in which the expression of only one point of view is tolerated have created a climate of opinion on some campuses very hostile to the principles of academic freedom as I have defined them. The situation is exacerbated by the intolerance of radical extremists among student bodies who refuse to permit the expression of views with which they are unsympathetic. It would hardly be an exaggeration to say that since the so-called Free Speech Movement at Berkeley, there is no longer freedom of speech for anyone, even invited scholars, publicly to present and uphold the views of the American government. Contrast the treatment meted out to Jeane Kirkpatrick, the violent disruption of her meetings, and the friendly reception accorded to Communist Angela Davis, the notorious apologist of the Soviet Gulag and other oppressive Communist regimes. Not so long ago the President of Harvard had to plead with the Cambridge academic community to extend the traditional courtesies of a hearing to visiting officials of the American government. These violations of elementary, political, and civic freedoms continue primarily as a result of faculty unwillingness to discipline disrupters in accordance with principles of due process worked out in collaboration with student bodies of recent years.

Even more widespread, continuous, and educationally disastrous is the conversion of many classrooms, especially in the humanities and social sciences, into political pulpits sometimes on matters unrelated to the theme of the course, and outside the field of competence of the instructor. Almost always the bias of the teaching and preaching is directed in one way—*against* American policies and institutions, without a scholarly, fair, or balanced presentation of the issues. Horror stories about such excesses abound. One English instructor whose area of specialization has nothing to do with political or foreign affairs teaches his class that there is currently more injustice in America than in Nazi Germany. Another instructor in history converts his class into guerilla theater to attack American policy in Nicaragua. A professor holding a joint appointment in psychology and anthropology teaches there are three varieties of racism of which Zionism is one. Another professor alleges that the holocaust of the Jewish population in Europe is a Zionist myth.

How can such violations of the ethics of teaching and scientific inquiry be combatted without opening the door to other and possibly worse evils? I repeat: certainly not by legislative investigation or action on a state or national level. This threatens the relative autonomy of the university and the whole conception of academic freedom which has developed to serve us well in this country only in our century.

Nor by a proposal recently presented by a group called Accuracy in Academia. This calls for the organization of concerned students and others on campuses to monitor the classrooms of teachers. Using tapes and notes they plan to record the statements of teachers which they deem seriously in error and send them to a central source where they will be vetted. If the statements are regarded as ill-founded, the professors will be requested to correct them in class, failing which wide publicity will be given to the offending remarks.

Those who have advanced this proposal are unwittingly damaging the cause of academic freedom and are playing into the hands of the very individual whose excesses have arroused their sense of outrage.

First of all, most teachers will justifiably resent the assumption that what they say will be monitored and judged by persons who have no professional standing. Secondly, in pursuing and analyzing an idea, new or old, it may be necessary to explore critically positions and statements that may be at great variance from accepted views, even if they are ultimately rejected. Thirdly, anyone with any academic experience knows how hazardous it is to rely on students' notes to determine what has been said, and in what context. Fourthly, teachers with heretical views will be discouraged from expressing their judgments lest a hue and cry be raised by some hysterical devotee of orthodoxy thus depriving both students and the community of insights that challenge accepted doctrine. Finally, the grant of academic freedom carries with it a trust in the *bona fides* or the qualified teacher which is challenged in advance by this proposal.

Already among the most vehement critics of Accuracy in Academia have been the very persons who are committed to a propagandistic, illiberal, and predominately anti-Western stance in their teaching, and who are shouting that academic freedom is threatened while they continue to violate its duties and responsibilities. Others have rushed into the fray with hackles flaring who just recently kept a discreet silence when free speech and academic freedom were being denied to Jeane Kirkpatrick, as Jefferson Lecturer, at Berkeley, and at Minnesota and other universities. At Stanford University, one of the leaders of the movement to deprive the Fellows of the Hoover Institution (whose scholarship and recognized achievements are beyond his range) of their academic freedom on the alleged ground of their conservative orientation, now paints himself as a target of victimization. In the hubbub that has been raised by this thoughtless proposal, public attention will be distracted from the actual sapping and undermining of the principles of academic freedom that have accompanied the growing politicalization of American universities.

Where does this leave us? If we reject any legislative oversight and forego the shortsighted and self-defeating proposals of Accuracy in Academia, how shall we combat the multiple abuses of the academic ethic?

By exercising our academic freedom *publicly* to criticize its violations on the campuses on which they occur, by insisting that administrations enforce the guarantees of free speech to visiting scholars and other invited academic guests, and by initiating disciplinary action against those guilty of disruption. If administrations persist in their policies of self-defeating appeasement and refuse to enforce the provisions of the disciplinary codes established on most campuses by joint student-faculty committees, resort should be made by concerned faculty, to the Civil Rights Law.

In the last analysis the academic health of the university and the integrity of the academic ethic can only be upheld by the faculties themselves. So far it seems that those members of the faculties who seek to subvert the academic mission, who deny that there are objective standards of scholarship, who insist that all teaching is a form of propaganda, seem to show more courage in proclaiming these absurdities and peddling their nostrums than those who disagree with them. On some campuses it may court unpopularity publicly to criticize the mouthings of radical fanatics and the duplicities of ritualistic liberals who deny that there is any danger to intellectual and political freedom from the left. But unpopularity is a small price to pay to recall the university to its mission.

Ultimately we must rest our faith in the intelligence of our students to assess for themselves the truth of conflicting claims. But they must be aware of the *existence* of conflicting claims; they must hear the other side; they must hear the criticism of the nonsense about the Nazification of American culture by the apologists for Gorbachev, Castro, Ortega, and their similars. Our students must be reassured that as a group their teaching faculties do subscribe to a tested body of knowledge painstakingly wrested from ignorance by our forebears; that they do actively participate in the process by which we differentiate between what is probably true from what is demonstrably false; that they are willing to stand up and defend the intellectual and scholarly legacy entrusted to them against politically inspired attacks, regardless of the political spectrum from which such attacks originate. Scholars cannot entrust to others the chores of intellectual hygiene. Compared to what other scholars have endured resisting the march of totalitarianism, in foreign countries, whose first victim is academic freedom, unpopularity is a small price to pay.

[1986]

## NOTES

1. American Association of University Professors, *New School Bulletin* 10, no. 19 (5 January 1953): 2.
2. Alan Wolfe, "The Myth of a Free Scholar," *The Center Magazine* (July 1979): 77.

# 22

# IN DEFENSE OF THE COLD WAR

## NEITHER RED NOR DEAD

The strongest justification of the Cold War between the U.S. or the West and the Soviet Union is that it prevented a hot war and the triumph of Communism in Western Europe. It did not prevent a hot war in other areas of the world, but these did not directly involve the Soviet Union or threaten Western Europe. The tendency has been therefore in Western Europe to assess the Cold War narrowly without regard to the potential effects of the conflicts in other areas of the world on the prospects of its survival as a relatively free society. Indeed this tendency has developed to a point where it would hardly be an exaggeration to say that influential sectors of public opinion in Western Europe regard what they call "the cold war mentality" as a greater threat to their security than the intense, unabated campaigns of subversion, propaganda, and political pressure which the Soviet Union has been waging against the free world for decades. It is as if the Cold War were a set of activities initiated by the West or practiced only by the West while the actual expansion of the Soviet Union, directly or through its proxies, although deplored, is explained as a response to Western Cold War activities.

This is very strange because the ostensible and declared purpose of the Western proponents of the Cold War was one of containment of Communism, an essentially defensive strategy. The strategy of containment was itself adopted after the U.S. policy of accommodation proved unable

From *Marxism and Beyond* (Rowman and Little Field, © 1983) "In Defense of the Cold War: Neither Red nor Dead," by Sidney Hook, chap. 16, pp. 187–96. Reprinted with permission of the publisher.

to halt Soviet expansion. This policy was slow in emerging. In the interest of historic justice, because of present-day revisionist interpretations, one should point out that at the close of World War II the U.S. demobilized its troops in Europe and dismantled its defense establishment, cutting its outlays from $81 billion in 1945 to $13 billion by 1948, while the USSR retained the bulk of its forces in place; that the U.S. offered Marshall Plan aid to all European nations, including those under Russian occupation, which was brusquely rejected by the Soviet Union, and that, when it had a monopoly of atomic weapons, the U.S. offered to surrender it to an international authority, the Baruch-Lilienthal plan, an offer spurned by the Soviet Union. So generous were the provisions of the Baruch-Lilienthal plan that Bertrand Russell at the time unwisely urged that the United States atom bomb the Soviet Union if it refused to accept the proposal. For Russell was convinced that the Soviet refusal presaged a renewed attempt to impose its way of life on the world as soon as it acquired atomic weapons. Fortunately the United States turned a deaf ear to Russell's pleas, and Russell himself as if to prove that the opposite of an absurdity could be just as absurd, became an ardent advocate of unilateral disarmament by the West.

Whatever the justifications of the policy of containment, a sober assessment of the situation today reveals that the containment policy has not been successful. The Soviet Union directly and through its proxies expanded into areas beyond its theater of national interest and indeed into regions that exceeded the reach or even concern of the czarist empire. Accompanying this expansion has been an absolute and relative decline in American defensive power. As the proportions of the GNP not only in the U.S., but in Europe devoted to defense declined (from the early sixties to the late seventies) the proportions of the Soviet defense expenditures to its GNP increased. One of the ominous consequences of this reversal of military power between the U.S. and the USSR is that the latter is now within easy striking distance of the oil fields and sea lanes on whose flow Western Europe and Japan are presently heavily dependent. Accompanying this has been the manifest decline and failure of American intelligence capacities, conspicuously illustrated in recent events in the Near East and Middle East but by no means restricted to these areas.

The upshot of all this, and of cognate developments on the diplomatic and economic front, has been a widespread perception among American allies, especially in Europe, of an erosion in the American will and capacity to defend the free world against aggression by an increasingly powerful Soviet Union both in conventional military weapons as well as nuclear ones. This in turn has naturally intensified the fears of many Europeans of needlessly exposing themselves by measures of concerted self-defense that might provoke Soviet punitive measures against them, especially as the deterrent power of the Western nuclear umbrella loses credibility.

We must also recognize that despite the fact that the balance of terror—which is not the same thing as the balance of power—has kept the peace in Europe, in recent years there has emerged in Western Europe powerful movements favoring unilateral disarmament, political neutralism, and even outright pacifism. The relative prosperity of Western Europe, compared to the immediate post–World War II years, has dulled the sense of history and blotted our consciousness of the basic values at stake in the struggle against Communism leaving only the obsessive fear of war in which even military victory may be catastrophic. The ancient illusion that passive disobedience may be more effective than armed resistance to aggression is being revived as well as the misleading citation of the Gandhian example which overlooks the crucial facts that Gandhi appealed to values that were integral to the ethos of the British, whereas passive or nonresistance on a small scale to totalitarian dictators has led to mass butchery. Another comfortable illusion that has nurtured pacifist fantasies is that, in the event of a Communist takover, the worst eventuality would be a decline in both the standard of living and the loss of political and cultural freedoms to the level of the Soviet satellites today. This is extremely questionable. Once the countervailing presence and power of the contrasting example of functioning open societies is removed, there is nothing to prevent the culture of the Gulag Archipelago or, more accurately, the standard of life and repression within the Soviet Union from becoming general. Where all resistance and threats of resistance to its global power are removed, the Soviet Union is not likely to countenance a higher level of existence or greater freedom of expression in its satropies than within its own borders.

There is an alternative to capitulation and all-out war. Properly waged this is the Cold War, which in effect was abandoned when the policy of detente was introduced. Basic to the strategy of the Cold War is the development and deployment of the means of military defense which would make extremely problematic all-out aggression against the free world. This strategy rests on the reasonable assumption—reasonable because based on historical evidence and the geography, so to speak, of the Communist mind—that, unless their domestic spaces are invaded, the leaders of the Soviet Union will not undertake a war they are uncertain to win, or one whose costs are so heavy as to make even a technically favorable outcome a pyrrhic victory. The cold war of containment is designed to deny them any such assurance and therefore is a policy of peace. And why indeed should the leaders of the Soviet Union think otherwise? Unless the disproportion of strategic forces in their favor is so overwhelming that resistance on the part of the West would be minimal or hopeless, why should the Communist high command incur unnecessary risks?

Even without all-out general war, the power and influence of the Soviet Union on a global scale, despite occasional setbacks in some areas and despite domestic difficulties, are growing. Extrapolation in human affairs is dangerous because it assumes the constancy of key variables, but some of the key variables have changed. Whenever there was a risk of war in the past, notably at the time of the Berlin airlift in 1948 and the Cuban missile crisis in 1962, the Kremlin has exercised what used to be called Bolshevik realism, and climbed down. Unfortunately for us today the present danger has developed because of the reversal in the positions of overall military strength between the two super powers. Unless that disproportion is reversed and the balance of strategic weapons is restored, the danger will grow that the leaders of the Soviet Union may abandon the cautious strategy of the past. In 1973, at the time of the Yom Kippur War, the 1962 positions of the U.S. and the USSR were reversed. One year after the ten point "Declaration of Basic Principles of Relations Between the U.S. and U.S.S.R." was signed in Moscow, in which both nations pledged themselves not to stir up conflicts in troubled areas of the world and obtain unilateral advantages at the expense of the other, the USSR encouraged Egypt and its allies whom it had rearmed, to attack Israel. After the initial defeats, Israel reversed the tide and by a pincers movement of its invading armies was about to destroy the Egyptian Eighth Army. At that point the Soviet Union threatened to intervene with its own armed forces. The U.S. protested. Soviet forces then went on a nuclear alert to which the U.S. responded with its own nuclear alert. The situation was every whit as serious as the confrontation in 1962. But a special meeting of the National Security Council informed President Nixon that the U.S. was no match at the time for the USSR. The result was that the American government brought pressure on the Israelis who reluctantly and under protest released the Egyptian Eighth Army from the grasp of the Israeli military forces. (Admiral Zumwalt is the source of this story, which has been confirmed by leading dignitaries at the time in the American defense establishment.)

This defeat, instead of being a signal to restore the equilibrium of strategic nuclear power, was a preface to detente. The domestic paralysis produced by Watergate had more to do with the failure to arrest the decline of American military power in the mid-seventies than the consequences of Vietnam.

Redressing the balance in military power on all levels—conventional as well as nuclear—will be a long, arduous, costly process in which the Welfare States of the West may have to sacrifice some hard-won social gains. I do not agree with some pessimistic voices who lament that it is already too late. But it is obvious that it will be extremely difficult to achieve, in the face of Soviet diplomacy that seeks to create rifts in the Western alliance and strong domestic currents of opposition, the necessary increased defense expenditures as well as the punitive commercial actions that break the economic ties with the Soviet Union established during the period of detente. These ties were supposed to bind the Kremlin with cords of self-interest and prevent it from pursuing adventurist policies that would upset the *status quo*, but in effect they seem to have bound certain Western economic interests to acquiescence in Soviet actions in other areas of the world that weaken the West. One thing should be clear although it may be impolitic to make much of it. The U.S. cannot undertake to redress the balance of strategic power without the whole-hearted cooperation of its European allies. This cooperation will be difficult not only because of increasingly onerous costs but because it requires a psychological reorientation in order to make nuclear deterrence effective.

The major psychological reorientation requires an understanding of the nature of the deterrent effect of nuclear weapons. The mere presence of these weapons is not sufficient to deter a potential aggressor. He must be convinced of the will and readiness to make *defensive* use of them, otherwise they lose their deterrence and end up contributing to a deceptive sense of security. There are several ways of communicating the presence and strength of this will and readiness—by frequent drills accompanied by preparedness for civilian air defense. The paradox which seems hard to accept in some quarters is that the more effectively is this will and readiness communicated, the more likely is it that these weapons will never be fired.

Further, the Cold War until quite recently, and this is still true among America's European allies, has been conceived as having its locus primarily in Europe—the region of the greatest threat. Defense planning both for strategic forces and theater nuclear forces has been geared to this eventuality. But in recent years the growth of Soviet military power together with the extension and intensification of its political power have made other areas peripheral to Western Europe highly vulnerable. But some of these other areas are vital to the security and industrial vitality of the West, particularly the Persian gulf. The resources of the U.S. are not sufficient to counter the Soviet threats, their power and maneuverability have increased in virtue of the fact that geopolitical changes have strengthened Soviet interior lines of communication. In their own interest America's European allies must broaden their conception of the Cold War and actively participate in the devising of common measures to deal with threats outside Western Europe.

I want to stress that in my view the primary responsibility for the failure to keep abreast with Soviet military power in Europe and to block its political incursion in other areas, rests with the United States. Its policy of detente signaled a change, welcomed by its European allies, that in effect represented an abandonment of the Cold War of containment for one of accommodation and appeasement. The very expressions "Cold War" and "Cold Warrior" became epithets of disparagement in the West. The situation was symbolized by the refusal of President Ford, on the advice of Kissinger, to receive officially Aleksandr Solzhenitsyn during the week in which Brezhnev was receiving Gus Hall, head of the American Communist Party. From the point of view of the West, it is certainly not true that the policy of detente was the continuation of the Cold War waged by other means. Such a characterization applies more accurately to the Soviet conception of detente. In November 1980 in an address in Madrid, Ambassador Max Kampelman quoted from a speech by a leader of the Soviet Union in Prague in 1973 in which the latter made clear that the policy of detente was a strategy to effect a decisive shift in the international balance of power. Said the spokesman for the Soviet Union: "We have been able to achieve more in a short time with detente than was done for years pursuing a confrontation policy with NATO. . . . Trust us, Comrades, for by 1985, as a consequence of what we are now achieving with detente . . . we will be able to extend our will wherever we need to." Even discounting for exaggeration, there is a grain of truth in the observation.

The adoption of the policy of detente by the U.S. was bipartisan. Its abandonment today should be equally bipartisan. But it seems to me still an open question whether our European allies have abandoned the policy of detente. There are disquieting signs that as the burden of the mounting costs of upgrading military defense becomes more onerous, especially in a period of economic retrenchment, the illusions that the status quo in Western Europe can be preserved without increasing sacrifice, born out of fear of a nuclear holocaust, will revive. The program adopted by the British Labour Party as well as the current orientation in international affairs of the Socialist International, may be harbinger of the drift of dominant European opinion. This could spell the end of NATO and I fear the reversion of American public opinion toward an isolationist foreign policy and the illusion of a Fortress America psychology rationalized by the consideration that one cannot defend the freedom of people who are unwilling to risk anything in their own defense. The withdrawal of American troops from Europe whose presence is now a guarantee that the fate of Western Europe and the United States is intertwined, would follow. The ghost of Senator Mansfield's proposal to call U.S. troops home who are now stationed in Europe still stalks the halls of Congress.

There is a misconception that the prosecution of the Cold War and negotiations on arms reduction and other issues are incompatible. This is a profound error. It has often been pointed out that the limited nuclear test-ban treaty was signed in 1963 at the height of the Cold War. This indicates that specific peace initiatives can be proposed and negotiated in an illusionless Cold War atmosphere. But there are negotiations and negotiations. Agreements must be strictly reciprocal and *verifiable*. It is not true that compliance can be monitored by satellite, sometimes called "natural means of verification." There must also be mutual *on site* inspections. As Eugene Rostow has observed: "No camera can tell how many separate war heads are carried by a single missile, or measure its thrust, its accuracy, or the explosive power of the weapons it carries. . . . Nor can it identify missiles in warehouses and underground." It is a commonplace but it has ever-relevant practical implications—the broadcast of knowledge of violations of agreements entered into in an open society, where the press and public opinion are independent, is almost a matter of course. In a closed society, however, violations of agreements by contracting governments can be carried out with impunity. The West should make it clear that when the Soviet Union fails blatantly to live up to its obligations under existing treaties as is the case in the current flagrant violations of the provisions of Basket Three of the Helsinki Final Act, the other signatory powers should declare that they are relieved of their obligations under the Final Act—including the *de jure* recognition of the Soviet boundaries so coveted by the Soviet Union that it professes to accept Basket Three, which it has systematically violated.

So long as the ramparts of freedom are abundantly defended the Cold War will not become transformed into a hot war between the U.S. and the USSR. The conflict for the minds of men and women will go on. There will not be a final conflict but one long drawn out in the hope—so far nugatory—that changes within the Communist world will lead to a degree of liberalization that will significantly modify its totalitarian character. The Cold War, as I conceive it, should be designed to achieve this result—to accept the fact that both systems are in a state of competitive peaceful coexistence struggling to win the allegiance of mankind.

It is sometimes said that facts, especially the facts of power, are ultimately more decisive than ideals and ideologies. But it is just as true that the weight and effects of power often depend upon our perception of them, and our conceptions of legitimacy and justified authority. The propaganda of all totalitarian countries recognizes this. Communist societies are particulary vulnerable to their own rhetoric and propaganda, especially in their proud claim of being a worker's state, committed to disarmament and peace, and human welfare. From this point of view (until very recently) the behavior of the West is a history of lost opportunities in exposing the weaknesses and hypocrisies in the roots of the totalitarian Communist structure itself. Next in importance to containing and frustrating Soviet expansion, is this effort at ideological destabilization of the potentially restive populations of Communist regimes not by inflammatory rhetoric but by the sober propaganda of truth—even truth about some of our own shortcomings. Its success may inhibit the appetite for foreign adventure among the Communist leadership.

The exodus of hundreds of thousands of Cubans at the risk of life and limb from Castro's island paradise was mishandled from the point of view of its educational potential, as well as other mass flights of refugees from Communist countries. Not enough has been done to expose the absurdity of equating the political and civil rights of the UN Declaration of Human Rights with the social and economic rights of the workers, for in the absence of the first, the second are uncertain and in times of crisis, nonexistent. In the absence of political freedoms, not even a slave system can provide security.

The Polish situation is a paradigm case of the bankruptcy of Communist professions of being a worker's state. No matter what the specific outcome of that situation will be in Poland, from now on it will be a perpetual reminder to all Communist satellite nations and to the workers of the Soviet Union itself that free and independent trade unions are incompatible with the monopoly of political power by a dictatorial Communist minority, and that a nation physically unarmed but spiritually mobilized—symbolized by slogans like "while there is death, there is hope"—may moderate the severity of totalitarian rule in the direction of a more humane order. Beyond that we cannot see at the present moment. Of one thing we can be confident. No words of support to Solidarity or contributions of food or clinical supplies, despite *Pravda*, will be a pretext for the Kremlin to do what it would not have done otherwise.

The Polish situation was a pitiful revelation of the unreadiness of the Western world, particularly the U.S., to wage an effective Cold War which the Communist authorities and their spokesmen in the West ungratefully charge the U.S. of engaging in. The decision of the AFL-CIO to contribute to the Polish Workers Aid Fund threw Washington, not the Kremlin, into panic and led the State Department to supererogative assurances to the Kremlin that the American government was not involved in the charitable efforts. Perhaps it was a hangover from previous administrations, but it seemed as if the Sonnenfeld doctrine was still active, although its own author had repudiated it, and that the West, as Tom Kahn caustically observed, "had developed a vested interest in the stability of the Eastern bloc." I am not well informed about the reaction to the Polish events in Western Europe, but my impression is that they were met with more alarm than elation. I have been informed that some Social Democratic figures showed a fine sense of international solidarity by proclaiming, "the U.S. out of El Salvador and the USSR out of Poland." There is something preposterous in this equation between several divisions of Soviet soldiers in full armor with a handful of American technicians aiding the government to carry out its plans for land reform against reactionary right-wing terrorists and left-wing terrorists of a Communist-dominated coalition fueled and armed by clients and proxies of the Soviet Union.

It is not inconceivable that if the situation in Poland develops along pluralistic lines that reveal the lineaments of the human face some heretical Communists talk about but so far have nowhere produced that the West should actually help to ease Poland's economic burdens. It would be well worth the cost of an example that might inspire instability in other satellites and similar liberal developments. Hopefully the appetite for freedom will grow upon what it feeds and even infect the rank and file of the captive trade unions of the USSR. The exact form of that cooperation cannot be forseen now, but it is not beyond imaginability that the kind of support extended to hard-line Yugoslavia under Tito at the first manifestations of Communist polycentrism be directed toward Poland if its free trade union movement is permitted to flourish.

In contradistinction to hot war, Cold War is not a monopoly of government. Private groups can wage it, sometimes, as in the case of organized protest against the systematic harassment of Sakharov, even more effectively. The refusal of American scientists and mathematicians to meet with their Soviet counterparts until the persecution of Sakharov ceases, by itself may seem a slight form of pressure that, the Soviet Union can shrug off. Multiplied and extended to other areas of science and scholarship this intellectual and cultural boycott may prove costly enough to occasion second thoughts in the Politburo.

I want to conclude by stressing a proposition that I believe can and should be a focal point in current Cold War agitation on which Western public opinion and Western governments can unite, to wit, that the Brezhnev doctrine is incompatible with the spirit, text, and principles of the Helsinki Final Act Accords just as much as the censorship, imprisonment, exile, and confinement in psychiatric institutions of dissidents. The Brezhnev doctrine that no satellite of the Soviet Union has the right to modify its current political and social structure in the direction of greater democracy and pluralism was never freely voted on by any people to whom it has been applied. It is a naked assertion of *Faustrecht*. Let us challenge it before the conscience of the world not only at Madrid but wherever East and West meet.

[1983]

# 23

# HUMAN RIGHTS AND SOCIAL JUSTICE

**T**his year there will be a universal celebration of the twentieth anniversary of the adoption of the UN Declaration of Human Rights. There is a certain irony and fatuity in the fact that in many countries which have subscribed to the Declaration, the human rights promulgated by our Declaration of Independence and the French Declaration of the Rights of Man and Citizen are completely disregarded and often openly violated by their governments. This raises a number of interesting questions about political semantics and political sincerity that cannot be pursued here.

In our own country the celebration of the Declaration of Human Rights comes at a time when there is increasing concern about social justice. In the past, declarations about the rights of man focused primarily on political and civil rights. Today, however, in official documents and declarations bearing on human rights we find specific references to whole clusters of social, economic, educational, and cultural rights. In some areas of the world, this emphasis upon social and economic rights has become the justifying ground—in the eyes of some observers, the pretext or rationalization—for sacrificing existing political and civic rights of dissent or for postponing their introduction to a time in the future when war will be among the institutions studied in the museums of antiquity. Unfortunately, this may be a long time to wait.

From *Revolution, Reform, and Social Justice—Studies in the Theory and Practice of Marxism* (New York: New York University Press, 1975). Reprinted by permission of the Estate of Sidney Hook.

What I propose to do is to explore some problems which grow out of the tensions, paradoxes, and indeed "conflicts" among the complex of human rights that enter into that comprehensive and controversial expression, "social justice."

I shall not spend much time on the difficult questions of definition. When we speak of human rights we are speaking of rights that are broader than legal rights and narrower than the morally right. Human rights are more inclusive—perhaps broader or more fundamental—than legal rights because they serve as criteria of what should or should not be the basic legal rights enforced by the state. And, obviously, there are many legal rights, like the right to sue for damages or for specific performance if a contract has been breached, that will not be found on any list of human rights. On the other hand, there are many things that are morally right to do, like helping someone in distress or telling the truth, which would hardly appear on a schedule of human rights. By and large, when we use the expression "human rights" we mean by it a justifiable claim to certain powers or goods and services, to certain modes of treatment, especially freedom from interference, which upon reflection we acknowledge we have an obligation or duty to respect. And this irrespective of whether they are enshrined in a constitution or not.

*Why* these claims are justified is a very difficult question to which philosophers have given incompatible answers—religious, metaphysical, and psychological. I shall not discuss these justifications, save peripherally, because it is clear that most human beings are much more convinced, e.g., that men have a right to a fair trial, to worship God according to their conscience, to freedom of speech, to property, to educational opportunity, etc., than they are about the justifications of these rights. This is analogous to the fact that we are more convinced that "proposition $x$ is truer than $y$," that "policy $a$ is better than $b$," than we are of any definition of "truth" or "good." Indeed, we test the adequacy of any definition in terms of its conformity to the usage of the terms "true" and "good" as revealed in our pragmatic, reflective commonsense judgments. All knowledgeable persons will admit the truth of the statement "Bread is more nourishing to humans than stones" but they will quarrel about the meaning of "truth." All sensible persons will grant that "a divorce is better (or a lesser evil) than a murder," but it is not likely they will agree about the meaning of "good" and "bad."

There is one characteristic of schedules of human rights that is noteworthy. They vary from age to age. And in the same age different rights receive different emphasis. This proves not, as some skeptics assert, that they are nonexistent or arbitrary expressions of individual wish but that they are *historical*, to be understood in the context of their time and place, and rooted in what is experienced as an urgent need, signifying either distress or hope for better things, and crying out for remedy, reform or, if improvisation fails, revolution. This emphasis upon the importance of historical considerations is essential if we are to avoid fanaticism in the pursuit of human rights and social justice.

If the phrase "human rights" is ambiguous, the expression "social justice" is even more so. The evidence for this lies at hand: everyone asserts that he believes in social justice even though the conceptions of social justice vary so widely. At one end of the spectrum is the view that society or the state should do nothing but set down and enforce fair rules to regulate the universal quest for welfare or happiness. At the other is the view that the state or society should do everything it can to guarantee that in the race for welfare or happiness everyone is a winner. But it is obvious that these views are also ambiguous. What are *fair* rules of a race? Does this mean that all start from scratch—the halt, the maimed, and blind as well as the healthy and vigorous? Or, to be fair, must we give handicaps to the handicapped? And on what basis? Do fair rules in the distribution of educational opportunity require that we spend more on the dull than on the bright? Why? And if we sincerely desire that the community do what is necessary for everyone to come in a winner— what shall we do when not everyone can win? Does it really make sense to speak of a winner without there also being losers?

To think of human beings as losers, in a life they did not choose and in a world they never made, may offend our moral sensibilities. Abandon then the very conception of social life as a race for victory or struggle for survival! Excellent! But the problem remains no matter how we conceive of society, to wit, *Where there does not exist more than enough of everything in the way of desirable goods, services, and opportunities that can be made available to everyone at the same time, by what rule shall we distribute them?*

Regardless of the ambiguities in the conceptions of "human rights" and "social justice" two characterizations of them are obviously valid. They presuppose that we are dealing with social relations, that where a man lives by and for *himself* alone, it is senseless to talk of human rights and/or social justice. Secondly, whenever we discuss these concepts we are committed to a belief in *equality* of some sort. Every pronouncement in favor of human rights stresses some principle of equality. Every proposal to do justice to a person is a proposal to treat him with equality in some respect. F. H. Bradley and some other philosophers define justice as the impartial application of a rule to all cases that fall within its jurisdiction. As we shall see, these notions are necessary but not sufficient to under-standing justice. After all, it would take considerable hardihood to declare that any rule, whatever its character, if impartially applied, was just.

Actually, there is another expression not synonymous with "social justice" that nonetheless has a bearing on it, and suggests that there is something else that must be taken into consideration. We sometimes speak of "natural justice," more often of "natural injustice" when, through no fault of their own, human beings suffer pain and misfortune from physical evils. Sometimes this is referred to especially in the writ-ings of Dostoevski, as "cosmic injustice." From time immemorial one can hear mingled with the cries for social justice cries for cosmic justice or surcease from cosmic injustice. It can be heard in the Indian Upanishads, in the chorus of Sophocles's *Oedipus Coloneus*, in the Book of Job—in the laments of anyone born blind or crippled or ugly or in any natural state which is the source of human anguish. There is a sense of "unfair" intimately related to being "unlucky." One curses the time in which he is born: bemoans the fate of being thrust into the world in a condition of servitude or in a benighted country or in an impoverished and loveless family There is a saying attributed to an Eastern sage who proclaimed: "Only a few enjoy the high privilege of not being born." That life itself is a sentence of punishment from which death is a welcome release is sug-gested by Socrates's last words in the *Phaedo* enjoining his disciple, Crito, to sacrifice a cock to Aesculapius, the Greek God of medicine. (How strange that the philistine-genius Hegel should have interpreted this as a reminder by an honest man on his death bed of a debt he owed a neighbor!)

Behind *this* cosmic lament on every level and at all times is the expe-rience of suffering, pain or agony, spiritual humiliation, in the sense of an evil *imposed* without justification, discriminatory because not shared universally, and therefore an ever-present source of resentment. A *uni-versal* calamity seems more easily endurable to most human beings than a merely *personal* one even if the totality of suffering is greater in the first. These cosmic or natural injustices are indirectly taken note of by all theories of social justice in a manner that suggests the recognition of the fact that "equality" does not exhaust its meaning, that another dimension is involved. For every theory of social justice makes special provision for, or extends special consideration to, the "victims" of natural injustice, for those who are handicapped or disadvantaged at birth or by accident. It is as if in applying the rules of social justice we wish to compensate for the privations and hardships that, but for the grace of God, or Chance, or Accident (name it what you will!), might have befallen us. It is as if we were trying to do something to *equalize* or diminish the burden of discomfort or suffering in giving differential privileges to the handicapped and deprived not out of philanthropic zeal or compassion but as if it were their due.

That is why it is not enough to define social justice as equal treatment or equality before the law or the impartial application of a rule to its domain. It is not enough because of the difference between saying: "Justice consists in *treating* everyone equally" and "Justice consists in *mistreating* everyone equally." The difference goes to the heart of our conception of social justice—as distinct from legal justice. It is recognized in the spontaneous judgments mature adults make in humorous as well as tragic situations. The child who startles her pious mother, when taken to the museum to see the well-known picture of the Christian martyrs thrown to the lions, with her exclamation: "Look, Mummy, there's one poor lion who has no Christian!" has taken too literally the principle of equality as a sufficient guide in determining just treatment. The invader who in retribution orders every tenth hostage shot is not acting less unjustly but more so, when on reflection, to avoid the reproach of not being fair, he orders all the hostages to be shot.

What I am saying is that there is a built-in demand either for the diminution of acute human suffering or for the expansion of human welfare in the very demand for social justice. Sometimes there is a conflict between the components of equality and welfare—but not for long when great human suffering may be avoided by sacrificing or modifying the *formal* rules of equality. When it is not a question of great human suffering, short of a reflective analysis of the whole situation and a consideration of the consequences of alternative possibilities of action, decision is difficult. I know of no one rule or one value that can guide us in making this decision.

Let us recognize at the outset, although this means we can offer no clean, clear-cut solutions to difficulties, that in the concept of social justice two notions are involved (but not fused)—equality and human welfare.

It is necessary now to look at the concept of equality more carefully.

It is a commonplace that no one can take literally the phrases in the great historic documents that state or imply that all men are created or are born equal. Even when this is acknowledged, we often find a desperate and subtle search for some property, apparent or recondite, natural or supernatural, which is presumably common to all men, and therefore can serve as a basis or justification for the equality of treatment that is due men if they are to be treated justly. Sometimes it is said that all men *have* intrinsic dignity or a spark of divinity in them or a common fate of mortality or some other basic attribute. And further, that unless they possessed this common attribute, the whole notion of justice as equality of treatment would be fatuous or even senseless.

It seems to me that this approach is profoundly mistaken. I am not convinced that there is any trait which is equally common to all men. It is obvious that if there were any such trait, you could not deduce from it any specific mode of equality of treatment. (One could release all the hostages or destroy them all.) This is true also of alleged nonnatural traits possessed by men. Even if all men are equal in the sight of the Lord, equally sinners or beloved children, this would be compatible both with the belief in, and practice of, the divine right of kings to rule on earth, and with the equal democratic right of sinners to participate in a government based on consent. Be the natural or supernatural constitution of man what anyone believes it to be, what makes one method of treatment wiser or better or more desirable than another is the upshot or fruits of the differential treatment. Put another way, the justification for treating human beings in relevant circumstances equally is not to be found in the possession of some antecedent trait but in the *consequences* of treating them equally contrasted with the *consequences* of not treating them equally.

What does it mean, however, to treat human beings equally or justly—aside from the question of whether all human beings possess an inherent equality? How shall we characterize the policy or proposal of equality of treatment, granted that we are not presenting it as a description of equality?

The first response made to this question is misleading because we sometimes confuse the equal with the uniform, the equal with the identical. The demand, for example, for "equality before the law" is one of the oldest expressions of the demand for human rights. Assume an incorruptible judge. Is it just to impose equal punishment on a youthful stripling and a mature adult both apprehended committing the same crime? Is it just to mete out the same sentence to a first offender and a fourth offender even if both are mature adults? Shall we hold all offenders charged with the same offense in equal bail—even if it means that the wealthy man walks free and the poor man must languish in jail until trial? Shall we fine the millionaire and the driver of the Good-Humor truck the same amount for going through the traffic light?

What is a just tax bill? A flat tax for everyone? That would be absurd because it would not lead to *equality of burdens*. Shall it be a percentage tax? But Engels' law shows the poor may have to do without necessities if they pay the same percentage of their income as their wealthier brethren because they spend a larger percentage of their income on food, clothing, and shelter. A progressive income tax? How do you know when you have equalized the burdens?

Consider situations not related to taxation or courts but in which I want to be fair, e.g., in teaching.

Shall I assign the best teacher to the best students (or class) or to the poorest students?

Shall I address myself in my class to the dullest? the brightest, or to the mediocre?

Actually isn't the best or ideal teaching situation one in which I adjust the teaching to the individual needs of the individual student—the tailor-made curriculum?

This individualization means, of course, *not* treating everyone alike but differently.

Doesn't justice also require, because of the different histories of the defendants at the bar and their different capacities for suffering, etc., individualization of punishment? Similarly for medicine.

Where then does this leave us? We started out by saying that justice consists in treating individuals under a rule *alike*. Now we are saying it consists in treating them *differently*.

Well, we correct ourself. We say that justice consists in treating everyone in identical circumstances equally. Who is really in *identical* circumstances? We must modify that to read in *similar* circumstances. But even that isn't enough. The similar circumstances must be *relevant*.

Now we are getting closer to the nature of social justice. But it is obvious that what is relevant depends upon the *situation* in which a rule is being adopted and the *purpose* of the rule. *Treating people justly in relevant circumstances does not require that we treat them uniformly but only that we must have a good reason for treating them differently, for making exceptions. These good reasons are derived from our desire to increase human weal and avoid human woe, to diminish suffering and to maximize welfare.*

We follow the rule of equality but we know that there can be legitimate and illegitimate grounds for *discriminating*. Many illustrations come to mind. In cases of great distress and scarcity rationing of supplies by the community is adopted, but often we make—and should make—special allowance for the *aged* or for the *infant* or for the *sick* but not for those whose religion or race or creed or friends are like ours.

We speak of equal rights for women but we have social welfare laws which forbid the employment of women in some kinds of hazardous work like mining, etc. *Sex* may then be a ground for fairly excluding some from work—but race may not be a ground. If the Equal Rights Amendment becomes law social welfare legislation in behalf of women may be abolished, but it is not likely that sex differences will be altogether disregarded in the administration of laws. Except in some special cases men will not be granted paternity leave from work comparable to the maternity leave extended to women.

Perhaps the best illustration of equality of treatment which is compatible with *justified differences* of treatment is found in the behavior of a dedicated physician toward his patients. Not only does he treat his patients differently when he gives them equal medical consideration—in a crisis situation he may give a patient in an acute condition or on verge of death *more* consideration than others, and we understand why and accept it.

Even more apt is the illustration of parents who treat their children with an *equality of concern* that does not, of course, presuppose an equality of talent among the children. What parent on the basis of the discovery that the children range in IQ from 80 to 140 would therefore conclude that this justified denial of food, clothing, decent shelter, and medical treatment to any of his or her children?

This provides an analogue for our approach to the organization of society. Assuming that there is an equality of concern on the part of the community for all its citizens to develop to their fullest growth as persons—which is the cardinal ethical belief of democracy as a way of life—then what is wrong is not inequality of treatment but unwarranted or unreasonable inequality. The democratic task in a society whose history reflects the inescapable heritage of class societies of the past is to replace inequalities of treatment which are unreasonable by those which are reasonable. It must replace *discriminations* that are irrelevant to the tasks in hand by discriminations that are relevant. (If, e.g., the task is to construct a great symphony orchestra, it must select musicians not by their color or religion or creed but by their ear, their sense of pitch, and their related skills.)

So far our considerations have been abstract. I want to bring them to bear upon some of the concrete problems of American life. I can only touch briefly on them because detailed analysis is impossible in short compass. What I have been saying is not unrelated to the commitments which the United States as a nation has made in its historic documentary professions of faith. We have rejected all the historic notions of an elite society and are committed to the political institutions of a selfgoverning community. We have prided ourselves that the democratic political and legal rules of the game have permitted the possibility of an equality of opportunity for all citizens to live the life of free men in it in accordance with their capacities. It was the philosopher-statesmen of the American Republic, particularly Thomas Jefferson and James Madison, who realized long before Karl Marx how difficult it was to preserve effective freedom for all in the face of great disparities in wealth. Where property is power, and where insufficiency of power deprives the masses of independence, the freedom of political institutions is imperiled. What Jefferson and Madison failed to see was that the disparities produced by the concentration and centralization of wealth could not be controlled without the government interventions they feared, and that the preservation of the mechanisms of freedom depended upon a healthy economic and social organism.

When one analyzes the concept of "equality of opportunity" one discovers that if it is taken seriously it is a truly revolutionary principle which would require the remolding of social institutions to a point where we could speak of the *revolution en permanence*. Actually it was Plato who first realized how revolutionary the principle of "equality of opportunity" was because he argued that children could be provided with equality of opportunity to develop their best talents and personality only if they were brought up by the best possible fathers and mothers. He therefore proposed to wipe out the family and have all children educated by those who had a professional genius for parenthood. Not all who are biologically fit to be parents are educationally, morally, or socially fit—a proposition no one can reasonably doubt.

However, one need not go so far as Plato (or even Freud) in this analysis of the family as an institution which makes for *inequality* of opportunity to recognize that where no provision is made for decent housing, adequate schooling, readily available health facilities, and, above all, proper nourishment and subsistence, there can be no meaningful talk about equality of opportunity. And today it is commonly recognized that those who *inherit* poverty and its consequent social deprivations are the victims of social injustice even if we dispute about the causes. This is certainly true of the *children* of those of whom we may be tempted to say that they deserve their misfortune. Even conservative thinkers acknowledge that there is a floor or level of subsistence below which we regard it as unseemly for a human being to sink. The principle of a negative income tax advocated by proponents of free enterprise like Professor Milton Friedman is testimony to the strength of the common conviction that where there exists sufficient affluence to distribute to those in want, justice as well as prudence requires that their basic needs be met, independently of merit or desert. This seems to be particularly true when there is a superfluity of goods and potential resources that go to waste or remain unused unless distributed. There is even talk of a guaranteed income as a floor with a rising slope depending upon the development of technology.

In the area of public health we are recognizing to an increasing degree that the same principle which justifies the extension of police protection to citizens independently of their worth or merit or ability to pay, also justifies the extension of medical protection, both preventive and remedial. If all citizens have a right to protection against human agents who threaten their safety and survival—whether on the grounds of equality of opportunity to live freely or to reduce insecurity or human suffering—why have they not a right to protection against the natural, nonhuman agents of destruction that threaten their health and life? A child who is ill or hungry certainly does not possess opportunities to develop himself equal to those normally enjoyed by his healthy and well-fed fellows. Why should people be expected to pauperize themselves before receiving medical protection any more than when they receive police protection? Of course where there are insufficient resources to make either police or medical services available to all, certain costs may be imposed.

This principle of equality of concern for all citizens in a democracy to develop themselves to their fullest as persons enables us to find a guide—if only roughly—in determining the locus and limits of permissible and impermissible discrimination—a theme about which so many individuals are confused today. Essential to the notion of a free man or free person is the right to choose, the freedom to develop his taste, his judgment, and the overall patterns of his life. Consequently in those domains of experience that are inherently or predominantly personal— friendship, family, cultural pursuits,—we must be free to discriminate, and legally protected in that freedom, even when our moral judgments are insensitive, capricious, or defective. For freedom to develop carries with it the right to err and to impoverish oneself.

Where, however, in fields in which discrimination prevents the development of personality in *others*, or erodes and undermines equality of opportunity, it is morally blameworthy and should be legally enjoined. Discrimination cannot therefore be tolerated in any of the public institutions that exist to serve the purposes of the governed, or in the domains of citizenship, housing, vocation, schooling, etc., since they grossly obstruct or interfere with the right and power of the person to live his own life.

Granting, however, that we are motivated by an equality of concern for all persons to lead the best life of which they are capable, there still remains the question of what *specific* rules to follow in the distribution of the social product in a given society at a given time. Granted that the distribution of goods and services cannot be literally or absolutely equal, except in limiting cases of extreme scarcity, but only *proportionately* equal. What should be the yardstick or criterion of the proportionate distribution? Many canons of distribution have been proposed. Merit or desert, basic needs, effort or willingness to work, etc. And if we take merit or desert as a criterion, what should be the measure of a man's desert? The *price* his services command in a free market? The *value* of the product determined by other than market considerations—say the quantity and quality of what is produced? Or its contribution to what is regarded as of greater social usefulness at the moment, whether it be a great symphony or medical discovery or inventions to guarantee national security against an atomic Pearl Harbor?

I do not believe there is any one canon of distribution for all types of situations. In an effort to achieve an overall equality it may be necessary to recognize the desirability of short-run inequalities of reward for highly skilled work or dangerous work or sacrificial work required to meet an emergency. If we are awarding *prizes* in a competition, what other criterion for the award can we follow except merit—at least as a necessary condition? After merit has been considered, we may assess as relevant the magnitude and urgency of economic need. Once minimal criteria of merit have been met, there is no one overriding principle that can guide us in all situations.

It is clear that in every situation where there is a scarcity of goods and services, over and above those necessary to preserve life and health, some principle of differential reward must be adopted. Necessities may be distributed on the basis of need or lot or chance but what about "luxuries"—using the word in the comparative or relative sense?

There are some who argue with Locke that in all situations natural justice requires that a man has a right to what he *produces* or to the full *product* of his labor—whether he be baker, tailor, farmer, sailor, or teacher. But the very enumeration of these professions—and the difficulty of determining *what* they produce, shows the inapplicability of any principle of natural justice. Take Locke's own illustration of the *loaf of bread* whose value is produced by labor. Whose labor? By the baker's labor, of course! But not by his labor alone! There is the labor of the miller and the farmer who produced the flour and the labor of the journeymen who made the things that entered into the gathering, storing, and transporting of the crop; and the services of the soldiers and sailors and others who prevented the country and crop from being despoiled; and not only these, but the labor of a long line of others who invented the ovens, and discovered the techniques of baking. The upshot of this line of inquiry is that in a sense *the whole of society produced that loaf of bread and not the unaided effort of one man however worthy.* Indeed, it is hardly an exaggeration to say that the debt of any individual to society in terms of what he receives from it, as a rule, is far greater than he can ever discharge by his own contributions to it.

To be sure, one may retort, it is true in some far-fetched sense to say that society produces the loaf of bread and everything else in the society but it is also true that not all elements of society produce it or anything else *to the same extent*. Some produce more than others both quantitatively and qualitatively, and therefore justice requires that more be given to them than to others. Does this mean that whoever takes this position is committed to the view that it is just to enjoy the social privileges or rewards that result from the possession of natural inequalities of strength, intelligence, beauty, or what not? This conception of justice may be challenged. Why should some individuals be rewarded *socially* for the natural luck or grace of being born better endowed than others? Why should others be penalized for their natural infirmities of strength

or intelligence? If people are to be socially rewarded over and above the
satisfaction and pleasure of enjoying the unearned *natural privilege of
talent*, why not reward human beings for being born more beautiful than
others? But that is precisely what we do! Think of the rewards we shower
on the beautiful! Yes—but who would undertake to defend this differential treatment of a beautiful woman on the ground of *injustice*? A better
case could be made perhaps for the justice of rewarding the woman's
less-beautiful sisters. "To them who hath shall be given—and from them
who hath not, shall be taken away" is certainly a fact of life! But only a
cynic will say that it is a rule of justice! It may be that the natural distribution of talents for which no one is responsible should be regarded as
a matter of luck rather than of justice, assuming that there is no God
whom we can praise or blame for it. The compensation for those who are
victims of bad luck, natural or social, may be justified either on grounds
of compassion or of some insurance principle.

My point is not that differential performance or merit should never
be rewarded but that when we do so the justification must be found in
some other principle than that of the natural fact of inequality itself.
Even those who espouse an extreme egalitarianism of treatment must
recognize that in some situations there may be good and sufficient reasons in terms of overall utility and individual advantage to accept as a
supplementary principle—differential rewards.

Assume a situation in which all members of a group are receiving
equal shares of the total social product for whose output they are responsible with equal dedication and zeal. Assume that an individual hits upon
an idea or invention that would enable the group to more than triple its
total output. The inventor refuses to disclose his new technique unless
he receives considerably more payment than anyone else. And this
despite the fact that he owes his scientific education to the community,
to its cumulative traditions, to its legacy of skills, and that he would have
honor enough for his discovery even if he did not receive a differential
natural reward. If your choice were between one scheme of distribution
in which all would share *equally* in poverty without the benefit of the
invention, and another in which all except one, the inventor, would
share an affluence, and that one, the inventor, enjoying a greater affluence than all the others, which scheme of distribution would you
choose? I think wisdom would dictate the choice of the second scheme.
Only a conception of justice rooted *exclusively* in envy and resentment
would prefer a literal or mechanical equality of deprivation to one of dif-

ferential distribution after a minimal acceptable standard for each individual has been met.

When individuals prefer that everyone go without rather than some enjoy more than others, it is only because the differential distribution becomes the source of invidious and patronizing judgments. There is a sense of rejection, inferiority, lack of status—as in children's response to comparable situations. But where the individual is convinced that he is as much an object of care and concern as anyone else, inequality loses its sting and bite. It requires sensitivity, intelligence, tact, empathy, and sympathy to apply policies so that licit inequalities of treatment are not misunderstood but are properly construed as flowing from an equality of concern. But as difficult as it is to implement this policy, which is central to the conception of social justice, it indicates the direction in which we must go—if social justice is a genuine goal.

So far I have been discussing the requirements of social justice without using high-level abstractions like "capitalism" or "socialism." My experience has been that once these terms are introduced they block fresh thought because so many individuals react viscerally to them. I am confident that we can get greater agreement if we avoid large terms like "capitalism" and "socialism" and concentrate on a pragmatic approach to specific problems. These problems may require large-scale changes like that of a guaranteed annual wage or unemployment insurance for all who are willing and able to work. We should be able to count on a much firmer commitment to human rights and social justice than to any economic theory.

The problem of implementing our analysis is very difficult because there are so many different agencies concerned on so many different levels with the task of removing the obstacles to equality of opportunity for all American citizens to lead a good life. There is need for coordination of energies. Although much remains to be done on local levels, the Federal government must shoulder the main responsibility.

I said earlier that questions of social justice are historical because we never begin with problems from scratch or as they were at the Garden of Eden but always in *this* time and in *this* place. When we tackle *present problems* we must face up to *present* alternatives. And when we do this we must disregard even if we cannot forget the historical evils of the past, and not try to punish the living for the failure of moral responsibilities, alleged and real, of the dead. There is a curious attitude developing among those who think they are repudiating liberal blandness for radical sincerity which sees the problem of social justice today bound up with *historical* justice, conceived as undoing, or compensating for, the evils of the past. Because a great many wrongs in the past have been done to the Indians in this country, to the Negroes, to Mexicans, and other ethnic groups, it is argued that the white race must *today* atone for it, and be punished for the evils of the past. One priestess of the new politics of absurdity, Miss Susan Sontag, has declared that "the white race is the cancer of human history." She does not say whether the cancer should be cauterized by flame or knife but leaves little doubt that she approves a violent solution to problems of social justice as they affect the descendants of those presumably guilty of American "genocide." Fortunately, the American Indians today who are probably more numerous than they ever were in the past, despite the many problems they still face, have no truck with Miss Susan Sontag's irresponsibility. Unfortunately, however, something of her mood has infected some highly articulate but hardly representative members of the Negro community who have been abetted in these sentiments by the so-called New Left. Thus at the historic Chicago National Conference on New Politics held not so long ago, the ultimatum of the Black Caucus was adopted as the official program of the Conference. One of the thirteen demands of the ultimatum reads: "Make immediate reparation for the historical, physical, sexual, mental and economic exploitation of Black people."

Edmund Burke found it difficult to draw up an indictment against a whole people. Contemporary rhetoricians of violence find it easy to draw up an indictment of a whole race. They accept without qualms the very doctrines of collective guilt and guilt by association that have done so much mischief in the past. They fail to see that morally human beings are guilty only for those consequences which *their* actions or failure to act have caused. Whatever the crimes in the past may have been; they do *not* justify any crimes in the present. Otherwise we may as well hang a man today because his grandfather was a horse thief! No nation, no people, no race is free of guilt in the perspective of the past. But this is not relevant to the present.

The prospects for the achievement of some progress in coping with the difficult problems of social justice are difficult enough without prejudicing them with invitations to violence in the name of historical right. No historical injustice of the past can be remedied by violating the rights of individuals in the present, without compounding another injustice which by the same illogic of reprisal for reprisal generates an historical feud that continues until it ends in a mutual destruction of all parties.

Whatever social justice is in this world it can never achieve absolute justice. We must recognize that even when we attempt rectification of evils, absolute justice is unattainable. Its pursuit and persistent refusal to settle for anything less may lead to wrecking the possibilities of getting more and better results here and now. The whole loaf in human affairs can never be achieved.

The program of social reconstruction to be achieved in order to further the equality of human concern essential to the commitment to social justice is vast. It requires large-scale and small-scale, piecemeal and yet bold, planning. But success depends upon the continuous exercise of those political and civic freedoms which are integral to the democratic community.

That is why despite the attempt to downgrade the importance of political rights among the schedules of modern human rights, I regard the political rights of a free society as of paramount importance. There is no such thing as "two kinds of democracy"—political democracy in contrast with economic democracy or any other kind—but only a more complete and less complete form. Social justice is a completer form of democracy than one in which only political rights are recognized and guaranteed. For in the absence of social justice, the expression of political rights is often blunted and frustrated. But social justice without political democracy is impossible, since the greatest injustice of all is to impose rules upon adult human beings without their consent.

[1975]

# 24

# TOWARD
# GREATER EQUALITY

The concept of equality has moved into the center of intellectual and cultural interest in recent years. In some quarters it has become a verbal fetish, used synonymously with terms like "democracy" and "social justice." Reflection will show, however, that when it stands by itself, "equality" or the demand for equality is an incomplete and ambiguous expression. If we want to move "toward greater equality" we don't know what it is we want unless we can specify *what* we want in greater equality. In a country in which members of group A have the vote while members of group B have not, we can move toward greater equality either by granting members of both groups the vote or by *denying* it to both groups. If we stress only equality we could not distinguish between saying that "justice consists in treating all persons alike" and "justice consists in mistreating all persons alike." At best, then, equality is a necessary but not sufficient condition of a just society—since human beings can be equal in poverty or affluence, equally enslaved as well as equally free. That is why a just rule or law must go beyond mere impartial application. The rule or law itself must be morally valid.

My starting point, which I am assuming is common for all of us, is that we are interested in furthering greater equality of participation in democracy as a way of life. The commitment to democracy as a way of life does not entail a belief that all men and women are physically and

From *Philosophy, History, and Social Action* (© 1988 by Kluwer Academic Publishers) "Toward Greater Equality," by Sidney Hook, pp. 235–43. Reprinted with kind permission of Kluwer Academic Publishers.

mentally equal, but the postulate that, whatever their differences, they are *morally* equal. The recognition of the moral equality presupposed by democracy as a way of life is expressed as an *equality of concern* for all members of the community to develop themselves to their full capacities as human beings. This makes it obligatory for the democratic community to equalize opportunities for its citizens regardless of race, color, religion, sex, and national origin. Toward greater equality, then, means toward greater equality of opportunity, for persons in all areas, especially education, housing, health, and employment, required for individuals to develop their best potential as human beings.

It is obvious that as long as the family and different home environment exists, as well as extreme genetic variations in capacities, *absolute* equality of opportunity is unattainable. But this is no more a justification for abandoning the continued quest for equalizing the conditions of opportunity than our failure to achieve absolute health, wisdom, and honesty undercuts the validity of these ideals. Properly understood, equality of opportunity commits us to programs of continuous reforms. It is the *revolution en permanence*.

But is equality of *opportunity* enough? Are competence and merit, which determine awards and rewards when careers are truly open to talents, sufficient? It is sometimes argued that equality of opportunity necessarily converts social life into a race or battlefield in which the consequence of the victor's triumphs is invidious defeat of his competitors. This is a non sequitur. If we remember that our controlling moral postulate is equality of concern for all persons to reach their potential, not all forms of competition are desirable; neither are all forms of competition undesirable; not all forms of competition need result in disaster for those who are not winners, and especially for their children. After all, we do not tolerate or encourage opportunity, no less equal opportunity, for many kinds of antisocial actions. Our moral postulate commits us at the very least to see that the basic human needs for food, clothing, and shelter are gratified for all, regardless of the outcome of social programs geared to merit. It commits us to provide a floor or level of life, whose extent and nature is a function of our technological capacities, beneath which human beings should not be permitted to sink through no fault of their own.

It is further objected: if careers are to be open to talents, what about the fate of the untalented? To which I reply: it is a tolerable fate provided that there are opportunities of employment for all; provided that no persons, regardless of their vocations, are regarded as second-class citizens

442     SIDNEY HOOK ON PRAGMATISM, DEMOCRACY, AND FREEDOM

of the political community; and provided that all citizens have the assurance that the community in diverse ways will seek to equalize the opportunities open to their offspring.

So I cheerfully acknowledge that equality of opportunity is not enough because it does not absolve us from the responsibility of responding to basic human needs; and because, as Jefferson realized, not all the possible consequences of equal opportunity, especially extreme disproportions of wealth and power, are acceptable, particularly if their operation undermines through monopolies of press and other strategic goods and services, equal opportunities of development for subsequent generations.

Nonetheless because equality of opportunity with all its institutional reinforcements is not by itself adequate for an enlightened social philosophy, it does not in the least follow that we must supplement it or substitute for it, or use as a test of its presence the principle of equality of *result*. It is strange logic that argues from the undesirability of *some* extreme inequalities of result to the desirability of equal results in every form of social distribution, or seeks to justify equality of results as essential to social justice or to genuine democracy. In a world in which men and women vary in all sorts of ways, how can equality of concern eventuate in equality of result except by chance or ruthless design? The expectation is as absurd as the presumption that equality of medical concern for those who are ailing necessitates the same medical prescription or regimen for them all—the unfailing sign of a medical quack. Equality as a moral postulate envisages the moral equality of the different and not merely of the same; the application of an equal desirable standard to those relevantly situated, regardless of their differences. It was none other than Karl Marx who reminded us that since a right by its nature consists in the application of an equal standard, applied to different individuals, "and they would not be different individuals if they were not unequal . . . every right in its content is one of inequality." It is a gross misconception of the socialist ethic to interpret its principle of distributive justice as aiming at equality of result or situation regardless of merit, variations in need, responsibility, and social utility. After basic needs have been met, with respect to goods and services that are scarce, i.e., relative luxuries, it is not unfair to distribute these on the basis of desert. This makes it more likely that the availability of such goods and services will increase.

How shall we apply these general considerations to the concrete situations we face in the United States today? I start with the assertion that among the very highest items on the agenda of unfinished business of American life is the final elimination of all practices of civil, social, and economic discrimination against any citizen on grounds of race, color, sex, religion, or national origin. We can move toward this objective by vigorous enforcement of all federal, state, and local statutory prohibitions against discrimination, not only in the field of civil and political rights but in public and private employment with respect to remuneration, promotion, and tenure, and in access to education, housing, recreation, and other areas that affect the development and fulfillment of human capacities.

It goes without saying that vigorous enforcement of existing laws against discrimination will not by themselves achieve the objective of equal opportunities. Where there are no opportunities, there is little solace in the assurance of equal opportunity to fill them. If decent housing is not available, equal opportunity of access to it is literally equal opportunity of access to nothing. It is therefore incumbent upon the federal government to commit itself to a program of full employment at a decent wage level. For those able and willing to work there must be posts for all who are qualified, and also for the unqualified, granting that the posts will naturally by different. In all areas, if private enterprise is unable to meet public need, public agencies must move to meet them. In education, particularly, special supplementary programs should be established to permit all *individuals* who have been disadvantaged in the past to make up for opportunities lost or denied to them. The basic strategy for realizing equality or opportunity is a combination of rational public and private policies, whose detailed nature we cannot explore here, that will expand opportunities for all. If there are not enough places in law school for all *qualified* students, where that has been determined on objective grounds, then instead of preferential racial or religious selection, let us establish more law schools. The same goes for medical schools. What we must avoid is, first, policies that discriminate *in favor* of any group at the cost of discriminating *against* some other group on grounds irrelevant to the objectives of the policy and, second, policies that fail to consider the rights and needs of the individual person, considering him or her only as a representative of a group. We must avoid them precisely because it has been such policies that in the past have resulted in gross injustices to racial and religious minorities and women. We are inconsistent, as well as insincere, if in attempts to rectify the arbitrary and invidious discrimination of the past we practice arbitrary and invidious discrimination in the present. Morally illicit proposals for such types of rectification have been made by partisans of preferential hiring, of quota systems, of schemes which require that "numerical goals and timetables" be mandatory for all institutions that have contractual relations with the government.

Let us consider this issue which currently divides those who are opposed to the patterns of prejudice and discrimination of the past.

It is sometimes denied that it is arbitrary to give preferential treatment to someone who has been the victim of preferential treatment. And with this we can agree. Any particular person who has suffered in consequence of injustices toward him or her is certainly entitled to compensatory treatment as an individual. But morally it is altogether different to say that since *other* individuals of his or her group have suffered in the past because their qualifications were disregarded that therefore individuals who belong to that group in the present, who were not themselves discriminated against, should be judged not on the basis of their qualifications, but on the basis of their group membership, even if this means barring individuals who are better qualified.

I say that it is altogether different because it violates the very principles of equity that justify compensatory treatment for the individual victimized by past discrimination. What I am asserting is that granting the evils of past and present discrimination, the remedy is *not* bureaucratically prescribed "numerical goals" and "time-tables," a quota system, imposed on educational institutions and other organizations. Such remedies are advanced on the basis of a highly questionable assumption, to wit, that a society of equality is one in which all the various groups and subgroups within that society are represented in all disciplines and professions in precise numerical proportion to their distribution in the total pool of the population, or in the community pool, or in the pool of those potentially utilizable. The additional assumption behind such remedies is that any statistical evidence that reveals a marked variation from these proportions is proof of a policy of discrimination.

Not only are these assumptions highly questionable, we never make them in other situations where abuses have been checked or abolished. No one would reasonably argue that because many years ago blacks were deprived of their right to vote and women denied the right to vote that today's generation of blacks and women should be compensated for past discrimination against their forebears by being given the right to cast an extra vote or two at the expense of their fellow citizens or that male descendants of some prejudiced white men of the past be deprived of their vote. Take a more relevant case. For years, blacks were shamefully barred from professional sports, until Jackie Robinson broke the color bar. Would it not be absurd to argue that, therefore, today in compensation for the past there should be discrimination against whites in professional athletics? Would any sensible and fair person try to determine what proportion of whites and blacks should be on basketball or football teams in relation to racial availability or utilizability? Do we not want the best players for the open positions regardless of the percentage distributions in proportion to numbers either in the general population or in the pool of candidates trying out? Why should it be any different when we are looking for the best qualified mathematician to teach topology or the best scholar to teach medieval philosophy? If we oppose all discrimination, why not drop all color, sex, religious, and social bars in an honest quest for the best qualified—no matter what the distribution turns out to be? Of course the quest must be public and not only fair, but must be seen to be fair.

One might even consider the situation with respect to athletics as a paradigm. Since there should be equal opportunities for health and recreation, the community has the responsibility for providing facilities for all citizens to engage in sport and other exercise and, in fact, many communities are moving in this direction. There are still areas of discrimination here with respect to women. There is a neglect of their legitimate athletic interests, especially in competitive sports with men, and they have not yet cracked the sex bar in professional athletics. The law can properly prevent some types of discrimination in budgeting appropriations to enlarge the field of opportunity for women. The rest ultimately depends on them. In time, as more and more women participate in sports, and the social stereotypes about women in this field disappear—as they have in tennis and swimming—I am confident that opportunities will open to women in professional sports as they have to blacks. Were a woman to appear who bats almost as well as Hank Aaron or who steals bases as well as Lou Brock, it would not be long before she broke into the big leagues. Where there is a vested interest in victory, one standard for everyone will sooner or later prevail. In a free and open society one standard for everyone should prevail, regardless of any vested interest.

We may even draw an analogy with equality of educational opportunity. On the basis of the principles I have outlined, we can support pro-

grams of open enrollment, in the sense that the community should provide opportunities for all young men and women to enter some institutions of higher or tertiary education, and beyond that to *compete* for
entry into *any* educational institution. However, the right to receive an
education, and to the schooling required for that education, does not
carry with it the right to enter any specific institution at any specific
time. But it does carry with it the right to be judged and evaluated by the
same standards as all others who have been admitted.

There are some institutions that seek to staff themselves with the
most talented faculty available, with the aim of serving the ablest students, engaging themselves in an educational experience and in a process
of learning and discovery of inestimable social value and human benefit
to the entire community. Provided that one standard of excellence is
applied to all applicants, when all the programs of remedial and special
training and coaching to enhance the skills of those who need this support to compete have been concluded, the percentage distributions of students in various ethnic groups or among men and women are irrelevant.

But of course these are not the only kind of students that should be
of educational concern to us. The ordinary students, even the dull students, have the same right to the best educational experience for their
aptitudes as have the superior students. That is why there must be a provision for various types of educational institutions for students of various
interests and capacities. That is why there must be provision for continuing education. After all, not all teachers can be the most talented nor all
students the ablest. There is a uniqueness about every student that must
be respected. That respect is perfectly compatible with the application of
a single standard of achievement or award in any given institution. We
may and should guarantee the basic needs of food, shelter, education,
and, whenever possible, vocation, too, but we cannot guarantee anyone
against educational failure.

It should be obvious that my whole approach is based on the belief
that it is the individual who is the carrier of human rights and not the
ethnic or national or racial group. Once we disregard this universalist
approach which is blind to color, deaf to religious dogma, indifferent to
sex, where only merit should count, we practically insure the presence
of endemic conflicts in which invidious discriminations are rife and tensions mount until they burst with explosive force. The pluralist society
then becomes a polarized society. A pluralistic society is one in which
the *individual* is a member of many different associations, in which he

does not stand stripped of all ties and parochial loyalties before the power of the all-encompassing State. A pluralistic society is *not* one in which individual rights are bestowed by different contending groups or possessed by virtue of membership in these groups. Such a society, whether it is called multi-ethnic or multi-racial, whether it be Malaysia, Northern Ireland, Cyprus, South Africa, Uganda, and other areas where persons do not enjoy equal rights unless their mothering groups possess equal power, is in an incipient state of civil war.

There are many cultural and psychological side effects that derive from employment practices based on membership in groups rather than from individual merit. First, there is a tendency to dilute and debase academic and professional standards in order to accommodate members of groups who, it is feared, would not make the grade. There is something offensively patronizing in assuming that members of some groups, even when given educational opportunities commensurate with others, cannot, without preferential treatment, compete on equal terms with their fellow citizens. Second, a double standard of status begins to emerge among the personnel of institutions recruited in this way. Invidious distinctions are drawn between those who have made it strictly on their own merits, selected by their professional peers in open competition, and those who have made it by virtue of membership in some group. Qualified members of disadvantaged groups who have succeeded without benefit of preferential selection have been quite eloquent on that score.

I want to conclude by presenting a program of nondiscriminatory hiring for institutions of higher learning—the institutions I know best— and by recommending the underlying principle, *mutatis mutandis*, to all other institutions of our society.

Let us assume for the moment that institutions of higher learning have been asked and have agreed to comply with the following rules:[1]

(1) that they publicize in the most open and evenhanded way all their academic and other job openings;
(2) that they recruit applicants from *all available* sources;
(3) that they maintain fully nondiscriminatory hiring procedures and keep full records of such items as interviews;
(4) that they comply fully with nondiscriminatory promotion and tenure policies;
(5) that they abolish all rules and regulations which are discriminatory with regard to pay, leave, or fringe benefits.

448 SIDNEY HOOK ON PRAGMATISM, DEMOCRACY, AND FREEDOM

Let us also assume that our colleges and universities:

(1) open up fully their respective institutions to all qualified student applicants;
(2) recruit their student body evenhandedly from *all* secondary schools and other possible preparatory channels;
(3) maintain vigorous remedial programs for entrants who wish to remove deficiencies;
(4) maintain comprehensive counseling and other auxiliary programs to facilitate the entry of disadvantaged students into the mainstream of academic life.

Let us further assume that there be maintained a *simple, speedy*, and *effective* complaint and grievance mechanism made inside and outside the academic institutions (lower and appellate levels) to handle promptly complaints involving alleged discrimination on grounds of race, sex, or creed.

Let there be academic and mixed academic/nonacademic study groups and standing commissions to investigate continuously the employment *possibilities* and *practices* and, when necessary, recommend censure and the withholding of government funding.

Here is a practical program of positive commitments, remedial measures, and monitoring bodies that constitutes a plan as comprehensive as any in existence to combat discrimination—without demanding "numerical goals," "timetables," or quotas of any kind.

I ask: wherein is it lacking? In what respects is it unfair? Why will it not work if it has the active support of all persons of conscience and good will?

[1988]

## NOTE

1. These are substantially the proposals made by University Centers for Rational Alternatives, through its Executive Secretary, Prof. Miro Todorovitch, to HEW [the former Department of Health, Education, and Welfare].

# 25

# THE INTELLECTUAL
# IN AMERICA

I t is hard to define an "intellectual." Although ideally all intellectuals should be intelligent, not only are many intelligent people not "intellectuals," which is as it should be, but unfortunately all too many "intellectuals" seem to lack intelligence.

The "intellectual" is, to borrow a phrase from W. E. Johnson, most comprehensively and least controversially defined as a member of what used to be called "the intelligentsia." He is a person professionally concerned with general ideas and values—their nature, application, and criticism. A politician may be an intellectual if he is more than a machine boss or a disciplined member of a political caucus; in that case he borders on being a statesman. There are obviously few such in America at present, but there is some reason to hope that as the years go by their numbers will increase. All literary men, novelists, poets, dramatists, essayists, editors, and critics are intellectuals by virtue of their calling, some of them obviously only by courtesy judging by their concern with ideas. Teachers, scholars, and other denizens of the academy whose writings have more than narrow vocational interest are also intellectuals.

As the rate and quality of literacy grows and as appreciation develops for the simple truth that intelligence is a *sine qua non* for survival in the modern world, we can expect the intellectuals to be held in higher esteem in America. Directly and indirectly it is likely that they will exert more

From *Political Power and Personal Freedom: Critical Studies in Democracy, Communism, and Civil Rights* (New York: Criterion Books, 1959).

influence on the centers of power even if they cannot share the responsibility for the exercise of that power save as they appraise and criticize it.

The "intellectual" is the natural guardian of quality in the life of mind and the natural critic of shoddy. He is the partisan of the ideal. That is why, if he is faithful to his calling in the imperfect world and culture in which he lives, he cannot become the poet-laureate of the *status quo*.

Today, as in the decade when Fascism was the chief danger, he must be active on two fronts: against the powerful threat that would destroy, root and branch, the free society which makes his vocation possible, and against the multiple evils within the free society that compromise its ethos and undermine the integrity of free men. This was a commonplace when Hitler was knocking at the doors of Western civilization. It required no soul-searching agonies to understand that one could oppose *both* the racial genocide the Nazis practiced and our own racial segregation. This could be done without making an absurd equation between the two, without assuming either a posture of Olympian neutrality toward both or a position of hostility toward both as evils of equal magnitude between which there could be no reasonable order of emphasis or priority. The truth is that the struggle against Hitlerism made more poignant to Americans realization of their own failings and what they owed to those who had been excluded from the democratic community. The defeat of Hitlerism was a signal for a great advance toward political and social equality for all minorities.

What was grasped without difficulty when Fascism challenged the survival of free institutions has become a complex and thorny problem to not a few intellectuals today in face of the challenge of Communist totalitarianism. They are acutely aware of the inequities and vulgarities of American culture which they judge not historically but from the standpoint of a European elite to whom the United States is nothing but "a semi-barbarian superstate of the periphery." So the Greeks might have regarded the Romans. Yet the legacy of Greece was saved for the world not by the Greeks, unable to unite in a genuine commonwealth, not by those elevated spirits who condemned equally the barbarians of the East and West, but by the Romans who stood firm against the autocracy of Asiatic Byzantinism. Corresponding to "the new failure of nerve" a decade or two ago, one can observe among intellectuals of our decade "a failure of political intelligence."

I cannot understand why American intellectuals should be apologetic about the fact that they are limited in their effective historical choice between endorsing a system of total terror and *critically* supporting our own imperfect democratic culture with all its promises and dangers. For after all within our culture they are not *compelled* to choose whereas in the Soviet world neutrality or even silence is treason. Surely, this should count for something even with those who, although dependent upon the protective security of our relatively free culture for their neutralism and cultivation of purity, regard its struggle for survival as a vulgar battle of ideologies. Nor is it clear to me why an appreciation of the values of American life is incompatible with vigorous criticism of its many deficiencies and with determined efforts to enhance both its chances of survival and the quality of its cultural experience by more enlightened domestic and foreign policies. And if there are any seers or prophets among us, let them make their visions known!

The political and moral issues of our time are no different for the intellectual classes, the writers, artists, and scholars, than they are for the working classes who recognize that even under the dislocations of our mixed economy, they enjoy more bread and freedom than the working classes anywhere else in the world. If anything, one expects the intellectuals to see even more clearly that the relative autonomy of their craft is threatened by Soviet totalitarianism more completely than by any other social system in history.

I must also confess to some perplexity in understanding laments about the "alienation" of the creative artist in American culture if this means that he faces more obstacles to doing significant work or finding an appreciative audience than was the case fifty or a hundred years ago. Surely, compared with his forebears, he can have no complaint on the score of creature comforts, which he certainly deserves no less than other human beings. The notion circulated in some quarters that university life is the Golgotha of the intellectual spirit is absurd. It seems to me that the creative life in America suffers more from mediocrity than from frustration. Equally bewildering is the view that mass culture or the popular arts constitute a profound menace to the position of American intellectuals. Certainly those who love cream more than their work may drown in it. The only sense I can find in the violent garrulities of Ortega y Gasset is that the mass "kind of man" who threatens the individual, is the man who lurks inside of anyone who fears to be himself. That mass "kind of man" in one form or another has always existed. And he sometimes is present in the man who strives and strains to be different as distinct from one who genuinely feels and thinks differently from his fellows.

There are all kinds of alienations in the world and one can get star-tling effects by confusing them. Hegel understood by self-alienation the process of dialectical development by which the individual conscious-ness progresses from innocence to maturity, from the simplicity of bare perception to the richly funded comprehension of a complexly interre-lated system. Remove the mystification about the Absolute Self, drop the consolatory, religious overtones about the meaningfulness of the Whole, and what we get in the language of a barbarous literary psychology is an account of the travail of spiritual growth in any culture—not only for the artist but for every human being.

Marx's notion of self-alienation is historically circumscribed and has much less sweep than Hegel's. It applies primarily to the worker who is compelled to labor at something which neither expresses nor sustains his own needs and interests as a person. The unalienated man for Marx is the creative man. He is anyone who, under an inner compulsion, is doing significant work wrestling with a problem or striving to articulate a vision. The artist for Marx is the unalienated man par excellence to the extent that he does not produce *merely* a commodity. Remove the Utopi-anism of believing that all work in an industrial society can make a call on man's creative capacities, and of imagining that everybody, once a market economy disappears, will be able to do creative work, and what Marx is really saying is not obscure. The more truly human a society is, the more will it arrange its institutions to afford opportunities for cre-ative fulfillment through uncoerced work. Man humanizes himself through work, which in association with others, is the source of speech. Man is dehumanized by *forced* work. There are some echoes of Rousseauistic myth in this and by a strange un-Marxian lapse Marx refers to a society in which there is no forced labor as a more natural society. From this point of view, the workers attending a conveyor belt, feeding a machine, endlessly filing orders or names are far more alienated than those intellectuals who have chosen their vocations and enjoy some freedom in setting their own goals or selecting their tasks.

There is a third conception of alienation popular with some sociolo-gists and Bohemians which is applied to the artist who breaks with the conventions or norms of his family, society, or class. He is pitied and sometimes pities himself because he has no market or patron or reputa-tion on the assumption that this is a necessary consequence of his non-comformity despite the fact that other nonconformists created their own audience and following and feel unalienated in the Marxian sense even when hostile critics ignore or rage against them. This is the most popular conception of the alienated artist in America and the shallowest. Why it is so popular I do not know unless it be that many individuals mistake the indifference of the world or their private creative agonies—which may very well be due to lack of creative capacity or to an ambition altogether incommensurate with their talents—for unerring signs of election to an alienated elite. But all a free culture can do is to provide opportunities for revolt: it cannot guarantee professional success.

No one knows the secret of significant creativity. We do know it cannot be mass produced and that it cannot emerge under conditions of extreme privation. But since the material lot of American artists has improved considerably in the last few decades and since the cultural atmosphere in America is much more receptive to the notion of total dedication to a creative calling—the son's announcement that he refuses to enter business or a profession but wants to be a writer, artist, or musician no longer causes a family crisis—I must confess I do not know why the American arts are more anemic than the arts abroad *if* they are. And I suspect that no one else knows. Certainly, American work in science, scholarship, and medicine does not lag behind European achievements. The hypothesis that mass culture and the popular arts—the Hollywood trap!—threaten the emergence of a significant culture of vitality and integrity because they constitute a perpetual invitation to a sell-out seems very far-fetched. Unless one is an incurable snob (I am old enough to remember intense discussions by otherwise intelligent people as to whether the cinema is an art), the forms of mass culture and the popular arts should serve as a challenge to do something with them. There are "sell-outs" of course but there are two parties to every "sell-out." The writer who "sells out" to Hollywood or the slicks cannot absolve himself of responsibility on the ground that he wouldn't be able to live as plushily as if he did. Why should he? I shall be accused of saying that I am sentencing artists and writers to starvation. But if scholars can live Renan's life of "genteel poverty" and do important work so can those who don't go to Hollywood.

Finally, I see no specific virtue in the attitude of conformity or nonconformity. The important thing is that it should be voluntary, rooted in considered judgment, an authentic expression of some value or insight for which the individual is prepared to risk something. "Conformity" or "nonconformity" are relational terms. Before evaluating them I should like to know *to and with what* a person is conforming or not conforming and *how*. Under the Weimar Republic, Stefan George, Spengler, and Hitler were nonconformists: under the Czarist regime Dostoevsky in his most fruitful years was a conformist. To the greatest of men the terms "conformist" or "nonconformist" have singularly little relevance—Shakespeare, Milton, Goethe, Plato, Aristotle, Kant, or Dewey.

Particularly inexplicable to me is the broad question of whether the American intellectual should continue the tradition of critical nonconformism. The social function of the American intellectual is to think, and to act in such a way that the results of his thinking are brought to bear upon the great issues of our time. The cardinal attribute of the life of thought—its proper virtue—is the capacity to discriminate, to make relevant distinctions. He is no more un-American when he is intelligently critical of the United States than he is chauvinistic when he is intelligently appreciative. Many American intellectuals are unaware of the extent to which the social climate and objective possibilities for a democratic welfare state have improved in the last twenty years. Some still think of socialism as a good in itself. Having made a religion of a form of economy, they are incapable of learning from experience. They comfort themselves with a superior terminological intransigence in the belief that their sincerity atones for their stupidity. Their opposite numbers now regard socialism as an evil in itself. Socialism is no longer a form of economy for them, but the principle of welfare or social control itself. Like the most orthodox of Marxists they believe that any economy uniquely entails one political way of life. Fortunately, more and more intellectuals are beginning to understand what they could have learned from John Dewey long ago, that democratic process is more important than any predetermined program, and that persons and values are the test of adequate social relations not conversely.

Outside their own immediate craft too many intellectuals are irresponsible, especially in politics. They don't know enough, don't think enough, and are the creatures of fashion. It is sufficient for the majority to believe anything, for them to oppose it. They are too conscious of "public relations." Some are exhibitionists who are always washing their hands in public, Mary Magdalenes making a cult of purity. The lowest form of intellectual life is led by left-bank American expatriates who curry favor with Sartrian neutralists by giving them the lowdown on the cultural "reign of terror" [*sic!*] in America.

Most American intellectuals still do not understand the theory, practice, and tactics of the Communist movement. Because McCarthy made wild and irresponsible charges, too many are inclined to dismiss the Communist danger in its total global impact as relatively unimportant. American intellectuals were more frightened of Franco in 1936 and of Hitler in 1933 than they are of Krushchev today. In 1933 and 1936 they did *not* say that, after all, there were few Fascists in America, fewer Fascists than there ever were of Communists since 1919. As country after country has come under the Soviet knife, concern in the colleges, in literary circles, even scientific quarters has *not* increased. The term "anti-Communist" has not got the same overtones as "anti-Fascist." It is not enough to say that McCarthy and reactionary demagogues have ruined the term "anti-Communist." Why didn't the Communists ruin the term "anti-Fascist"? They were just as vehement in their anti-Fascism as McCarthy was in his anti-Communism and even more irresponsible, because they called men like John Dewey and Norman Thomas "Fascists."

The task of the intellectual is still to lead an intellectual life, to criticize what needs to be criticized in America, without forgetting for a moment the total threat which Communism poses to the life of the free mind. Our own vigilantes and reactionaries are much more like witches and straw scarecrows than are the paid and unpaid agents of the Kremlin who constitute the membership of the Communist Parties in all countries. They can be cleared out of the way by a little courage and a sense of humor. They have nuisance value especially because of their effects abroad.

We face grim years ahead. The democratic West will require the critical support, the dedicated energy, and above all, the intelligence of its intellectuals if it is to survive as a free culture. With the possible exception of the technical arts and their theoretical ancillaries, great creative visions, conforming or nonconforming, can today flourish only in the soil of a free culture. It was not always so. But modern totalitarianism is not the same as ancient absolutisms.

Let the neutralists of the world remember. In the West nonconformists, no matter how alienated, can always win a hearing, even if they do not win a place in the Academy or earn the Order of Merit. In the land of Purges and Brainwashing, the only thing a nonconformist can earn is a bullet in the neck. This is the historical premise of our age whose recognition is binding on all humanists whether they are democratic socialists or civil libertarian conservatives or members of the alienated avant-garde.

[1959]